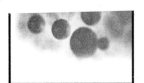

Quick CORBA™ 3

Jon Siegel

Wiley Computer Publishing

John Wiley & Sons, Inc.

NEW YORK · CHICHESTER · WEINHEIM · BRISBANE · SINGAPORE · TORONTO

In loving memory of my dad, Armand Siegel—
professor, teacher, thinker.

Publisher: Robert Ipsen
Editor: Robert M. Elliott
Assistant Editor: Emilie Herman
Managing Editor: John Atkins
Associate New Media Editor: Brian Snapp
Text Design & Composition: Publishers' Design and Production Services, Inc.

This book is printed on acid-free paper. ☺

Published by John Wiley & Sons, Inc.

Published simultaneously in Canada.

Library of Congress Cataloging-in-Publication Data:
Siegel, Jon.
   Quick Corba 3 / Jon Siegel.
     p.   cm.
   ISBN 0-471-38935-8
   1. Object-oriented methods (Computer science)   2. CORBA (Computer architecture) I. Title.
QA76.9.035 S55 2001
005.1'17—dc21   2001017809

Printed in the United States of America.

10 9 8 7 6 5 4 3 2 1

OMG Press Advisory Board

OMG Press Books in Print

(For complete information about current and upcoming titles, go to www.wiley.com/compbooks/omg/)

- *Building Business Objects* by Peter Eeles and Oliver Sims, ISBN: 0471-191760.

- *Business Component Factory: A Comprehensive Overview of Component-Based Development for the Enterprise* by Peter Herzum and Oliver Sims, ISBN: 0471-327603.

- *Business Modeling with UML: Business Patterns at Work* by Hans-Erik Eriksson and Magnus Penker, ISBN: 0471-295515.

- *CORBA 3 Fundamentals and Programming, 2nd Edition* by Jon Siegel, ISBN: 0471-295183.

- *CORBA Design Patterns* by Thomas J. Mowbray and Raphael C. Malveau, ISBN: 0471-158828.

- *Enterprise Application Integration with CORBA: Component and Web-Based Solutions* by Ron Zahavi, ISBN: 0471-32704.

- *Enterprise Java with UML* by C.T. Arrington, ISBN: 0471-386804

- *The Essential CORBA: Systems Integration Using Distributed Objects* by Thomas J. Mowbray and Ron Zahavi, ISBN: 0471-106119.

- *Instant CORBA* by Robert Orfali, Dan Harkey, and Jeri Edwards, ISBN: 0471-183334.

- *Integrating CORBA and COM Applications* by Michael Rosen and David Curtis, ISBN: 0471-198277.

- *Java Programming with CORBA*, *Third Edition* by Gerald Brose, Andreas Vogel, and Keith Duddy, ISBN: 0471-247650.

- *The Object Technology Casebook: Lessons from Award-Winning Business Applications* by Paul Harmon and William Morrisey, ISBN: 0471-147176.

- *The Object Technology Revolution* by Michael Guttman and Jason Matthews, ISBN: 0471-606790.

- *Programming with Enterprise JavaBeans, JTS, and OTS: Building Distributed Transactions with Java and C++* by Andreas Vogel and Madhavan Rangarao, ISBN: 0471-319724.

- *Programming with Java IDL* by Geoffrey Lewis, Steven Barber, and Ellen Siegel, ISBN: 0471-247979.

- *UML Toolkit* by Hans-Erik Eriksson and Magnus Penker, ISBN: 0471-191612.

About the OMG

The Object Management Group (OMG) was chartered to create and foster a component-based software marketplace through the standardization and promotion of object-oriented software. To achieve this goal, the OMG specifies open standards for every aspect of distributed object computing from analysis and design, through infrastructure, to application objects and components.

The well-established Common Object Request Broker Architecture (CORBA) standardizes a platform- and programming-language-independent distributed object computing environment. It is based on the OMG/ISO Interface Definition Language (OMG IDL) and the Internet Inter-ORB Protocol (IIOP). Now recognized as a mature technology, CORBA is represented on the marketplace by well over 70 Object Request Brokers (ORBs) plus hundreds of other products. Although most ORBs are tuned for general use, others are specialized for real-time or embedded applications, or are built into transaction processing systems where they provide scalability, high throughput, and reliability. Of the thousands of live, mission-critical CORBA applications in use today around the world, more than 300 are documented on the OMG's success-story web pages at www.corba.org.

CORBA 3, the OMG's latest release, adds a Component Model, quality-of-service control, a messaging invocation model, and tightened integration with the Internet, Enterprise Java Beans, and the Java programming laguage. Widely anticipated by the industry, CORBA 3 keeps this established architecture in the forefront of distributed computing, as will a new OMG specification integrating CORBA with XML. Well-known for its ability to integrate legacy systems into your network, along with the wide variety of heterogeneous hardware and software on the market today, CORBA enters the new millennium prepared to integrate the technologies on the horizon.

Augmenting this core infrastructure are the CORBAservices that standardize naming and directory services, event handling, transaction processing, security, and other functions. Building on this firm foundation, OMG Domain Facilities standardize common objects throughout the supply and service chains in industries such as Telecommunications, Healthcare, Manufacturing, Transportation, Finance/Insurance, Electronic Commerce, Life Science, and Utilities.

The OMG standards extend beyond programming. OMG specifications for analysis and design include the Unified Modeling Language (UML), the repository standard Meta-Object Facility (MOF), and XML-based Metadata Interchange (XMI). The UML is a result of fusing the concepts of the world's most prominent methodologists. Adopted as an OMG specification in 1997, it represents a collection of the best engineering practices that have proven successful in the modeling of large and complex systems and is a well-defined, widely accepted response to these business needs. The MOF is OMG's standard for metamodeling and metadata repositories. Fully integrated with UML, it uses the UML notation to describe repository metamodels. Extending this work, the XMI standard enables the exchange of objects defined using UML and the MOF. XMI can generate XML Data Type Definitions for any service specification that includes a normative, MOF-based metamodel.

In summary, the OMG provides the computing industry with an open, vendor-neutral, proven process for establishing and promoting standards. The OMG makes all of its specifications available without charge from its Web site, www.omg.org. With more than a decade of standard-making and consensus-building experience, the OMG now counts about 800 companies as members. Delegates from these companies convene at week-long meetings held five times each year at varying sites around the world to advance OMG technologies. The OMG welcomes guests to their meetings; for an invitation, send your email request to info@omg.org.

Membership in the OMG is open to end users, government organizations, academia, and technology vendors. For more information on the OMG, contact OMG headquarters by phone at +1 (781) 444-0404, by fax at +1 (781) 444-0320, by email at info@omg.org, or on the Web at www.omg.org.

Contents

Introduction

This book collects descriptions of the Object Management Group's most powerful new CORBA and modeling specifications into a single volume. These specifications combine to give CORBA the capabilities it needs to support advanced Internet and enterprise computing. It includes almost all of the ten specifications originally labeled CORBA 3 (most of which have already been issued by the OMG as part of various CORBA 2.X point releases), and adds important new ones including the XML/Value mapping that represents an XML document as a multiply linked list of CORBA **valuetype**s. It also includes descriptions of OMG's modeling standards: the Unified Modeling Language (UML), Meta-Object Facility (MOF), and XML Metadata Interchange (XMI). With these infrastructure and modeling specifications, OMG defines the state of the art in distributed enterprise and Internet computing.

There are two groups of people who should read this book:

First, if you are an experienced CORBA programmer or architect, curious about OMG's newest specifications, this is the book for you. As I just mentioned, it describes the new CORBA specifications that you need to know about, plus OMG's modeling specifications. Since the book does not include an introduction to basic CORBA, it is an "advanced" book even though the presentation of each specification is no more advanced than the presentation in my introductory book *CORBA 3 Fundamentals and Programming*. It provides experienced CORBA users with a book that discusses OMG's new specifications without yet another introduction to IDL, or how IIOP and the IOR let a CORBA client invoke an operation on another vendor's CORBA server over the network.

Second, if you are an enterprise architect and are considering using CORBA for your infrastructure, even if you haven't studied basic CORBA, you can benefit from this book as well but in a different way. The specifications described in this book give CORBA the capabilities it needs to play in the the enterprise and Internet worlds—in fact, they put it in the forefront. You will be able to understand the capabilities of the specifications from the descriptions and figure out how they fit into your enterprise architecture. But you will find the technical (as opposed to architectural and functional) parts of the descriptions opaque, so you should go back and study basic CORBA after you're done to fill in the blanks. As much as possible, I've kept the technical and programming aspects towards the end of each chapter so that architects can read farther into each chapter before coming to programming detail. (On the other hand, if you're a programmer and you find the beginning of a chapter a little thin technically, this is your clue to skip towards the end!)

If you're new to CORBA, you'll need to read another book first unless you're only interested in the capabilities and architecture of the specifications and not in programming details. If you're a programmer and you haven't studied basic CORBA, perhaps now's the time. You need to learn how OMG Interface Definition Language (OMG IDL) separates interface from implementation, how the CORBA Object Reference makes invocations location transparent, and other aspects of the CORBA infrastructure. My previous book, *CORBA 3 Fundamentals and Programming*, is a good place to learn this.

If you're an experienced CORBA programmer or distributed-systems architect, you may want to skip through this book and read the most interesting (to you!) parts first. Except for XML/Value and the CORBA Component Model (CCM), there are few dependencies from one chapter to another. (XML/Value in Part I, Chapter 2 depends on the **valuetype** presented in Part I,Chapter 1, and all of Part III builds to the presentation of the CCM in its final chapter.)

Here's how it's organized:

The book starts with a **Prologue**, which pulls together the many parts of CORBA 3 from an architectural point of view, covering both client and server sides. The prologue also lists all of the specifications originally included in the original CORBA 3 press release, plus the others presented in this book, and tells when each was adopted and formally issued by OMG as part of a numbered CORBA release. (More on this below.)

Part I covers **Integration with Java and the Internet**, including the **valuetype**, the reverse Java-to-IDL mapping, the XML/Value mapping, which lets you manipulate XML documents (including those described by DTDs) as a collection of native CORBA types, and the Interoperable Naming Service.

Part II covers **Quality-of-Service Control**, including asynchronous and messaging mode remote invocations, setting policies for timeout and priority control, and the three specialized CORBA modes: Real-Time, Fault Tolerant, and minimumCORBA for embedded systems.

Part III leads up to and presents the **CORBA Component Model (CCM).** The first two chapters present the Portable Object Adapter (POA) and Persistent State Service (PSS). The last presents the CCM itself, starting with a programming example and moving on to a description of all of its parts.

Part IV presents **OMG's modeling specifications**, starting with UML and the MOF, and finishing with OMG's new Model Driven Architecture (MDA). A recent extension to OMG's basic architecture (as I write this, OMG members have just voted to authorize drafting of technical documents that would enable this extension to be adopted as the organization's direction), the MDA defines services and facilities as a platform-indendependent UML model first, which it then maps to the various platforms for either implementation or interoperability. The end of this book, this chapter represents a new beginning for OMG, which soon expects to be adopting specifications for facility interfaces, based on platform-independent UML models, on a variety of middleware platforms such as EJB, XML/SOAP, COM/DCOM/MTS, .Net, and others.

Even though OMG may not have released a volume labeled CORBA 3 when you first pick this book up in your bookstore, the specifications described here are real. As already mentioned, the label CORBA 3 was first used in a 1998 press release from OMG declaring that 10 specifications—including most of the ones in this book, of course—would be issued, together, under that label sometime during 1999. All of the specifications were adopted on schedule or nearly so, but formal release (a subsequent step which requires a maintenance revision of the original adopted specification, and a vendor commitment to produce and market an implementation) occurred in stages, rather than all-at-once. The first few (including the important **valuetype**, foundation for the XML/Value mapping) were formally issued with CORBA 2.3 in June 1999; several more as part of CORBA 2.4 in late 2000. As this book goes to press, it appears likely that others will be issued as part of a CORBA 2.5 point release around mid-2001 (although this is developing too late for mention anywhere else in this book except here!), preceding the formal release of the few remaining (mainly the Persistent State Service and CORBA Component Model) as CORBA 3.0 late in the year. The CCM is being implemented in quite a number of places; check out www.ditec.um.es/~dsevilla/ccm/ for details. (After the page comes up, search for "CCM implementations.")

I've collected information on release dates (mostly in the past!) for all of these specifications and put them in the Prologue, where they appear both in the text and in a table.

Some of the material in this book was taken from my previous book, *CORBA 3 Fundamentals and Programming*, published in mid-2000 by John Wiley and Sons. These chapters are new: The XML/Value mapping which lets you manipulate an XML document as a collection of native CORBA types, Fault Tolerant CORBA, minimumCORBA for embedded systems, and OMG's new Model Driven Architecture. The discussion of the Interoperable Naming Service was updated to take into account a maintenance revision to the specification, as was the chapter on Real-Time CORBA.

Thank you for picking up this book. It collects my descriptions of the most powerful new CORBA specifications into a single slim (well, compared to my other books!) volume. I hope you enjoy reading it as much as I enjoyed putting it together.

Jon Siegel
Director, Technology Transfer
Object Management Group

Acknowledgments

It's not possible to acknowledge all of the people who contributed to this book. It's based on the OMG specifications, and hundreds of skilled people from hundreds of companies around the world have participated in their creation. Five times every year, more than five hundred CORBA experts gather at a hotel somewhere in the world at an OMG meeting to advance OMG's suite of standards. I can't name them all here, but I can at least start by acknowledging my debt to these people for their fine work.

Enthusiastic support from the Object Management Group made this book possible. In particular, I want to thank OMG CEO Dr. Richard Soley for his good advice and support. Others around the OMG offices who provided support and encouragement include COO Bill Hoffman, Technical Director Andrew Watson, Liaison Director Henry Lowe, Director of Standards Fred Waskeiwicz, Dody Keefe, and the rest of the staff. However, all of the opinions in the book are mine, and neither anyone else's nor OMG's.

Many thanks to Dan Frantz (BEA Systems, Inc., www.bea.com) who wrote the technical and programming sections of the POA chapter. (I wrote the beginning sections and Santa Claus story myself, and don't want Dan to get blamed for them!) Also thanks to Ed Cobb (BEA Systems, Inc.), Patrick Thompson (Rogue Wave Software, Inc., www.roguewave.com), and Patrick Ravenel (Persistence Software, www.persistence.com), who wrote the code for the mini-example in the CORBA Components section of Part III

Chapter 3 and reviewed my text for that section so many times, they might as well have written some of it themselves. Patrick Ravenel also wrote the PSDL code and reviewed the PSS writeup in Part III, Chapter 2, and so gets double thanks. Michael Cheng of IBM Corporation (www.ibm.com) started out helping with the C++ mapping for valuetypes but, by the time he was done, had also contributed the example for the Java mapping and the RMI/IIOP code example. I had a lot of help with the XML/Value mapping chapter, and want to mention in particular Alan Conway (one of my co-authors on *CORBA 3 Fundamentals and Programming*) and Darach Ennis of IONA Technologies (www.iona.com), and Patrick Thompson (already mentioned for his help with the CCM chapter). Alan and Darach wrote the code for the dynamic mapping example and checked my IDL for the static mapping; Patrick contributed some essential and very timely help with the static mapping.

On the Analysis and Design side, thanks to Cris Kobryn of TeleLogic (www.telelogic.com) for contributing Part IV, Chapter 1 on UML. Cris is one of the authors of the specification, and he chairs the current UML Revision Task Force at OMG. Also, thanks to Sridhar Iyengar of Unisys, Inc. (www.unisys.com) for Part IV, Chapter 2 on the MOF and XMI. Sridhar is the principal author of these specifications, and known around OMG as "Mr. MOF." I'm proud to have these two authorities contribute to this book.

Many thanks to the OMG members who reviewed my writeups of the various specifications. These reviewers get credit for the consistent correctness of the descriptions, but I take all of the blame myself for any errors that might have crept in while they weren't looking. Dock Allen of The Mitre Corporation (www.mitre.com) reviewed the Real-Time description. Vic Giddings and Bill Beckwith of Objective Interface Systems (www.ois.com) helped with minimumCORBA. Louise Moser and Michael Mellior-Smith of Eternal Systems, Inc. (www.eternal-systems.com), principal authors of the Fault Tolerant CORBA specification, reviewed that chapter. And finally, Jishnu Mukerji of Hewlett-Packard Corporation (www.hp.com) and Dave Frankel of IONA Technologies reviewed the chapter on the MDA.

Since books tend to be written during evening, weekends, and even vacations, authors' families contribute noticeably to the success of a project such as this one. I want to thank my wife Nancy and our younger son Adam for their support and patience during the writing and editing of this book. Their help and forbearance made this work possible. Even our older son Josh, who is off on his own (working as a programmer, of course!), managed to help out here and there and gets his own "thank you" too.

This is an exciting time for CORBA and OMG. Even after the additions presented in this book, CORBA continues to grow. I just checked OMG's Web site where 15 technology adoptions (out of the 100 currently in process) will extend CORBA's capabilities in one way or another. Another 20-plus processes will add new CORBA-based facilities in OMG's domains. But the big news is about the Model Driven Architecture described in the last chapter, which provides big benefits to enterprise computing everywhere by extending OMG specifications to middleware platforms beyond CORBA. That chapter, at the end of this book, is the beginning of a new chapter for OMG. I hope you get a lot out of this book, from beginning to end.

Enjoy!

About the Author

Dr. Jon Siegel is Director of Technology Transfer for the Object Management Group (OMG) where he has worked since late 1993. At OMG, he heads OMG's technology transfer program with the goal of teaching the technical aspects and benefits of the Object Management Architecture including CORBA, the CORBAservices, the Domain specifications in vertical markets ranging from healthcare, life sciences, and telecommunications to manufacturing and retail systems, and OMG's modeling specifications UML, MOF, XMI, and CWM. In this capacity, he presents tutorials, seminars, and company briefings around the world, and writes magazine articles and books. With OMG since 1993, Siegel was founding chair of the Domain Technology Committee responsible for OMG specifications in the vertical domains.

Before joining OMG, Dr. Siegel performed research and development in Computer Science for Shell Oil Company where he championed the use of standards to reduce software development time and cost, and was an early developer of distributed object software. While at Shell, he served as its representative to the Open Software Foundation for four years, and to the Object Management Group for two years. He holds a Ph.D. in Theoretical Chemistry from Boston University.

Dr. Siegel lives in rural eastern Massachusetts, about 40 miles outside of Boston, with his wife Nancy and their younger son, Adam. His older son, Josh, left the family nest a few years back and is now working as a computer programmer (of course!). Siegel's hobbies, which he abandons while working on a book, include bicycling and astronomy.

Trademarks

CORBA®, The Information Brokerage®, CORBA Academy®, IIOP® and the Object Management Group logo® are registered trademarks of the Object Management Group. OMG™, Object Management Group™, the CORBA Logo™, "The Middleware That's Everywhere™", the CORBA Academy logo™, XMI™, MOF™, CWM™, OMG Interface Definition Language™, IDL™, CORBAservices™, CORBAfacilities™, CORBAmed™, CORBAnet™, UML™, the UML Cube Logo, "We're Known By The Companies We Connect™", Model Driven Architecture™, MDA™, OMG Model Driven Architecture™, OMG MDA™, "The Architecture of Choice for a Changing World™", and Unified Modeling Language™ are trademarks of the Object Management Group.

Enterprise JavaBeans, Java, Java Server Pages, and JDBC are trademarks or registered trademarks of of Sun Microsystems, Inc., in the United States and/or other countries.

Microsoft, MS, MS-DOS, Windows, Windows NT, COM, DCOM, MTS, and .Net are either trademarks or registered trademarks of Microsoft Corporation in the United States and/or other countries.

CORBA and Distributed Computing Grow Up Together

In the 11 years since the Object Management Group (OMG) first defined the Common Object Request Broker Architecture (CORBA), the standard has moved from the periphery of computing to the preferred architecture for enterprise and internet server applications. Hundreds of mission-critical applications, documented at www.corba.org, attest to the suitability of CORBA for applications that must be scalable, reliable, transactional, and secure.

CORBA and distributed, networked computing grew up together. In the early 1990s when CORBA was young, the internet was still a curiosity used by a small number of scientists to exchange email and send files using ftp. Desktop computer users were more likely to exchange files via floppy disks than networks, which were expensive, unusual, and hard to use.

And, network programming was difficult. There were a few network programs—telnet, FTP, and SMPT—that satisfied basic needs. To go beyond this, programmers needed to code directly to sockets or some other primitive abstraction of the network. Even Remote Procedure Call (RPC) implementations were off in the future.

Following the OSF's Distributed Computing Environment (DCE) to market by only a year or two, basic CORBA added advanced features characteristic of object orientation: *Location transparency* divorced objects not only from their location on the network, but even from the need to be on the network at all: objects could just as easily be local to the client that

---

WHAT ABOUT BASIC CORBA?

You need to understand basic CORBA first (and rather well, in fact) in order to understand the CORBA 3 extensions that are the subject of this book. But, we're not going to cover these basic aspects here; this is an intermediate-level book written for the thousands of architects and developers who have already mastered basic CORBA and deserve a book that doesn't force them to wade through (and carry around!) chapters of stuff they already know. If you aren't familiar with basic CORBA, we suggest that you switch to our basic-level book, *CORBA 3 Fundamentals and Programming*, ISBN 0-471-29518-3 (John Wiley & Sons, 2000).

---

called them. *Cascaded calls* allowed applications to be built up from componentized building blocks. *Instantiation* allowed the creation of instances when they were needed, and their destruction when they were not. Interfaces defined in OMG *Interface Definition Language* enabled programming language independence even if the first language binding was for the distinctly non-object–oriented language, C.

In this environment, it was a virtue that CORBA hid networking details from the programmer almost totally. Distributed application programming was difficult enough. Starting slowly, programmers generated the first useful business CORBA applications nearly as soon as vendors provided them with the basic tools.

As the 1990s progressed, intranet and Internet computing grew up together. Following a brief period of experimentation with a number of incompatible proprietary protocols (does anyone out there remember DECNET?), TCP/IP emerged as the transport protocol of choice and, with the arrival of inexpensive and easy-to-install twisted-pair cabling, offices everywhere began to replace "sneakernet" with ethernet. Wide-area-network providers that started by coupling thermal-printing terminals via 300-baud modem connections to text-based mainframes morphed into high-speed infrastructures that coupled powerful desktops and laptops with color displays and high-bandwidth DSL or cable connections to the millions of servers on the World Wide Web.

Everyone noticed the emergence of HTTP as the application protocol (that is, the protocol that ran over TCP/IP) of choice over the Internet link from client to server, since that was what users came into contact with. Less obvious was the protocol that linked together the numerous machines that comprised the business infrastructure, which grew too big to run on a single machine even if it was a huge mainframe.

SETTING THE STAGE

With the additions collectively known as CORBA 3, the suite of Object Management Group (OMG) specifications keeps up with enterprise requirements in distributed computing. These first few pages describe how networked computing and CORBA grew up together. We'll keep the history short, and get to the architectural overview in the introduction to Part I. This high-level overview will establish the context for the rest of the book.

With the formal adoption of the CORBA Component Model (CCM) in June 1998, all of the CORBA 3 specifications became adopted OMG technology. However, this did not mean that the OMG issued a CORBA 3 specification book right away. To ensure that implementing companies have a robust specification to work from, OMG requires all newly-adopted specifications to undergo their first maintenance cycle before they are given a release number and issued as a formal document. Since the specifications that make up CORBA 3 completed this mandatory maintenance step individually rather than all at once, their releases happened the same way: A few specifications were issued early as part of CORBA 2.2; a few more in releases 2.3 and 2.4; and finally the remainder—including the key CORBA Component Model—in CORBA 3.0 scheduled for release in late 2001. We review the details of this event sequence in this Prologue.

This is where CORBA predominated. In this heterogeneous world where scalability and reliability were crucial, CORBA provided a tight, reliable, and secure coupling that enabled even transactional reliability in applications that spanned the enterprise and, where necessary, beyond it. CORBA 2 applications scaled to thousands of transactions per second and powered Web sites in electronic commerce and financial trading in public view, and some of the largest manufacturing installations in less visible situations.

But by the end of the 1990s, networks were no longer the curiosity they had been, and network programming experience had become a common skill. This was fortunate, because the network had morphed from a simple wire that linked client and server to a key infrastructure component that enabled the linking of business units in powerful new forms of commerce.

As the network changed, CORBA had to change. The pure location transparency that was such a benefit when networks were new and unknown, became a hindrance to programmers when they tried to take advantage of network characteristics in new and powerful server designs. And, when networks became overloaded, taking advantage was replaced by coping as Quality of Service control became essential.

As networks allowed more users to access popular servers, programmers developed techniques that allowed these servers to scale to meet the need. Proprietary at first, by the end of the decade these techniques had become common enough to be standardized and they, too, became a part of the new CORBA, particularly through the Portable Object Adapter (POA) and CORBA Component Model (CCM). OMG decided to collect these advances in a major release they planned to label CORBA 3.

P.1   The Power of CORBA 3

There's a lot to CORBA 3 (as you know just from scanning the table of contents of this book); so much so that if you look only at the details, you can miss the point—a "forest-and-trees" effect. To avoid this, we'll start here with a broad view of the power of CORBA 3; once we're done, we'll use the rest of the book to back up the promises and assertions that we'll make in this section.

P.1.1   The CORBA 2.0/2.1 Client

We've already introduced the CORBA 2.0/2.1 client: It's a simple construct with no view of the network. It invokes and passes objects by reference only, and invokes synchronously using either the Static Invocation Interface (SII), using stubs compiled from IDL, or Dynamic Invocation Interface (DII), using stubs interpreted at runtime from the IDL. Some programmers used the DII to make *deferred-synchronous* invocations—a polling-mode invocation that required polling to retrieve results.

P.1.2   The CORBA 3 Client

In contrast, the CORBA 3 client has a very sophisticated view of the network, and of other distributed resources hidden from (or, in some cases, not yet available to) its CORBA 2 ancestor. This client:

- Can invoke either synchronously or asynchronously on any CORBA object, using either SII or DII
- Can make time-independent invocations—that is, operate in CORBA's new loosely coupled networking environment
- Can take advantage of CORBA's newly defined reliable network infrastructure
- Can negotiate a quality-of-service level with the network and a server

- Can invoke and pass CORBA objects by reference, and CORBA Value-types by value
- Can find services using URL-format object references
- Can invoke operations on RMI/IDL Java objects
- Can deal with firewalls
- Can use both Factory and Finder patterns to interact with CORBA components (and objects)
- Can navigate among the multiple interfaces of a CORBA component

Originally defined to let clients take advantage of local compute cycles while server operations executed remotely, asynchronous invocation plays a much more important role in enterprise computing: Combined with a reliable network infrastructure—that is, CORBA invocations over a messaging-like protocol—this mode allows CORBA clients and servers to operate in the loosely coupled way that inter-enterprise computing requires.

Other capabilities—URL-like object references, coping with firewalls, and interoperability with RMI/IDL Java objects—further integrate our client with the world of the Internet and of enterprise computing. And the last two capabilities—using Factory and Finder patterns, and navigating among a component's multiple interfaces—equip our client to deal with important new capabilities of CORBA 3 servers.

P.1.3   The CORBA 2.0/2.1 Server

Programmers have been writing huge, scalable, reliable CORBA servers for years (OMG has a collection of writeups on its success story Web site, www.corba.org). So CORBA's ability to support these servers has never been in question. What has been questioned, however, is the amount of low-level programming skill needed to produce these servers, and the difficulty of finding this skill combined with the business knowledge needed to make them function in the enterprise. Programming this kind of capability into a CORBA 2 server did, we admit, require a certain amount of skill. In addition, infrastructure support for making an object's internal state persistent, and for associating the persistent state with the executing instance, was not fully developed.

P.1.4   The CORBA 3 Server

The salient advancement in CORBA 3 on the server side is the simplification of the programming model. Embodied mainly in the CORBA Component Model specification, with help from the Persistent State Service (PSS), CORBA 3 defines an environment that lets every capable business developer produce servers with the characteristics required by enterprise computing. In addition to simplifying the programming model, CORBA 3 standardizes the mechanisms that make servers scale, and the interfaces to these mechanisims. The CORBA 3 server:

- Simplifies server programming with new declarative languages for server-side functions and characteristics

- Automatically generates, for CORBA Components, a type-specific home object that implements class-like methods including instance creation and destruction and client-visible identity, and provides a place for queries across the extent of a type

- Allows CORBA Components to bear multiple interfaces, and supports client navigation among them

- Integrates object persistence, transactionality, security, and event handling into the CCM as *run-time* constructs, rather than *coding-time* constructs, relieving business programmers of the responsibility for dealing with them

- Integrates with Enterprise JavaBeans (EJB) and is, as we'll show in Section III.3.3.13, a *superset* of EJB

- Supports many flexible patterns of resource control for *servants* (a servant is the executing image of a CORBA object instance), with differing qualities of transience or persistence

- Associates an ObjectID with the Object Reference, allowing a servant to find and retrieve its persistent state on activation, and properly store it on deactivation

- Can negotiate quality of service with the network and the client

- Can deal with firewalls

- Can be specialized for small embedded systems, or for Real-Time applications, in addition to its capabilities in large scalable server applications

Aimed at enterprise servers—CORBA's most demanding environment—these new capabilities make CORBA one of the biggest of the big boys on the enterprise end of the wire. Supported by new capabilities in persistence handling, and working with the server-side analogues of the networking functions we examined on the client side, the features on this list define a very capable programming and execution environment indeed. What else could we possibly want? How about applicability to specialized environments, provided by minimal (for embedded systems) and Real-time CORBA, mentioned in the last bullet. Already used in mission-critical (read "life and death") applications including fly-by-wire and chemical process control, Real-Time CORBA brings standardization to the previously proprietary world of distributed real-time systems. We'll describe some of the most exciting applications in Part II, Chapter 3.

P.2 The Many Parts of CORBA 3

CORBA 3 was pre-announced by the OMG in a September 1998 press release. The release predicted that 10 new distinct but related specifications would be adopted nearly simultaneously and issued together. As we will show in the rest of this book, all of the predicted specifications and several more closely related ones were in fact adopted and issued, although not together. In fact, the 10-plus specifications spread over three point releases (CORBA 2.2, 2.3, and 2.4) and the major release 3.0, which was scheduled for late 2001 as we went to press. We've summarized the release schedule for all of these specifications in Table P.1.

The press release divides the specifications into three categories. This division fits so logically that we've used it to organize this book, which is

Table P.1 Release of Specifications Originally Grouped as CORBA 3

RELEASE	DATE	INCLUDED SPECIFICATION	ORIGINALLY ADOPTED
CORBA 2.2	Feb. 1998	POA	June 97
		IDL-to-Java Mapping	July 98
CORBA 2.3	June 1999	Valuetypes	May 98
		Java-to-IDL Mapping	Aug. 98
CORBA 2.4	Late 2000	Messaging	Sept. 98
		Interoperable Naming Svc	Mar. 99
CORBA 3.0	Early 2001	CORBA Component Model	Late 99
		CORBA Scripting	May 99
		Real-Time CORBA	May 99
		Minimal CORBA	Nov. 98

divided into a Part for each category plus a final one describing OMG's modeling specifications. The three categories, and our additional Part, are:

- Improved integration with Java and the Internet, presented in Part I
- Quality of Service control, presented in Part II
- The CORBA Component Model, presented in Part III
- OMG's modeling specifications, presented in Part IV

Here's a closer look at each category, with a list of the specifications included in each one and where (and whether) it appears in this book.

P.2.1   Improved Integration with Java and the Internet

The 1998 announcement included three specifications in this category. We're not going to follow the original categorization in this book. In fact, we won't present two of the original specifications (for the reasons given below), but we've moved one here from the third category and added two new ones. We present this category in Part I. Here is our revised list of specifications in this category:

- *Objects passable by value* (**valuetype**s): The press release mentions this specification in the third category along with the CCM, but we've moved it to here where you'll find our presentation in Part I, Chapter 1. It definitely improves integration with Java, and also serves as the basis for the XML/Value mapping. It was formally released as part of CORBA 2.3.
- *Java-to-IDL Mapping*: Based in part on the **valuetype**, this mapping allows Java RMI objects to interoperate over the network like CORBA objects. They have CORBA object references and emit the IIOP protocol. The Java-to-IDL Mapping was mentioned in the press release in this category; we present it in Section I.1.4 right after **valuetype**s. This specification was also released as part of CORBA 2.3.
- *XML/Value Mapping*: This mapping of the popular data language XML to CORBA **valuetype**s wasn't even in the plans when the original CORBA 3 press release was issued, but because XML is so important to Internet commerce, we're including it in this book and in this category. It standardizes the representation of an XML document as a collection of native CORBA types. The specification lets you take advantage of a DTD if you have one, but works perfectly well for DTD-less (that is, dynamic) XML documents if you don't. In this book, we present the mapping along with a programming example in Part I, Chapter 2. This

specification is brand-new as we go to press; although adopted, it has not yet been issued as part of a numbered CORBA release.

- *CORBA Firewall Specification*: This specification will allow firewalls to be configured for CORBA, passing IIOP traffic when they're supposed to and keeping it out when they're not. The firewall specification, although adopted, was undergoing a major revision as we went to press, so we decided not to include a chapter on it even though the press release mentions it in this category. Check the OMG Web site for information as the work progresses, and look for our writeup in a later book.

- *Interoperable Naming Service*: Another specification not mentioned in the press release, this service is key to allowing newly discovered CORBA objects to be invoked over the Internet. So we've added it to this category, where you'll find it in Part I, Chapter 3. All of the provisions of the Interoperable Naming Service were added to CORBA core in release 2.4.

- *DCE/CORBA Interworking Specification*: This one is mentioned in the press release and passed its OMG Platform Technology Committee (PTC) vote in September 1998, but wasn't embraced enough by the marketplace to become a fully adopted specification or rate a chapter of its own in this book.

P.2.2 Quality of Service Control

In the press release, this category included three specifications. OMG adopted one more in this category since then, so we've added it to this section. This category is presented in Part II. It includes these specifications:

- *CORBA Messaging*: This comprehensive specification encompasses both asynchronous and messaging-mode invocations (which you'll find in Part II, Chapter 1) and Quality of Service Control (Part II, Chapter 2). This specification was added to CORBA in Release 2.4, where it appears as Chapter 22.

- *Real-Time CORBA*: This specification extends the CORBA architecture to give Real-Time applications the resource control they need to guarantee end-to-end predictability for distributed applications built on Real-Time operating systems, running in a controlled environment. We describe it in Part II, Chapter 3. This specification was added to CORBA in Release 2.4, where it appears as Chapter 24.

- *Fault Tolerant CORBA*: New since the press release, the Fault Tolerant CORBA specification standardizes redundant software configurations and systems that, when run on redundant hardware, give CORBA the robust and reliable performance that Enterprise applications need. Our description appears in Part II, Chapter 4. More recent than Real-Time and minimum CORBA, this adopted specification has not yet appeared in a numbered release.

- *minimumCORBA*: Aimed at embedded and card-based systems, this specification defines a small-footprint CORBA configuration by omitting dynamic features (DII, interface repository) not needed in a predictable environment. minimumCORBA is presented in Part II, Chapter 5. This specification was added to CORBA in Release 2.4, where it appears as Chapter 23.

P.2.3   The CORBA Component Model

The press release mentions four specifications in this category. We've moved one, the **valuetype**, into the first category. Another, multiple interfaces for CORBA objects, was absorbed into the CCM specification itself, and we've absorbed a third one, CORBA scripting languages, into the CCM chapter even though these are distinct specifications. Still, there are three chapters in Part III of this book, and they describe:

- *The Portable Object Adapter* (POA): Added to CORBA in release 2.2, the POA forms the basis for scalable CORBA servers. The CCM Container is a specialized POA. We've devoted Part III, Chapter 1 to the POA to ensure that we've presented the background necessary to understand the CCM, coming up two chapters hence.

- *The Persistent State Service* (PSS): Not mentioned in the original announcement, the PSS is another important building block in the foundation of the CCM. Replacing the now-deprecated Persistent Object Service, the excellently designed PSS is used by the CCM Container to store the state of persistent objects when executing code is deactivated between calls. (It's also available for programmers to invoke directly, of course, in both CCM and non-CCM CORBA applications.) The PSS was adopted in late 1999 and is scheduled for inclusion in a formal CORBAservices release before the end of 2001, intentionally synchronized with the formal release of the CCM as part of CORBA 3. We present the PSS in Part III, Chapter 2.

- *The CCM*: Considered by many to be the essence of CORBA 3 (even though so many other important specifications were included in the original announcement!), the CCM packages up transactionality, persistence, event handling, security, and POA-based server resource control into a development and runtime package that business programmers can handle. Intentionally matched feature-for-feature with Enterprise JavaBeans (EJBs) as far as they go, the CCM fulfills the last promise made by the Java and Internet integration theme that started our three categories. The CCM was adopted by OMG in late 1999 and is scheduled for formal release before the end of 2001 as the numbered release CORBA 3. The CCM, and a brief description of CORBA scripting languages, comprise Part III, Chapter 3.

These three categories, and the specifications we've listed, include everything originally labeled CORBA 3. But because modeling plays a key role in the success of the large software projects that benefit most from CORBA, we've added a fourth part devoted to OMG's modeling specifications, including the world standard for representation of Analysis and Design, the Unified Modeling Language (UML).

P.2.4   OMG's Modeling Specifications

There are three chapters in this part. The first two cover OMG's existing modeling specifications, and the last looks ahead at what OMG members expect, as we go to print, to be OMG's future direction: the *Model Driven Architecture* (MDA). Part IV covers:

- *The UML*: Part IV, Chapter 1 was written by Cris Kobryn, one of the authors of the UML specification. It introduces the UML and presents an example based on the programming example in our companion book, *CORBA 3 Fundamentals and Programming*. Although Release 1.3 of UML was current as we went to press, Release 1.4 had just been completed and was working its way through OMG's voting process, and RFPs for a major revision to be designated UML 2.0 were scheduled to complete in late 2001.

- *The Meta-Object Facility* (MOF): Part IV, Chapter 2 was written by Sridhar Iyengar, principal author of the MOF specification. It describes this important foundation that defines the meta-models for almost all of OMG's specifications, and a standard repository for models and meta-models. Release 1.3 of the MOF was current as this book went to press, with Release 1.4 due soon.

- *The MDA*: This final chapter brings our book to a close with a look at OMG's future: the MDA. Basing future specifications on the UML, OMG members will build a library of standards that hold their value as the computing infrastructure under them changes over time. Retaining its requirement that standards be implemented as they are adopted,

OMG will further require that every UML model be mapped to and implemented in at least one middleware platform, which might be CORBA, Java/EJB, XML/SOAP, or some other existing or future platform. Part IV, Chapter 3 describes (in a general way, since work on the MDA is just getting started) how UML will model specific middleware environments as OMG-standard UML profiles, allowing standard mappings to define the route from a platform-neutral UML representation to a platform-specific set of interface specifications and, ultimately, the application itself.

P.3   OMG's Adoption Process and Timing

OMG's technology adoption process is defined in the group's policies and procedures. It starts with the issuance of a requirements document called a Request for Proposals (RFP), and ends its first phase with the adoption of a submission through a series of votes by various subgroups of members with varying (i.e., technical or business) interests. This part of the process typically takes 14 to 18 months, and is followed by an ongoing series of maintenance revisions of which the first is the most important (at least for our discussion here).

All OMG specifications are maintained evergreen by the group's members, and in particular by the companies that contributed the technology. During the last month or two before a new specification is adopted, its submission document is in flux as submitting companies attempt to merge their individual technologies into a "best of breed" common standard. In the haste to make deadline, there is not always time to check that these changes get all of the details right. As a result, the first maintenance revision of an OMG specification usually requires more than the usual amount of change in order to fix bugs that have become apparent during initial implementations.

Until October 1998, OMG had been calling the initial adoption of each of its specifications the 1.0 release, and the first maintenance revision the 1.1 release. Members and others who followed OMG closely knew to expect more than modest changes between the 1.0 and 1.1 releases, and to wait for the 1.1 release before coding or releasing a product based on a new specification. Just before the CORBA 3 specifications were adopted, however, OMG changed the designations of these first key releases. Instead of calling the first adoption the 1.0 release, it was designated an *adopted specification* and not given a release number. In spite of the lack of a release number, adopted specifications are fully adopted OMG technology and available to all on the group's Web site. But, to emphasize the implementability of the first revised version of a new specification, its release was designated an *available specification* and bore a release number.

Helpful to companies that otherwise might have invested time and money implementing preliminary versions of OMG specs, this change in labeling had the unfortunate side effect of lengthening the time between initial adoption of a new specification and its formal issuance with a release number. Although every specification had had an interval between adoption and availability of products, the market had previously been able to point to the issued (albeit buggy) OMG specification with its release number for reassurance that the new spec was really there.

This explains why, between the initial adoption of the CCM in late 1999 and the scheduled issuance of the formal CORBA 3 book with the revised specification in late 2001, CORBA 3 exists as a specification but not as a numbered release nor a product. During the longer interval starting with the issuance of the CORBA 3 press release in September 1998 and ending with the formal release of CORBA 3 book, the 10 specifications that ultimately constituted the specification finished their initial maintenance revisions at widely spaced intervals and became ready for issuance. Since it didn't make sense to hold technologies back from release once they were ready, OMG included them in a number of point releases during 1999 and 2000 as we listed in Table P.1.

We've included parts of CORBA 2.2 in the table, with the POA and IDL to Java mapping, because these specifications are the foundation for much of CORBA 3 even though they're not part of CORBA 3 itself.

CORBA 2.3 is the first formal release that includes specifications originally slated for CORBA 3: **valuetype**s and the reverse mapping of Java to IDL.

About six months later, CORBA 2.4 added Messaging and the Interoperable Naming Service.

CORBA 3.0—with the CCM, Scripting, Firewall, Real-Time, and Minimal CORBA—is scheduled for release in late 2001.

Integration with Java
and the Internet

Dissecting the Internet

The first major part of CORBA 3 we'll cover is integration with the increasingly popular language Java, and the Internet.

There's more to the Internet and to Internet computing than HTTP and HTML. Figure I starts to show the Internet architecture we're talking about. We've only shown one set of a servers from a single company on the slide, in the three rightmost columns, but suppose they represent all of the world's servers, and similarly that the individual PCs, set-top boxes, and PDAs on the left represent all of the hundreds of millions of connected devices in the world.

The rightmost two columns correspond to the bottom two tiers of a conventional three-tier architecture: storage at the base, and business logic next to it.

We've expanded the top client tier into the two columns on the left. The second column from the left is a mediating layer, which relays requests from the various client machines to the business logic layer and formats and delivers the replies from the business layers to the various clients. Although we've shown this layer running on its own hardware, this is not a requirement; after all, your database (bottom tier) and business logic (middle tier) may share hardware resource without any problem today. If the mediating software runs on the same infrastructure as the servers, this layer will be very thin (or absent); if not, it will have more to do.

At the extreme left is a column of clients. Do not assume that client and "PC" are synonomous; companies are realizing that *any* device capable of connecting to a digital network is a potential client, and there are a lot more television sets, telephones, and pagers in use than there are PCs. More and more, customers expect to access their same data in different ways—for example, bank account data may be accessed via a home PC over the Web, a cellular phone, a wireless PDA, or on a screen at the ATM at the Country Cupboard down Main Street. And the customer expects to see the balances as he left them the last time, even if that access used a different mode.

Client and Server Execution Environments

There are a couple of big differences between the environment of servers on the right and of clients on the left. About the servers on the right, we notice that:

- They are outnumbered by client machines by many orders of magnitude, even though there are many servers and a greater variety.

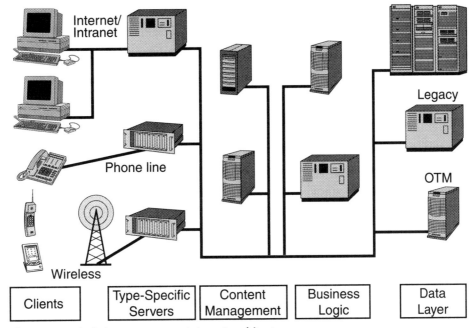

Figure I Today's heterogeneous Internet architecture.

- When a server fails, even for a short time, impact may be severe both on the business that owns it and on the potentially large number of clients it was serving.

- Because of this, server hardware and software are designed and run to be reliable even though this is costly.

- Servers typically run in controlled environments and are administered 24×7 by trained staff.

- Although a server may count millions of other machines as its clients, it works with only a few other (also closely controlled) machines as peers, relying on them for help in getting its business done.

About the clients on the left, we notice that:

- There are many of them—in the hundreds of millions or more; certainly too many to count.

- When a client machine fails, the impact is confined to itself and its user.

- Because of this, and because client hardware and software are typically bought by households, small businesses, or individual offices (without their own IT support), the economic model for this end of the network connection favors low cost over reliability. Using this model, vendors have expanded this market to a nearly unbelievable size.

- Client machines may run in any environment, typically uncontrolled, and may be administered by their users who are untrained in this task, or not administered at all.

- They may access a number of servers, in the role of client, but they depend on no other machine as a peer. Instead, whatever work they do without calling on a server, they do entirely on their own.

Seen in this light, it's evident why the common Web browser client model is so thin: It's uneconomic and impractical to move functionality from a single, reliable, administered server to many types and millions of instances of unreliable, unadministered client machines. However, you can sell a lot of merchandise with the same type of block-data–transfer interaction that we got used to in the 1970s and 1980s. (Do you remember 3270-type terminals? Do you get a sense of déjà vu when you fill in a CGI form and press "enter"? My kids play Internet-based games with much richer interoperability than I ever see when I fill out CGI forms and send them to a server over HTTP.)

Where Is CORBA?

Where is CORBA in this diagram? It's holding together the enterprise, where reliability is important and many different platforms and operating systems must work together to get the job done in the most robust way possible. Even though the desktop corner in the upper left dominates in sheer numbers of machines, the enterprise portion is where the action (and the money!) concentrates: *All* of the requests from *all* of the clients on the left, of every machine type, execute on the far smaller number of enterprise machines on the right.

These machines are going to be stressed: High volumes of network traffic and requests—coming from millions of machines of various types and shapes over radio, cable, fiber, and copper links—funnel down to these servers. If you're a provider of a service in this part of the diagram, you need two things: First, you need the freedom to pick the *best possible* hardware and software for your job, since second-rate just won't cut it in this high-pressure environment; second, you need platform-independent, scalable, robust interoperability so that your best-of-breed hardware and software integrate smoothly with the rest of your enterprise. CORBA gives this to you, and enterprise architects already realize this. If you can get this in an infrastructure that is transactional and secure, which CORBA is, so much the better.

CORBA OVER THE INTERNET

We've run CORBA applications over the internet. We noticed, right away, a richer experience due to the much tighter integration with the server. In fact, we didn't have the sense of being outside the server looking in through a data display window; instead, we felt that our computer, and we ourselves, had become part of the server environment—on the other side of the thin link to the client, as it were. And, in a very real sense, this was true. Computers built for home and office use have a lot of power, and downloadable code removes some of the system-administration obstacles to thicker clients. We don't think that every application needs a thick client; the success of the internet shows how much you can do with data display and a block-data–transfer reverse channel. But, this doesn't mean that these are enough. When you need a richer level of inter-action with your user, think of CORBA on the client as the way to deliver it.

What about other types of devices? Pagers and PDAs use device-type–specific or proprietary formats over their intrinsically unreliable wireless links (although OMG members are working on a standard protocol for CORBA over wireless), and cellular telephones use more protocols than we can count. We'd like to see more CORBA in this link too. There already is some; probably more than you imagine. The telecommunications industry has been relying on CORBA for years, primarily for network management, and is moving it into devices. Some set-top boxes are CORBA based. As we write this, the infrastructure supporting the lower left corner of this picture is not fully realized, and some of the blanks are being filled in with CORBA. We've spoken to and, we hope, influenced some of the people who are deciding what pieces of this layer will look like, a few years down the road. We hope that our words, and this book, have some effect there.

What about the link from the server complex to the client? As we head further into the new millenium (or towards it, for those who insist on lexi-cal precision), there is no single protocol that covers all of the various cli-ent machine types we've shown in Figure I. For PCs and equivalent machines (WebTVs, mainly), Internet interaction is based on HTML over HTTP: from the server to the client we have HTML, a data display format; from the client back to the server we augment this with a Common Gate-way Interface (CGI) block data transfer reverse channel.

CORBA and Java

There are many reasons why Java and CORBA work well together:

- Java, like CORBA, is object-oriented. In fact, the object models are surprisingly similar although (as we'll see) not identical.

- Java has a distribution facility, Remote Method Invocation (RMI), with parallels to CORBA.

- Both work well over the Internet as well as over intranets.

On the other hand, each has things that the other lacks:

- CORBA is a multilanguage environment, with all languages sharing OMG IDL through standard mappings and the common protocol IIOP, while Java—even distributed via RMI—is a single-language environment.

- Java has a large programmer base. Many programmers know Java RMI, but not CORBA and IDL, presumably just because they learned it first. (We don't think that CORBA interfaces are difficult to program; in fact, we think they're rather elegant, not to mention well-modeled and powerful.)

From time to time, someone will ask us, "Why do I need CORBA? Now that Java has RMI (or EJB, or transactions, or whatever), all I need is Java."

There are lots of reasons why CORBA is not going away—not just anytime soon; we mean anytime *ever*. One (or many, depending on your point of view) of those reasons is *legacy applications*. A wise and experienced systems analyst once described legacy applications as "applications that work". If you're a programmer or architect, you'll be smart to regard them as the applications that bring in the money that shows up in your paycheck at the end of the week. After years, or perhaps decades, of use, these applications are finely tuned to the work that they need to do, and your enterprise is finally adjusted to the way that they work, so treat them well.

Another reason is heterogeneity—the wide variety of hardware and operating system platforms that today's enterprise needs to get all of its work done. As we point out every time we talk about CORBA, different platforms are good for different things, and an enterprise needs to pick the platform best-suited for each use. Picking the second-best (or third, or whatever) platform because it's the only one that interoperates with your other systems is asking for trouble.

The final reason is the future. For a few years, Java was the latest language and it was possible (unrealistic, but possible) for people to say, "No language will ever replace Java. I'll just switch to Java and never have to worry about any other language." Then, in mid-2000, the new language C# came onto the scene seemingly out of nowhere and suddenly these same people were worrying about integrating their legacy Java applications with the ones they're about to generate using this new "silver bullet" language. When C# becomes a significant player in Enterprise computing, you can bet that OMG will standardize an IDL mapping for it, integrating it with the rest of the world's languages—including Java—via CORBA.

Java and CORBA

Because of the similarity of their object models and the popularity of Java, this language enjoys a special relationship with CORBA. We'll describe most of the couplings in detail as we work our way through CORBA 3. Here's a summary:

- Java is the only language with a reverse mapping from its objects' interfaces to OMG IDL.

- CORBA's **valuetype** aligns, in function, with the Java `serializable`. This enables implementation of the reverse Java-to-IDL mapping, which has to deal with Java objects sent over the wire. To retain programming-language independence, CORBA needed a solution that worked across language boundaries. The **valuetype** does this; we'll show how in Part I, Chapter 1.

- And the basic level of the CCM is aligned, quite intentionally, with the EJB specification.

The introduction of objects passable by value was the first major change that OMG members made to the CORBA architecture since adding the IIOP protocol in 1995. Like the Asynchronous and Messaging Interfaces that followed this specification, the **valuetype** exposes aspects of the remoteness of object instances to the client, and either allows or requires a client to treat objects differently depending on their location. This is a necessary part of the "growing up" that brought CORBA to its prominent position in the world of enterprise and Internet computing.

Coming Up in This Part

We'll start the section off with a description of the **valuetype**, acknowledging its role as enabler of the reverse Java-to-IDL mapping. This will take up most of Part I, Chapter 1, but we'll finish the chapter off with a treatment of the reverse mapping in Section I.1.4. Part I, Chapter 2 contains a detailed look at the XML/Value mapping—XML documents expressed as native CORBA types. Most of the chapter is devoted to a programming example, showing both what you can do with an XML document in CORBA and how you do it. To finish off this part of the book, we describe the Interoperable Naming Service in Part I, Chapter 3.

The valuetype, and the Java-to-IDL Mapping

CHAPTER PREVIEW

Of the two topics in this chapter, the valuetype has to come first. This new construct plays two important roles in CORBA: Most generally, the valuetype gives
CORBA programmers an alternative construct that passes by value, rather than
by reference. More specifically, because of the way the valuetype was defined
(and quite on purpose), it also gives CORBA a construct that parallels Java's
`serializable`. In addition, the valuetype's handling of NULLs fills another
gap in CORBA/Java relations.

These capabilities of the valuetype enable the Reverse mapping of Java
objects to OMG IDL which we will take up in Section I.1.4. Watch for other
CORBA/Java similarities to help throughout the discussion, too.

The **valuetype** and the reverse Java-to-IDL mapping presented in this
chapter are building blocks for several important CORBA specifications
coming up throughout this book: the XML/Value mapping (which represents an XML document as a tree of **valuetype**s); asynchronous invocations
(where the poller return type is a **valuetype**); and the CCM (which regards
EJBs as basic-level CORBA components).

CORBA BASICS

After an introduction and a chapter of stage setting, we're finally ready to dig into our first really technical material. We admit that was a long introduction, but we think it was worth it to clarify, at the outset, what's in CORBA 3 and when each part became an official OMG specification.

You need to understand how CORBA works in order to benefit from this chapter and the ones that follow. We haven't included that material in this book—we wanted it to remain a (relatively!) svelte tome dedicated, exclusively, to the new specifications originally designated CORBA 3.

If you need either an introduction or a brush-up on basic CORBA and how OMG IDL (Interface Definition Language) interfaces map to the various supported programming languages, there are a couple of places you can turn. For a complete description that starts at the very beginning, check out *CORBA 3 Fundamentals and Programming* by the same author and publisher as this book. On the Web, try the tutorials on OMG's Web site, starting at www.omg.org/gettingstarted. We wrote these too, so you should feel comfortable with the material and style there. For references to more books and tutorials, surf to the CORBA Resources page from the Getting Started tutorial.

Role of a Language Mapping

So, this next paragraph is more of a reminder than a summary. If you need more than you find here, run (don't walk!) to one of those references for more help.

In CORBA programming, you define the interface to each object type by writing it in OMG IDL. Then, to convert the interface to your programming language, you run the IDL through an IDL compiler, which converts it to a language-specific interface according to the OMG-standard mapping for that language. Standardized mappings for C, C++, Java, Smalltalk, Ada, COBOL, Lisp, PL/1, Python, and IDLscript ensure that all of these languages participate in CORBA integration; commercially or publicly available IDL compilers (albeit non-standard) for other languages extend CORBA to programming environments that lack, for whatever reason, a standardized mapping.

The role of IDL is central to CORBA. You need to understand it in order to understand what this chapter (and the rest of the book!) is talking about.

I.1.1 The valuetype

In the introduction, we pointed out that CORBA 3 was bringing big changes to the established architecture. Our first specification, the **valuetype**, brings this to the fore. Definitely inconsistent with CORBA's inviolate principle (until now!) of location transparency, the **valuetype** lets client and object move objects (albeit not CORBA objects, as we'll see) from one end of the wire to the other, explicitly, at will.

When we code our CORBA application to refer to and invoke objects identically, regardless of whether they are local or remote, we're following the principle of *location transparency*. But in our design, installation, and administration, we always pay careful attention to remoteness because we know that network transmission is never free—bandwidth is limited and latency is frequently longer than users want to wait. The reason we design and code in a location-transparent manner is that these problems have nothing to do with any particular application—they're characteristic of the network environment, and should be dealt with in the infrastructure layer wherever this is possible.

In part, issuing the RFP for objects passable by value was an admission on the OMG's part that some objects—with their states—need to be operated on in multiple locations with the performance you can only get with local invocations. Where resources are stressed, this may be the only way to get your work done while providing the service levels that your users expect. It doesn't matter whether your data structure is huge—gigabytes or more—or the network is so overloaded that even small payloads travel slowly. Whatever the reason, this is another tool in your CORBA programmer's toolbox that you can use to cope in special situations.

Here's another use of **valuetype**s: Recursive or cyclic graphs such as btrees, when represented by **valuetype**s, transfer properly over the wire and are guaranteed to be set up the same at the receiving end as they were at the sending end. Btrees are ubiquitous in computing: they can be used to index databases, keep track of the lines of text in an editor as the user adds and deletes at will, store filenames in a directory, and other tasks, typically involving storage and retrieval of quantities that need to be ordered but weren't when they arrived. CORBA uses a btree-like structure as the basis of its XML/Value mapping which we'll discuss in detail in the next chapter.

And, this specification does one more important thing: It unifies CORBA and Java, by providing a CORBA equivalent to the Java `serializable`. We'll see in Section I.1.4 how this enables the reverse Java-to-IDL mapping which has to deal with Java objects passed over the wire. In addition, **valuetype**s encode and send nulls over the wire as Java expects, whereas IDL types (which are not CORBA objects) do not—if you think that your CORBA code may ever be used with Java (and there isn't much code that could escape *that* net), then it would be a good idea to code your **strings**, structs, sequences, and arrays as valuetypes to keep Java from choking when it gets an empty one. Then, in Part III, Chapter 3, we'll see how this special relationship between CORBA and Java is expressed in the intentional consistency of Enterprise JavaBeans and basic-level CORBA Components.

But first, on to the valuetype.

I.1.1.1   valuetype Basics

The IDL keyword for an object passable by value is valuetype.

You can think of a valuetype as a "struct with functionality"—you can put any IDL datatypes that you want (including constructed types) into a valuetype. When you pass the valuetype as a parameter to a CORBA call, the ORB at the receiving end constructs a *local copy* and populates it with an exact copy of whatever data was contained in the original at the instant you either made the invocation or sent the reply that contained it (since valuetypes can be either in, out, inout, or return value parameters). At the receiving end, it becomes a *local programming-language object,* where it is invoked through the language mechanism and not through the ORB. Data at the two locations is *not* synchronized by any CORBA mechanism—as far as the system is concerned, there is no relationship between source and copy once the transferred data finishes its trip over the wire. If you want the copies at the two ends to update each other, you'll have to do all the work for this yourself.

valuetypes are *not* CORBA objects—they do not inherit from **CORBA:: Object**; instead they have their own base class, **ValueBase**. This allows valuetype implementations to stay lightweight, avoiding the baggage required by CORBA interface semantics—marshaling, POA support, and so forth. They don't even have object references. valuetypes can inherit singly (but not multiply) from other valuetypes, but can only *support* interfaces. We'll discuss *support*ing a little more at the end of this subsection.

Since there is no magic in CORBA (or anywhere else except on TV), you can't just pass a valuetype to any application and expect it to work. At the receiving end, the ORB must have a factory that it can invoke to create a running instance of the valuetype. After the factory creates it, the instance accepts the stream of state data that the ORB received over the wire and uses it to reconstruct its state, making it ready to accept calls. If you're using Java, you'll be pleased to know that the protocol provides for a look over the wire for downloadable code to create the running instance, although the ORB also looks for a local factory even in Java. And, if you plan to pass a valuetype from an application in one language to an applica-

TECHNICAL INSIGHT

Besides losing the baggage, there was another reason why this specification doesn't allow CORBA objects to be passed by value: Suppose CORBA objects could be passed either by value or by reference. Presumably, to be most flexible, the specification would allow the decision to be made at runtime: wherever you had an object reference, you could put an actual object whenever you wanted. Imagine what would happen when a pre-pass-by-value implementation found coming at it over the wire, instead of an object reference, an actual object, state and all.

By defining the valuetype to be different from a CORBA object, the specification avoids dealing with this. It also forces architects and programmers to partition objects into pass-by-reference and pass-by-value formats. If not for this, the specification would have had to invent a category of object that could never be passed by value (for your company's main accounting system CORBA object, for example) and for objects that could only be passed by value (btrees and the like), as well as the collection of "normal" objects that could be passed either way.

You can define an interface that accepts either the CORBA form or valuetype form of an object. Watch for the discussion of abstract interfaces later in this chapter.

tion in another, you'll have to write identical implementations in the two languages yourself—no magic is going to do this for you either.

Although **valuetype**s are active objects with callable methods, you can also use them to represent objects that only encapsulate data, or to pass large or complicated **struct**s. (A **valuetype** with no methods and only one data element is called a *valuebox*.) If your application passes the same **struct** data over the wire in repeated calls, the **valuetype** gives you an easy way to re-create the struct in the remote context where it remains accessible after the call that created it. As soon as the **valuetype** became official, new OMG specifications started using it in place of **struct**s wherever they could.

When we completed *CORBA 3 Fundamentals and Programming* in late 1999 and early 2000, only a few ORB products implemented **valuetype**s, so we recommended waiting before you designed them into your applications. Now we think the waiting is over: As we write this barely a year later, most of the major ORBs and many others implement **valuetype**s in both C++ and Java. So, now is certainly a good time to start experimenting with this new type and, if your environment includes only (or mainly) ORBs in this category, to consider deploying them as well. Even if you decide that it's too soon now, it won't be long before the **valuetype** becomes a standard part of every ORB and every developer's CORBA toolkit.

valuetype implementations require the mapping of their new IDL to different programming languages. As we wrote this, mappings were complete for C++, Java, Ada, PL/1, and Lisp, and new mappings were under way for Smalltalk and expected for C, ensuring that applications using these languages will be able to participate in the full suite of CORBA features. But, we admit, we don't know of plans to map this feature to COBOL.

What about interoperability? This book is not a good place to print interoperability test results that would become obsolete between the time we proofed them and when they printed, so we won't. But we did hear, informally, about successful Java/C++ **valuetype** interoperability demonstrations as early as mid-2000, indicating that the specification is tight enough that independent implementations interoperate across both vendor and language boundaries. And, we fully expect interoperability to become even tighter as second- and third-generation products come to market.

Considering the advantages that they bring to your applications—local access to data, easy handling of linked lists and complex structs, and integration with Java serializable types and NULL semantics—we think it will be hard to resist including valuetypes in your application's design. And, considering the rapid advances in implementations, we think there's little reason to.

I.1.1.2   valuetype Example

Let's analyze a **valuetype** definition, to figure out what's in there and how it works. This example, from the specification, also demonstrates the use of recursion, but first we'll concentrate on the three major parts of the declaration.

```
typedef sequence<unsigned long> WeightSeq;

valuetype WeightedBinaryTree {
     // state definition
       unsigned long weight;
       WeightedBinaryTree left;
       WeightedBinaryTree right;
     // initializer
       init(in unsigned long w);
     // local operations
       WeightSeq pre_order();
       WeightSeq post_order();
};
```

Following the single line typedef'ing **WeightSeq** comes our definition of a **valuetype** named **WeightedBinaryTree**. The three components of a **valuetype** declaration are, as shown, its state, zero or more initializers, and local operations.

When we defined CORBA objects, declarations served only to define types for use in invocations, which was the only place that these declared variables were realized. In a **valuetype**, this part of the declaration defines the type's actual *state*—that is, the state variables whose values will be sent over the wire when the **valuetype** is passed as a parameter of an invocation. These declarations commit us to declare space for these variables and to make them our implementation's state when we write it—far different from the situation when we wrote an implementation of an IDL interface. Don't get carried away though: This state only exists in memory, and does not persist. When your process terminates, it all goes away.

Following the state declaration come zero or more initializer declarations. Language mappings will define a constructor for each initializer you write. Unlike the IDL interface declarations, the operation **init** will be overloaded if you have more than one (all initializers are named **init**); this is OK since it's not a CORBA call (that is, it will only be callable from within your local language implementation). Watch out for different IDL-type arguments that map to the same language type because they can generate colliding constructors. The specification recommends that you vary the number of parameters to avoid this. (No, it doesn't give you another alternative.)

The final component of the declarations are the *local* language operations on a local language object in your running code.

Let's take a closer look at the recursion in this declaration, since it shows another of the advantages of **valuetype**s so well. A weighted binary tree is composed of nodes, each composed of a weight and two child nodes. This makes its declaration simple—what you see is all there is. In realization, at one end of the tree one node will be the root (no other nodes will point to it); at the other end of the tree will be many leaves (**left** and **right** will be null—that is, pointing to no other nodes). All other nodes will have at least one member (**left** or **right**) that is actually another node.

If each node were a CORBA object, accessing a btree over the network would be extremely slow; every reference would be one or more round trips. And an attempt to copy all these objects, keeping (or re-establishing) referential integrity in the new copy at the receiving end, would be complicated.

In contrast, passing the tree as a set of **valuetype**s is easy. When you pass the root node of your tree as a **valuetype**, its state gets passed automatically. (That's what **valuetype**s are for, of course.) Its state, it turns out, are the two WeightedBinaryTree nodes **left** and **right**, which are **valuetype**s in their own right, and they get passed too. When they do, their state nodes get passed, and so on down the line until all leaf nodes are passed. The system guarantees that, when the tree is reconstructed at the receiving end, the copy is an exact local replica of the original structure. You do have to be careful to pass the root node when you start this process, of course; if you start in the middle, all you get in the receiving context is the node that you passed, and the branches that grow from it.

In the next chapter, we'll see that CORBA maps XML documents to a structure that's a lot like a btree: It's composed of nodes, and each one contains child nodes as state. But, a node in an XML document may have more than two children, and each node contains its parent as state too, enabling traversal down as well as up the tree.

I.1.1.3   valuetype Details

Several advanced aspects of **valuetypes** are interdependent. First, **valuetypes** can be either concrete or **abstract**. Concrete **valuetypes** are the form that we just discussed—with state, constructors, and operations. Abstract **valuetypes** have no state or constructors, and are declared **abstract** instead of **valuetype**. (If you declare a **valuetype** with no state variables, it's not **abstract**—it's just a degenerate stateful **valuetype**.)

valuetypes can inherit, as we've summarized in Table I.1.1. Concrete **valuetypes** can only single-inherit from other concrete **valuetypes**; the authors of the specification believed (correctly, we think) that the complications of statefulness make multiple inheritance impractical. A **valuetype** is *truncatable* if it inherits *safely* from another **valuetype**, and may therefore be cast to a more general inherited type. Truncation for **valuetypes** is the analogue of slicing in C++. If this sounds like a bad idea to you, that's because it is. Don't use it.

Concrete **valuetypes** can multiply inherit from **abstract valuetypes**.

The specification also allows a **valuetype** to "support" an IDL interface. **supports** means that the **valuetype** does what you would expect if it had inherited the interface, but the mechanism is not the same as inheritance so the authors of the specification use the word "support" to avoid confusion. As an example, you could declare

```
valuetype Example3 supports ThisInterface { ... }
```

and your IDL definition would incorporate, through the **supports** mechanism, the types and operations of **ThisInterface**, in addition to everything that you declared in your IDL here, and the valuetype would have included them in its implementation. In Java, the IDL compiler uses a tie mechanism

Table I.1.1   valuetype Inheritance

MAY INHERIT FROM	INTERFACE	ABSTRACT INTERFACE	ABSTRACT VALUE	STATEFUL VALUE	BOXED VALUE
Interface	multiple	multiple	no	no	no
Abstract Interface	no	multiple	no	no	no
Abstract Value	supports	supports	multiple	no	no
Stateful Value	supports single	supports	multiple	single (may be truncatable)	no
Boxed Value	no	no	no	no	no

(defined in the language mapping in a standard way) to couple the implementations; in C++, a combination of virtual base classes and a POA skeleton provide the functionality.

Why not inherit? Using CORBA inheritance would allow **widen** operations to move between valuetypes and objects, a type-system error since the valuetype was defined to be a totally new type, and not derive from **CORBA:: object**.

Should you use **supports**? It's an advanced feature, and we were a little leary of it when we got on our soapbox in *CORBA 3 Fundamentals and Programming*, but now (late 2000) it's about a year later and there are a number of **valuetype** implementations with a track record on the market. You'll need **supports** if you ever declare an **abstract interface** and use it to pass **valuetype**s and CORBA objects interchangeably. We're still a little leary of a construct that not only can be passed by value, but also can be registered with a POA, given an object reference, and then be invoked and passed by reference. Even if it works, it is potentially confusing. (When you pass one of these by value, you have to register the new copy in the receiving context with a POA there and get a new object reference which will have no relation to the original's object reference.) If you think your new application needs something like this, go ahead. But be sure that your architecture is sound, and that none of your staff get confused about whose state is whose at runtime!

So, suppose your application deals with something with lots of instances—a **stockaccount** type, let's say—and it makes sense for some of these **stockaccount** instances to be CORBA objects and others to be **value-**

types. (The **valuetypes** can be passed to traders' computers, while the CORBA instances work well on the trading company's own network, for example.) In this situation, you will have many operations that should accept *either* the valuetype or CORBA object form of **stockaccount**.

To make this work, you can create an **abstract interface** named **stockaccount** that has all of the needed operations but no state. You then define a CORBA object that inherits this **abstract interface**, and a **valuetype** that supports it, as Table I.1.1 indicates. When you define the signature of processing objects that need to accept both forms interchangeably, you place the **abstract interface** into the signature instead of either concrete form. Then, at runtime, you can place either an object reference or a **valuetype** in the slot, and the system will do the right thing with either one.

I.1.1.4   The valuebox

A *valuebox* is a **valuetype** with only one data member and no inheritance, initializers, or methods (the opposite of an **abstract interface**, which has methods but no data). There's a one-line shorthand for declaring a valuebox. For example,

```
valuetype mystring string
```

is all it takes to declare the valuebox **mystring** to be a **string**. If all you're doing is encapsulating data, this form can save you a lot of typing. But, try to resist the temptation to replace all your database entries with valueboxes and think that you're object oriented—that's not what they're for, and it certainly isn't a good architecture. You need active CORBA objects with methods and state, and a well-designed architecture, to realize the benefits of object orientation.

I.1.1.5   Mappings to Java and C++

The **valuetype** is defined in OMG IDL, and of course is programming-language independent. In order to use **valuetypes**, we have to compile the IDL into programming-language code, and pass and invoke the **valuetypes** in our CORBA clients and objects. This part of the job is covered by the language mappings, and the new IDL that defines **valuetypes** required new language mappings as well.

As we mentioned in our introduction to this topic, mappings to Java and C++ came first. Although there are mappings to Ada, Lisp, and IDLscript also, the main players in this arena are C++ and Java. (C is another potential player, with interest re-kindled by the GNOME desktop project. Small-talk is another expected entrant.)

As we cover the mappings to Java and C++, look for the many parallels as well as differences owing to the ways that the two languages differ in memory allocation patterns.

I.1.2   valuetype Mapping to Java

An IDL **valuetype** is mapped to a public Java class of the same name. The class contains instance variables that correspond to the fields in the state definition in the IDL definition. Only private and public fields are supported in IDL. The public fields are mapped to public member variables, and private fields are mapped to default access instance variables (that is, package-level access). The operations defined in the IDL **valuetype** are correspondingly mapped to Java methods in the generated class. There is also a Java factory interface that declares methods used to create instances of the **valuetype.** Each `factory <ident>` declaration in IDL corresponds to a method of the same name in the factory interface.

For example, the Java language mapping for this **valuetype**:

```
valuetype MyValueTypeExample {
   private unsigned long aLong;
   public boolean isMonday;
   void op1(in string val);          // a method does not use "public" or "private"
   public MyValueTypeExample myValType; // recursive definitions allowed
   factory init(in string defaultValue);
};
```

is:

```
abstract public class MyValueTypeExample implements
 org.omg.CORBA.portable.StreamableValue
{
   int aLong;  // IDL unsigned long mapped to Java int.
               // Also note the default "package" protection
               // for private state members
   public boolean isMonday ;
   public MyValueTypeExample myValType; // Public -

   abstract public void op1 (String val) ;

     /* other emitted methods to help with marshaling/demarshaling*/

};

public interface MyValueTypeExampleFactory extends
```

```
    org.omg.CORBA.portable.ValueFactory {
      MyValueTypeExample init(String defaultValue);
}
```

You extend the abstract base class to implement the **valuetype**:

```
public class MyValueTypeExampleImpl extends MyValueTypeExample {

    public void op1(String val){
        /* user code */
    }
};
```

You also have to provide a concrete factory:

```
class MyValueTypeExampleDefaultFactory implements
MyValueTypeExampleFactory {
    public MyValueTypeExample init(String val){
        /* just an example */
        MyValueTypeExample obj = new MyValueTypeExample();
        obj.op1(val);
        return obj;
    }
};
```

A Java class supporting a **valuetype** must implement the `java.io.`
`Serializable` **interface**. A **valuetype** that supports an IDL **interface** must use
the TIE mechanism for its implementation.

`Holder` and `Helper` classes are also generated for the valuetype.

If you compare this to the C++ mapping for **valuetypes** (presented in the
next section), you will notice that the two are very similar. The two major
differences are:

- C++ does not have introspection, so you have to register value factories. For Java, there is a set of rules that the ORB uses to find the value factory.

- The wire format for Java **valuetypes** may contain a pointer to the actual URL location where the valuetype implementation is stored. This allows an ORB with missing Java **valuetype** implementations to automatically download the class files on the fly. Of course, you can't do this in C++.

This concludes our look at the Java mapping of the **valuetype**.

I.1.3   valuetype Mapping to C++

In C++, the lifetimes of **valuetype**s are managed by reference counting. Unlike the reference counting for CORBA object references which is implemented on a remote ORB and deletes only the reference and not the object when the count reaches zero, the reference counting for valuetypes is implemented by the object itself. When the count reaches zero, the object itself is deleted. As you already suspected, a **_var** type automates all of this for you.

We'll use the same code example that we just used for Java:

```
valuetype MyValueTypeExample {
    private unsigned long aLong;
    public boolean isMonday;
    void op1(in string val);
    public MyValueTypeExample myValType; // recursive definitions allowed
    factory init(in string defaultValue); //like a ctor
};
```

This **valuetype** maps to a number of C++ classes: First, the IDL compiler creates a C++ abstract base class with the same name as the **valuetype**. It has pure virtual accessor and modifier functions corresponding to the state members of the **valuetype**, and pure virtual functions corresponding to its operations:

```
class MyValueTypeExample : virtual public ::CORBA::ValueBase {

public:
    virtual  ::CORBA::Boolean   isMonday () const=0;
    virtual  void isMonday (::CORBA::Boolean _member) =0;
    virtual  ::MyValueTypeExample_ptr    myValType()
      const=0;
    virtual  void   myValType(
      ::MyValueTypeExample_ptr _member)=0;
    virtual  ::CORBA::Void op1(const char* val)=0;

    static MyValueTypeExample* _narrow
      (::CORBA::ValueBase *);

protected:
    virtual  ::CORBA::ULong aLong () const=0;
    virtual   void aLong (::CORBA::ULong _member) =0;

private:
    void   operator=(const MyValueTypeExample&);
     // private and unimplemented
};   // end of ::MyValueTypeExample
```

The mapping for **valuetype** data members follows the same rules as the C++ mapping for **unions**, except that the accessor and modifiers are pure virtual. Public state members are mapped to public pure virtual accessor and modifier functions of the C++ **valuetype** base class, and private state members are mapped to protected pure virtual accessor and modifier functions (so that derived concrete classes may access them).

The code that follows is just an example; vendors are allowed to differ in their implementations as long as they support the methods in the abstract base class `MyValueTypeExample`:

```
class OBV_MyValueTypeExample : virtual public MyValueTypeExample {

private:
    // states
    ::CORBA::ULong _aLong_;
    ::CORBA::Boolean _isMonday_;
    ::MyValueTypeExample_StructElem _myValType_;

public:
    virtual ::CORBA::Boolean isMonday () const;
    virtual void isMonday (::CORBA::Boolean _member) ;
    virtual ::MyValueTypeExample_ptr myValType() const;
    virtual void myValType(::MyValueTypeExample_ptr _member);

protected:
    virtual ::CORBA::ULong aLong () const;
    virtual void aLong (::CORBA::ULong _member) ;

protected:
    /* constructor */
    OBV_MyValueTypeExample();
    /* constructor */
    OBV_MyValueTypeExample(::CORBA::ULong _m_aLong, ::CORBA::Boolean
        _m_isMonday, ::MyValueTypeExample_ptr _m_myValType) ;
    /* destructor */
    virtual ~OBV_MyValueTypeExample();
private:
    void operator=(const OBV_MyValueTypeExample&);
}; // end of OBV_MyValueTypeExample
```

You subclass `OBV_MyValueTypeExample` to get a class that you fill in with your implementation of the virtual functions for the operations of the **valuetype**. `OBV_MyValueTypeExample` implements the state accessors and modifiers, so you do not need to reimplement them, although you may override them if you wish. For example, you could do this:

```
class MyValueTypeExampleImpl:
  virtual public OBV_MyValueTypeExample,
  virtual public ::CORBA::DefaultValueRefCountBase {
    // implement the operation op1
    void op1(const char *val){
        printf("op1: %s\n", val);
    }

    // over-ride the state setter for isMonday so that we
    // print a message whenever it's called.
    void isMonday(CORBA::Boolean isIt){
        printf("now calling isMonday %d\n", isIt);
        // parent call
        OBV_MyValueTypeExample::isMonday(isIt);
    }
};
```

The `CORBA::DefaultValueRefCountBase` is a mix-in class that supports simple reference counting for **valuetype** instances. This class will either be generated by your IDL compiler or available in your ORB library.

In C++, all factory `<identifier>` initializers declared for a **valuetype** map to pure virtual functions on a separate abstract C++ factory class. The class is named by appending "_init" to the name of the **valuetype** (e.g., type `MyValueTypeExample` has a factory class named `MyValueTypeExample_init`).

Here's the factory class for our example, as generated by the IDL compiler:

```
class  MyValueTypeExample_init:
  public ::CORBA::ValueFactoryBase {
  public:
    static MyValueTypeExample_init*
      _narrow(::CORBA::ValueFactoryBase *vf);

  virtual  MyValueTypeExample* init(const char*
    defaultValue)=0;

  protected:
    MyValueTypeExample_init();
};
```

You also have to subclass from `MyValueTypeExample_init` to provide a factory for the value. For example:

```
class  MyValueTypeExampleFactory:
  virtual public MyValueTypeExample_init{
  public:
    virtual  MyValueTypeExample* init(const char*
      defaultValue){
        MyValueTypeExample *newObj =
```

```
            new MyValueTypeExampleImpl();
        newObj->op1(defaultValue);
        return newObj;
    }
private:
    virtual CORBA::ValueBase* create_for_unmarshal(){
        return new MyValueTypeExampleImpl();
    }
};
```

You register this factory with the ORB using the `register_value_factory()` method, passing in a RepositoryID and a factory instance as parameters. Before it unmarshals a new valuetype's state, the ORB will locate the factory and call the `create_for_unmarshal()` method to create an instance of the **valuetype**. There is also a `lookup_value_factory()` method on the ORB that you can use to locate a value factory. Once it's located, you can call its factory methods to create your own instance of the **valuetype**.

I.1.3.1 Using a Valuebox in C++

As we pointed out in Section I.1.1.4, a valuebox is a shorthand that defines a **valuetype** with a single public state member. One advantage of using a valuebox is that you can pass along a NULL for the value, as expected by Java invocations. For example, you can pass a NULL in a **string** valuebox (or, if you wanted to do the extra work, in a **string valuetype**), but you can not pass a NULL in a **CORBA::string**.

If you are using a valuebox of `strings`, or `wstrings`, you will be interested in two types predefined in the CORBA module:

```
module CORBA {
    valuetype StringValue string;
    valuetype WStringValue wstring;
};
```

Here is the C++ mapping for `CORBA::StringValue`. The mapping for `CORBA::` `WStringValue` is similar:

```
namespace CORBA {

class  StringValue: virtual public ::CORBA::DefaultValueRefCountBase {

private:
    // state. Implementation may differ for ORB vendors
    char * _value_;
```

```cpp
public:
    StringValue();
    StringValue(const StringValue& val);
    StringValue(char* str);
    StringValue(const char* str);
    StringValue(::CORBA::String_var& var);
    StringValue& operator=(char* str);
    StringValue& operator=(const char* str);
    StringValue& operator=(const ::CORBA::String_var& str);
    const char* _value() const;
    void _value( char* _member) ;
    void _value (const char* _member) ;
    void _value( const ::CORBA::String_var& _member);
    const char* _boxed_in()const;
    char*& _boxed_inout();
    char*& _boxed_out();
    char&operator[](::CORBA::ULong index);
    char operator[](::CORBA::ULong index)const;

    static StringValue* _narrow (::CORBA::ValueBase *);

protected:
    ~StringValue();
private:
    void operator=(const StringValue&);
}; // end of ::StringValue

};
```

This finishes our coverage of C++. In the rest of this chapter, we'll go back to Java and cover the reverse mapping to OMG IDL.

I.1.4 The Reverse Mapping: Java-to-IDL

In the introductory chapters we talked, in broad terms, about the special relationship between CORBA and Java. The **valuetype**, with its special relationship to the Java `serializable`, was our first example of this relationship. Our examination continues with a look at the reverse mapping from Java to IDL, termed RMI/IIOP.

As we've mentioned in the introduction, the reverse mapping allows Java programmers to produce Java objects that look like CORBA objects to the outside world: They have CORBA object references, OMG IDL interfaces, and accept and emit IIOP protocol. They do not, however, have the internal characteristics of CORBA objects: They have no POA, and do not have the flexible resource management of CORBA objects (unless they are Enterprise JavaBeans, which are a subset of RMI/IIOP objects).

I.1.4.1 Mapping Details

Java programmers have to honor a few restrictions when they program their RMI objects to work over RMI/IDL and IIOP. CORBA programmers will discover, in turn, that the IDL interfaces of these objects are somewhat restricted on their side—for example, they will never include an **inout** or **out** parameter (all output comes back in the return value), or an **enum**. This is because Java doesn't allow **inout** or **out** parameters, and doesn't have an **enum**, so they never occur. Interfaces may have IDL **attributes**, however, cleverly constructed by the reverse compiler from a pair of set and get invocations in the base Java code. Because RMI/IDL is a strict subset of Java RMI, it neither creates an additional distributed programming dialect nor adds an additional incompatible distributed environment.

The RMI/IDL Specification defines five "conforming" Java types, whose values may be transmitted across an RMI/IDL interface. They are an inclusive bunch, comprising:

- **All of the Java primitive types.** These are `void`, `boolean`, `byte`, `char`, `short`, `int`, `long`, `float`, and `double`.

- **A conforming remote interface.** Conforming remote interfaces must inherit from `java.rmi.Remote` (although this may be indirect). They must throw `java.rmi.RemoteException` or superclasses of it; method exceptions must conform to exception restrictions (see last bullet in this list). At runtime, only conforming types may be passed as arguments or results. In addition, there are some fairly evident (and not serious) restrictions on method names, constant definitions, and method and constant names.

- **A conforming valuetype.** Conforming valuetypes must implement `java.io.Serializable` and not implement `java.rmi.Remote`. They may implement `java.io.Externalizable`. `java.lang.String` is a conforming RMI/IDL valuetype, but is handled specially in the mapping (although we won't give details here).

- **An array of conforming RMI/IDL types.** Arrays of conforming types are conforming types—'nuff said.

- **A conforming exception type.** Conforming RMI/IDL exceptions must inherit from `java.lang.Exception`, which extends `java.lang.Throwable`, which implements `java.io.Serializable`. Therefore, these exceptions do not have to implement `java.io.Serializable` directly since it's already done. Otherwise, all **valuetype** requirements apply.

If you've restricted your Java server interface and arguments to these types, and you're using a Java ORB, you can use your RMI compiler to generate RMI-style bindings that talk to the Java ORB. If you use this method to access RMI/IDL, you'll never see any CORBA stuff even though the ORBs are talking IIOP underneath the covers.

And, you can run your Java code through a reverse compiler to emit the IDL equivalent to your Java RMI interface, and from the IDL generate bindings that you can use in either Java or any other language to build CORBA clients that can access this Java object. Remember that any `Serializable` must have a corresponding implementation in the language of the binding. (This could be a big deal if you pass around lots of `Serializable`, which are mapped into the **valuetype** that we just discussed.) You have to use this method to access the object from non-Java clients, but you can use it for Java clients as well as long as the client and server are separated. (The RMI/IDL bindings conflict with the straight RMI bindings and get in each other's way unless you have this separation.)

1.1.4.2 Writing and Calling an RMI/IDL Java Object

For each RMI/IDL interface, there is a stub class invoked by the client that extends `javax.rmi.CORBA.Stub` and supports stub methods for all of its remote methods.

For the server, there is a Tie class that implements `javax.rmi.CORBA.Tie` and is called by the ORB with the incoming call. In addition, Java provides a class `javax.rmi.PortableRemoteObject` that your implementation objects may inherit from, unless you want to use the `exportObject` method directly to register them as server objects.

Here's an example. Let's use this Java interface, which conforms to the requirements we just reviewed:

```
public interface MyInterface  extends java.rmi.Remote{
   int op(int param) throws java.rmi.RemoteException;
};
```

Compare with this Java implementation, which also conforms to the RMI/IDL requirements:

```
public class MyInterfaceImpl extends javax.rmi.PortableRemoteObject
  implements MyInterface {
    MyInterfaceImpl() throws java.rmi.RemoteException{
    }

    public int op(int param) throws java.rmi.RemoteException{
        return param *2;
    }
};
```

First, you'll need to produce the `.class` files for the above, using

```
javac MyInterface.java
javac MyInterfaceImpl.java
```

Then you'll need to run the RMI compiler that came with your ORB to generate a special RMI stub for `MyInterface`, and a special RMI tie for `MyInterfaceImpl`. The stub is used by the client to make IIOP calls to the server. Its name is something like `MyInterface_Stub.java`. The Tie is used on the server side by the Java ORB to dispatch to your implementation. Its name might be `MyInterfaceImpl_Tie.java`.

On the server side, you'll have to create an instance of `MyInterfaceImpl` and export its object reference to the client. We'll show an example using JNDI, but you'll want to register the name in your enterprise's CORBA Naming Service if you're planning to use cross-language invocations:

```
public class MyServer {
    public static void main(String args[]){
        try {
            /* ORB specific initialization */
            ...

            /* create an instance of MyInterfaceIMpl */
            MyInterfaceImpl impl = new MyInterfaceImpl();

            /* bind it to a naming context */
            javax.naming.InitialContext ctxt = new
javax.naming.InitialContext();
            ctxt.rebind("MyInterfaceServer", impl);
            ...
        }
        catch(Exception e){
            System.out.println("got exception " + e);
        }
    }
}
```

The Java client can use Java Naming and Directory Interface (JNDI) to locate the object that was exported:

```
public class MyClient {
    public static void main(String args[]){
        try {
            /* ORB specific initialization */
            ...

            /* lookup up the server object from a naming context */
```

```
                javax.naming.InitialContext ctxt =
                   new javax.naming.InitialContext();
                java.lang.Object obj = ctxt.lookup("MyInterfaceServer");

                // Use the RMI/IIOP version of narrow
                MyInterface myobj =
                 (MyInterface)javax.rmi.PortableRemoteObject.
                    narrow(obj, MyInterface.class);

                int result = myobj.op(10); // call to method uses IIOP
                ...
           }
        catch(Exception e){
            System.out.println("got exception " + e);
        }
     }
  }
```

Up to this point, no IDL is involved, but the method invocation uses the
CORBA protocol IIOP, and the interface is accessible from non-Java
CORBA clients. To access `MyInterface` from one of the CORBA languages,
run the RMI-to-IDL compiler on `MyInterface`. This generates the following
IDL:

```
interface MyInterface {
   long op( in long arg0 );
};
```

You can compile this IDL on any ORB in any programming language it
supports, write your client in that language, and make calls on the RMI
interface of your Java server using CORBA and IIOP.

I.1.5 Summary

We've covered a lot of ground in this chapter, starting with the valuetype
and its mappings to the two most popular CORBA languages C++ and Java,
and finishing with the reverse Java-to-IDL mapping. The XML/Value mapping, coming up next, represents an XML document as a tree of **valuetypes**,
so your first opportunity to use what we just covered is coming right up. In
the asynchronous messaging specification, the poller return type is a **valuetype**, and the CCM relies on the reverse mapping to enable EJBs to interoperate with CORBA Components. All this is coming up, but first, on to the
XML/Value mapping.

Mapping XML to CORBA

CHAPTER PREVIEW

OMG's XML/Value mapping defines a representation for an XML document as native CORBA types. It's extremely elegant and deserves to be the way everybody—and not just CORBA fans—works with XML documents in their applications. This chapter starts with a description of what XML is and, just as important, what it is not. XML documents' structure may be described by a separate Document Type Definition (DTD). The OMG mapping can be applied to XML documents with either dynamic (no DTD) or static (DTD) structure; the static mapping takes good advantage of the extra information in the DTD. Even though more applications will use the static than the dynamic mapping, we open with the dynamic mapping because it defines all of the functions used in the static version.

So, our presentation of the XML/Value specification proper starts with a programming example of the dynamic mapping, using the brief purchase-order XML document introduced in the opening descriptive part of the chapter. The example shows how to do everything you'd ever want to do with or to an XML document: create a new one, open and parse an existing one, prowl through its structure, edit content, create new content, send it over the wire, and serialize and output it in the familiar text-based format you're used to. The next section presents IDL definitions for the various operations used in the example.

> Then, on to the static mapping. Using the DTD, a programming tool will generate both IDL interfaces and some template code for an application tailored to the element names and types defined in the DTD. This part of the chapter presents the IDL for the DTD corresponding to the purchase order that we worked with already, and shows how a few of the operations differ when specialized for the purchase order. Compared to the generic operations in the dynamic mapping code, the static operations code is easier to work with and analyze.
>
> The chapter closes with a brief look at the flyweight design pattern, which streamlines storage and transmission of XML documents as trees of valuetypes, and a few advanced features of the specification.

As we write this, XML is the interoperability Silver Bullet *du jour*. No technology stays king of the Silver Bullet hill for long, but for a time businesses are (or were, depending on when you read this) trying to use XML as the interoperability key for just about every purpose, in just about every area of business and commerce from manufacturing to healthcare, finance to utilities. So, in honor of XML's current status, we'll describe it and its connection to CORBA in some detail in this chapter.

One of the first things we'll talk about early on in this chapter is that XML is a *document format* and neither a programming language nor an RPC. Because XML documents are character-based, we can manipulate them using a text editor, but (another thing we'll learn early on) because they may be complex, are totally intolerant of error, and are likely to be extremely long, that's not really practical.

The XML specification defines a document structure but does not provide an API into it. (It doesn't provide a lot of other things either, as we'll discover throughout this chapter.) But, the World Wide Web Consortium (W3C) has supplemented XML with an API dubbed the Document Object Model (DOM). (W3C has supplemented XML with a lot of things, it turns out, probably because of all the things XML itself doesn't provide.) Because W3C wanted their API to be programming-language and platform independent, they wisely defined it in OMG IDL. They say, in their specification, that they did this not to encourage CORBA implementations, although these are certainly possible. They did it because the use of OMG IDL allowed them to define and maintain one set of interfaces that is usable from many programming languages, on many platforms.

With a CORBA API into XML already defined, why do we need a new OMG specification and a chapter in this book? Because CORBA objects are not the best way to represent elements in a structured document, that's why. CORBA has a much better tool for this, and we learned about it in the previous chapter. It's the **valuetype**, and it seems tailor-made not only to represent an XML document's structure tree in a way that lets us manipulate it, edit it, and navigate up and down it in a most effective and efficient fashion—it also lets us ship the entire document (or parts of it, with a little effort) around the network with all of the delightful aspects of its in-memory structure preserved.

So, in this chapter we'll investigate OMG's XML/Value mapping and all of the things it lets us do with our XML documents. It's more than just a bridge between XML and CORBA, although it certainly is all of that. The **valuetype**s and their structure provide such an elegant API into the XML document—structure and content alike—that this deserves to be the way everyone works with XML content from a program, even in a non-CORBA environment. Here's what we'll do with our XML document in this chapter:

- Create a new XML document from scratch in our program.
- Read an existing XML document in from storage or from the network.
- *Parse* the document into a multiply-linked-list of CORBA valuetypes executing in memory:
  - Parsing can be done dynamically if there is no DTD with structural information about the document.
  - Parsing can take advantage of a DTD if there is one.
  - And, if the document and DTD versions are out of synchronization, the parsing can take advantage of the DTD as far as it goes.
- Edit the document, including adding or deleting elements; adding, deleting, or changing attributes; and editing text.
- As a linked list of valuetypes, the document may be sent around the network in CORBA calls with its structure intact. This includes secure, transactional CORBA calls or asynchronous calls using CORBA messaging (Part II, Chapter 1). This is a great way to make an invocation using XML as data.
- *Serialize* the in-memory representation, generating a revised version of the character-based XML format document that you're used to.

So, in order to understand what's going on, you have to understand what XML is (and what it is not) and know something about the DOM. If you're not familiar with the DOM, have no fear—it's taken over so faithfully by the OMG specification that you'll pick up most of what you need from our presentation although a look through the DOM documents referenced in Appendix A is probably a good idea. (You also need to understand **value-types**, but we presented them so lucidly in the previous chapter that we barely need to mention that here—right?) We're not going to present a basic tutorial on XML and the DOM here—it would be out of place in a book about CORBA. We have neither the time nor the space, and people who know these technologies better than we do have written much better XML and DOM tutorials than we ever could and put their output up on the Web where you can read it. We've collected a number of URLs about XML and the DOM and put them in Appendix A.

What we will do in this chapter is present just enough about XML to ensure that we're all on the same page, and get on to the XML/Value mapping as quickly as we can. We'll say a little about the DOM along the way and point out where the CORBA specification borrows directly from it. Watch for use of valuetype details that we presented in Section I.1.1. The mapping converts an XML document into a multiply linked list of value-types that uses the technique we presented in Section I.1.1.2.

One last thing before we start: Throughout the chapter, we will refer to an XML data file as a "document." This is in part to as a reminder that XML is a collection of text strings and also to maintain parallel terminology with the Document Object Model on which the XML/value mapping is based. We realize that many (most, perhaps) XML "documents" contain data and will never be printed out or read as a document by a person, but the restriction to string representation and the lack of a type system combine to make document a better label than any other. XML files are documents, even when they contain data.

I.2.1 World's Shortest Introduction to XML

XML "stands for" (since our industry insists on using a non-initial in this acronym) *eXtensible Markup Language*. It's a data language, *not* a programming language, that defines an extensible structure for the representation of structured data as a file of characters. *Dynamically structured XML* is simple and most compact: a single document simultaneously defines a structure and presents content. *Statically structured XML* defines structure in a *DTD* or *Document Type Definition* distinct from the document that contains the text. XML is a specification from the W3C; the official specification and many tutorials and papers on XML are available on the Web. We've put a collection of XML references into Appendix A for you.

I.2.1.1   Dynamically Structured XML Documents

Computers represent data as binary bits. Internally they typically represent numbers as binary integers (with or without a sign) or as floating point values; some business languages (COBOL, for example) have an extended or effectively infinite precision fixed-point format as well. XML, on the other hand, represents every data element the way a person would read it—as a string of characters. This way we can read the values but, if we intend to calculate anything with the numbers in our XML document, we'll have to convert them to computerese. This is one place where XML's lack of a type system becomes a worry; watch for it later in the chapter.

Structured data is nothing new: in order to be useful to a computer, data *must* be structured whether the data are located in memory, on persistent storage, or traveling down a wire. The structure may be imposed only by the sequence of `write` statements that creates a data file and realized by the `read` statements that read it in, and the structure may be useful or illogical (to us humans, anyhow), but the data *are* structured.

What XML brings to the table is a combination of four attributes, none brand-new but synergistic in the way they combine. Here they are:

- An XML document's structure is *flexible*: The XML specification does *not* define the tags and their meanings, unlike (for example) HTML. XML is a *tabula rasa* on which industry groups, companies, or even individuals may scribe whatever structure they want. This can be good: If an entire industry gets together on a common structure, widespread interchange-ability of XML documents results. But it is not always good: If different factions define alternative and conflicting structures, or some individual companies define their own formats and refuse to use the group's standard (especially if the uncooperative companies have substantial market share), interoperability is compromised.

- An XML document's structure is *dynamic*: You can add, delete, change, or rearrange structural elements in an XML document and it remains a valid XML document—in that sense, at least, nothing is broken. Of course, changing the structure probably renders it broken with respect to all of the programs that expect to read it in and use it, but at least it's not broken with respect to the XML standard itself.

- An XML document's structure is, to some extent, *self-describing*. Although there is no official requirement that XML structure tags describe the element they identify, the custom is to do exactly this. And, because XML documents contain only text characters, these descriptive tags and the contents of the elements that they identify can be read on-screen or in a printout.

(Don't assume, just because you can read the tags in an XML document, that you can read and understand the document itself, even though you'll be able to understand the extremely simple document that we use for an example throughout this chapter. Try reading a real XML document and figuring out what it means. There's an interesting example at

```
http://zowie.metnet.navy.mil/~spawar/JMV-TNG/XML/OMF-sample.xml.
```

Even this is a sample, so it's short. It could just as easily have been twenty, thirty, or several hundred pages long. And, don't assume that you can *write* XML documents either. The XML specification is totally unforgiving of mistakes: If an XML document contains even *one* structural error, no matter how trivial, the entire document *must* be marked invalid and rejected by a parser. Do you think you could type our entire Navy weather XML example into a text editor without making a single mistrake? Neither do we. XML documents are meant to be written and read by *machines*, not people; even the W3C Web site says so. So why are they expressed inefficiently in characters instead of efficiently as binary bits? Beats us.

■ And finally, XML is *popular*. There are many reasons for this, starting with the ones we've just listed: A flexible, dynamic, self-describing, text-based data structure sounds attractive (especially to people who don't appreciate the value of an infrastructure-enforced type system, or who own stock in companies that manufacture disk drives). Other factors contribute: XML looks like HTML, the language of Web documents, so it must be cool—right? And, because of this similarity, it can ride on top of HTTP, the most widely used protocol on the Internet. And, because HTTP typically transports data that will be used only for display and will probably not execute anything, most firewalls allow XML/HTTP packets through without examination. (Is this a good thing? Stay tuned.)

In an XML document, the data's structure is imposed by a series of *tags*— text identifiers enclosed in angle brackets < >. A start tag and an end tag delimit an *element*; they share an identifying text string that allows a parser to match them up, and the end tag prepends a slash / to it. Elements may be nested. Here's the example XML document that we'll use throughout this chapter. It represents a purchase order (PO).

```
<purchase_order company="Enjay Manufacturing" number="01239876">
  <ship_to_address>
```

```
              <street>21 Pine Street</street>
              <city>Cleveland</city>
              <state>OH</state>
              <postcode>44113</postcode>
          </ship_to_address>
          <POitem_list>
            <POitem>
              <POitem_name>bolt</POitem_name>
              <POitem_number>BO1420</POitem_number>
              <POitem_size>1/4X20</POitem_size>
              <POitem_quantity>120gross</POitem_quantity>
            </POitem>
            <POitem>
              <POitem_name>nut</POitem_name>
              <POitem_number>NU14</POitem_number>
              <POitem_size>1/4</POitem_size>
              <POitem_quantity>120gross</POitem_quantity>
            </POitem>
          </POitem_list>
      </purchase_order>
```

Elements may have *attributes*. Each attribute has a name and a value. You attach an attribute to an element by including it in the opening tag in the form attribute="value". The quotation marks let us incorporate spaces into the character data that makes up an attribute value. In our purchase order, company and number are attributes.

Elements may contain, besides other elements, data. In our example, the elements <street>, <city>, <state>, <postcode>, <POitem_name>, <POitem_number>, <POitem_size>, and <POitem_quantity> contain data. In XML, all data, even if it consists only of numerals and decimal markings and is supposed to represent a numerical quantity, is composed of character data and regarded as text, and none of it is formally typed.

Although there are more structural details and a way to define a static element structure outside of an XML file (which we'll present in the next section), *this is basically all there is to XML itself.* So, don't look for a type system to double-check your values, a way to specify an operation that you want performed on the data in the file, or a protocol for transferring XML files around. All of these things have to be defined *outside of the XML specification.* All you get from XML is a document format, containing only characters (Unicode plus ISO/IEC 10646, basically), with some characters acting as tags and others acting as content. Nevertheless, as even our short example hints, the XML format has potential despite (that is, if we can overcome) these shortcomings. There are different ways to do this but, because this is a CORBA book, we'll concentrate on the CORBA way, of course.

I.2.1.2   Statically Structured XML Documents

There is a difference between structure and content, but our dynamically defined XML example doesn't help us take advantage of it. Sure, you can infer structure from our example document and create a new one with the same structure, but suppose we built each document using the preceding one as an example and made a mistake somewhere in the middle of generating hundreds or thousands of POs. (We wouldn't even have to make an actual error: Suppose we generated a "blank" PO with zero items for someone else to fill in later. This version, of course, wouldn't include any information on how to format the items in the list!) So, we could easily end up with a collection of inconsistent documents if we lack something that defines our "official" structure.

So, to overcome the disadvantage of too much "dynamic" in our dynamic document structure, XML provides the *Document Type Definition* (DTD). The DTD expresses the structure of an XML document, compactly and definitively (and statically!), separately from any content. Here is a DTD for our example document:

```
<!ELEMENT street ( #PCDATA ) >
<!ELEMENT city ( #PCDATA ) >
<!ELEMENT state ( #PCDATA ) >
<!ELEMENT postcode ( #PCDATA ) >
<!ELEMENT POitem_name ( #PCDATA ) >
<!ELEMENT POitem_number ( #PCDATA ) >
<!ELEMENT POitem_size ( #PCDATA ) >
<!ELEMENT POitem_quantity ( #PCDATA ) >

<!ELEMENT ship_to_address
    ( street
    , city
    , state
    , postcode
    ) >

<!ELEMENT POitem
    ( POitem_name
    , POitem_number
    , POitem_size
    , POitem_quantity
    ) >

<!ELEMENT purchase_order
    ( ship_to_address
    , ( POitem )+
    ) >

<!ATTLIST purchase_order company CDATA number CDATA #REQUIRED>
```

Element definitions within a DTD are enclosed in angle brackets, just like XML document elements. `!ELEMENT` introduces the definition of an element. The element's tagname follows the declaration, and `#PCDATA` says that it will contain character data. Alternatively, its declaration may be followed by a list of its children. A list (which may be a single element or a group enclosed in parentheses) may be followed by a + to indicate one or more copies allowed, a * to indicate zero or more, or a ? to indicate zero or one. Absence of a symbol indicates exactly one is required.

There's a lot more to DTDs, but we're not going to turn this section into a tutorial; check out the XML specification for details. DTDs do not let you type your content (Is it a string or a number? Is the value restricted to a range?) or specify how many times an element may occur more precisely than the zero, one, many that we mentioned already. There is something called an XML schema, also specified by W3C, that lets you do this, but it's an optional add-on and not part of XML itself like the DTD.

In spite of its shortcomings, the DTD format collects a lot of structural information into a single place. We will use it to generate a content-specific mapping that's a lot more useful than the restricted one we get when we use dynamic information only. We'll introduce the static mapping in Section I.2.6.

I.2.1.3   A Word on Data Modeling in the Enterprise

Let's take a closer look at something else about DTDs: Since our XML documents contain data, and a DTD describes a set of XML documents, a DTD contains *data about data*. (Data modelers would call it *metadata*, but that's just a name so don't let it scare you.) In our example, this DTD might either:

- *Define* purchase order for our company, or
- *Follow* our company's existing definition of purchase order, or
- *Conflict with* our company's definition of purchase order, or
- (Even worse) *our company might not have* a definition of purchase order, and must deal with multiple versions—on paper, electronically via XML or email, or by phone, or FAX, or whatever.

What's the point? For one thing, handling purchase orders is *expensive*. A large enterprise handles hundreds, thousands, or sometimes hundreds of thousands per year. At $10 to $20 for handling and computing costs alone, this may run into millions of dollars of pure expense. And, because multiple formats multiply costs, a company needs to be aware of every format it uses, and avoid creating inconsistent versions.

But we're not mentioning this just because we think purchase orders are important, although they are: When you construct a DTD, you are *constructing a data model*: the DTD determines which data are used and which are stored; what they are called; and how they are expressed. Advanced data modeling capabilities let you specify how different data elements relate to each other. The DTD then becomes the key to data in conforming XML documents, unlocking it to staff who have the DTD or who know how to access it. Your enterprise will have models for crucial business data elements such as customer, supplier, and product, in addition to the purchase order that we're working with here. Customers are where your money comes from, so it's helpful to be able to store, retrieve, and analyze your customer data and that's one thing that a data model lets you do.

What a great capability—to be able to create and edit data models using only a text editor, any time you want! Until now, you needed to learn how to use a database in order to construct a data model, which was represented as a collection of tables with column headers. How elitist—restricting data modeling to skilled database staff. Data modeling is too important for that. Thanks to DTDs, now anyone with a text editor or word processor can construct a data model in DTD format, and anyone with a browser can be a data model critic! And, DTD data models look like HTML so they must be cool, just like the Web! (In case anyone failed to notice, yes, we have our tongue planted firmly in our cheek here.)

*Just because DTDs make it easy to define data models in a cool format that looks like HTML, using just a text editor or word processor, does **not** mean that it's a good idea.* Your enterprise will live or die based on how much profit you can squeeze out of your archived data: customers and their buying habits; suppliers and their cost and delivery histories; other data that you can mine for opportunities. The quality of your data models—the entities that they represent, how they represent these key entities, and the relationships among them—can make the difference between business success and failure.

So, before you get carried away and start work on your collection of DTDs, stop and think about what you're doing: if you do this, your enterprise data model will be expressed as a collection of flat DTD text files, and your enterprise data collection will be a directory full of flat files in XML format, conforming (if you enforce it) to the DTD. Aren't there better formats to store data models than flat-file DTDs? And better ways to archive them than as directories of flat-files, described by file and directory names? Do you really want your data modelers to build their models with a text editor? Databases and data modeling tools form a multi-billion dollar industry, and they didn't achieve this volume selling copies of NotePad. These tools are extremely sophisticated, and customers buy them because they're worth it.

And how about the data in the files: How much has your company spent on databases? Databases are a good investment, allowing you to store and retrieve data quickly and keeping the task practical as data volume grows unbelievably large. Have you ever tried to do a `select` or a `join` on a directory of XML files? Many enterprises store multiple gigabytes—in some cases, *tera*bytes—of data in databases. How would you deal with this much data stored as XML documents? How much of this space would be consumed by tags? When you store a piece of data in a table, the table and column names tag it quite nicely and take care of its mates in the rest of the column too without using any additional disk space. In an XML archive, each data element *instance* requires its own label. (Of course you can compress XML data and trade CPU cycles for disk space if you want.)

Data integrity is another key attribute of data that is unsupported by these *ad-hoc* text-based storage/retrieval methods. How will you manage relationships across data models on different DTDs? What about traceability?

Summing up our message about data modeling: Don't go overboard extending DTD and XML usage beyond the areas where they add value. A sophisticated data model, the kind that lets you get every last dollar out of the data archive that is an e-business enterprise's greatest asset, needs to be constructed by experts using specialized tools. And enterprise data needs to be stored in a facility tailored to its requirements: databases do this; any other storage format does not.

You should view XML DTDs and XML documents as *secondary*—as *uses* of data, rather than primary stores. XML is OK for data in transit, if you insist, so extract parameters from your enterprise database when you need to and copy them into XML format for your message, following your DTD. (Alternatively, you could make a type-safe, secure, transactional CORBA invocation but we'll skip the details here since this is a chapter about XML, even though it is a book about CORBA.)

To get the most out of your data archive, standardize your enterprise's meta-model and then standardize a data model based on it. Do the modeling work on tools built for the purpose, use UML (the industry's standard modeling language; look ahead to Part IV, Chapter 1 for details) to model your application and CWM tools to model your data, and archive your meta-model reference and data model in a specialized repository. The established industry standard for this type of repository is the Meta-Object Facility (MOF) from OMG, which we describe in this book in Part IV, Chapter 2.

And, OMG's XMI standard (also described in Part IV, Chapter 2) lets you transmit any of these models over the network as, of all things, an XML document described by an XMI-standard DTD.

Let's take a closer look at our list of alternatives in this light: The first alternative, using a DTD to *define* your purchase order, is a bad idea for all of the reasons we've just mentioned. And anyhow, the DTD is too lightweight for this. The XML schema specification adds enough to get a tight definition, but its format is not suitable for archiving the definitions of the business processes that make your company successful. We recommend, instead, using OMG's Meta-Object Facility. Using it, you can define your data model in an environment that also provides archival storage. The definitive copy, stored in the MOF, can be output in many formats including as a DTD or as an XML document.

The second alternative is the one to use, especially if you store the authoritative definition in the MOF, as we just mentioned.

The third and fourth alternatives are variations on a theme. In the first, your company has a definition of PO but ends up with a DTD that is inconsistent. There are at least two ways this could happen: The person or committee that writes the DTD could be careless and adopt one that is inconsistent with your established definition, or you could adopt a DTD from an external source (an industry group or a service provider) without comparing it to the definition you've been using. In the second, you haven't even thought about data modeling and are really behind the eight ball. Either way, your IT and accounting departments will end up servicing multiple PO definitions, at increased cost in both money and confusion.

Before we leave this topic, one more aspect to the DTD story: Many industry organizations are standardizing DTDs for various e-commerce transactions. Of course it's essential to agree on the form and format of the data that companies exchange, but that's not all there is to it: On the data side, each participating company has to relate the data in each DTD to its own data element definitions. And on the process side, companies have to agree on what gets done with the message and the data when it arrives and what gets sent back, and on the messaging semantics. (Is it an invocation or just a message? What protocol? Is it secure, or transactional?) XML is just a start. Each industry, and each company within each industry, will have to decide for itself whether or not XML is a start in the right direction, and if it is, what to add to XML to complete the e-commerce environment. It takes years to design, build, and refine a distributed computing infrastructure, as OMG members have already done with CORBA. You can save years by adopting an existing infrastructure instead of building a new one from scratch. Don't undertake this task lightly!

I.2.1.4 XML Over the Wire

Once we've agreed on a structure and set of tags for our XML dataset, we need a way to send it to a destination and a way to specify what we want the destination to do with or to it once it arrives. We may even want to receive a response. None of these functions are part of the XML standard.

Because an XML dataset contains only text, it can be sent via email and, in fact, that's what many XML-based applications did, especially in the early days. Or, because of its similarity to HTML (Hyper-Text Markup Language, the language that describes web pages), XML can ride on HTTP without much trouble. Firewalls typically pass XML when it travels this way, allowing it to be used for inter-enterprise e-commerce.

Once the XML gets to its destination, what do we want it to do? For some XML datasets—a purchase order, for example—it may be obvious: process it! But what if the dataset contains data about a person, and it arrives at a hospital. Is this person a patient, or a doctor, or a salesperson, or a job applicant? Of course there are lots of ways we could incorporate the information telling which it is, and what we want done with the data, and that's the problem: too many ways. At minimum, sender and receiver have to agree on one way; at best, the world will agree on a single standard allowing any enterprise to send an XML message to any other enterprise and know, for sure, that the receiver will do what they're supposed to with it and send the expected response back.

There are enough XML-carrying protocols in existence and in preparation that you don't have to worry about any standards body forcing you to conform to any particular one, but that probably means that you ought to be prepared to deal with a few at least. Here's a snapshot of what the industry was working on in early 2001:

SOAP, the Simple Object Access Protocol, carries XML over the wire and incorporates an RPC-like operation specifier. It got a lot of press, but was only a W3C submission (that is, nothing official) when we wrote this. XP, the XML Protocol, had its own working group at the W3C but, as we write this, they were still working on a requirements document and hadn't started on the specification. They have posted an interesting matrix that lists *over 20* XML protocols. ebXML from the international standards body UN/CEFACT and backed by OASIS, BizTalk from Microsoft, and OMG's own XMI are on the list. We're not going to describe XML protocols in any more detail, though. (SOAP looks a lot like HTTP to a firewall and tends to go through security barriers that think they're passing display data going to a browser. Once inside the protected enclave, a SOAP message can trigger an operation on a networked server. The business folks, who can now trigger operations on computers across the firewall barrier, are typically happy. Firewall administrators, who understand the risks that this creates, do not necessarily share this attitude.)

And what about security, speaking of firewalls? Since there's no security in the XML specification (XML is a text data file. It doesn't do *anything* by itself, so it can't do security either), any security functionality has to be layered on top of whatever protocol you use to send XML around, and access control on XML-triggered actions has to be layered on top of whatever RPC mechanism is developed and adopted for this purpose as well.

Another aspect of enterprise computing is transactionality. We won't describe CORBA's Object Transaction Service (OTS) in this book because we're concentrating on new OMG standards, and the OTS is many years old and well-established not only in products but also in enterprise installations all over the world. Of course there's no transactionality in XML (data files can't do transactions). The SOAP specification points out that it has a place where you could put a transaction context, if you wanted to run distributed transactions over it. We're sure that other protocols will be happy to let you re-invent distributed transactions also. CORBA has been doing distributed transactions since about 1995.

While we described the things that XML lacks, were you thinking:

- "XML is almost there—all we need is to plug in RPC, security, transactions, a little type checking, and a few other things, and we're home free!"

Or were you thinking:

- "XML doesn't have *any* of the things that CORBA has today—Why is everyone re-inventing all of these services that are well established in CORBA already? Why not just use CORBA?"

That last point of view makes a lot of sense to us. The alternative does a lot of unnecessary re-inventing of business computing infrastructure, which typically takes several generations and years to mature. At OMG, we know how long it takes to establish a secure, transactional networked environment because we've *done* it, and we have one. Believe us, it's not something that you'd undertake lightly.

If this last point of view makes sense to you too, and you'd like to combine the expressiveness of XML with the robustness of CORBA, read on in this chapter and we'll tell how OMG is doing this. But first, we need to touch quickly on W3C's Document Object Model or DOM.

I.2.2   W3C's Document Object Model (DOM)

If we're going to manipulate XML document elements in a program, we need an API—that is, a set of interfaces to operations that access, change, and otherwise manipulate our XML data. Fortunately for OMG members, not only was this work done for us by the W3C (just not in the XML specification itself, of course), it was done in OMG IDL! It's called the Document Object Model (DOM), and is a W3C standard.

We've already mentioned this interface set in the chapter. When we did, we also mentioned that any content-independent API to XML would have to be very generic, and the DOM is, as we'll see. But, if we have a set of XML documents that share a structure even without benefit of a DTD, we can still program to the structure and benefit from API access.

In order to maximize the benefit, we need to stabilize our document structure by establishing a DTD. Using information in the DTD, we can tailor the document element representations in our program as CORBA types adjusted to the way each is used and manipulate them in appropriate ways. We can even (albeit not automatically) deal with conversion of data from character strings to integers or floating point numbers for elements where this is required. We'll show how this works for our PO example starting from its DTD in Section I.2.6. But for now, here's a summary of what we'll be able to do with our XML document using the DOM interfaces.

I.2.2.1   Using the DOM Interfaces

The DOM specification itself lists some of the useful things you can do with it.

Without an API, the only way to manipulate XML documents is with a text editor. Yuck! It's not just that XML documents are difficult to read (and write); they are so sensitive to errors that you're not even *expected* to do anything to them by hand: The XML specification *requires* that an XML parser stop when it encounters an error. This is quite unlike the typical HTML parser—your Web browser—which tries to plow through as many errors as it can, doing the best it can with whatever a Web server sends it, mistakes and all.

Using the DOM API, not only the user but even the programmer can manipulate documents easily. New XML documents can be created in the DOM, and existing XML documents can be read into a DOM implementation via a parser (added through the courtesy of the XML/Value mapping first, but coming to the DOM in Level 3). Through the implementation, all of the elements in the XML document are available to any application that your programmer writes.

If you're using an established XML structure, with a known set of tags (especially if they're recorded in a DTD), you can do a lot with this. Consider the purchase order XML document that we first showed in Section I.2.1.1. A DOM application with a GUI interface could collect information from a clerk and generate an XML purchase order with the same form as our example. Internally, the application would have invoked the **createDocument** operation to create the PO, and then invoked the **createElement** operation as many times as needed, supplying the proper tag string each time, to generate a PO with the expected format. Done this way, the format of the PO is actually recorded in the sequence of executable statements in the application. If there is a DTD for the PO, a program would refer to that instead.

At the other end of the wire, once the PO has been transmitted to a supplier and read into an application, it is straightforward to retrieve a list of `<POitem>` nodes, count them, and process each one.

Originally, programmers manipulated HTML and XML documents with scripts written in such languages as Javascript, ECMAscript (a version of Javascript), and Python. Without a standard interface to HTML and XML elements, it was impossible to port scripts from one platform to another. The DOM provides the standardization needed for portability and enables programmer skills to port from one platform to another. OMG's XML/Value mapping goes way beyond that, as we'll see.

I.2.3   OMG's XML/Value Mapping

In the first section of this chapter, we listed the things we needed to do with our XML document: The list started with reading in an existing document or creating a new one, went on to list various editing tasks, and finished up with outputting the new or edited document in the familiar XML character-based format.

If we can do all of these things, we will have combined the flexibility of XML with the distributed capabilities of CORBA. And, as we'll show in the rest of this chapter, we can do it.

The XML/value specification maps the DOM interfaces to CORBA value-types—the same types that we just defined and described in Part I, Chapter 1. And, the document and all of its nodes are collected in a multiply-linked list of **valuetypes**, using the technique we first presented in Section I.1.1.2. Not present in the DOM (which was only defined up to Level 2 when the

OMG specification was adopted) were methods to parse from an XML document to a node tree and serialize from a node tree to an XML document. Anticipating DOM 3, the OMG specification adds these functions now.

We'll start by showing Java code to parse and manipulate our PO as a dynamic document—that is, without using its DTD. Once we've completed this code example, we'll look at OMG's standard IDL interfaces for the XML elements that we used. There are two reasons to examine the IDL: It not only explains the code that we just showed in the dynamic example, but it's also the basis for the static mapping that we'll detail right after. And, we're sure that the static mapping will be the way that programs most typically work with XML documents, far more popular than the dynamic. We'll examine the complete IDL generated by the static mapping from the PO DTD next and have a look at a few code fragments to see exactly how they differ (for the better, of course) from the dynamic code. To conclude, we'll briefly review some other features of the dynamic mapping and skim over a few W3C additions to DOM Level 2: The Events, Traversal, Range, and Views interface specifications.

I.2.4   Working with a Dynamic XML Document

Before we get into the nuts and bolts of the XML/Value mapping, let's work with the nuts and bolts of our Purchase Order example and examine the code we'd have to write in order to manipulate it as a set of CORBA value-types. Since this is code, and not IDL, we have to pick a language. We've picked Java, although you could do everything here in C++ now if you prefer it, and in the other CORBA-mapped languages soon.

I.2.4.1   Initializing and Reading the Document

Before we do anything, we have to call **XMLinit** to initialize the system, locate and read in the document as an **XMLstring** (Unicode, actually, as we mentioned before), and define a document. First off, we have to import the Java `net` and `io` libraries, and the `XMLValue` libraries (one is named `dom`). Next, we define a convenience function that converts Java strings to **DOMStrings**. (XML uses Unicode, as does Java, but CORBA can't assume that every language understands Unicode and so maps a **DOMString** to `sequence<unsigned_short>`, which in Java is a sequence of `Int`).

One more thing before we get started. The XML/Value specification is brand new and hasn't been through even its first maintenance revision at OMG. A few things were left out of the version that we have to work from, including a way to retrieve initial object references for the **DOMStringValue-Factory**, **XMLinit** factory, and a few other routines. When you see a comment in our code that starts out "Insert code to retrieve the Java object reference for...", that signals a spot where the specification was unclear. We suspect that some of these will come back from `resolve_initial_references`, or that `resolve_initial_references` will return an object that provides the other references. In any case, the revised specification and the documentation that comes with your XML/Value product will tell you what to do.

Here's a quick review, in case you forgot how IDL **attributes** work: If you declare a variable to be an IDL **attribute**, the IDL compiler generates a **get** and **set** operation for it automatically unless you declare it **readonly**, which eliminates the **set** operation. The Java mapping overloads the **get** and **set** operations on the name of the variable: If you include an input argument, it's a **set**; leave it out and it's a **get**. The IDL for the **DOMString** declares the string that it contains to be an IDL **attribute**. The variable's name is `data`. Watch for it to be **set** in this code block. This IDL shortcut will get used a lot as we work our way through this chapter.

Here's the java code that gets us started:

```
import java.net.*;
import java.io.*;

import XMLValue.*;
import dom.*;

class Example;   // wrap everything in a class so it compiles

  /** Convenience function to create a DOMString from a Java String. */
  private DOMString makeDOMString(String str)
  {
    short[] xmlString = new short[str.length()];
    for (int i = 0; i < str.length(); ++i)
    {
      xmlString[i] = (short)str.charAt(i);
    }

    // Insert code to retrieve the Java object reference for
    // a DOMStringValueFactory here:
    DOMStringValueFactory factory = whatever;

    DOMString dom = factory.create();
    // set the value of IDL attribute data:
    dom.data(xmlString);
    return dom;
  }
```

The first thing we will have to do is read in our Purchase Order XML document. We've implemented the read operation as a function named, aptly enough, readPODocument(). We've posted the document at the URL in the code, so you can try this code as it stands if you want. We plan to post a working version of the code at this book's Web site, after the specification has finished its first maintenance cycle and products come onto the market. Here's the code to read in the document:

```
private DOMString readPODocument()
{
  try
  {
    // Open a connection
    URL url = new URL("http://www.omg.org/library/corfun/po12345.xml");
    URLConnection conn = url.openConnection();
    conn.setUseCaches(false);
    InputStream stream = conn.getInputStream();
    BufferedReader in = new BufferedReader(
      new InputStreamReader(stream));

    // Download Purchase Order XML file into a string
    StringBuffer sb = new StringBuffer();
    String tmp;
    while ((tmp = in.readLine()) != null)
    {
      sb.append(tmp + "\n");
    }
    return makeDOMString(sb.toString());
  }
  catch(MalformedURLException mue)
  {
    throw new Error(mue.toString());
  }
  catch(IOException ioe)
  {
    throw new Error(ioe.toString());
  }
}
```

We admit, all of the code so far is setup and hasn't actually used the XML/Value mapping yet. But, finally, we're done setting up and ready to work. This first code section initializes the XML/Value package, reads in the XML document, and parses it into the multiply linked list of **valuetype**s that we access it from.

We're going to wrap all of this section in a class named dynamicCode that starts here. We'll point out when we get to its end.

```
private void dynamicCode() throws
    XMLValue.XMLException, dom.DOMException
{
  // First things first: Initialize the XML/Value package:
  // Insert code to retrieve the Java object reference for
  // the Initializer here:
  XMLInit initializer = whatever;
  initializer.init ();

  // Insert code to retrieve the Java object reference for
  // a parser here:
  XMLParser parser = whatever;

  // It takes only two lines of code to read in our XML document and
  // parse it into a tree of valuetypes, using the readPOdocument class
  // that we defined, and the parser that comes with our XML/Value
  // implementation.
  // The first line declares a DOMString and reads the entire
  // document into it:
  //
  DOMString PO_Stream = readPODocument();

  // The second line declares a new Document - the root
  // node of our valuetype tree - and parses the document
  // into a tree of valuetypes starting at this node. The
  // parser will allocate the additional nodes that hold
  // the document elements:
  //
  Document PO_doc = parser.parse(PO_Stream);
```

In a triumph of expediency over good programming practice and good sense, we haven't performed *any* error checking here. The XML specification *requires* a parser to return an error, with no partial results, if a document contains *even one* XML structure/format error. (It doesn't care if you had the price of the bolts wrong, though.) The OMG specification is well prepared for this, with its definition of **exception XMLException** and 38 specific parsing error codes (numbered 2 through 39, of course). Do as we say, not as we do, and check for these errors on return from **parse**.

On return from **parse**, if the routine found no errors during parsing, our document is stored in a multiply linked list of valuetypes starting at the root node PO_doc. Now let's do some things with it. We can change existing elements, add new elements, and delete elements.

I.2.4.2   Editing the XML Document

If we're the company that is writing the PO, we need to edit it—adding or deleting items, changing quanities or POitem numbers or names, or whatever. To our programmer, the XML/Value mapping structures the PO data to make it all easily available; using these program structures, he will present the data to our clerk for editing via a GUI. The operation `getElementsBy-TagName` returns a list of Elements by Tag Name (duh!), so he would probably start by retrieving all (that is, both) of the `POitem`s this way:

```
DOMString name = makeDOMString("POitem");

// Retrieve items in Purchase Order

NodeList elms = PO_doc.getElementsByTagName(name);
```

Now `elms`, a sequence of `Node`s, contains two elements—the two items in our Purchase Order. Each one contains four child elements—the `POitem_name`, `POitem_number`, `POitem_size`, and `POitem_quantity`. We could easily display a `POitem` in a window for editing, or count the number of `POitem` nodes that we got back and display the number on the screen, or print it for confirmation when we print the PO.

I.2.4.2.1 Changing the Text in an Element

To demonstrate how we can change the text associated with a particular element, let's change the quantity of Bolt `POitem_number` B01420 to 150 gross. Here's the code in a single block, with a few comments. The rest of this section explains it in more detail:

```
// Modify any Bolt items gross values to 150 gross
// where their POitem_number is 'BO1420'
DOMString checker = makeDOMString("BO1420");
DOMString change  = makeDOMString("150gross");
// Loop over the items in our PO:
for (int i = 0; i < elms.length(); i++)
{
  Element poItem = (Element)elms.item(i);
  // ino is the POitem_number element for this poItem:
  NodeList ino =
    poItem.getElementsByTagName(makeDOMString("POitem_number"));
  // iqty is the POitem_quantity element for this poItem:
  NodeList iqty =
    poItem.getElementsByTagName(makeDOMString("POitem_quantity"));
  if (ino.length() != 1 || iqty.length() != 1)
  {
    System.err.println("Invalid purchase Order");
    System.exit(1);
  }
  // This next line is explained in detail in the text
  if (((Text)(ino.item(0).firstChild())).data().equals(checker))
```

```
      {
        // Compare successful: this poItem needs its gross changed
        ((Text)(iqty.item(0).firstChild())).data(change);
      }
    }
```

After defining two DOMStrings for use later, we start our loop over `poItems` in `elms`. `elms.item(i)` returns the ith `Node` in `NodeList` `elms`. (The operation name `item` comes from the XML/Value specification and has nothing to do with the fact that we're retrieving a `poItem`.) `elms.item` returns a `Node`; we have to cast the return value to an `Element` in order to assign it to `Element poItem`.

Each `poItem` element has four children, tagnamed (from the strings in our XML document) `POitem_name`, `POitem_number`, `POitem_size`, and `POitem_quantity`. `getElementsByTagName` returns a list, so we declare `ino` and `iqty` to be `NodeLists` even though we're certain that only one element is going to come back from each call here. After checking that we have a valid `poItem` (even though we didn't bother to check that we had a valid PO!), we're ready to check and change the number of items we want to buy.

One of these lines of code (at least!) needs a little explanation. It's this one:

```
    if (((Text)(ino.item(0).firstChild())).data().equals(checker))
```

The four `Element` valuetype children of poItem that we're working with here do *not* contain text—they have *children* that contain the text. Why? Because an XML `Element` is allowed to contain multiple text blocks separated by `#PCDATA`, or to contain text blocks of different types. The `Element` node–`Text` node structure is necessary to represent these cases. Even though our elements contain only one text block each, they still have this structure because it's part of the DOM. Here's how we burrow down to the text itself:

`ino` is a one-`Element` `Nodelist` containing our `POitem_number`. `item` is the operation defined on `Nodelist` that returns an item in the list by index number. So, `ino.item(0)` returns the first `Element` in our (one-`Element`!) list.

Fortunately for us, this `Element` (and its brothers and sisters) has only a single `Text` `Node`, so we can retrieve it using the **get** operation of **readonly attribute Node firstChild** defined on the `Element`. In Java, the **get** operation for an **attribute** maps to the name of its parameter so the operation `firstChild` **get**s that node. The `firstChild` is a `Text` `Node`, so we have to cast it to `(Text)` in order to retrieve the text from it.

Now, the text that it contains is in **attribute DOMString data**, so we can retrieve it using the **get** operation for **data**, which in Java maps to the operation name `data`. Fortunately it's a `DOMString`, the same type as `checker`, so we don't have to do any more casting in order to do the comparison.

Of course we've strung all of these fetch operations together in a single line of code to show you how elegantly you can program with this specification!

In the next line of code (not counting the comments), we use the **set** operation of the **data attribute** of the `Text Node` of the `POitem_quantity` Element to set the new quantity. Except for this, the tricks in this line are the same ones as in the line above it.

We realize that this code, with its loop and conditional test, isn't particularly realistic and that a more typical example would use a GUI. But this isn't a chapter on GUI-writing, so this primitive algorithm will have to do for an illustration. It does demonstrate, in a relatively few lines, how to access and modify the contents of individual elements that were created originally by our generic parser and, by extension, how to edit a document in general.

I.2.4.2.2   Adding a New Element

In this section, we'll present the code to add a `poItem` when our user presses the "New Item" button on the screen.

Operations to create new **Node**s of all types—that is, **Node** factories—are defined on our document, so we invoke on `PO_doc` to create `Element`s and the `Text` **Node**s. When you create an `Element`, you specifiy its `tagName`; when you create a `Text` **Node**, you pass in its text `data`.

`appendChild` does just what its name says; because each child node of our PO poItem has its own `Text` **Node**, we have a lot of appending to do:

- Each `Text` **Node** is appended to its parent `Element`.

- All of the four new `Element`s (name, number, size, quantity) are appended to our new `poItem`.

- Finally, our new `poItem` is appended to our `POitem_list`.

Watch for each of these appends in the code. And, one reminder: we've already defined `name` to be a **DOMString** containing `"poItem"`.

```
// Create a new PO poItem
//
Element poItem = PO_doc.createElement(name);

// Create each Element with TagName, and its text Node with text.
// Append Text Node as child of Element.
//
```

```
Element i_name = PO_doc.createElement(makeDOMString("POitem_name"));
i_name.appendChild(PO_doc.createTextNode(makeDOMString("nail")));

Element i_number = PO_doc.createElement(makeDOMString("POitem_number"));
i_number.appendChild(PO_doc.createTextNode(makeDOMString("NL4590")));

Element i_size = PO_doc.createElement(makeDOMString("POitem_size"));
i_size.appendChild(PO_doc.createTextNode(makeDOMString("1/4")));

Element i_quantity = PO_doc.createElement(
                              makeDOMString("POitem_quantity"));
i_quantity.appendChild(PO_doc.createTextNode(
                       makeDOMString("200gross")));

// Attach the four Elements as children of our new poItempoItem:
//
poItem.appendChild(i_name);
poItem.appendChild(i_number);
poItem.appendChild(i_size);
poItem.appendChild(i_quantity);

// Finally, append the new poItem at the end of our list of items:
//
NodeList poItemList =
       PO_doc.getElementsByTagName (makeDOMString("POitem_list"));
poItemList.item(0).appendChild(poItem);
```

I.2.4.3   Passing the Document in a CORBA Invocation

Suppose we have a roomful of cubicles (no Dilbert jokes, please) where clerks with desktop client machines read in XML-format purchase orders that arrive in various ways: embedded in an email message, or as an attachment, or via FAX (which we have to OCR—good grief!), whatever. Suppose, in addition, that orders are processed on a server machine that is separate from all of the client machines but connected to them by a network.

Our clerks' client application can send the XML PO, as a tree of **value-type**s, over the network from one application to another by including it in a CORBA invocation. To do this, our server might support the operation **PlaceOrder** with this IDL:

```
Interface PurchasingServer {

   Document ThisPO;
   boolean PlaceOrder(in dom::Document order);
};
```

In this operation, **ThisPO** is a **Document** valuetype, and is an *input argument* to the CORBA invocation **PlaceOrder**. (We're *not* executing one of the **Document** methods.) When our client application invokes, in Java,

```
{
  // Retrieve a purchasing server object reference
  // from the naming service...
  PurchasingServer server = whatever;
  // Set up the document root of our PO tree structure:
  //
  dom.Document thePO = whatever; // set equal to our PO document root
  // Here we go...
  if (server.PlaceOrder(thePO))   // this line sends the entire document
  {
    // Success!
  }
  else
  {
    // Whoops.
  }
}
```

even though we've only included the root **Document** node of our purchase
order in the argument list of PlaceOrder, the *entire* purchase order tree gets
sent over the wire to the server where it gets reconstructed exactly as it
was in the client application. Here's why. (This is review. If you remember
this from Section I.1.1, you can skip the next paragraph.)

When a valuetype is sent over the wire *as the argument to a CORBA call*
(as we show here), it gets reconstructed at the receiving end *exactly* as it
started out, state included. Although you may think of state as only numbers and text, for our XML tree the state also includes other valuetypes.
(This type of recursive structure, with valuetypes including other valuetypes as state, is referred to as a *linked list*. Because our base node structure includes its parent, as well as its children, as state, it is formally a
multiply linked list.) For our XML Document **Node valuetype**, state includes
the list of top-level children that Document inherited from **Node**, and its parent. So, all of the children in the list go over the wire and, along with them,
their state. Because the children go, their state goes too, and so on up (and
down, if we hadn't passed the root **Node** in the call) the tree. We won't trace
through the tree element-by-element, but you can see that even the text
data nodes get packed up and set to the server by the time our system is
done tracing through the structure.

I.2.4.4 Passing Part of a Document

In the previous section, we passed the entire PO to our server for processing. Suppose we wanted to pass a part of it—just a single `poItem`, for example. How would we do that?

It turns out that the specification doesn't let us pass a part of a document by passing the node at its base. If the structure were a simple binary tree like the one we showed as an example in Section I.1.1.2, we could just pass the node at its root. But, if you look at the **Node** definition, you'll see that its parent **Node** is included in its state along with its children. That means, even if you chose a non-Root **Node** to pass in a CORBA invocation, your *entire* XML document would be sent over the wire and reconstructed at the receiving end. (Programmers who work with typical linked lists are used to sending a branch of a tree by including the base of the branch, instead of the root of the tree, in their argument list. But, typical linked lists include only children, and not parents, in the state of each **Node**.)

There's a reason for this: XML defines an *entire* XML document to be a unit. To XML, a piece of a document does not conform to the specification and therefore has no meaning, so there's no reason to ever be able to do anything with a fragment. (There's a Fragment element in the XML mapping specification, but it contains its parent **Node** as state so even this form can't be sent anywhere without the entire rest of the document following along.) The mapping conforms with this idiosyncrasy of XML, and won't let you send a piece of a document without bringing along the rest of it.

So, there's only one way to send partial content of a document over the wire, and that is to create a *new* document, copying only the part of the document that you want into it, and include this (entire!) new document in your invocation. The new document, and your intent, conforms to the XML specification.

Taking advantage of the nodal structure of your XML document, you can code the partial copy operation fairly easily. We're not going to show how, but it's an obvious loop structure and the methods on the Node and other valuetypes help you along the way. An alternative is to use the Range facility defined in DOM Level 2. We don't describe this in detail, but do mention it in Section I.2.8 and point to its URL in Appendix A.

I.2.4.5   Writing Out the New or Revised XML Document

Once your user finishes editing the PO, you can either write it out as an XML dataset or transmit it via a CORBA invocation. We've already sent it, so now we'll write it out as an XML document.

The CORBA mapping provides a simple invocation for this. It doesn't exist in the DOM at either Level 1 or Level 2 so don't look for it there; DOM Level 3 is supposed to introduce this functionality when it arrives.

In CORBA, you'd invoke

```
// Insert code to retrieve the Java object reference of the
```

```
// serializer:
XMLSerializer  serializer = whatever;

// Serialize our edited Purchase Order into a DOMString that we
// could output as an XML file:
makeDOMString NewPO = serializer.serialize ( PO_doc );
```

After this call, NewPODocument contains the new purchase order in XML format. We can print it out, or save it to disk and send it to our supplier as an email attachment. If we printed it out, it would look like the PO example we started with except for the items our clerk just added.

There's an **XMLShutdown** call that can save you some resource, so it's a good idea to give it a call if you're done with the XML/Value package but not done with your application. And, once we've shut down, we can close the brace on class `DynamicCode`, which we opened up in Section I.2.4.1:

```
// If we're done with the XML/Value package for now, we can
// save some resource by shutting it down:

// Insert code to retrieve the Java object reference of the
// Shutdown:
XMLShutdown shutdown = whatever;
shutdown.shutdown ();
}
```

This concludes our example. Next we'll present details of the XML/Value IDL interfaces, pointing out the ones we used in the example along with those that will come in handy for other functions. When we've finished, we'll go on to the static mapping, which works from our document's DTD. Even if you're only interested in the static mapping, you should read this section since every **Element** and **Node** in the static mapping inherits from a corresponding **Element** or **Node** in the dynamic.

I.2.5   IDL for the Dynamic Mapping

We expect that, because so many XML documents used in e-Commerce will be based on DTDs that are more or less standard, OMG's static mapping will be used a lot more than the dynamic. But, we're going to present the dynamic IDL interfaces and valuetype definitions next because, it turns out, the static valuetypes are exactly the dynamic valuetypes but with names and structure derived automatically from your DTD.

We're not going to present all of the IDL—we don't have the space to turn this book into a programming guide for all of the OMG specifications! But we will cover the core of the specification in enough detail to show you how all of the important parts work together and, more importantly, to prepare you for the static mapping that's coming up. Then we'll point out what the other parts are, without going into the same level of detail.

I.2.5.1 The DOMString

Going beyond the DOM's treatment of strings, the specification defines a DOMString with a number of attributes and operations. Virtually everything we touch uses **DOMString**: **nodeNames**, **tagNames**, character **data**, and just about everything else. And a **DOMString** uses the **typedef XMLString**:

```
// Introduced for XMLValues
  typedef sequence<unsigned short> XMLString;
```

That is, it's a sequence of 16-bit quantities with UTF-16 encoding. Case sensitivity follows the DOM rules, of course.

valuetype DOMString contains its string as an **XMLString**, like this:

```
valuetype DOMString
{
// Attributes
attribute XMLString data;
// State
private XMLString s_data;
. . .
```

Because the string is an IDL **attribute**, your IDL compiler will automatically generate **set** and **get** operations on it. (We've seen these already in our Java example—they are named `.data` because the attribute's data is named `data`.) The specification goes on to define nine operations on the **DOMString**: **appendData**, **insertData**, **deleteData**, **substringData**, **clone**, **at**, **length**, **compare**, and **equals**. You'll get the signatures in the documentation that comes with your XML/Value implementation , so we won't list them here. But you get the idea: **DOMString** is a very capable construct.

I.2.5.2 The Node

To avoid forward references in our chapter text, we're going to depart from the order that elements are presented in the DOM and XML/Value specifications and present **Node** first.

In the DOM and XML/Value specifications, the XML document is represented as a tree of **Nodes**. Everything from the **Document** and **DocumentType** to **Elements**, **Attrs** (that is, XML attributes), **CharacterData**, and **Comments** inherits from **Node**. (There's a complete list of **Node** types at the beginning of the **Node** IDL.) In this section, we'll present all of the functionality that lets **Node** play this key role in the way things work.

A **Node**'s state includes everything you need to navigate the tree around that **Node**, *and to transmit the tree as a unit when it appears as a parameter in a CORBA call*: State includes all of its **childNodes**, plus its **parentNode**, **previousSibling**, and **nextSibling**, as well as its attributes stored as a **NamedNode-Map**, and its **ownerDocument**. In addition, its **firstChild** and **lastChild** are listed explicitly in its state in addition to their appearance in the list of **childNodes**.

In the previous chapter, we demonstrated how you could create a linked list of valuetypes and send the whole thing over the network by placing the root node in a parameter list of a CORBA call. The XML/Value specification takes advantage of this: Because of the way each **Node** contains its children as state, when you pass a Doc in a CORBA call to a remote object, the *entire* document gets passed: DocumentType, root element, children, everything, structured *exactly* as it was in the original process. We've already demonstrated how to do this, in Section I.2.4.3.

Node operations include all of the childcare basics: **insertBefore**, **replace-Child**, **removeChild**, **appendChild**, **hasChildNodes** (returns a boolean; some **Node** types, such as text **Nodes**, aren't allowed to have children and others may just turn out not to), **cloneNode**, and **Normalize** (merges adjacent Text **Nodes** and eliminates empty ones, useful after an editing session).

All of the allowed **Node** types inherit from this definition; the constant defined in the list at the beginning of the definition identifies each one. We don't have space to present the IDL for every **Node** type, so we'll concentrate on the **DOCUMENT_NODE**, **ELEMENT_NODE**, **ATTRIBUTE_NODE**, and **TEXT_NODE** in the sections that follow this one.

For all of these definitions, we're going to list only public IDL. Many of these valuetypes have **private** state, mainly used to implement the Flyweight metadata pattern that we describe in Section I.2.7. We'll tell you how to take advantage of this but won't show the IDL that supports it because it's available only to the service implementor.

Here is the IDL definition of **Node**:

```
valuetype Node
{
  // XML Node Types
  const unsigned short ELEMENT_NODE = 1;
  const unsigned short ATTRIBUTE_NODE = 2;
  const unsigned short TEXT_NODE = 3;
  const unsigned short CDATA_SECTION_NODE = 4;
  const unsigned short ENTITY_REFERENCE_NODE = 5;
  const unsigned short ENTITY_NODE = 6;
  const unsigned short PROCESSING_INSTRUCTION_NODE = 7;
  const unsigned short COMMENT_NODE = 8;
```

```
const unsigned short DOCUMENT_NODE = 9;
const unsigned short DOCUMENT_TYPE_NODE = 10;
const unsigned short DOCUMENT_FRAGMENT_NODE = 11;
const unsigned short NOTATION_NODE = 12;
// DOM1 Attributes
readonly attribute DOMString nodeName;
attribute DOMString nodeValue;
  // raises(DOMException) on setting
  // raises(DOMException) on retrieval
readonly attribute unsigned short nodeType;
// NOTE: nodetype computable via repository id
readonly attribute Node parentNode;
readonly attribute NodeList childNodes;
readonly attribute Node firstChild;
readonly attribute Node lastChild;
readonly attribute Node previousSibling;
readonly attribute Node nextSibling;
readonly attribute NamedNodeMap attributes;
readonly attribute Document ownerDocument;
// DOM2 Attributes
readonly attribute DOMString namespaceURI;
attribute DOMString prefix;
  // raises(DOMException) on setting
readonly attribute DOMString localName;
// DOM1 Operations
//
Node insertBefore(
  in Node newChild,
  in Node refChild
)
raises(DOMException);

Node replaceChild(
  in Node newChild,
  in Node oldChild
)
raises(DOMException);

Node removeChild(
  in Node oldChild
)
raises(DOMException);

Node appendChild(
  in Node newChild
)
raises(DOMException);

boolean hasChildNodes();

Node cloneNode(
  in boolean deep
);
// DOM2 Operations
```

```
//
void normalize();

boolean _supports(
    in DOMString feature,
    in DOMString version
);
}; /*! valuetype Node */
```

I.2.5.3   The DOMImplementation

The **DOMImplementation** valuetype bears operations and answers queries that are independent of the DOM tree instance. It stores the version number of the implementation and a list of its features, to enable this.

It's the entity that you call to create a **documentType**. **documentType** operations refer to the static mapping, to XML documents whose structure is expressed in a DTD. The **documentType** contains a **NamedNodeMap**, which contains a list of the DTD definitions for your statically defined document, but, as the DOM level 2 specification admits, standardization of XML schema and DTDs is not advanced enough for this to be really useful. Essentially, the **documentType** functionality here is a placeholder; look for it to develop in later versions. **documentType** is a **valuetype** and inherits from **Node**, a key piece of functionality as we just showed.

It's also the entity that you call to create a **Document valuetype**. Every XML document that we work with will have a **Document valuetype** as its root **Node**. The **create** operation returns a new **Document**, which is a valuetype that inherits from **Node**, and which we'll present next.

I.2.5.4   The Document Node

The **Document Node** is the command center for your document. First off, it's the root **Node**—the base element in your XML document is its child—so this is where you start your navigation through the contents.

In addition, the operation to create every type of **Node** is an operation on the **Document**, making the **Document** the owner of all of the **Node**s. (This doesn't make the **Document** the parent; you set the parent with an **appendChild** or **insertChild** operation on another **Node**. But it does let the **Document** cache information on the number and types of **Node**s that it contains. **DocumentMetadata** is a **struct** that contains this information. We'll explain a little more about it when we explain how the specification uses the Flyweight pattern to optimize metadata storage and transfer, in Section I.2.7)

Because it's central to document handling, here is the complete IDL for the **Document valuetype** (except for its private state):

```
valuetype Document : Node
   {
   // DOM1 Attributes
   readonly attribute DocumentType doctype;
   readonly attribute DOMImplementation implementation;
   readonly attribute Element documentElement;

   // Introduced XMLValue Attributes
   readonly attribute DocumentOptimizationType xv_docOptimizationType;
   readonly attribute DocumentMetadata DocMetadata;
```

Next come the operations to create all of the valuetypes that make up our document tree:

```
// DOM1 operations
//
Element createElement(
   in DOMString tagName
)
   raises(DOMException);

DocumentFragment createDocumentFragment();

Text createTextNode(
   in DOMString data
);

Comment createComment(
   in DOMString data
   );

CDATASection createCDATASection(
   in DOMString data
)
   raises(DOMException);

ProcessingInstruction createProcessingInstruction(
   in DOMString target,
   in DOMString data
)
   raises(DOMException);

Attr createAttribute(
   in DOMString name
)
   raises(DOMException);

EntityReference createEntityReference(
   in DOMString name
)
   raises(DOMException);
```

The operation to **getElementsByTagName** is defined on the **Document**:

```
NodeList getElementsByTagName(
    in DOMString tagname
);
```

Level 2 of the DOM specification, which we won't discuss here, defines some advanced features that are included in the specification. You can import a **Node** into your document, either deep or shallow, and you can use DOM Namespaces:

```
// DOM2 operations
//
Node importNode(
    in Node importedNode,
    in boolean deep
)
raises(DOMException);
```

DOM Level 2 adds XML Namespace recognition to the DOM, and this carries through to this specification. Operations whose names end with **NS** are tied to the Namespace that you input as a parameter to the operation. The DOM specification (on which this is based) cautions you not to mix Namespace and non-Namespace operations on the same Element. If you're going to associate an Element with a Namespace, be consistent about it!

```
Element createElementNS(
    in DOMString namespaceURI,
    in DOMString qualifiedName
)
raises(DOMException);

Attr createAttributeNS(
    in DOMString namespaceURI,
    in DOMString qualifiedName
    )
raises(DOMException);

NodeList getElementsByTagNameNS(
    in DOMString namespaceURI,
    in DOMString localName
);

Element getElementById(
    in DOMString elementId
);
}; /*! valuetype Document */
```

We're not going to say anything else here about **Document**. We think that the IDL says it all, and very clearly too.

I.2.5.5   The Attribute Node

We'd like to present the **Element Node** next, since our document structure will be based on **Elements**. But, because an **Element** is a **Node** with Attributes, we're going to define the Attribute before we use it. In the specification, an **Element**'s Attribute is an **Attr**. Don't get confused; an XML **Attr** is *not* an OMG IDL **attribute**!

As the IDL shows, an **Attr** is a **Node** with a **name** (the Attribute name, that appears between the chevrons < > in our XML) and a **value** (that appears in quotes in our XML). You set the **name** when you create the **Attr** with an operation on the Document, but you set the **value** by operating on the **Attr** itself. **Attrs** are not children of anything; they're officially just a part of an **Element**. So, they have no **parentNode**, **previousSibling**, or **nextSibling**. They do have a pointer to their **ownerElement**, and their owner has a **NamedNodeList** of them. (**NamedNodeList** is just what you think. We're not going to give details in this book—enough's enough, after all.)

Here is the IDL:

```
valuetype Attr : Node
    {
    // DOM1 Attributes
    readonly attribute DOMString name;
    readonly attribute boolean specified;
    attribute DOMString value;
    // raises(DOMException) on setting

    readonly attribute Element ownerElement;
};
```

I.2.5.6   The Element Node

Now that we've defined our **Document** and the **Attr**, we can define an **Element**. valuetype **Element** inherits from **Node**, adding a **tagName** and support for DOM Attributes—that is, **Attrs**. All of the **Attr** operations have Namespace and non-Namespace forms; as we pointed out before, for each **Element**, decide whether or not it's based on a Namespace and be consistent!

Here is the IDL for **Element**:

```
valuetype Element : Node
    {
    // DOM1 Attributes
```

The **tagName** is a **readonly** IDL **attribute**, so this IDL generates a **get** operation. In Java, the operation will be named `tagName`:

```
readonly attribute DOMString tagName;

// DOM1 Operations
//
```

You can set and get DOM attributes either by name, or as **valuetype**s. These operations take **DOMString**s as arguments:

```
DOMString getAttribute(
   in DOMString name

);
void setAttribute(
   in DOMString name,
   in DOMString value
)
   raises(DOMException);

void removeAttribute(
   in DOMString name
)
   raises(DOMException);
```

And here we have a set of operations that take or return **Attr**s instead:

```
Attr getAttributeNode(
   in DOMString name
);

Attr setAttributeNode(
   in Attr newAttr
)
   raises(DOMException);

Attr removeAttributeNode(
   in Attr oldAttr
)
   raises(DOMException);

NodeList getElementsByTagName(
   in DOMString name
);

// DOM2 Operations
//
DOMString getAttributeNS(
   in DOMString namespaceURI,
   in DOMString localName
```

```
    );

    void setAttributeNS(
        in DOMString namespaceURI,
        in DOMString qualifiedName,
        in DOMString value
    )
        raises(DOMException);

    void removeAttributeNS(
        in DOMString namespaceURI,
        in DOMString localName
    )
        raises(DOMException);

    Attr getAttributeNodeNS(
        in DOMString namespaceURI,
        in DOMString localName
    );

    Attr setAttributeNodeNS(
        in Attr newAttr
    )
        raises(DOMException);

    NodeList getElementsByTagNameNS(
        in DOMString namespaceURI,
        in DOMString localName
    );

    boolean hasAttribute(
        in DOMString name
    );

    boolean hasAttributeNS(
        in DOMString namespaceURI,
        in DOMString localName
    );
}; /*! valuetype Element */
```

I.2.5.7   The CharacterData Node

Now that we have **Elements** and **Attrs**, we need to insert **Text**. For this, we need to follow a two-level inheritance trail: **CharacterData** inherits from **Node**, adding basic text-handling functions. Then **Text** inherits from **CharacterData**, adding the capability to split into multiple **Text Node**s.

CharacterData stores its text data as an IDL attribute, allowing you to **set** and **get** the full contents by invoking the operations generated automatically by your IDL compiler. Then it adds operations to edit in more specific ways. Here's the IDL; look through it to see all of the operations that **Charac-terData** supports on its contents:

```
valuetype CharacterData : Node
  {
  // DOM1 Attributes
```

Here's the data (appropriately enough named `data`) in our **CharacterData** Node. It's an IDL attribute:

```
attribute DOMString data;
  // raises(DOMException) on setting
  // raises(DOMException) on retrieval
readonly attribute unsigned long length;

  // DOM1 Operations
  //
```

And here are the operations we can perform on the `data`, if we don't want to just replace it entirely:

```
DOMString substringData(
    in unsigned long offset,
    in unsigned long count
  )
    raises(DOMException);

  void appendData(
    in DOMString arg
  )
    raises(DOMException);

void insertData(
    in unsigned long offset,
    in DOMString arg
  )
    raises(DOMException);

  void deleteData(
    in unsigned long offset,
    in unsigned long count
  )
    raises(DOMException);

  void replaceData(
    in unsigned long offset,
    in unsigned long count,
    in DOMString arg
  )
    raises(DOMException);
}; /*! valuetype CharacterData */
```

I.2.5.8   The Text Node

Finally, we can define our **Text Node**. This addes one operation to **Character-Data**: The capability to split the contents into two **Nodes** at a specified **offset**. On return, the original **Node** contains all of the content from the beginning up to but not including the character at the specified **offset**. Then a new **Node**, created by the operation, contains this character and all that follow. Here's the IDL:

```
valuetype Text : CharacterData
{
// DOM1 Operations
//
Text splitText(
   in unsigned long offset
)
   raises(DOMException);
};
```

I.2.5.9   IDL Summary

This is not all of the XML/Value IDL, but it is all that we're going to present at this level of detail. We think that these basic operations give a good idea of what the service can do and were well worth the space. And, based on these, we'll be able to explain the static mapping in the next section.

This specification has a number of advanced capabilities that we will present in summary form. But, because they're rather technical, we're going to postpone this part until the end of the chapter. Right now we're going to describe the static mapping, which is the part we think will be the most widely used.

I.2.6   The DTD-Based Static Mapping

The DOM defines a very general structure, ensuring that we can read *any* XML document into our program. But if we've already locked down the structure of our document by writing (and following!) a DTD, there's a lot of structural information that we could use in our program to make the document easier to work with.

The XML/Value *Static Mapping* does this by fixing the valuetypes, and their names, that must be produced to conform to an XML DTD. So, instead of getting nodes named "Node" that we can only differentiate by retrieving tagname attributes, we actually get nodes named **POitem** and **ship_to_address** and all of the other tagnames that we saw in the purchase order. In addi-

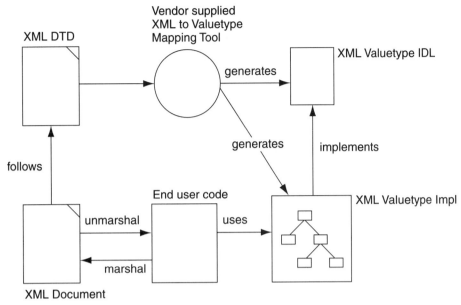

Figure I.2.1   Using the Static Mapping.

tion, because the mapping uses the document structure as dictated by the DTD to define the nodes available in our code, the DTD structure is imposed on us to a large extent, and consistency is enforced by the generated code.

There is enough information in the DTD to define all of the valuetypes in the document and to produce an implementation of them. So, that's what the specification defines, as we see in Figure I.2.1. Vendors will build a tool that takes your DTD as input. From your DTD, the tool produces two things: First, it produces IDL defining **valuetypes** tailored so precisely to your DTD that each has a type name that corresponds to its tag name. Second, the tool produces an *implementation* of these valuetypes. All that's left for your programmer to code is the logic that calls the valuetypes and functions that the tool produced.

Following the pattern we established already in this chapter, we'll start by working our way through the static mapping of our PO DTD and seeing what it does to our example XML purchase order document. Because the static mapping produces IDL, we'll look at that and not language code. When we're done with our example, we'll have a look at a few of the features of the static mapping that it didn't show.

I.2.6.1   Static Mapping for the Purchase Order DTD

To understand the order that the mapping declares things, remember that everything has to be declared before it can be used. So, there's a lot of setting up in the first half of the file, and a lot more using of declarations towards the end.

The mapping starts by declaring our module, with a name derived from the name of our DTD. We've named the DTD and the module **purchasing**. We were careful not to name it **purchase_order**, because that's the name of our document valuetype, and IDL doesn't allow these name collisions. The final specification will dictate name-mangling for cases where the DTD name and an element name are identical, but the initial release that we worked from didn't provide for this.

After it declares our module, the IDL declares all of the primary elements that we declared up front in our DTD. These are the ones that contain text data:

```
#include <value_xml.idl>

module purchasing  {

valuetype street                : truncatable dom::Element {
     dom::text getPCDATA ( );
     void setPCDATA (in dom::text t);
};
valuetype city                  : truncatable dom::Element {
     dom::Text getPCDATA ( );
     void setPCDATA (in dom::Text t);
};
valuetype state                 : truncatable dom::Element {
     dom::Text getPCDATA ( );
     void setPCDATA (in dom::Text t);
};
valuetype postcode              : truncatable dom::Element {
     dom::Text getPCDATA ( );
     void setPCDATA (in dom::Text t);
};
valuetype POitem_name           : truncatable dom::Element {
     dom::Text getPCDATA ( );
     void setPCDATA (in dom::Text t);
};
valuetype POitem_number         : truncatable dom::Element {
     dom::Text getPCDATA ( );
     void setPCDATA (in dom::Text t);
};
valuetype POitem_size           : truncatable dom::Element {
     dom::Text getPCDATA ( );
     void setPCDATA (in dom::Text t);
};
valuetype POitem_quantity       : truncatable dom::Element {
     dom::Text getPCDATA ( );
     void setPCDATA (in dom::Text t);
 };
```

Did you notice the big difference between this and the dynamic mapping? Here, our **Elements** all have type names that correspond to their **Element** names: No longer do we work with anonymous **Element valuetype**s, fetching their **tagName**s to see which ones we have. Instead, we operate on **street**s, or **city**s, or **POitem_name**s!

All of these are **Elements** by inheritance, with different names and operations to **get** and **set** the children for those suitably blessed. Inheritance is always declared **truncatable** by the mapping, but we recommend that you code carefully to avoid ever causing truncation to occur. Our advice about truncatable inheritance from Section I.1.1.3 applies here, even though the mapping didn't listen to us!

So why does everything in the static mapping inherit **truncatable**? This allows you to pass a statically mapped document tree to an application that only knows the dynamic mapping. When you do this, all of your sophisticated static types—**street**, **city**, **state**, **ship_to_address**, and all the rest—are turned into dumb **Elements** as they arrive at the far end of the wire. To analyze document-specific structure, the application must use the metadata that was stored when the document was parsed, and the primitive methods that we demonstrated in Section I.2.4. But, this capability can let you upgrade a set of applications from dynamic to static mapping one at a time. If you're going to do this, check that your valuetype implementation supports **truncatable**—it's an advanced feature, so early releases of some implementations may not support it.

The text is, as we saw in the dynamic mapping, held in **Text Nodes** that are children of their **Element**. Because our **Elements** contain only one **Text Node** each, the operations are named simply **getPCDATA** and **setPCDATA**. If we had an **Element** with two **Text Node**s, the operations on the first would be **getPCDATA1** and **setPCDATA1**, and on the second, **getPCDATA2** and set **PCDATA2**.

Now that our static IDL has declared these **Text Elements**, it can declare the **Elements** that contain them—**ship_to_address** and **POitem**. These are also DOM **Elements**, and each has operations to **get** and **set** the **Elements** that they contain. As soon as the mapping has defined **POitem**, it will typedef **itemlist** which will be used in the **purchase_order**:

```
valuetype ship_to_address : truncatable dom::Element {
street              getstreet ( );
void                setstreet ( in street Arg0 );

city                getcity ( );
void                setcity ( in city Arg0 );

state               getstate ( );
void                setstate ( in state Arg0);
```

```
postcode                        getpostcode ( );
void                            setpostcode ( in postcode Arg0);
};

valuetype POitem : truncatable dom::Element {
POitem_name                     getPOitem_name ( );
void                            setPOitem_name ( in POitem_name Arg0 );

POitem_number                   getPOitem_number ( );
void                            setPOitem_number ( in POitem_number Arg0 );

POitem_size                     getPOitem_size ( );
void                            setPOitem_size ( in POitem_size Arg0);

POitem_quantity                 getPOitem_quantity ( );
void                            setPOitem_quantity ( in POitem_quantity Arg0);
};
```

```
typedef sequence<POitem> POitemSeq;
```

Now, finally, the mapping can declare our **purchase_order**. If you check back to the original DTD, you'll see that **purchase_order** contains a list of items. The + on the list signifies that it contains one or more, without limit. The mapping implements this as an unbounded sequence. Because the list is declared within the **purchase_order** in the original DTD, it is implemented as private to the **purchase_order** element, which contains all of the operations that manipulate list entries.

The `purchase_order` DTD also bore two attributes (XML attributes, not IDL attributes): `company` and `number`. These show up here too, with operations to **get** and **set** them.

Here's what the **purchase_order** IDL looks like:

```
valuetype purchase_order : truncatable dom::Element {
    //State Declaration
    private POitemSeq thePOitemSeq;

    //Attribute access operations
    dom::DOMString getcompany ( );
    void  setcompany (in dom::DOMString arg0);
    dom::DOMString getnumber ( );
    void  setnumber (in dom::DOMString arg0);

    //Element access operations
    ship_to_address getship_to_address ( );
    void  setship_to_address ( in ship_to_address Arg0 );

    POitemSeq getPOitemSeq              ( );
    void setPOitemSeq                   ( in POitemSeq Arg0 );
    POitem getPOitemSeqAt               ( in long index );
    long getPOitemSeqSize               ( );
    void replacePOitemSeqAt             ( in POitem arg0, in long index );
    void appendPOitemSeq                ( in POitem arg0 );
    void insertPOitemSeqAt              ( in POitem arg0, in long index );
```

```
        void removeFromPOitemSeq        ( in POitem arg0 );
        void removeFromPOitemSeqAt      ( in long index );
        void clearPOitemSeq             ( );
    };
```

The mapping isn't done yet. Although **purchase_order** holds all of our content, it's an **Element** and not a Document. It needs to define a Document to wrap everything up. The **purchase_orderDoc** bears all of the Factory operations to create **Elements** and to start our traversal at the root. And, once it has defined the **purchase_orderDoc**, it can declare interfaces to **parse** and **serialize** our XML document as well. And once these are declared the mapping is, indeed, finished generating IDL. Here's the last fraction of the file, generated from the DTD:

```
    valuetype purchase_orderDoc : truncatable dom::Document {
        purchase_order    getpurchase_orderRoot ( );
        void              setpurchase_orderRoot ( in purchase_order docRoot );
        purchase_order    createpurchase_orderElement ( );
        street            createstreetElement ( );
        city              createcityElement ( );
        state             createstateElement ( );
        postcode          createpostcodeElement ( );
        POitem_name       createPOitem_nameElement ( );
        POitem_number     createPOitem_numberElement ( );
        POitem_size       createPOitem_sizeElement ( );
        POitem_quantity   createPOitem_quantityElement ( );
        POitem            createPOitemElement();
    };

    local interface purchase_orderParser : XMLValue::XMLParser {
        purchase_orderDoc  parsepurchase_order
                            ( in XMLValue::DOMString XMLStream)
            raises (XMLValue::XMLException);
    };

    local interface purchase_orderSerializer : XMLValue::XMLSerializer {
        dom::DOMString serializepurchase_order
                            ( in purchase_orderDoc XMLStream)
            raises (XMLValue::XMLException);
    };
};
```

I.2.6.2 Additional Static Mapping Features

The static mapping defines a few more things, mostly aspects of features that we covered in the example. It defines different mappings for the *, +, and ? quantities that map to zero or more, one or more, and zero or one respectively. It also defines mappings for sequences and choice lists (both simple and complex). And, it specifies that the mapping appends numerals to duplicate names to distinguish them.

There are several pages of mappings for **Element** Attributes, which can contain either strings, Element IDs, references to IDs of other elements, or enumerations. We won't go into the mappings here; we'll just reassure that if you use these constructs in your DTD, it will map.

One thing that you have to do before you map your DTD: Resolve conditional sections. The mapping won't produce conditional IDL!

I.2.6.3   Working with the Static Mapping

We're not going to re-present all of the dynamic mapping code with the type-specific names that the static mapping defines. The two modes are too similar. But, we will reprise the changing of the quantity of one of the items. Here's the static-mapped version of the code:

```
// Modify any POitem with POitem_number "BO1420" to have
// an POitem_quantity of "150gross"
DOMString searchFor = makeDOMString("BO1420");
DOMString setToQuantity  = makeDOMString("150gross");

purchase_order order = PO_doc.getpurchase_orderRoot();
for (int i = 0; i < order.getPOitemSeqSize(); ++i)
{
  POitem thePOitem = order.getPOitemSeqAt(i);
  POitem_number number = thePOitem.getPOitem_number();
  if (number.getPCDATA().data()._equals(searchFor))
  {
    POitem_quantity quantity = thePOitem.getPOitem_quantity();
    quantity.getPCDATA().data(setToQuantity);
  }
}
```

Once we finish setting up our `searchFor` and `setToQuantity` variables, we start working with type names that we recognize from our DTD. Our document is a `purchase_order`, not just a **document**. And, because we have a sequence of items in our PO, the static mapping has generated operations on the sequence. (Did you notice them, two pages back?) These operations are available to us, so we've used them to loop over items in search of the one we want to change. The operations have suggestive names: `getPOitemSeqSize, getPOitemSeqAt(i)`.

Ours is a particularly simple example, with a single sequence and only two hierarchical levels of **Elements** that contain text. If our DTD had defined 20 times the number of element types, and our document were 100 times the length, the identification by element name would shift from a convenience to a necessity for error-free programming.

Here's a code fragment that creates and populates a new **POitem** in the static mapping:

```
// Create a new POitem
//
POitem newPOitem = PO_doc.createPOitemElement();
newPOitem.getPOitem_name().getPCDATA().data(makeDOMString("nail"));
newPOitem.getPOitem_number().getPCDATA().data(makeDOMString("NL4590"));
newPOitem.getPOitem_size().getPCDATA().data(makeDOMString("1/4"));
newPOitem.getPOitem_quantity().getPCDATA().data
                                    (makeDOMString("200gross"));
```

If we were coding in the dynamic mapping, we would have had to create all of the subordinate elements—POitem_name, POitem_number, POitem_size, and POitem_quantity—individually and append them to the new-POitem as children. However, because the static mapping knows from the DTD that a POitem has exactly one child Element of each of these types, the generated code creates and appends them automatically. And, each of these elements has a single Text Node child, as we expect. All we have to do is fill in the data.

By the way, the reason why all of the operations are gets instead of sets in the lines that set the values for the new item is this: In the first of these lines, for example, we getPOitem_name to get the POitem_name **Element** and then getPCDATA to get its **Text Node**. It's the operation data on the **Text Node** that is overloaded: With an input argument, it's a set; without an argument, it's a get and the string comes back as the return value. Here, there is an input argument so this last operation in the line—data—is a set operation.

I.2.7   Flyweight Design Pattern

For a purchase order that only has two items, we wouldn't begrudge the few bytes taken up by the string attribute names POitem_name, POitem_number, POitem_size, and POitem_quantity, even if the strings were stored separately as part of the state of each element. However, if our purchase order grew to hundreds or thousands of items (as it could, if generated by a computer), we would be able to save a lot of space in memory, and transmission time over the network, by eliminating the redundancy.

The XML/Value mapping does this using the Flyweight Pattern. This is an extension provided by the CORBA specification and not part of the DOM.

Use of the Flyweight Pattern may be enabled or disabled by setting **s_doc-Metadata** in your **Document valuetype**. It's a **MetadataSwitch**, typedef'd to **bool-**

ean. If you set it to TRUE, which you should, the XML/Value implementation will store only one copy of each Element and Attribute name, in a list with a key, which maps to an `int` in Java and occupies only four bytes, the equivalent of two characters of Unicode. (It's an `unsigned long` in C++.) Each instance of that **Element** or **Attr** then stores just the key. The **valuetypes** that stores the key/name lists and bear the operations to store and retrieve them are part of the document's state, so they go over the wire with the rest of the document when you send it as a parameter in a CORBA call, as we demonstrated in Section I.2.4.3. There are three separate valuetypes and list structures, one each for **Elements**, **Attrs**, and **Nodes**.

You don't have to do any special programming to use this optimization. And, if you're going to send long XML documents with many repeated elements over the network, you'll benefit by reading them into a string of **valuetypes** first, enabling the Flyweight optimization, and sending them in CORBA calls.

I.2.8   DOM Level 2 Features

We haven't said much about mappings for features added to the DOM in level 2, although we've mentioned support for XML Namespaces, which is the most significant to the basic manipulations that we've showed so far.

The mapping also supports DOM Level 2 Events, Traversal, Range, and Views but does not support DOM Level 2 features for HTML manipulation, StyleSheets, and CSS (Cascading Style Sheets).

Events may be triggered by UI devices (keyboard, mouse), logical UI events (focus change), and document mutation. Events "bubble" (in the terminology of the specification) through a target's ancestors after they are handled by the target. Or, an event may be "captured" (again, in the terminology of the specification) and handled by one of the target's ancestors before it reaches the target. The interfaces may well help you build an application that edits or manipulates XML documents.

The Traversal extension defines **TreeWalker**, **NodeIterator**, and **Filter** interfaces for traversing DOM trees. The **Filter** interface lets you define sets of conditions that divide your nodes into two groups, accepted and not.

Walking your document tree with the **TreeWalker** is a lot like navigating its structure directly, but with a **Filter** applied.

The **NodeIterator** constructs a one-dimensional array of **Nodes**, possibly **Filtered**, in an order defined by the DOM specification. An application then moves forward and back in this array to access **Nodes**, instead of moving through the tree structure. For some documents, and some purposes, this can be easier.

A **Range** identifies a range of content in a **Document, DocumentFragment**, or **Attr. Range** definition supports editing, especially using a GUI: a **Range** is what you select from your document when you drag the mouse, for example. We're not going to describe the IDL that supports this.

Finally, a **View** of a document is a computed presentation. A document may have multiple views, depending on the style sheet that was applied or the adjusted size of a window. Editing programs, which must identify where in a document a mouse or pointer lies, will be concerned with views. The **Views** interface standardizes dealing with different views.

We know that this cursory treatment does not do justice to the capabilities of these features of the DOM. Our excuse is that they're not part of the mapping of XML to CORBA *per se*. But, we admit, they look like a pretty good place to start if you're writing an application that presents or edits XML content. We realize that the world has more than enough generic editors, and we don't expect many readers of this book to start work on yet another one. Instead, we're referring to the many content-specific XML applications as editors: the purchase-order editor that we sketched out in our example is one candidate in this category. And, every time an industry or organization standardizes a DTD, there's an opportunity for someone to run it through a Static Mapping tool, produce an IDL file and valuetype implementation, and wrap a DTD-specific editor around it.

I.2.9 Summary

In this chapter, we've seen how to work with both dynamic and static XML documents in CORBA. Represented as a tree of **valuetype**s, the in-memory structure made it easy for us to do everything we could possibly want to the document: create, read and parse, modify content, and output the result. And the static mapping took full advantage of the DTD to create a structure-specific tree of **Node**s to represent our XML document.

This concludes our discussion of the XML/Value mapping. We've devoted a lot of space to it, but XML promises to be widely used in enterprise and business computing so we think this treatment was warranted. We hope you'll give this facility a try and see for yourself how CORBA helps you manage your XML documents.

In the next chapter, we'll see how the CORBA URLs defined by the Interoperable Naming Service help us use CORBA over the Internet.

Interoperable
Naming Service

CHAPTER PREVIEW

The Interoperable Naming Service *est omnis divisa in partes tres*. (Have you forgotten your second-year Latin already? "The Interoperable Naming Service is divided into three parts.")

The first two parts were incorporated into the CORBA Core specification starting with Release 2.4. The first part defines human-readable object references: corbaloc to identify standard services including the Naming Service, and corbaname to retrieve a name from a remote Naming Service. The second part of the specification enhances the ORB's handling of object references for standard services at startup: The original initialization service standardized the interfaces that a client used to get references for these services from its ORB at startup; this specification standardizes three ways for the programmer, user, or sysadmin to enter the references that the client will ultimately retrieve.

The third part standardizes the textual representation of an object's name. Although the original Naming Service standardized the representation as a hierarchical structure of identifier/kind pairs during execution, it did not standardize separator characters for the occasion when a name might be written down or sent to someone in an e-mail or fax.

This chapter presents all three parts of the Interoperable Naming Service, in that order.

The final new specification in this category, helping to integrate CORBA with the Internet, is the interoperable naming service. Providing some new functionality as it solves a few nagging interoperability problems, this addition to CORBA clears up some things that users have been asking about for years. Specifically, the new service definition:

- Defines two URL representations for the object reference that give your ORB access to the Naming Service, Trader Service, or any object that you know the name of, at any available remote site, using standard DNS or IP address forms that you already know how to use (the CORBA equivalent of the Web's familiar format, www.omg.org)

- Lets you configure, in a standard way, any vendor's ORB to initialize using the naming context instance you want, so that, for example, all the ORBs in your company or department can see the same naming hierarchy. In fact; these extensions to run-time configurability go beyond the Naming Service, as we'll see in Section I.3.2.2.

- Defines a standard syntax for the compound object name, so you and all the CORBA 3 clients that you exchange email with will write and read the same name in the same form, and your programs will know what to do with it.

In this chapter, we'll cover these extensions in order. When we're finished, we'll also be finished with CORBA integration with Java and the Internet, and ready to start on our second major section, Quality of Service control.

I.3.1   Universal Resource Locators (URLs)

One thing that's great about the World Wide Web is how you can guess the Web address of a place from its company name, type it in the address window of your Web browser, and (most of the time, anyhow) get to its Web page right away. Here's a good example—OMG. You start out by guessing that we use our initials, OMG, and you know we're a not-for-profit organization so our extension should be .org (signifying that we're not-for-profit on purpose, unlike so many .coms!); so you put these together and guess that our Web URL is www.omg.org.

You type this into your browser address bar and, without your ever having to look anything up yourself, OMG's homepage appears in your browser window. This works because OMG runs a Web server on the host machine whose IP address, 192.67.184.5, corresponds to www.omg.org. But web servers are not the only server type—there are already FTP servers, mail servers, and an increasing number of CORBA servers. Wouldn't it be even nicer to be able to access a CORBA server or object by typing in a URL? The specification is in place, and soon you'll be able to do just that.

To see how this will work, first consider the analogy we made to the Web. On the Internet there's a network of domain name servers which your computer used to convert our domain name, www.omg.org, to our Web server's IP address, 192.67.184.5. By convention, this computer is listening to HTTP requests on its port number 80, so your browser sent its request to port 80 of our computer, asked for our homepage, and back it came.

I.3.1.1 URLs for Services Delivered Using CORBA

To make this work for CORBA, *almost* all we need to do is put a CORBA server on a well-known port of a machine with a domain name and address. What else do we need? Web servers hold lots of different pages and serve them up one at a time, identifying them by a page or file name ("getting-started/overview.htm" or whatever) following the domain name and separated from it by a slash. Analogously, CORBA servers serve lots of different objects so we need to put an object key or object name on to the end of our object URL. The object key or object name identifies the service or exact object we want an object reference for.

`corbaloc` is the keyword for the CORBA URL format that translates to the object reference of an object instance, typically providing a service, at a location. Here's an example:

```
corbaloc::MyGiganticEnterprise.com/NameService
```

Taking advantage of defaults (we'll get complicated later), this URL starts with the identifying string `corbaloc::`, followed by a domain name (here, MyGiganticEnterprise.com) or an IP address, a forward slash, and an object key which in this case is `NameService`.

I.3.1.1.1 *The Object Key*

The object key is the part of the IOR that the ORB uses to identify the exact instance that is the target of an invocation. Until now—that is, in ORB-generated object references—CORBA had standardized neither the form nor the content of any object key: ORB-generated object keys are only useful for, and used by, the ORB that generated them, so there was no reason to standardize here. In a sense, these object keys are like elves: They live inside the Interoperable Object Reference and never come out where they can be seen in daylight even by programmers, never mind users.

The interoperable naming specification defines URL-format object references with Object Keys that actual humans can read. (The Object Keys that

---

IS IT "NAMING SERVICE" OR "NAME SERVICE"?

That depends on what part of the specification you're reading.

- The title of Chapter 3 of the CORBAservices book is *Naming Service*. The entire chapter refers to the service, consistently with only one or two exceptions, as the Naming Service.

- But, the string used by list_initial_services, resolve_initial_references, and `corbaname` (if you default the object key) is `NameService`.

This is enough confusion for us. We're going to use the term *Naming Service* everywhere in this book. If you find us using *Name Service* anywhere except in the `list_initial_services` string, consider it a typo.

By the way, the service that is the subject of this chapter is the *Interoperable Naming Service*. It only has one name, so there's no reason for confusion. Phew!

ORBs create for non-URL-format IORs are probably just long strings of computer numbers, but we'll never know for sure because they never come out into the light. Maybe they really *are* elves.)

The `corbaloc` part of the interoperable naming specification does not standardize object keys for remote access to standard services (or anything else, for that matter), although the document does use common names as examples and we think this is good practice: `NameService`, `NotificationService`, `TradingService`. `corbaname` (which we'll present in the next section) goes a little further, standardizing `NameService` as the default object key for the Naming Service, used by your client if you don't include an explicit object key in the URL as we show in Section I.3.1.2.

The object key doesn't have to be a single word; it can be any string that the server responds to. Everything that follows the slash after the domain name or IP address is the object key. The specification suggests, by example, that object keys may be strings separated by slashes although this is not an official notation. (Later in this chapter we'll present the new official notation for object names which uses slashes for separators, but this isn't it.)

I.3.1.1.2   `corbaloc` *for IIOP Protocol, with Defaults*

So, if we combine the object key with the IIOP-**protocol** `corbaloc` format, we get URL-format object references that look like these:

```
corbaloc::YourDomain.org/dev/sandbox/NotificationService
```

where the object key is `dev/sandbox/NotificationService`, and

```
corbaloc::MyShoppingSite.com/pub/Catalog
```

where the object key is `pub/Catalog`.

Because the `corbaloc` portion of the specification says nothing about the contents of the object key, there's no official equivalent of a "home page" or `index.htm` for `corbaloc` invocations. `NameService`, the default object key for `corbaname` invocations, is as close as the specification comes. If you're setting up a `corbaloc` server, we suggest you use `NameService` as your object key (or one of your object keys, since nothing prevents a server from responding to a number of keys). And when you browse the web for CORBA servers using a CORBA 3 client browser, we suggest you start with `NameService` as the key that you type into your `corbaloc` URL.

I.3.1.1.3   `corbaloc` *for IIOP Protocol, Full Form*

Let's take a look at the full form of the `corbaloc` URL, specifying every field instead of using defaults:

```
corbaloc:iiop:1.2@MyGiganticEnterprise.com:2809/pub/NameService
```

After the URL key string `corbaloc:` with its single colon comes the protocol specifier. `iiop:` is the default protocol; you can either spell it out followed by a colon, or just put the second colon as we did in the previous section. There will be URL formats for many protocols but right now there are only two: `iiop`, as we've seen, and `rir` for Resolve Initial References. We'll give details about the `rir` form in Section I.3.1.1.4 later in this chapter.

Addressing information goes between the colon that ends the protocol specifier and the slash that starts the object key. The address format is protocol specific, of course, since each protocol specifies the information that it needs to find a target. For IIOP, which runs over TCP/IP, the address field includes an optional IIOP version identifier followed by @, the host specifier as either a domain name or an IP address, and optionally a port number preceded by a colon.

If you're not sure of the domain name, or if your target is available via two different addresses, or you have two domain names and either one will do, you can include both. The ORB will use your list of addresses "in an implementation dependent manner" (quoting the spec) to access the target. Check your documentation or ask your ORB vendor to find out how your ORB uses the list. Multiple addresses are separated by commas, like this:

```
corbaloc::MyGiganticEnterprise.com,:CORBA.MyGiganticEnterprise
.com:2809/NamingService
```

TECHNICAL NOTES: REGISTERED PORTS AND THE IANA

If you're planning to implement or use `corbaloc`, you'll find these few details helpful:

- First, IANA (The Internet Association Naming Authority) has assigned ports for other CORBA invocations as well as `corbaloc`. The best-known are 683 for IIOP connections, and 684 for secure IIOP. We've even mentioned these ports in connection with `corbaloc`, back before port 2809 was assigned for this purpose. Now, with this assignment, 2809 is *the* default port for `corbaloc`.

- Second, for a few months up to mid-August 2000, the specification document available from the OMG server misprinted the port number as 2089. We discovered the discrepancy as we were researching this chapter, and had it fixed in the original document right away. If you have an old copy with 2089, you should either fix it up or download a copy of the latest version.

- To download the latest version of the specification, surf to `www.omg.org/technology/documents/index.htm`.

- To review the complete list of IANA well-known and registered port numbers, go to `ftp://ftp.isi.edu/in-notes/iana/assign-ments/` and download the document `port-numbers`. (No, there's no extension on this filename.)

IANA—the Internet Association Naming Authority—has assigned the registered port number 2809 to OMG for `corbaloc`. Invocations default to this port if you don't specify another.

I.3.1.1.4 `corbaloc, rir` *Protocol*

In addition to IIOP, the specification defines an `rir` protocol. The `rir` protocol gives you access to your ORB's configured initial services through a URL. For example, passing

```
corbaloc:rir:/TradingService
```

to **string_to_object** returns the same object reference as passing `Trading-Service` to **resolve_initial_references**. The object key in an invocation of `corbaloc:rir` can be any of the keys defined for **resolve_initial_references**; if you leave out the object key, the system inserts `NameService`.

When we get to `corbaname`, we'll use the `rir` capability to resolve a name against our ORB's default configured Naming Service in a single call.

I.3.1.1.5 `corbaloc`*, Other Protocols*

The specification only defines addressing information for IIOP, but points out how this could be specified for additional protocols. For example, an ATM URL *might* look like this:

```
corbaloc:atm:E.164.358.400.1234567/TraderService
```

This is not an official OMG form for an ATM URL, or for anything else. It's just an example of what a future ATM URL *might* look like. It does show that, when protocols besides TCP/IP become popular enough to rate a URL of their own, this specification is ready for them.

What if an object or service is available over more than one protocol? You can mix addresses with different protocols in your list, *except* for rir: rir doesn't share — if you use it, you can't use any others at the same time.

I.3.1.1.6 *Coding and Using* `corbaloc`

How do you code this into your client, and how does it work? The URL is a string, and every ORB already has a standard interface that turns a string into an object reference—it's **string_to_object**. (**string_to_object** is a part of basic CORBA, which we don't cover in this book.) The INS assigns the new functionality we've just covered to this same function. When you pass a `corbaloc` object reference string to **string_to_object**, the ORB resolves the domain name into an address, creates an invokable object reference, and hands you back a session reference for it.

You will have to **narrow** the session reference to whatever interface type it's supposed to be—**NameService, TraderService,** or whatever your object key corresponded to.

If you are the server programmer and these invocations are coming at you, there are (at least) two ways you can respond to them: A normal CORBA name or trader object instance will recognize the incoming request and do the right thing, so you can just run yours on your main host IP address at the registered `iioploc` port 2809. Or, if you don't want to run your server on your gateway machine, you can run a lightweight software agent that listens there and replies to **request** messages with **LOCATION_FOR-WARD** replies, and to **LocateRequest** invocations with **LocateReply** responses. Any standard CORBA client will re-issue its request to the location you've forwarded to, allowing you to shift this load away from your gateway host

TECHNICAL NOTES: corbaloc **IN ACTION**

You don't know, because the specification doesn't dictate, the order in which these actions occur. Your ORB will have to complete at least one round trip to the server in order to construct a usable object reference, but doesn't have to do any of these steps in order to return a session reference in response to a call to string_to_object.

So, when your client calls string_to_object with a corbaloc URL, most ORBs will probably just save the string. You'll get an apparently usable object reference as the return value, but the ORB won't have checked anything out. Then, when you actually make an invocation using that object reference, your client's ORB will do the real work—converting the domain name to an IP address, invoking the object identified by the object key by sending a request to that host and port, and following any LOCATION_FORWARD responses.

This means that it's wise to check for errors not only after the return from string_to_object, but also after the return from your first invocation of the object. If you want to check things out before you make this invocation, you could try invoking non_existent or validate_connection first. These will get you closer (validate_connection will force its way past any LOCATION_FORWARD replies to the actual servant's ORB), although even success on either of these operations does not guarantee success on your invocation of the corbaloc object itself.

to a more suitable server. In any case, you will have to run your server on a CORBA 3 ORB that lets you define textual object keys.

So, now you can set up your CORBA 3 server on a machine with a domain address, run the Naming Service, Trader Service, or another one of the standard services, or anything else you want, and have your customers or clients access it *without* having to obtain a stringified CORBA object reference first. Compared to the stringified object reference, which is a long, imposing stretch of hexadecimal characters, the corbaloc URL format is very user-friendly indeed.

In order for this to be useful, people must have clients for the objects that are served at these sites, but this isn't so far-fetched since most uses will be for standard CORBAservices and clients for these services are both common and easy to write: The first use will probably be for the Naming Service, which has standard interfaces so any CORBA programmer can write a client for it. The next common service will probably be Trader, because you can browse a Trader to see all the neat stuff that's available, and an object's Trader entry can point to a downloadable client for it so you can try it out right away. OMG Task Forces have already defined standard services in finance, electronic commerce, telecommunications, manufacturing, transportation, and health care; standard CORBA clients written to these interfaces could easily be adapted to find services through CORBA URLs.

I.3.1.2   URLs for Objects by Name

One more thing: Objects with persistent state store their ObjectID and POA names in the IOR. When you call **string_to_object** with an object URL and your ORB creates an object reference, it won't contain any of this information because there's no way to get it. Therefore, this technique can only create generic object references and is useful only to access standard services that run constantly and know what to do when they receive a simple request. So how do we access a specific named object on a foreign server if `corbaloc` won't let us? We use a URL to invoke the Naming Service on the server, get back a real IOR for the object, and invoke it. `corbaname` is the new URL that we use for this. Here's how it works.

I.3.1.2.1   `corbaname`

It's great to be able to initialize our ORB to use our enterprise directory for object names, but sometimes we need to be able to resolve names on *any* server, anywhere, directly. For that, OMG has added a URL format—`corbaname`—that lets you invoke the Naming Service on a remote computer without getting its IOR first.

Here's a sample corbaname URL:

```
corbaname::MyGiganticEnterprise.com/Pub/Catalogs#
Year2000/Menswear/Outdoors.obj
```

Up to the pound sign (#), it's a corbaloc URL except that the identifying string is now `corbaname`. After the #, it's an object name in the newly standardized OMG format that we'll present in Section I.3.3.

When you pass this to **string_to_object**, your ORB resolves the `corbaloc` part to a **NamingContext** object instance. (All Naming Services are provided by **NamingContext** instances.) We've specified a particular **NamingContext**— `Pub/Catalogs`— in our object key because we knew in advance that this particular server ORB would recognize this particular key. The specification does *not* allow clients to use arbitrary NamingContext objects as keys!

Your ORB then invokes **resolve** on the **NamingContext** instance to resolve the name part of the URL.

For our example, the client ORB would attempt to resolve the name `Year2000/Menswear/Outdoors.obj` on the **NamingContext** instance `Pub/Catalogs` on the ORB server at `MyGiganticEnterprise.com`, listening on port 2809. If it finds that **NamingContext** at that address using that object key, and the name resolves, the object reference comes back to your client's ORB and you get it as the return value from **string_to_object**. Of course it's of type **object**, so you still need to **narrow** it to whatever type `Outdoors.obj` is.

If you leave out the starting context, the object key (for that's what it is, at this spot in the `corbaname` string) defaults to `NameService`. Here's an example:

```
corbaname://MyShoppingCompany.com#OnlineShopping
```

asks the Naming Service running at `MyShoppingCompany` to resolve the name `OnlineShopping` in its top level `NamingContext`.

You can use the `rir` protocol with corbaname. For example,

```
corbaname:rir:/NameService#pub/Catalog/Fall2001/Shirts.obj
```

resolves the name `pub/Catalog/Fall2001/Shirts.obj` in the **Naming-Context** returned by `resolve_initial_references("NameService")`.

If you leave out the object key, it defaults to NameService. So,

```
corbaname:rir:#pub/Catalog/Fall2001/Shirts.obj
```

is the same as the previous example, but simpler to type.

Don't get the impression that this is only useful with computers that have their own domain names. Although only a small fraction of computers have domain names, every machine on the Internet or on your company's enterprise network (if it's running TCP/IP) has an IP address. You can run a Naming Service with corbaloc access on any CORBA 3 ORB that does the right thing with the string form of the object key and, when you do, your co-workers or anyone else who knows your machine's IP address can take advantage of it.

For example, if you were running a Naming Service at IP address 192.168.1.141 on the standard corbaloc port 2809, we could resolve the name /RootObj/Catalog/Clothing/Winter/Blouse1584389.obj with the URL.

```
corbaname::192.168.1.141#RootObj/Catalog/Clothing
    /Winter/Blouse1584389.obj
```

Security permissions willing, *any* running Naming Service instance on a CORBA 3 ORB and accessible to your client can be invoked this way. (By the way, the IP address we used for the example—191.168.1.141—is not an

Internet address. It's part of a block of numbers restricted for private net-work use. If you attempt to invoke a service at that address and some machine responds, it's one on your company's private network and not on the Internet!)

I.3.2 Client Initialization

At start-up time, after it initializes, a CORBA client needs to locate that first object—the one that lets it get started working, or find the object instances that it needs to do what it's supposed to do. After years of hard-coding access to environment variables or vendor-specific solutions, OMG mem-bers realized that they needed to standardize this essential bootstrapping function. The result was the initialization service, with two new ORB oper-ations: **list_initial_services** and **resolve_initial_references**. These operations did what they were supposed to, allowing client code to initialize these services in a standard and portable way. What it did not do was solve the other half of the problem: allow the references that are returned by these invocations to be *set* by someone in a standard way. As a result, ORBs differed widely in the amount of control they gave the user or even the site administrator or programmer at initialization time, and in the functions used to set the object references for initial services returned at client initialization.

There are many cases where this type of control is useful. Let's use the Naming Service as an example: A site might want all of its end-user clients to initialize to the same root naming context, allowing users to exchange object names by email and have them work regardless of the client that resolved them. Developers, on the other hand, might need either their own individual root naming context, or a workgroup context, depending on how their work was structured. Some will need one root context for one project, and another for a second. Administrators, also, will need control and flexi-bility in this setting.

The Interoperable Naming Service standardizes ways to configure the ini-tial services returned by an ORB. Needed most for the Naming Service, the new interfaces not only allow you to set the object references returned by all the services returned by **list_initial_services**, but also let you define and set object references for new services that haven't been defined yet. These set-tings may use the `corbaloc` and `corbaname` URL formats, so we had to cover them first. In order for these names to resolve properly, CORBA needs a standard format for name strings and, until now, it hasn't had one. (Hard to believe, but true!) The interoperable naming service defines one, finally, and we'll go over it in Section I.3.3.

I.3.2.1   Finding Initial Services and References

Once you've initialized your ORB (a basic CORBA function not covered in this book), you still need your first object reference in order to do anything useful. The obvious way to get this is from the Naming Service, but since the CORBAservices are optional components of the standard, the OMG did not want to mandate including a full-blown service with every ORB just to get things started. (There's a good reason for this. ORBs are being built into just about anything, and some hardware that contains embedded ORBs is really small—those on wristwatch-sized pagers, for example, or switches in a telephone network. Manufacturers of this equipment want the benefit of an industry standard, but have to keep memory footprint to an absolute minimum. The CORBA specifications take these needs into account.)

To meet these requirements, initial object references are provided by the ORB via operations that are modeled after, but not provided by, the Naming Service. It's really a mini-Naming Service implemented within the ORB itself, with two operations. The first (**list_initial_services**) returns a list of available service names; you then pass each service name to the next operation (**resolve_initial_references**), and it returns an object reference that gets you started with that service. Currently, these service names are defined for return from **list_initial_services**:

- `NameService`
- `TradingService`
- `InterfaceRepository`
- `SecurityCurrent`
- `TransactionCurrent`
- `DynAny Factory`
- `ORBPolicyManager`
- `PolicyCurrent`
- `RootPOA`
- `POACurrent`
- `ComponentHomeFinder`

Clients will surely want the Naming Service, and may use any of the others except the two POA-related services, depending on their environment. Object instances may use all except the first two. (If an object instance uses the Naming or Trading Service, it's acting as a client, of course.) Clearly, **list_initial_services** is an ORB service that is useful to both clients and objects.

I.3.2.2   Configuring Initial Services and References

list_initial_services and **resolve_initial_references** are great for finding and retrieving your initial references, but our concern in this chapter is the other end of this problem: How did these initial references get in there in the first place? The original client-side initialization specification that defined **list_initial_services** and **resolve_initial_references** covered how to pull 'em out pretty well, but left the stuffing 'em in part to the ORB vendors' discretion. As a result, some ORBs that came with their own Naming Services initialized to them and left no way for programmers or users to change this setting, while others didn't initialize to anything unless you set it in an environment file or command-line argument at startup.

The INS RFP required the specification to cover the *setting* of initial object references for the Naming Service and, while they were at it, the authors of the specification extended it to cover all initial services. They provided three hierarchical settings, which we'll detail in the next sections. They are:

- Administrative setting
- ORBInitRef
- ORBDefaultInitRef

Once we've described all three, we'll tell how they interact as your ORB starts up.

I.3.2.2.1 Administrative Setting

First, the specification requires, in about these words, that an ORB be administrably configurable to return an arbitrary object reference for non-locality-constrained objects—that is, the standard services that reside outside of the ORB. (It wouldn't make a lot of sense to let a system administrator redefine the object reference of the RootPOA, after all!)

The specification doesn't elaborate on this one, but it's easy to figure out some ways to meet it: Environment variables are a good way; command-line arguments would work too but are more a user tool than an administrative one.

I.3.2.2.2 ORBInitRef

Second, you can set the object reference for a service by passing to the ORB at startup an argument pair of the form

```
-ORBInitRef <ObjectID>=<ObjectURL>
```

`<ObjectID>` may either be a string from the list of initial services, or a new ObjectID: that is, you may define a new initial service ID that wasn't there when the ORB was written.

`<ObjectURL>` can be any of the URL schemes supported by `CORBA::ORB::string_to_object`, including the ones we've just discussed in addition to the stringified IOR.

Here are some example settings:

```
-ORBInitRef NameService=IOR:00230021AB08FA123...

-ORBInitRef NotificationService=corbaloc::TelecomSvcCo
                        /NotificationService

-ORBInitRef TradingService=corbaname::MyISP/Dev/Trader
```

The first example specifies a stringified IOR for a Naming Service. Your ORB will convert this to a session reference of type **Object** that it will return in response to your invocation of `resolve_initial_references` ("NameService").

The second example specifies a corbaloc-format object reference which will be converted to a session reference that will be returned in response to your invocation of `resolve_initial_references` ("NotificationService").

And the third example specifies a corbaname-format object reference that will be converted to a session reference and returned in response to your invocation of `resolve_initial_references` ("TradingService").

I.3.2.2.3   ORBDefaultInitRef

`ORBDefaultInitRef` lets you define the default host for all of your services to be one or a cascading series of locations represented by a URL-format object reference. You provide all of the URL except the slash "/" character and object key; your ORB appends the slash and the appropriate key string and feeds the resulting string to **string_to_object**. For example, if you input

```
-ORBDefaultInitRef corbaloc::MyServiceHome.com
```

at ORB startup, and then called `resolve_initial_references` ("NotificationService"), your ORB would add a slash and object key to generate the now-complete URL

```
corbaloc::MyServiceHome.com/NotificationService
```

and pass it to **string_to_object** to obtain the session reference for the service, which it would then return to you. As you continued to **resolve_initial_references**, each new request would generate a URL with the appropriate key string, and your ORB would resolve just as it did the Notification Service in this example.

You can specify multiple addresses in your URL, such as

```
-ORBDefaultInitRef corbaloc::MyServiceHome.com,
    MyServiceBackup.com/Pub/Local
```

As specified in the definition of `corbaloc`, your ORB will attempt to resolve each of these in turn, after appending the slash and key string.

I.3.2.2.4 Resolution Order

These three methods are resolved in a strict order, but the order depends on how your ORB is configured. The default order is:

- First, attempt to resolve using `-ORBInitRef`. If you didn't specify an `ORBInitRef` for this service at initialization, or if the resolution attempt fails,
- Attempt to resolve using `-ORBDefaultInitRef`. If you didn't specify an `ORBDefaultInitRef`, or if the resolution attempt fails,
- Attempt to resolve using the administratively-configured settings.

There are cases where you don't want an ORB to use the default setting to divert certain services. The specification suggests, for example, that an ORB using a proprietary `ImplementationRepository` may not want to be diverted to use one from another vendor, or one that doesn't work in the way that ORB expects or requires. To prevent this, an ORB is allowed (but not required) to ignore the `ORBDefaultInitRef` argument when it resolves services that do not have a well-known service name accepted by **resolve_ initial_references**. The ORB is not, however, allowed to ignore *any* setting specified by `ORBInitRef`—only `ORBDefaultInitRef`.

I.3.3   String Form of CORBA Names

The original CORBA Naming Service specified how names were stored inside your program, but provided no standard format to print them out. That meant you couldn't print out a name and send it to a friend or coworker and expect him to use the literal string unless you both had the same ORB and used the same code. (Your friend could parse the name into pieces and enter each piece individually if his GUI allowed it, but this is not a friendly way to deal with names!) Another reason to fix this deficiency: `corbaname` requires a standard representation for the string form of a compound name. The revision of the Naming Service fixes this by specifying a string representation for CORBA names, which it refers to as *stringified names*. (Do not confuse a stringified name with a stringified object reference! They're very different beasties.)

The bottom line is that CORBA object names are Unix-format directory and file names applied to objects. If you're more used to DOS directory and file names, change the backward slashes to forward slashes—everything else is the same. If you're used to Windows names, change the backward slashes to forward slashes *and don't use spaces*. There are some other differences but they're subtle, and you can skip them if you're only interested in the higher-level structure. If you are interested in the details, read on.

The basic unit of the CORBA object naming structure is the naming context. A Naming Context is a CORBA object; you can think of it as a subdirectory for names, combined with the CORBA object functionality that stores and resolves them. A naming context has its own name and contains as many entries as you care to cram into it. Each entry in a naming context has a name and can be either another naming context or a CORBA object. As we just said, this is how your file system works if you're using any one of the popular computer operating systems.

Because naming contexts are CORBA objects, they are identified by CORBA object references. You can register a naming context in your Naming Service even if it resides in another Naming Service on another computer (and even though the naming context is already registered there too, probably under a different name!). This is called Federating, and the Naming Service will resolve a compound name by following its links wherever they lead.

At each level or naming context, CORBA object names—whether for another naming context or an object—already consist of an identifier or ID (the main part of the name) and a kind (the minor part). In the newly defined standard name string, these two parts are separated by a dot and the different naming contexts are separated by slashes. Just in case you wanted to put dots and slashes into your object name, OMG defines *escape characters* that you can use to tell the system that the next dot or slash is really part of the name and not a separator. Instead of telling you how to do this and what the escape character is, we're going to give you a piece of advice. Pardon us, we're going to shout, so cover your ears: DO NOT EVER EVER ESCAPE DOTS OR SLASHES IN YOUR OBJECT NAMES! It's a really stupid thing to do. If you ever feel like you really have to do this in a commercial or business system, take a long break instead. Go for a walk. Drink a non-caffeinated, non-alcoholic beverage slowly and deliberately. Don't go back to your terminal until the urge has totally passed. Your boss and your co-workers will appreciate your consideration.

When you represent a name as a string, if the kind field at a level is empty, you leave out the dot. If both the ID and kind fields are empty, you represent the missing level as a dot between the two bounding slashes. (This can happen if you're representing X.500 names, which are not hierarchical, in the CORBA scheme, which forces a hierarchical representation, albeit temporarily. X.500 names do not require an entry for every possible field. Don't worry, a Naming Service implementation based on X.500-format names will deal with this format properly.)

Two stringified names are equal if every identifier and every kind in one equals the corresponding name and kind in the other. Comparisons are case-sensitive. If the two strings are equal, the names are equal. Simple enough?

I.3.3.1 Converting among Object Name Formats

A new interface, **NamingContextExt**, inherits from the **NamingContext** interface and extends it with operations that convert among the forms of object names:

- **to_string** converts from an object name in its original CORBAservices name-and-kind structure to a name in the new CORBA string format.

- **to_name** accepts a stringified name and returns a CORBAservices name-and-kind structure name.

- **resolve_str** is a convenience operation that accepts a stringified name and performs a **resolve** operation on it. It's the equivalent of **to_name** followed by **resolve**.

- **to_url** takes two parameters: a `corbaloc` address/object key combination, and a stringified name, and returns a fully formed URL string.

The Names Library, one of the least thought-out features of the original Naming Service, was removed from the specification by the interoperable naming service specification. Not just deprecated, totally removed.

I.3.4 Summary

As promised, we've covered all three parts of the Interoperable Naming Service: `corbaloc` and `corbaname` URLs; finding initial services and references; and the standard format for stringified object names (*not* stringified object references!). With this presentation, we've completed our presentation of specifications that enhance integration with Java and the Internet. Now we'll shift gears and start the next part of this book, on Quality-of-Service control.

PART

II

Quality-of-Service Control

My dictionary lists two definitions for *quality.* A thing's quality, by the first definition, is its *essential characteristics or features.* By the second definition, a thing's quality is (as you might have expected for the first definition) its *degree of excellence.* Combining those definitions, the phrase *Quality of Service Control* means that CORBA 3 lets you control both the essential characteristics or features of the services it provides, and the degree of excellence of the services you choose—a most delightful prospect.

So, in this section of the book, we'll show how you can control the characteristics of your CORBA environment, or select a specialized version of CORBA, to tune it precisely for any one of a number of specialized application areas.

Here's what we're going to cover, and how we've arranged it:

- *Invocation modes* (covered in Part II, Chapter 1): The Asynchronous Messaging Specification adds both callback and polling-mode asynchronous invocations to the CORBA invocation repertoire, allowing CORBA to play in distributed environments that require a looser coupling between client and server.

- *Invocation Quality of Service* (covered in Part II, Chapter 2): For both synchronous and asynchronous invocations, under CORBA 3 you can prioritize invocations, and set timeouts, and control other characteristics, making CORBA robust in environments that become overloaded or stressed.

- *Real-Time CORBA, Fault-Tolerant CORBA, and Minimum CORBA* (covered in Part II, Chapter 3; Part II, Chapter 4; and Part II, Chapter 5): These three specialized versions of CORBA meet the requirements of environments with strict requirements for reliability (in two senses of the word: reliability in time, and reliability in actions) and footprint. Applications in all three of these markets now benefit from the standards-compliant distributed computing that CORBA provides.

CORBA 3 Application Areas

In the chapters that make up this section, we'll present these specifications. But first, in this introductory section, we'll look at the big picture—how these specifications let CORBA play in more industries and more markets.

B2B and Loosely Coupled Interoperating Systems

CORBA 2 integrates your distributed objects into a tightly coupled application. Synchronous invocations work well in this environment: With all of the servers under your control, you (typically) have confidence that the services they provide are available when you need them.

But, business-to-business (B2B) applications (which cross enterprise boundaries), and even some business-to-consumer (B2C) applications, do not fit this pattern. Your business partner's server is an unknown quantity to you; even if they gave you a help desk number to call when things go wrong, you know they will prioritize internal requests higher than yours. Under these conditions, it's not prudent to issue synchronous calls where any trip to their server may not return for seconds, minutes, or perhaps hours. And, this is not an environment conducive to shared distributed transactions.

The Messaging Service, which we present in Part II, Chapter 1 and Part II, Chapter 2, lets CORBA play in the markets that use messaging services now. With its asynchronous invocation modes and reliable store-and-forward invocation transmission, this service does the waiting (and the nagging!) for your client when you invoke on a server that's temporarily unavailable. Combined with CORBA's new ability to transmit requests described in XML (described in Part I, Chapter 2), this loose coupling produces an environment ideal for B2B e-Commerce.

Coping with Limited Resources

In principle always, and in real life most of the time, *location transparency* brings a host of benefits. It lets any client access any instance, anywhere, using the same invocation. At the server end, the object instance responds to every client in the same egalitarian way. This simplicity enables complex systems to be built using straightforward coding schemes. Designed into CORBA from the beginning, location transparency provides many benefits to programmer, administrator, and end user alike.

But, we all face limited resources from time to time, and the way we cope is to prioritize. For example, consider a company running a large accounting system on an overloaded mainframe or server. This machine should have been replaced years ago, but the company needed to upgrade its e-commerce servers for quicker response and didn't have resources to spare for back-office applications that were running well enough to get by. If this system treated all invocations equally, customers might have to wait while the market research department ran next year's projections, or the VP of marketing might have to wait for his reports while trial balances finish up for the clerks in the accounting department, since they got into the queue first.

This company needs to run customer transactions first in order to capture orders before customers get impatient and surf their browsers over to the competition. Remaining cycles need to be partitioned carefully, so that vital business functions get done before less important ones. In order to do this, they need to be able to prioritize requests.

So, to enable CORBA to play well in environments where resources may be stressed from time to time, the Messaging Specification includes a comprehensive section on QoS.

Time-Critical Applications

Many application areas require that invocations complete within a certain time. Some (the most exciting ones, such as aircraft fly-by-wire) require that execution also be *fast*, while others (altering a satellite's orbit today to avoid a collision tomorrow) require only that the invocation complete within a window, which may be an hour long, or more. Regardless of the time scale required, the defining characteristic of these Real-Time (RT) systems is that execution of commands is, in the temporal sense, *predictable*. The price of predictability is control, and we will see in Part II, Chapter 3, that RT CORBA systems can control their resources in many ways.

RT CORBA could be (and is!) also used in flight or engine control, plant security or building environmental control (heating and air conditioning), and data acquisition for scientific use or feedback in industrial systems. Financial quotes used in programmed trading may be worthless if delayed more than a certain time, sometimes measured in seconds or less. Architects and designers want to use CORBA in these systems, which almost always involve heterogeneous distributed hardware and software, but they cannot unless they can control every resource that their application uses.

The first Real-Time systems included a single CPU and its peripherals, but did not extend to the network. Addition of a network, whose load and latencies may not be entirely under the control of the RT system, makes it more difficult to provide the guarantees that characterize these systems. Nevertheless, if the load on the network is stable enough and everything else is carefully controlled, distributed systems can deliver RT performance.

Real-Time CORBA standardizes the architecture of a distributed RT system and the interfaces an application uses to control available resources and guarantee end-to-end predictability. It's being used today in many systems, from military to flight control. In July 2000, the OMG attracted 140 participants to its first workshop on CORBA in RT and embedded systems where they heard reports of case studies in software-defined radio, industrial machinery, military applications, and more. Enthusiastic support from vendors and end-users alike bodes well for the future of this specialization of CORBA. If you're interested in attending a future workshop, surf to www.omg.org/news/schedule/upcoming.htm.

From here, we'll go in two directions: Fault-Tolerant CORBA provides extra reliability in systems that add extra hardware and software, while Minimum CORBA shrinks the footprint of software that has to fit into the smallest possible space. (Yes, there are systems that have to fit into small spaces and simultaneously provide extra reliability but we won't discuss them here.) We'll discuss both, with Fault Tolerance first.

Fault-Tolerant Systems

Any individual piece of computer hardware or software can fail. That's why we back up our hard drives. (Hard drive failures can happen to anyone. When the hard drive on my laptop failed last year, I restored from a recent backup tape. Your drive is backed up now—right?)

The tape backup of my hard drive got me back up and running in a few days. That's the time it took to get a replacement drive and re-load my files. But some systems can't afford to be down for a few days, or even a few hours, or sometimes even a few minutes. For example:

- 911 telephone systems, which deal with situations critical to people's life and health.

- Medical monitoring systems which, similarly, deal with health-critical information constantly.

- Fly-by-wire systems must act in Real-Time, and must not fail (as you'll attest if you've ever flown in an airplane).

- When widely-used e-Commerce systems fail, companies lose thousands of sales and possibly thousands of customers who may never come back.

- Financial trading applications may lose unbelievable amounts of money for both customers and the responsible company if they go down, even for a short time, at a critical moment (which is, usually, when the load is highest and potential for failure is greatest).

My tape backup provided *redundancy*: a second copy of my critical data. It was an exact copy; the awkward delay in getting back up and running occurred because the redundant data were off-line and the redundant hard drive was stored off-site. (OK, what really happened is that I bought a new drive the day after my old one failed.) Systems that can't afford a delay, including the ones we just listed, achieve reliability through the use of *on-*

line redundant hardware and software. To avoid even a moment's down-time, they keep their redundant copies on-line, running. This costs more but, as the popularity of FT systems proves, it's often worth it. In fact, it's the only way to be sure (well, nearly sure) that your system will never (well, very, very rarely) go down. Why are we so hesitant to say "never"? If a failure occurs due to something intrinsic to a hardware system, or a defect in the software, every part of a redundant system may fail simultaneously for the same reason. Careful testing can minimize these occurrences, but not eliminate them. There are other ways that systems could fail in spite of redundancies. Look for our list in Section II.4.2.

FT CORBA standardizes a number of ways of providing redundancy in distributed systems. This means that application areas that depend on high availability—including the ones we listed above—can now depend on CORBA. In Part II, Chapter 4, we'll show how.

Small-Footprint Systems

CORBA defines a rich and flexible programming and execution environment. The features that give CORBA this flexibility, including the Dynamic Invocation Interface (DII) and Interface Repository (IR or IFR), occupy memory, of course. Where they're used, that's no problem. Also, on large systems such as mainframes, the amount of memory they occupy may be insignificant compared to large data structures so, again, no problem. But, when you're trying to cut an application's footprint down to the bare minimum in order to burn it into a dedicated chip, and you've already cut your data structures down as far as you can, the memory occupied by these CORBA features looms large.

Embedded systems is a large market, espcially when you talk about numbers of units. Compared to the systems we think of as "conventional"—desktops, laptops, servers, and mainframes, which total in the few hundreds of millions at most—embedded systems loom large, numbering in the billions: Some estimates predict that, if you include applications as small as the nearly disposable "system-on-a-chip," more than 10 billion will be sold in the next few years.

We're all familiar with embedded systems: They run your TV, VCR, or even high-end refrigerator or dishwasher today. For these systems, space and price constraints allow reasonably sized systems. There is another category of "systems-on-a-chip" that has much more restrictive space, power, and (sometimes) price requirements. This category includes a network of sensors that may be, for example, set free on an ocean current, attached to a wild animal and released into the rain forest, or dropped onto a battlefield, with little or no hope of recovery for quite a variety of possible reasons.

To enable CORBA to play in this market, OMG members have completed one specification and are working on another. Minimum CORBA defines an ORB environment that sacrifices the DII and IFR, among other things, in favor of a smaller footprint. Going even further, a new specification for micro-level networked systems, termed "Smart Transducers" in its RFP, is in the works. We'll describe the Minimum CORBA specification, and (briefly!) the Smart Transducers RFP, in Part II, Chapter 5.

Here We Go

In this section, we've introduced what each of these specifications does and the application areas they enable. The detailed explanations and technical details come in the next five chapters, starting with the Messaging Service.

Additions to CORBA Interoperability

CHAPTER PREVIEW

We've split our presentation of the CORBA Messaging specification into two chapters: this one covers asynchronous invocation and the next covers Quality-of-Service control.

CORBA's messaging model, presented in this chapter, itself divides into two parts: a programming model and a communications model. The programming model offers a choice of callback or polling mode result return, while the communications model offers a choice of direct or routed communications. By picking the right combination from these sets of alternatives, an application can achieve the loosely coupled but reliable invocation semantic that B2B e-commerce requires. By choosing other combinations, you'll be able to tailor your communications semantic to just about any type of application.

The chapter starts out with a description of the programming model, with its callback- and polling-mode invocations. To accommodate the architects who use messaging semantics to design enterprise systems, we've moved the programming details from this initial descriptive section to their own section at the end of the chapter. Before we get to the programming details, we present the communications model, including the role of CORBA routers. Once architectural and descriptive aspects of every part of the service have been presented, we finish up with programming details for callback- and polling-mode asynchronous CORBA invocations.

II.1.1 CORBA 3 Interoperability Modes

Under CORBA 2, support for non-synchronous invocations was not well developed. If you declared your invocation to be **oneway** in your IDL, your client would get control back from an invocation right away but you couldn't get results back (**out** and **inout** parameters are not allowed, and the return value must be **void**) and no exception informs you if your invocation fails to get through or to execute. There is a *deferred synchronous* invocation but it's only available through the Dynamic Invocation Interface (DII) and only supports polling-mode result return.

Under CORBA 3, things have gotten a whole lot better. The new CORBA Messaging Specification makes CORBA a fully equipped player in the asynchronous and messaging arena. If you want to do it asynchronously, now you can do it with CORBA. Here's what you get:

- A messaging architecture that cleanly separates the asynchronous programming model from the over-the-wire communications model.

- A flexible asynchronous **programming model** (described in Section II.1.1.1) with automatically generated, standard interfaces for result retrieval by either callback or polling.

- A separate **communications model** (described in Section II.1.1.2) with three distinct routing policies and types of network configurations, allowing the same application to automatically adapt to take best advantage of networks with different routing/staging capabilities and QoS support.

- QoS settings that let you tailor invocation characteristics to the needs of your application and your site, and prioritize tasks when your system and your network get overloaded.

- Callback-mode result return that allows "fire-and-forget" programming *and* optionally allows results to be returned to a different CORBA context than the client that made the invocation—even a totally separate application, running on another computer.

- Polling-mode result retrieval that allows a client to fetch results when it's ready for them, and optionally (depending on the features installed on the network) allows results to be retrieved in a different CORBA context than the one that made the invocation.

- An extended Transaction Service, able to handle asynchronous invocations within a transaction (Section II.1.1.4).

- Clearly defined semantics for the **oneway** invocation, with four different client-selected QoSs available (Section II.1.1.5).

There's more good news: These additions have *no effect* on existing CORBA applications. If you're content with the synchronous invocations that your client has been making all along, you won't have to change anything. For non-transactional applications, all of the changes are on the client side so you can have asynchronous access to your existing CORBA servers just by rewriting the clients. The basic CORBA programming model is unchanged, and the new interfaces are defined in OMG IDL. GIOP remains the standard wire format, and IIOP remains the standard protocol, although GIOP receives a minor addition. However, the specification has been designed in a protocol-independent way so that it can be used with protocols other than IIOP.

CORBA 3 terms this capability *Asynchronous Method Invocation* (AMI). It's provided primarily by extending the current programming model with a ReplyHandler object for callback-mode result return, and a Poller value-type for polling-mode result return. We'll cover the architecture of these additions in the early parts of this chapter (Section II.1.1) and detail the interfaces at the end (Section II.1.2).

Going beyond AMI, the specification defines *Time-Independent Invocation* (TII) by adding a store-and-forward routing capability and protocol to standard GIOP. This allows a client to make an invocation on an object instance that is currently unavailable for whatever reason, and gives objects the corresponding capability for replies. By adding persistent storage to routers, we can make the network as reliable as a transactional system. This enables a number of scenarios that require the reliability of CORBA invocation combined with the loose-coupling provided by messaging environments, such as B2B e-commerce. We'll describe the routing capability starting in Section II.1.1.2.3.

In this book, we'll use the term AMI as a shorthand for the programming model, which is virtually always unchanged by whether we use routed or non-routed network transport. If anything about an interface or mechanism is affected by routing, we'll point it out.

The easiest way to learn how AMI and TII work is by studying the programming model and the network communications model separately, since the specification was designed this way. We'll start with the programming model but only examine its architecture at first, leaving the programming details for the last part of our discussion. Then we'll look at the communications model and see how the different policy settings interact with our programming model to deliver the flexibility that we need for modern distributed applications. We'll postpone the programming details until later, to allow the nonprogrammers to stay with us as long as possible. If you're not interested in the programming details, skip all of Section II.1.2—when you get to it, move ahead to Part II, Chapter 2 and resume reading with Real-Time CORBA. (On the other hand, if you're *only* interested in coding, you can skip the explanations and page ahead to Section II.1.2 now!)

II.1.1.1 Asynchronous Programming Model

Under CORBA 2, you had to program using the DII using the deferred-synchronous invocation mode to get non-synchronous invocations. Under CORBA 3 using AMI as we're describing now, you have equal access to every asynchronous mode regardless of whether you use the SII or DII. Since most programmers use the SII when they have a choice, and now that they're equal in asynchronous access you have this choice all the time, we're only going to describe the SII interfaces in this book.

The taxonomy of the programming model is simple (see Figure II.1.1): At the top level, you can pick between the synchronous client-stub interfaces of basic CORBA and the asynchronous interfaces that we will describe here. If you pick **synchronous**, you have to program to your operation's stub, but there is still a choice left: You can declare the invocation to be **one-way** in the IDL. If you don't (that is, you choose the default two-way), your invocation will block until it completes; when you get control back, the results will be in the return value, **out**, and **inout** parameters. If you choose **oneway**, you will probably get control back sooner depending on the QoS you set (see Section II.1.1.5 for details).

If you pick **asynchronous**, there's an additional level of choice: callback or polling mode result return. **Callback** is fire-and-forget programming for the invoking client. The advantage of callback is that your client doesn't have to do anything about the invocation while it's outstanding; the result calls you when it's ready. However, if a result arrives when your program is busy doing something else, no matter how important, it will stop its processing and service the callback (or, at least, devote a thread to it if you're multithreaded). With **polling**, on the other hand, your program chooses when it wants to fetch and examine results. This suits some applications well, and others not so well. Another difference: Because polling mode does not use a callback object, it lets you link your client with only the smaller client-side library, producing a much smaller executable. If you're programming for a small device, such as a cell phone or pager, this could be

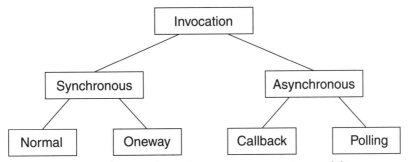

Figure II.1.1   Synchronous/Asynchronous programming model taxonomy.

significant. We'll present architectural details on both modes in the next two sections.

II.1.1.1.1   Callback-Mode Asynchronous Invocations

There's something unusual about how you get the response to a callback-mode AMI invocation. The CORBA model, up to now at least, is that a client makes a request, the target object receives it and does whatever while the client waits, and the object returns the result to the waiting client. In asynchronous mode, however, the client sends out the request and *doesn't wait*. The target object receives it, does whatever, and gets ready to return the result only to find that *nothing is waiting for it*. The original client is off doing something else, and there's no way to interrupt it with the response. How can we get the response to the client, or wherever it's needed?

Here's how: In callback mode, we *turn the response into an invocation.* That's what callback mode is all about—calling something with the result so it doesn't have to keep polling to see if it's ready. Invocation is the mechanism we have in CORBA for calling something. By using it, we don't have to invent anything new.

The name for the CORBA object that receives the reply is the **ReplyHandler.** A CORBA 3 IDL compiler will generate skeletons for **ReplyHandler**s for every operation if you set the switch for it, but you have to program each **ReplyHandler** yourself to do whatever needs to happen when it is invoked with the result. It's a regular CORBA object with an object reference, created and instantiated on a POA in any of the usual ways. You have to create the object reference for it on your POA before you make the request, since that object reference is one of the arguments to the callback form of the AMI.

When the AMI designers turned the response into an invocation, they created an opportunity and took advantage of it: Since the **ReplyHandler** is a regular CORBA object, it can be *anywhere on your network*, not just in the client process. This gives you a tremendous amount of flexibility in designing your distributed applications: Even if asynchrony is not an important aspect of an operation, you can use callback AMI to make an invocation whose result is routed to where it's needed by the system, instead of returning to your client where you will have to route it to wherever it's needed yourself.

We now have (at least) three different ways to make our invocations. Figure II.1.2 through Figure II.1.4 show the steps in each, letting us compare and contrast them:

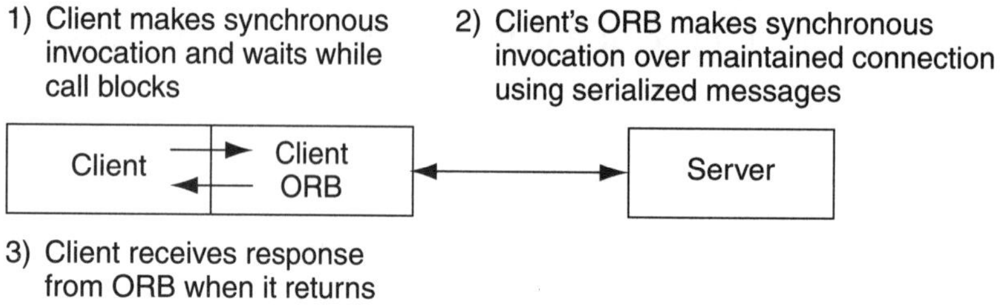

1) Client makes synchronous invocation and waits while call blocks
2) Client's ORB makes synchronous invocation over maintained connection using serialized messages
Client
Client ORB
Server
3) Client receives response from ORB when it returns

Figure II.1.2 Steps in a synchronous CORBA invocation.

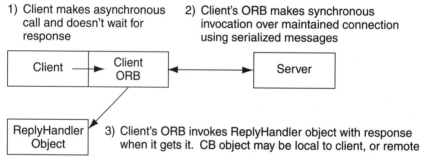

1) Client makes asynchronous call and doesn't wait for response
2) Client's ORB makes synchronous invocation over maintained connection using serialized messages
Client
Client ORB
Server
ReplyHandler Object
3) Client's ORB invokes ReplyHandler object with response when it gets it. CB object may be local to client, or remote

Figure II.1.3 Steps in an asynchronous CORBA invocation, non-routed network.

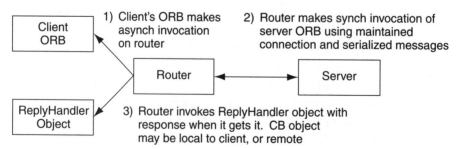

Client ORB
1) Client's ORB makes asynch invocation on router
2) Router makes synch invocation of server ORB using maintained connection and serialized messages
Router
Server
ReplyHandler Object
3) Router invokes ReplyHandler object with response when it gets it. CB object may be local to client, or remote

Figure II.1.4 Steps in an asynchronousCORBA invocation, routed network.

Figure II.1.2 diagrams the steps in a synchronous CORBA invocation using the IIOP protocol: The client makes an invocation, which it passes to its ORB (step 1). This also passes control of this active thread to the ORB, so client execution blocks until the invocation returns. IIOP invocations always go over TCP/IP connections so, if it hasn't done so already, the client ORB establishes a connection with the server ORB (step 2). The client ORB marshals the input arguments that it received from the client, and dispatches the invocation to the server ORB over the connection (still step 2). The server ORB unmarshals the arguments, passes the invocation to the servant, receives the output arguments back, marshals them, and sends them (step 3) back *over the same connection* (a requirement of IIOP) to the client ORB which unmarshals the return arguments and passes them to the client along with control of the running thread.

Figure II.1.3 diagrams the steps in an asynchronous callback invocation in a system without CORBA routers. (We'll explain CORBA routers fully in Section II.1.1.2.3.) At development time, we programmed a **ReplyHandler** object. Now, at run time, we instantiate one (step 1) so we can include its object reference in our invocation. Next, our client makes our invocation using **sendc_<opname>**, passing the **ReplyHandler** object reference and input arguments to the client ORB. (For more details on the programming interface, look ahead in this chapter to Section II.1.2.) The client gets control back right away and continues execution. Simultaneously, the client ORB marshals the arguments and prepares to invoke the server. As we pointed out in the last section, the server side is unchanged from CORBA 2.3 and so requires a TCP/IP connection (step 2) just as we had in the synchronous case. The client ORB marshals the arguments *into exactly the same form as it would have if they had come in via a synchronous invocation* and invokes the server ORB (step 4). The server-side action here is identical to the synchronous case, and marshaled arguments come back over the connection. Next, the client ORB unmarshals the return arguments into a callback-specific format and invokes the **ReplyHandler** object with them (step 3), regardless of where the **ReplyHandler** object might be. Summing up: In this case the client sees *asynchronous* invocation semantics while the server sees the same old *synchronous* semantics it's been used to. Something had to transform from one to the other; in this case it's the client's ORB.

To finish this set of explanations, we need to anticipate the introduction of CORBA routers. A CORBA router is not a network router; it's an ORB running on a networked computer with persistent storage—that is, an ORB running on a machine with a hard drive. Routers are client and server for a special object type that passes invocations over the network reliably using a store-and-forward algorithm. Section II.1.1.2.3 presents routers fully; for our purposes here that's all we need to cover.

Figure II.1.4 diagrams the steps in an asynchronous callback invocation in a system with CORBA routers. As in the previous case, we've programmed and instantiated our **ReplyHandler** object (step 1). Our client makes the invocation which passes to its ORB; the client again receives control back right away and continues executing while its ORB (perhaps using another thread, or in another process—the specification doesn't dictate) dispatches the invocation. In this case, however, the client ORB passes the invocation to a CORBA router (still step 1) using the CORBA routing protocol and then *forgets all about the invocation.* The invocation may pass along the network from router to router although we've only shown one in our diagram. The final router in the chain (step 2) *establishes a TCP/IP connection with the server,* just as the client ORB did in the synchronous case. The server thinks it's being invoked by a client ORB because the the router ORB does the same things a client ORB would do. This allows previous-generation CORBA servers to serve asynchronous CORBA clients, even in a routed environment. The router invokes the server, which does its usual thing and returns the result to the router over the same TCP/IP connection. The final router in the chain (thinking backwards, since this is the return!) *invokes the* **ReplyHandler** *object* (step 3) with the output parameters. Summing up: In this case, as in the no-router case, the client sees *asynchronous* semantics while the server sees *synchronous* semantics. Unlike that case, however, the transformation from one to the other is done by the combined efforts of the client's ORB and the router closest to the server.

If the **ReplyHandler** object is not co-located with the calling client, there's no reason for the reply to go through the client's ORB as it did in our no-router example, so a system with properly located routers can be more efficient.

There are two new aspects to exception handling in callback invocations: First, because the system turns responses into invocations on a **ReplyHandler** object, exceptions raised in the invoked object during execution can't be handled in the usual way since exceptions can only be raised by a reply. (You make a synchronous invocation in a try/catch loop; exceptions thrown in the object on the server side are caught in the client after the return.) To handle this, the system creates an **ExceptionHolder valuetype** that contains the exception as its state and has operations that raise the exception in the **ReplyHandler** context. You will have to do some of the programming that checks and calls the valuetypes to raise the exceptions. Second, even though you're used to throwing exceptions when you program a CORBA object and returning them to be raised in the client when the result returns, you can't throw a CORBA exception in a **ReplyHandler** object since it's never going to return anything anywhere, and it doesn't have a client. Remember, this object was called by an ORB or router with a result generated by an *object*, and not by a client, so the usual CORBA client-object relationship doesn't hold here! (Existentialists may want to pause here and ponder the ramifications of an object without a client. Where did the client go? If you wait long enough, will it show up? I know someone who programmed a client for a **ReplyHandler** object. He named it Godot. I don't know how he named a client. Isn't philosophy fun?)

There is one thing we haven't covered: What turns the response into an invocation on the **ReplyHandler**? This, it turns out, has no bearing on the programming model as long as it happens somewhere—it's actually part of the communications and messaging model, so we'll postpone discussion for now and meet up with it in Section II.1.1.2.

II.1.1.1.2 *Polling-Mode Asynchronous Invocations*

Remember how we said that the AMI programming model and communications model were independent? Well, it's really true for callback mode, but only *almost* true for polling. There are two modes of polling. In the simpler one, this programming model takes advantage of the environment to allow lighter weight clients suitable for small embedded systems, for example. (You select the extended model by setting your Routing QoS for Time-Independent Invocation; details later in Section II.1.1.4.) Here is the programming model for the simpler case.

When your client invokes an operation using AMI polling mode, it immediately receives control back along with a **Poller valuetype** as the return value. While the client goes about its other business, the ORB (either using a separate thread, or another process—the specification doesn't dictate these implementation details) makes its usual invocation, gets the results back, and stores them somewhere in memory.

The IDL-compiler-generated **Poller valuetype** defines a separate operation for you to invoke to retrieve the results from each operation in the original interface. Your client can attempt to retrieve the results of an operation anytime after invoking it. You can make a retrieval attempt either block or not by specifying a time-out value in milliseconds: 0 (zero) means don't wait—return immediately whether the result is ready or not. If it is ready, you get it; if not, you get the error **CORBA::NO_RESPONSE** and you get to try again later. A timeout of $2^{32} - 1$ tells the valuetype to block on this retrieval call until the result returns. Any value in between means you're willing to wait that many milliseconds for the result. When the result returns, the retrieval succeeds. You can only fetch the results once; subsequent attempts return the error **OBJECT_NOT_EXIST**.

In this simple mode, the **valuetype** is a locality-constrained object that will *not* work outside of the client process, so don't pass it to a friend somewhere else on your network and expect him to retrieve some result with it.

Why this constraint? The ORB libraries that we link with our CORBA applications are typically split into two, one containing (small, lightweight) client-side functionality and the other containing (larger, longer-to-load although still quick to execute) server-side stuff. In the simple polling mode, there's no **ReplyHandler** object so the client can link *without* the server-side libraries, making it lighter weight as we promised at the beginning of this section.

We can instruct the ORB to generate a **ReplyHandler** object by requesting the highest value of the routing QoS as we'll show in Section II.1.1.2.2 when we present the polling-mode AMI communications model. The **Poller valuetype** then contains the **ReplyHandler**'s object reference in its state and can be passed out of process and still work. This flexibility is the advantage; the price is that the client may now require the server-side library and may no longer be the svelte lightweight as in the previous case. The **ReplyHandler** in this scenario is the same as the callback **ReplyHandler**, except that it's generated by the ORB and is hidden from the client, which can only invoke its **Poller valuetype** wrapper.

That covers the programming *architecture*. We haven't presented the IDL interfaces for asynchronous callback and polling invocations yet because we want to cover the communications model before we scare off the non-programmers. We'll cover the IDL details at the end of the AMI discussion in Section II.1.2.

II.1.1.2 Asynchronous Communications Model

To get started, let's identify what we need to happen in order for AMI/TII communications to work. Here's the fundamental principle:

Before CORBA Messaging, the ORB expected to be invoked *synchronously* for *every* invocation. *The messaging specification does not change this, as we've seen. The server-side ORB still expects to be invoked synchronously for every invocation.* (Only the client cares about the synchronous/asynchronous distinction, so the Messaging specification avoided perturbing server-side architecture. This way, ORB and server implementations do not have to change. Only transactional server functions that must synchronize with the client during a commit or rollback are affected by CORBA Messaging.)

Here are some more details about what happens during a synchronous invocation: As we discussed when we examined Figure II.1.2, the invoking ORB establishes a TCP connection with the server ORB. Connections are maintained, so many invocations may use the same one over time and even simultaneously. The client ORB receives an invocation from a client through its stub, applies a serial number to it, sends it to the server ORB over the connection, and waits for the response to come back over the same connection. If one or both ends are multithreaded, or if the connection is pooled for use by multiple ORBs, there may be multiple requests outstanding simultaneously on the same connection; responses are numbered with the same serial as the request to enable client ORBs to sort out results when they come back.

Contrast this with the asynchronous AMI invocation model. We'll consider only the callback case right now to keep things simple. Since we're examining only client /server functions and not the network, it doesn't make any difference whether we have routers or not. The client makes its invocation and gets control back right away (see either Figure II.1.3 or Figure II.1.4). The invocation contains the reference for a callback object, not necessarily in the client's process, that gets called back with the result when it's ready. There isn't any need to maintain a connection, or even a serial number for that matter, since the connection between the invocation and response is maintained by the *client*, and not by the ORB, in this model.

Clearly, we need an agent to translate from the asynchronous model on the client side to the synchronous model on the server side. That is, something that accepts the invocation from the client and takes charge of it, invoking the server over a maintained connection, receiving the response and matching it to the invocation using its serial number, and invoking the callback object whose reference was received with the invocation.

This can be done by the client's ORB, as we showed in Figure II.1.3. There's no reason why a multithreaded or multiprocess ORB can't return control to a client immediately upon receiving an asynchronous invocation, make a normal synchronous invocation of the server, and invoke the callback object when the result returns.

Alternatively, the agent could be separate from both the client's and the server's ORB; that is, it could be a *Router* as we showed in Figure II.1.4. We'll present routers formally in Section II.1.1.2.3, but introduce them briefly here. Routers are software agents that either store and forward asynchronous CORBA invocations, or (for the router closest to the server) transform the invocation from asynchronous to synchronous and invoke the server as we showed in Figure II.1.4. They may be co-located on the same hardware as the client or server, or on dedicated hardware strategically located on a network. Routers co-located with the client and server can perform special functions, as we'll show shortly.

CORBA routers come in two flavors: without, and with, persistent storage. Routers transfer invocations from one to another with a reliable hand-off that ensures that the data are passed correctly; by adding persistent storage, they combine to form a network that transmits data as reliably as an OTS processes it since invocations and responses are not lost even if power loss or other fault causes a router to shut down, even abruptly, and boot back up. Routers' functionality and the interfaces they use to transmit messages are defined in the Messaging specification, but they are an optional conformance point. When you look at Messaging implementations on the market, you will almost certainly find that routing capability—whether persistent or not—is an add-on to the basic product, although we detect an expectation that many Messaging products will offer routing because of the additional capability that it offers.

There are three levels of QoS for routing of asynchronous invocations; as you might expect, you need to install routers to use any except the most basic. (We've collected details of all CORBA QoS settings in the next chapter, but include this summary here to round out our discussion of routers.) They are ranked, from minimum to maximum QoS, as **ROUTE_NONE**, **ROUTE_FORWARD**, and **ROUTE_STORE_AND_FORWARD**. You can set your **RoutingPolicy** to a range; if your minimum is **ROUTE_NONE** and your maximum is **ROUTE_STORE_AND_FORWARD**, your invocation will run anywhere and take advantage of the highest QoS of router it can. If your **RoutingPolicy** calls for a higher QoS than the physical network configuration can deliver, your invocation will fail with a **CORBA::INV_POLICY** exception. If your application requires a minimum QoS above **ROUTE_NONE**, you can go ahead and set it, but the only way to get the application to work on that network is to get together with the hardware folks and sysadmin, and buy and install CORBA routers.

That's our introduction to asynchronous CORBA communications. Now we'll see how the various levels of routing QoS combine with the callback and polling invocation modes, starting with the simplest "no routers" case and building up from there.

II.1.1.2.1 No-Router Callback Communications

In this simplest case, the client makes a callback-mode invocation that includes the object reference of an already instantiated **ReplyHandler** in its parameter list (Figure II.1.3). The client's ORB accepts the invocation and returns control to the client. Working either on a separate thread or in a separate process (the specification properly leaves these details to the implementor), the ORB places a serial number onto the request and invokes the server ORB over a stable connection. When the result comes back over the same connection, the client's ORB transforms it into an invocation of the **ReplyHandler** object, which it executes, regardless of whether the **ReplyHandler** is local or remote. Keep in mind that CORBA does not define exactly where the "ORB" is, and the ORB may do its thing in a distributed way, so this transformation and invocation of the **ReplyHandler** may happen within the client process or elsewhere. Details are immaterial as long as everything happens as the specification dictates.

So this architecture meets all of our requirements: The client uses the callback-mode AMI programming model, the server sees a normal CORBA invocation, and no routers are involved. All of the pieces of the callback API are there, including callback to a remote **ReplyHandler** whenever you want. You get this behavior, or at least this observable functionality, when you make a callback-mode asynchronous invocation with **RoutingPolicy=ROUTE_NONE**.

As we've already mentioned, many vendors provide ORB functionality in two basic libraries, one for client functionality and the other for server stuff. (There may be additional libraries as well.) Client libraries are typically small, and executables that include only client functionality can be lightweight with a small memory footprint. In contrast, server libraries are much larger and add significantly to the memory footprint of an executable. If you've made callback-mode asynchronous invocations, your client process includes one or more ReplyHandlers and has to include the server libraries, which rules out lightweight clients. However, if lightweight is a requirement, you can do it with polling, as we'll show next.

II.1.1.2.2   No-Router Polling Communications

When you program in polling mode, the client makes a callback-mode invocation that immediately returns control along with a **Poller valuetype** as the return value. Similarly to the callback case, the ORB (possibly in the same process on another thread, although possibly elsewhere; the specification does not dictate) proceeds in parallel to make a serialized invocation of the target object and to receive the reply over the same connection.

Where is the operation of the **valuetype** implemented? The ORB does it by implementing the operations itself. Although you could imagine a "virtual" ReplyHandler object, there's no reason for any real CORBA object to be instantiated on the client side—the ORB just stores the return values itself when they come back, and hands them to your client when you invoke the fetch operation on the **Poller valuetype**. Remember, the Messaging specification dictates that the Poller valuetype is constrained to your local process unless you've set **RoutingPolicy=ROUTE_STORE_AND_FORWARD**. There's a real advantage to this: As we just mentioned, most ORB products have you link a small, lightweight library for client-side functions, and a larger, heavier library for server-side functions. So, a client that makes only polling AMI calls and sets **RoutingPolicy=_ROUTE_NONE or ROUTE_FORWARD** (that is, non-TII) links only the smaller client library, thereby keeping its memory footprint small. In order to make this work, the model for this case deviates from our client-side programming model, which ordinarily allows the response to go anywhere instead of returning to the invoking client's process.

Of course this limits functionality: The **Poller valuetype** *cannot* be passed out of the client's process, since it has no state that refers back to the originating ORB so the retrieval functions won't work in a foreign process. And, the trick of switching from polling to callback mode while a request is outstanding will not work for the same reason. (We'll mention this briefly in Section II.1.2.1.5.) These limits go away if you have routers on your network and set **RoutingPolicy=ROUTE_STORE_AND_FORWARD**, but of course then you may have to link with the server-side library too, POA and all; details are coming up.

The bottom line on polling asynchronous invocations is this: Everything new happens on the client side, in process, small, and simple.

II.1.1.2.3   Adding Routers

As we've mentioned in passing (several times!), a *router* in CORBA Messaging is a software agent with three possible functions:

- Routers store and forward invocations and replies.
- Routers co-located with servers order and deliver invocations according to the QueueOrderPolicy in effect.
- Routers transform the asynchronous invocations that they receive from clients into synchronous invocations that they make on servers.

Some routers run on the same hardware as clients or servers; others run on separate hardware. Even routers on separate hardware may not have it all to themselves. Remember, routers are just applications with ORBs in them, the same as any other CORBA application.

Physically, CORBA Messaging recognizes two different types of routers: those without persistent storage, and those with it. Routers with persistent storage participate in a reliable, end-to-end network configuration that gives a transaction-like assurance to the transport layer. Routers without persistent storage are really handy to keep network traffic flowing, but are regarded by the Messaging specification as providing a lower level of assurance.

At the software level, you set **RoutingPolicy** to control the routing of your invocations. The policy takes a range, so you can set the minimum and maximum values. The choices are, from minimum to maximum, **ROUTE_NONE**, **ROUTE_FORWARD**, and **ROUTE_STORE_AND_FORWARD**. If your site has installed and configured routers with persistent storage, you may set your maximum value to any of these three levels. If your routers do not have persistent storage, the maximum you will get is **ROUTE_FORWARD**. Routing policy may be set at both the client and server ends; the policy used is the highest in the intersection of the two ranges with each other and physical reality. If you don't have any routers, the minimum you set must be **ROUTE_NONE** because this is the QoS you'll get and if it isn't in your range, your invocation will fail with an **INV_POLICY** exception.

If your network has persistent routers and you set **RoutingPolicy=ROUTE_STORE_AND_FORWARD**, your invocations fall into the category of Time-Independent Invocations (TII). In TII, both callback and polling mode asynchronous invocations may return values to locations remote from the client that made them. Invocations will succeed even if both client and server are disconnected from the network when the invocation is made and are never both connected to the network at the same time. The OMG specification document illustrates TII with a gee-whiz scenario in which a sporadically connected laptop client invokes an operation on a similarly sporadically connected laptop server over the Internet, using routers and staging in three places. This may be the ultimate in flexibility, but we think that the loosely coupled semantic is much better justified in B2B e-commerce where you want invocations to succeed even though, for instance, the two companies' machines may communicate over a slow or unreliable Internet connection, or the server machine may not always be available and the client user doesn't have access to the other company's helpdesk. An invocation made over TII will just wait patiently in the queue for the server machine to become available, instead of returning immediately with an error. (Like downloading and uploading e-mail while you work offline, CORBA using a disconnected *client* can be really handy, and we think that people will use this feature a lot for both enterprise and personal computing. However, we don't think that many applications will run servers on laptops or other computers that are disconnected on purpose a lot of the time. Think of this as being most useful for servers that are disconnected from time to time by accident. Perhaps you can think of one or two, without even straining.)

Consider these reasons to install and use routers in your CORBA network:

- With persistent routers, the robustness of your network matches that of your transactional servers.

- With persistent routers, invocations are preserved, not lost, when servers and network links/segments go down.

- With routers resident at or near your servers, invocations will be queued and delivered for processing in the order you specify, rather than the order in which they arrive.

- With persistent routers located at sites or enterprises located far apart and communicating over WANs or the Internet, all traffic is guaranteed to get through even though the interconnections may be slow, unreliable, or even totally down at times.

- With persistent routers, disconnected operation is supported at both the client and server ends of a CORBA invocation.

II.1.1.2.4 Example Router Configurations

Figure II.1.5 shows a configuration consisting of two LANs with various computers and interconnections. We've shown only clients on the left and servers on the right for clarity although, of course, clients and servers can connect anywhere on the network. At the client end, we've shown a desktop machine and a laptop. The laptop is running a local router while the desktop is not. We think it will be typical to run a local router on a disconnected client but not on a connected one; the specification (of course) doesn't prescribe either way.

Each LAN has a router. The LANs are interconnected by either the Internet or a WAN; it doesn't matter what we call it, the effect is the same: This link is not quite as reliable or as fast as our corporate network, but it's pretty fast and usually up. The LAN on the left services our office complex, and on the right, our remote information center building. On the right, we show two servers, one on a fixed machine and the other on a laptop (yes, so we can work through the gee-whiz disconnected laptops illustration. It's neat, whether it's practical or not). Both servers have local routers. The local router plays such an important role in server request queuing that every server will want its own if it can get one.

In the scenarios envisioned by the authors of the specification, servers may be disconnected for long periods of time, or frequently for shorter periods. There may be large numbers of clients, invoking on a number of serv-

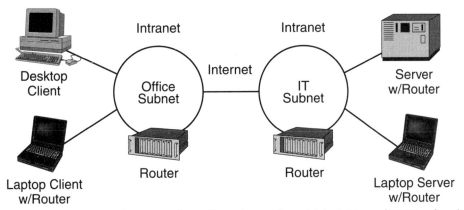

Figure II.1.5 Enterprise network configuration with multiple LANs and WANs, showing CORBA routers at likely locations.

ers. As a result, a router may hold outstanding requests for a number of targets. In this situation, the intermediate router is obliged to monitor either the target or some number of intermediate routers until it is able to forward the stored invocations. Solutions totally dependent on "pinging" do not scale, so the CORBA router architecture allows the target to specify a number of more highly available routers as temporary destinations for its requests. This decreases the number of destinations that the router has to monitor, while it makes it less likely that requests will stack up because the intermediate destinations are chosen and maintained for their reliability.

The target lists the routers that it knows about in a **TaggedComponent** of its IOR, where it is available to the client ORB as well as every router that may store and forward the invocation as it wends its way over the network. Routers are supposed to be listed in order from "most highly available" (closest to the target) to "least highly available" (closest to the Internet). There's no magic to this; when you install a CORBA 3 messaging system, you have to install the routers and configure their router tables.When you configure the tables for a server's router, do the best you can but don't worry if you can't figure out exactly which order is the best; in many cases the ordering will be fairly arbitrary.

When the client ORB makes an invocation, if the target is unreachable directly or if the QoS setting requires router use (i.e., does not include **ROUTE_NONE**), the client ORB looks in the sequence of routers in the **Tagged-Component**, chooses the most available first, and attempts to invoke it. If this works, fine; otherwise the target works its way down the list until it finds an available router. If the Internet is down (or whatever pathway connecting the client domain to the server domain), none of the routers on the list will be available. To handle this case, the client ORB is aware of routers in its own domain and selects one as the initial step of the transmission. The specification does not dictate the order in which the client ORB selects an intitial router; anything that works is OK. If the routing QoS setting requires persistent storage, the client ORB and each router along the way check each router before forwarding the invocation. If the client ORB can't find one, it raises the **CORBA::INV_POLICY** exception to the calling client.

Invocations and replies are transferred from one router to another in a reliable exchange. There's an IDL interface defined for the handshaking and transfer, but only ORB programmers write to it so we won't go into the details here. Suffice it to say that the sending ORB doesn't let go of its handshake until the receiving ORB acknowledges that it has received the entire message and committed it to persistent storage. Since we're describing only persistent routers in this section, that means the data are stored persistently while they await routing to their next stopover or their destination. (Techies take note: This IDL interface also gives you access to the ORB's marshaling engine, potentially useful for a host of purposes!)

The target router accepts the request message, delivers it to the target, and routes the reply back to the client or to the reply handler if there is a reply. This router may be co-located with the target, or deliver the request via a synchronous GIOP connection as we showed in Figure II.1.4. This is where QueueOrderPolicy is implemented; for details, look ahead to Section II.2.2.

To the laptop in Figure II.1.5, the routers enable disconnected operation: While the machine is disconnected, CORBA clients may make any invocations they wish using asynchronous **STORE_AND_FORWARD** routing, in either callback or polling mode. All will go to the router where they are stored until the machine connects to the network. Even though client applications shut down in the interim, the invocations remain stored on the router and will be dispatched the next time the machine connects. (If you've ever worked with an e-mail program that lets you type in messages while you're offline and "send" them to a queue where they wait until you connect up to your network or server, you understand how this works.) And, responses that come back while you're connected to the network are stored by the router until you restart the clients that sent them. When the clients start, the router sends them the responses immediately if they went originally as callbacks, or waits for a poll if they went in polling mode.

The desktop client machine has no need for an on-board router if its physical network connection is reliable at least as far as the closest network router. Its invocations all go directly to the network. Depending on the QoS settings and the condition of the network, they may go directly to the invoked servers, or to routers that queue and order them before delivery.

We can illustrate the use of the intermediate routers using this same figure and configuration. Suppose the fixed client attempts to invoke the server, but can't reach it or any of the routers listed in its IOR because the Internet connection is temporarily down. So, the client tries the router on its local WAN and succeeds, as far as it can; that is, the invocation is staged on the router and the client is free to go about its other business (since this level of QoS control is aviable only over an asynchronous invocation). The local router now attempts, as routers do, to relay the invocation to either the server's co-located router or the router on the distant WAN, and it eventually succeeds when the Internet link comes up. Most likely, access to both routers comes up simultaneously when the link is restored so the invocation is staged on the server's co-located router. From this point, the scenario proceeds exactly like the one before: When the invocation completes, the response routes directly back to the client unless that network link is down.

We think that routers will really shine in B2B e-commerce, where two totally independent applications—one on the buyer's end, the other on the seller's—need to interact quickly, assuredly, and much more frequently and rapidly than would be possible with hand-keyed browser entries. (Think of a mainframe application ordering thousands of different parts per day for an assembly line, instead of your sister ordering a blender for a wedding present.) Unlike similar interactions linking two applications within the same company, this scenario involves applications with little or no connection apart from the network: The person or department running the "client"—which is actually a server-like mainframe application—works for a different company than the person or department running the server, and the interaction needs a reliable yet loosely-coupled communications pathway.

If this sounds like EDI or XML, that's because we're describing the EDI or XML scenario worked with CORBA invocations. In the past, EDI datasets have been passed (for example) over e-mail, using SMTP. This gives the loose-coupling that we need, but without the reliability: There is no standard way to request a method execution over SMTP, no standard result return, and especially no standard way to return an error code if there's something wrong with the input data or other message contents.

Over CORBA, routers provide the same queuing and loose coupling that the mail queue provided for our EDI dataset transfer but with invocation/return semantics, type safety, and robust exception handling.

Finally, here's the disconnected client-disconnected server example. Suppose we're running a CORBA client on the laptop on the left, and a CORBA server on the laptop on the right, and the client wants to invoke an operation on the server. The client may, at any time, make the invocation, which goes to his router if the laptop is not connected to the network at the time.

(If made when connected, invocations bypass the router and go as far as they can to the server.)

When the user next connects his machine to the network, the router automatically goes to work, trying to execute all of the invocations it has stored up while offline. Presumably, any stored invocations for the fixed server, for example, execute during the session, and the responses either go back to the clients if they are running or get stored in the client's laptop's router if they are not. Invocations for the laptop server do not get executed because (we presume, in order to make this example interesting!) this machine is not connected when the client's machine is. The best that the client's router can do is transmit the invocation to the router on the MainOffice network where it sits, awaiting the laptop server. The client laptop now disconnects.

When the laptop server next connects, the IT network router notices, pulls the invocation out of its persistent store, and forwards it. (There is a protocol that routers use to contact each other that minimizes pinging, but we won't go into it in this book.) Depending on prioritization and queuing QoS levels in effect, the invocation may go either directly to the server or to its router where it is queued and delivered when its turn comes. Afterward, the server attempts to return the response directly to the laptop client but can't, since it's disconnected, so it routes the response as far as it can, which is the router on the office network where it sits until the laptop client next connects. You've already figured out what will happen when that machine connects, so we won't go over the details here. Right?

We think that the disconnected client part of this example is important, and will become a frequent pattern of CORBA use—if not quite as frequent as e-mail, almost as much. The application to a mobile sales force, already a frequent user of disconnected computing, is evident; so is the application to delivery services and other uses where work is done on a disconnected client machine and then uploaded to a business system. We don't think the disconnected server will be as prevalent, since companies will move all frequently accessed server applications to fixed machines where users do not have to wait for them to connect up. Nevertheless, the disconnected-server mode may be useful in some circumstances and requires little or nothing extra from the specification, so we're pleased that it's in there.

II.1.1.2.5 Callback Invocations with Routers

As we saw in the no-router callback example, something between the client and the server has to convert the asynchronous client invocation into a synchronous server invocation. Of course, the client and server are not involved in the siting of the conversion; we're discussing it here primarily to satisfy your curiosity about how asynchronous invocation works, and perhaps also to enable your system administrator to configure your routers better.

In the no-router example, the conversion was done by the client's ORB. If we have routers installed on our system but have full connectivity and do not require queue ordering (**Order=ORDER_ANY**), the conversion could still be done by the client's ORB although there are now other possibilities. The most logical place is the server's co-located router, because this allows replies to go directly to their destination even when they're not going back to the client that originated them. If we use queue ordering (**Order≠ORDER_ANY**), the routing and ordering functions would both be performed at the same place.

Of course, the specification is silent on this, and ORB vendors are free to configure their systems to convert wherever they think best. Since this has nothing to do with any application, it does not affect client or server code. Some products will expose these decisions to your sysadmins, allowing them to tune your system for best performance.

II.1.1.2.6 *Polling Invocations with Routers*

When you make a TII polling invocation, the system creates a **PersistentRequest** object on your behalf and returns a **Poller valuetype** that includes a method that queries the **PersistentRequest** object to obtain the result. Only if the invocation was made in TII mode (**RoutingPolicy=ROUTE_STORE_AND_FORWARD**) may the Poller be passed out of the client process and used *anywhere* on your connected system to obtain the result. This means that the **PersistentRequest** object must be accessible from anywhere, so your system will probably be configured to create it on a router on your corporate network. In this case, your polling client still does not need to link with the larger server-side library; however, if the **PersistentRequest** object gets created in your client process, you will need this library and your client will be larger.

The difference between polling in TII mode, which creates a **Poller valuetype** that functions anywhere including outside the client process, and polling in the other modes, where the poller only functions within, is this: In TII mode, the **Persistent_Request** object is a true CORBA object with an object reference, accessible from anywhere on your system. In non-TII mode, its functionality is provided by code within the ORB and accessed via **valuetype** APIs but no true instance is created.

Of course the poller functions exactly the same in TII as before: You invoke it to obtain the result, using the same **Timeout** variable to control whether you get control right back or wait if the invocation has not completed. There is a way to collect pollers into a set and query them all with a single call, but we won't give details here.

II.1.1.2.7 Unchecked Narrow

As we've mentioned several times, CORBA uses the type system built into object-oriented languages to enforce type safety on CORBA objects. The programming tool you use to cast an object reference from the generic type Object to its specific type is the **narrow** operation. This operation may need to know the full type hierarchy of the object in order to confirm that the requested typecast is proper, but this information may only exist at the target. If your client is making TII invocations in disconnected mode, the server access to perform the **narrow** (done by the client ORB on your behalf, possibly requiring a synchronous invocation of the server) would not take place until the machine next connected to the network; until that time, no further processing could be done and no invocations could be queued on the router unless there were another way to perform the **narrow**. Timing constraints may even hamper program operation in situations where a response delay in a normal asynchronous call is acceptable but the result of the **narrow** is needed immediately.

To allow you to deal with this situation, the Messaging specification defines a new operation, **unchecked_narrow**. Unlike the **narrow** function, **unchecked_narrow** does not check that the requested interface is supported by the target instance, and immediately returns an (apparently!) valid object reference. Using the result, you will be able to queue up a TII for your object right away. If your **unchecked_narrow** was proper, you'll get the answer back when the object becomes available; if it wasn't, you'll receive a **BAD_OPERATION** exception return.

II.1.1.3   What about the Four Invocation Modes?

In some write-ups of CORBA Messaging, you may see invocations divided into these four invocation modes:

- Synchronous invocations
- Deferred-synchronous invocations
- Asynchronous invocations
- Time-independent invocations

Although we've used some of these terms, we've avoided the assumption that every CORBA invocation fits neatly into just one of them. Instead, we've analyzed each invocation according to its programming model as we showed in Figure II.1.1, and independently (well, mostly) on its communications model QoS as we discussed in Section II.1.1.2 and its subsections. Overall, we found that it wasn't helpful to try to stuff all of this detail, permutations, and combinations into four overall categories, so we haven't done it. That's all; there's no mystery.

II.1.1.4 TII and Transactions

We're not going to include any background in on-line transaction processing (OLTP) or on the CORBA Object Transaction Service in this book. The OTS is covered in *CORBA 3 Fundamentals and Programming.* We list this and a number of references for basic OLTP in Appendix A.

The classical transaction processing scenario involves a *synchronized* collection of actors and resources, all proceeding through a transaction (which may be financial but doesn't have to be) at the same time. This way, if one participant is unable to complete its part, it can notify the others that it is rolling back so that they do too. In this kind of transaction, either all participants commit, or none of them do.

OMG's Object Transaction Service (OTS) extended this pattern, which was first established on mainframes, to CORBA, following a standard set originally by X/Open. Established long before CORBA Messaging, OTS executed over synchronous CORBA calls and spread the single transaction previously confined to the mainframe over a collection of distributed objects. This model didn't need a name at the time since it was the only model we had, but now we refer to it as the **shared transaction model**. That is, there is only one transaction, and it is *shared* by all of the participants, regardless of where they are located.

It's pretty obvious that we can't run shared transactions over TII invocations. In a shared transaction, every player ties up resources while the transaction is pending, and releases them (hopefully in a new state) when it completes with either a commit or a rollback. When invocations are made via TII, there is no guarantee that the invocation will complete within any length of time—the originating machine may be a laptop that only connects for a few minutes each day, as we saw in one example in this chapter, and it is impractical for transaction systems to tie up resources for so long. (Remember, transaction systems that support successful businesses may run several tens or hundreds of millions of transactions per day!)

So, CORBA Messaging adopted the **unshared transaction model** for use over TII. First we'll go over how it works, then we'll tell what it's good for. It's easy (now that we know how TII works), so hold on and here we go.

Recall that we said that invocation propagation over a network with persistent routers was transactional. Now we get to take advantage of this. There is no single transaction that covers both the client and transactional server in this model. Instead, the client creates a transaction that only covers the transfer of its TII invocation to the network. The invocation transfers along the network transactionally from router to router until it reaches the router closest to the server, which conducts a transactional invocation and waits (in its synchronous way, since the invocation is synchronous at this point) for it to complete. When this is done, the result snakes its way, transactionally again step by step, either back to the TII client or to wherever the TII client decided to route the result.

What is this good for? After all, it doesn't look anything like a shared transaction. As it turns out, it's good for lots of things.

One common purchase pattern that fits this model is the purchase of a vacation. Airline tickets, hotel room, and car rental must all be purchased for the same week. If you get the plane tickets and the car, but you can't get a hotel room for that week, you can't go; but the plane, hotel, and car rental all come from different companies so you know you can't involve them all in a single shared transaction. The solution is to conduct three separate transactions serially. As each succeeds, you go ahead to the next. If one fails, you go back and undo (*not* roll back; the previous transaction has already committed) the reservations you've made so far and start again on a different week.

Another common unshared transaction pattern is "memo posting." This is what a bank does when it records teller transactions durably (which used to mean recorded by hand) during the day and reconciles all of its accounts with a batch run of the accounting system overnight. The recording of the teller visit during the day is one transaction, while the adjustment to the customer's account at night is a separate one.

The unshared transaction model gives you a way to implement this type of scenario in your distributed CORBA applications.

One new characteristic of this model is the way you cope with failure. In a shared transaction, all of the parties roll back simultaneously, and when it's over, it's over. In the unshared model, each part finishes up and commits individually. When one part fails, the *application* has to go back and pick up the pieces, backing out whatever it needs to explicitly with application logic. Remember, each individual piece has committed as part of its own transaction, so it's too late to roll anything back.

This is clearly a different model from shared transactions, but no less useful. It is not designed to extend the original shared distributed transaction model to TII—if you need to roll back on failure, you'll have to conduct your business using a single shared transaction and stay connected long enough to invoke synchronously. Instead, the unshared transaction model lets you transactionalize new business dealings that already have some of the aspects of disconnected operation—between departments or enterprises with separate transactional systems, for example—with the reliability of CORBA transactions but the flexibility and freedom of TII.

II.1.1.5   oneway Invocations

Under CORBA 2, the only way to make a stub-based invocation and get control back right away was to declare it **oneway** *in your IDL*; that is, the operation had no **out** or **inout** parameters, and a **void** return value. Delivery was, according to the definition of **oneway**, "ORB best effort," and the meaning of the phrase was defined by your ORB provider.

CORBA Messaging preserves the **oneway** semantic, adding the capability to control the QoS of this previously vague but potentially useful mode. Because this feature falls more in the domain of QoS than communications, we've postponed it until the next chapter where you'll find it in Section II.2.2.1.

II.1.2   Programming Asynchronous Invocations

Now that we've covered all of the various architectural features of the invocation space, it's time to proceed on to programming details. In the next several sections, we'll cover interfaces for callback and polling invocations, reply handlers, and pollers. When we're finished with this, we'll also be finished discussing the new Messaging specification and will go on to cover Quality of Service options in Part II, Chapter 2.

The specification coins a new term for the way it expresses the interfaces for AMI: "implied IDL." They're expressed in IDL because the asynchronous invocation signatures need to be defined in every programming language that supports CORBA—that is, every language with an IDL language mapping. The Messaging specification can take care of this in one shot by expressing them in IDL, so that's what it does.

But why "implied"? There are several differences between these generated interfaces and the IDL that we originally wrote. Let's examine them.

One difference is that true IDL interfaces map to both client-side and object-side signatures, and have to be implemented in our servant. But these additional interfaces do not have to be implemented on the object side, since they call the signatures on the object side that came from the mapping of the original true IDL. So, the client invokes the implied IDL signatures to make an asynchronous invocation, but the servant receives the invocation on the original, true IDL signature that it has used all along to receive synchronous invocations. Conversion from the client's asynchronous implied-IDL format invocation to the servant's true-IDL format invocation takes place either in the client's ORB or in a router, as we've seen. It's all automatic; you don't have to do any of the work. As we've stated before in this chapter, this has several advantages. The servant doesn't know or care whether an invocation is synchronous or asynchronous. And, servant programming style and existing servant code don't have to change to support asynchronous invocation. (Exception: Certain transactional invocations will notice the difference between synchronous and asynchrous invocations.)

Another difference: The new invocation formats (such as **sendc_<opname>**) do not generate new entries in the interface repository. But, when the reply arrives, the new IDL creates entities that behave just like IDL that you write yourself. For example, **ReplyHandler** objects are a new type registered in the IFR, with a real skeleton generated from IDL created according to the AMI specification. Poller valuetypes act similarly, at least in this respect.

II.1.2.1   Interfaces for Asynchronous Invocations

In CORBA 2, the IDL compiler generated a single synchronous client stub for each operation you defined.

In CORBA 3, if you set your flags properly, the IDL compiler will generate an additional *asynchronous* stub, with two additional signatures: one for callback-mode asynchronous invocations and another for polling mode. You'll probably have to set a compiler switch to get these interfaces (since so many modules will not use them), but the compiler does all the interface generation, so it's no sweat for you. These stubs, and the ORB routines that support them, do most of the extra work that's necessary to make your asynchronous invocations go, but you will have to do a little more than you're used to for a simple synchronous invocation.

So, for both callback and polling-mode asynchronous invocations, we'll have to cover two aspects, each with its own distinct signature: making the invocation, and obtaining the result. That's because, while our synchronous invocations came back as the return to the same operation that made them, the return from asynchronous invocations will come back to a different routine, through a different interface, that has a different signature. In fact, even though asynchronous invocations are still made by clients, callback-mode responses come back to *servants*. Polling-mode responses don't come back at all—you have to go get them.

Before we get into the programming details, we want to point out a few things that we won't describe in detail until the next chapter on QoS:

- Don't forget to set *all* of your QoS policies before you make your invocation.

- Remember that you'll probably have to reconcile client-side and server-side policies.

- You'll have to bind to the server first with a **validate_connection** call to get the actual server's actual policies. If you don't, and your client policies don't overlap with the server's, your invocation will fail with an **INV_POLICY** exception.

What if you want to use the DII? Since the DII doesn't use stubs, the IDL compiler isn't involved, and you don't get the invocation forms we're about to present. DII interfaces have been extended to access all of these invocation modes, and the old deferred-synchronous invocation is still valid, too. (Deferred-synchronous invocation is not exactly the same as any of the asynchronous cases we've presented so far.) Since the DII isn't used as much as the SII, we aren't going to present any of the DII interfaces and language mappings here. You can get the details in the documentation of your CORBA 3 ORB, and that will tell you what to do.

II.1.2.1.1 *Asynchronous Details—Callback Mode*

For callback-mode invocations, you will have to program a **ReplyHandler** object to receive the results. Your IDL compiler will generate a skeleton and, optionally, a template for this object whose signature is defined by the Messaging specification, but you'll have to fill in the working code. This is where you program in whatever your client-side application needs to do with the result. The **ReplyHandler**'s object reference is an input parameter to the invocation, of course, so that your ORB knows where to call when the reply completes. This means you'll have to get a reference for the object from your POA *before* you make your invocation. We'll examine the IDL interface of the **ReplyHandler** object when we see how to receive asynchronous replies.

Remember the two special aspects of a **ReplyHandler** object: Since it was called by an object, and not by a client, it cannot throw a CORBA exception, and it does not `return` in the usual sense. (Execution of its `return` statement just returns control of its thread to the ORB.)

As we just said, for asynchronous invocations there are two signatures that we have to be concerned about: one for the invocation, and another for the reply. The IDL compiler generates these signatures by converting your IDL to a specific form and then generating programming language code following the mapping for each programming language.

II.1.2.1.2 Asynchronous Callback-Mode Invocations

The implied IDL signature for callback-mode asynchronous invocation of an IDL operation consists of:

- **void** return type (always); followed by

- **sendc_<opName>**, that is, an operation name that starts with **sendc** and concatenates an underscore and your operation name; followed by

- The object reference of your reply handler, with the parameter name **ami_handler;** followed by

- Each **in** and **inout** parameter, with a parameter attribute of **in** and the type and parameter name as in the original IDL.

- **out** arguments do not appear. (**out** and **inout** parameters will be returned to the reply handler, as we'll see shortly.)

For attributes, the operation names are **sendc_get_<attributeName>** and **sendc_set_<attributeName>**. The **get** form has no arguments except for the reply handler, while **set** has one named **attr_<attributeName>**, as you might expect.

As we pointed out just a few paragraphs back, the IDL compiler generates the skeleton for the reply handler. Its interface name is generated from the name of our interface, by prepending **AMI_** and appending **Handler**. The compiler also generates a set of operations for this interface, one for each operation in the original, and (easy enough for us) using the original operation names. We'll list the arguments in the next section.

Here's an example to make this all concrete. In our other book, *CORBA 3 Fundamentals and Programming,* our example IDL file included the **interface OutputMedia** with one operation:

```
interface outputMedia {
    boolean output_text (in string string_to_print );
{
```

If we ran this through a CORBA 3 IDL compiler (with the switch set to generate the additional asynchronous interfaces, of course), it would produce, in addition to the synchronous-invocation stub we're used to, an asynchronous stub *as if* we had also input this "implied" IDL operation:

```
void sendc_output_text (
        In AMI_OutputMediaHandler ami_handler,
        In string string_to_print );
```

So, each time we invoke the operation **output_text** in our client, we have a choice. We can either make a synchronous call by invoking the standard stub, or we can make an asynchronous callback-mode invocation by calling the stub **sendc_output_text**, which was also generated by the IDL compiler. (We could also make a polling-mode asynchronous call, as we'll see in the next section.)

II.1.2.1.3 *Asynchronous Callback-Mode Replies*

Here's our second new operation signature. For our reply, the IDL compiler has generated a complete new interface with operations. Its name is **AMI_<ifaceName>**, where **<ifaceName>** is the name we originally gave to this interface.

For every operation we defined on our original interface, the IDL compiler generates a new operation with a signature defined by this template:

- **void** return type (again, always); followed by
- The operation name which is the same as the original name of our operation; and then
- If the original operation had a non-**void** return type, it is returned as the first parameter named **ami_return_val** and typed as it was in the original IDL. If the original return value was **void**, this parameter is omitted. This is followed by
- Each **inout** or **out** parameter, with its original type and name, as it was declared in the original IDL.
- **in** parameters do not appear.

So, an asynchronous call to **output_text** would result in a reply, after it completes, which causes the ORB to invoke the operation "**output_text**" on the **AMI_OutputMediaHandler** object running in our client code:

```
Interface AMI_OutputMediaHandler  {
        void output_text (boolean ami_return_val);
}
```

The return value is the first parameter, with its original type and the name **ami_return_val** (since return values aren't assigned names in the IDL). Since we had no **out** or **inout** parameters in the original operation, nothing else appears inside the parentheses.

Some programming details: Since we're working in an asynchronous environment, we can have multiple calls outstanding, all returning to the same reply handler servant. To identify the calls when they return, even though all return to the same servant, we can use the POA to assign different **ObjectIDs** to the object references we generate. Since the **ObjectID** is accessible to the servant, it will have no trouble figuring out which reply is which.

If you're concerned with the details (and a little existentialism, as we mentioned), you'll want to consider this: The reply handler IDL generates a true object skeleton, but no client stub. In fact, even though the skeleton is invoked, no client ever exists for its IDL. Instead, this skeleton is invoked with a response from an object, that was transformed from response form to invocation form by an ORB or a router.

So, there are two normal "object-implementation" things that this object can never do: First, it cannot `return`—there's no client for it to `return` to. When it finishes processing, it does `return` but this only returns control of its thread to the ORB; no output parameters or return value go anywhere. Second, it cannot raise CORBA exceptions, which are typically thrown in the object and caught in the client: There's no client to catch them!

If any exceptions were raised in the execution of the invocation, we want them raised in the **ReplyHandler** context. To enable this, the IDL compiler actually generates a separate operation for each exception. Since you never see either the IDL or the reply handler component that implements them, we won't show their forms here. You do have to write code to raise the exceptions once they come back your way, but we won't show this either.

II.1.2.1.4   Asynchronous Polling-Mode Invocations

Just as with callback-mode invocations, polling-mode invocation signatures are defined by implied IDL converted from the original. In place of **sendc_**, polling-mode signatures start with **sendp_** (no surprise there, right?). Unlike the callback-mode signature, however, polling-mode signatures do have a return value: It's a **valuetype**, a CORBA object passed by value, which will contain the return values when the operation completes. We'll invoke an operation on this **valuetype** to check if our invocation has completed, and fetch the output values.

Why a **valuetype**? Because **valuetypes** execute as programming language objects that cannot be invoked remotely, and this fits the polling programming model. Since **valuetypes** have the operations and characteristics we need, they're a logical construct to use here. And, a **persistent poller** type can even be derived from them for TII invocations that allow responses to be obtained outside of the client process.

We'll define the **poller valuetype** more completely in Section II.1.2.1.5. For now, we'll just say that its name is derived from the name of the original interface, and it bears operations with the same set of names, but with arguments rearranged in a manner similar to the asynchronous reply handler.

The signature of the implied-IDL operation in polling mode is:

- The **poller valuetype** for this operation as the return value, followed by

- The operation name, **sendp_<opName>**, where _<opName> is the name of the operation; followed by

- Each of the **in** and **inout** parameters, in their original order, all with the parameter attribute **in** and with their original types and names.

- The operation's original return value, if it has one, and **out** arguments do not appear. The **poller valuetype** will deliver them in the output.

For attributes, the operations are named **sendp_get_<attributeName>** and **sendp_set_<attributeName>**. The **set** operation has a single argument, **in <attrName>attributeName.**

Our same example in polling form would generate the implied IDL:

```
AMI_OutputMediaPoller sendp_output_text (
    in string string_to_print );
```

The operation signatures in each programming language would follow the corresponding language mapping.

II.1.2.1.5 Asynchronous Polling-Mode Replies

The advantage of polling-mode invocations is that you can wait to fetch the reply until you're good and ready. The disadvantage is that you *have* to fetch the reply, since it's not delivered to your application, and you may have to try several (or many!) times if it hadn't come back when you asked for it the first time, or the next, or the time after that, or . . .

The base functionality that makes an object pollable is embodied in the **interface CORBA::Pollable**, from which all pollers derive. This interface has an operation **is_ready**, which returns **TRUE** if the reply is available, and **FALSE** if the reply has not yet returned from the target.

Generic poller functionality is embodied at the next level, which defines a generic poller **valuetype**. Poller has three interesting IDL attributes: the target object reference, the operation name as a **string**, and a **boolean is_ from_poller**, which describes exception returns: **TRUE** means that a system exception was generated by the polling operation itself, and **FALSE** means that it was generated by your method execution. There's another attribute, **ReplyHandler**, which supports (of all things!) switching between polling and callback mode while the invocation processes. Not only can you do this, you can switch back and forth as many times as you can manage while your invocation is out there processing on the server machine, or waiting in the queue on your network. We haven't figured out why you'd even want to do it once, so we won't use any space in this book describing how. We will let on that you have to make your original invocation in polling mode, and you have to code for both return modes yourself, in order to use this "feature."

Finally, our type-specific poller IDL is generated based on these types. The **valuetype** interface name is **AMI_<ifaceName>Poller**, where **<ifaceName>** is the name of the original interface. For each operation in our original IDL, this **valuetype** bears an operation with the following signature:

- The return type **void**; followed by
- The original name of the operation; followed by
- A timeout parameter, described below; followed by
- The original return value, as an **out** parameter, with its original type and the name **ami_return_val**; followed by
- Any **out** or **inout** parameters, all declared here as **out** parameters, in their original order with their original types and names; followed by
- A **raises** clause, citing any exceptions that were declared in the original IDL, and one more, **CORBA::WrongTransaction**, which may be raised by certain transactional invocations.

The **timeout** parameter, an unsigned long representing milliseconds, lets you control how your polling executes:

- If you set **timeout** to 0 (zero), your poll is non-blocking and returns the exception **CORBA::NO_RESPONSE** if the reply is not available.
- If you set **timeout** to $2^{32}-1$, no **timeout** will be used. Your polling call will block until the reply is available.
- If you set **timeout** to some value in between, your poller will return the response to you as soon as it is available unless it is not available after **timeout** milliseconds, at which time the poller will return the exception **CORBA::TIMEOUT.**

Exceptions will be raised in your client on return from the poll, if any were raised during the invocation.

Here's our example, as a type-specific poller **valuetype**:

```
valuetype AMI_OutputMediaPoller : Messaging::Poller {
                    void output_text (
                In unsigned long timeout,
                Out boolean ami_return_val)
                Raises (CORBA::WrongTransaction)
    }
```

Since this is a **valuetype**, we will invoke it locally as a programming-language object using the mapping for the language we use to implement.

II.1.3 Summary

This concludes our discussion of the messaging part of CORBA Messaging. We've spent a considerable amount of space on this, but we felt it would be worthwhile since communications is key to distributed computing and this is CORBA's (and your!) interface to the communications layer. We also believe that the specification is a good one, containing all of the enhancements that programmers and users have been asking for, wrapped up in a well-architected package. We're looking forward to working with some of these asynchronous invocation modes ourselves as products arrive on the market, several as we were finishing up this part of the book.

We've reserved discussion of the QoS parts of the CORBA Messaging specification for the next chapter. Following that discussion, we'll move to three specifications that are almost pure QoS: Real-Time, Minimum, and Fault-Tolerant CORBA.

Quality-of-Service Control

CHAPTER PREVIEW

This is the second half of our presentation of the Messaging Specification. The chapter starts with a description of CORBA's QoS framework, explaining how QoS policies are selected on the client and server sides; how these are reconciled; and how they affect execution. With this established, the chapter goes on to describe QoS policy types affecting timing and time-out, routing of non-synchronous invocations, prioritization, and the special case of oneway invocations.

II.2.1 QoS Framework

The QoS portion of the CORBA Messaging specification starts out by defining a general QoS framework based on *policies*, using the policy object defined in the CORBA module where it is part of the POA. (We describe some of the POA interfaces in Part III, Chapter 3.) The authors tried to formulate a comprehensive set of QoS policies but did not presume that they had covered everything, so they set up a framework that was extensible as well.

Both clients and servers can set policy values, although not for every policy type, of course. The specifications tell which policies are client-set, which are server-set, and which may be both (and, for these, how conflicts are resolved). We'll present some of these details later on in this section.

On the client side, QoS policy values are scoped to three levels:

- **ORB-level QoS policies** are the broadest. The ORB PolicyManager, returned by **ORB::resolve_initial_references**, allows setting and retrieval of ORB-level policies. In your call to **resolve_initial_references**, you would ask for "**ORBPolicyManager.**" Your ORB may set default values here, but beware: OMG has *not* set standard defaults, so the values set by different vendors' ORBs will probably be, well, different as well. Remember this when you read the warning about defaults later in this section.

- In the middle level are **thread-level QoS policies**, defined by a **PolicyCurrent** object, which override ORB-level policies. Again, you turn to **ORB::resolve_initial_references** for the reference to this object, asking for "**PolicyCurrent**"; this object bears interfaces that allow you to set policies at this level.

- Finally, we have **object-reference-level QoS policies**, which override thread-level policies. These are set by extensions to interface **interface Object**, and affect individual instances.

By starting with the ORB-level policy, and considering overrides at the thread level and object level in turn, your system comes up with what is termed the *effective client-side policy*—that is, the QoS value that your client wants to use, for each policy type, that controls invocation of a particular instance of a CORBA object. This evaluation is done separately for each policy type, for each instance, providing a high degree of control.

However, clients cannot use any values they please—servers have rights too, and their policy values must be reconciled with clients' values in order to determine the actual values used for an invocation. Server-side QoS policy is set the same way we handled every other type of server-side policy, by setting POA policy values at POA creation time. QoS settings derive from **interface Policy** for just this reason. Some server-side policy type settings affect client-side requests or constrain the values that client policies may use in requests; these are included in the object reference created by the POA and become available to the client's ORB and, through the call to **get_policy**, to the client itself. Other policy types affect the server only. The specification tells which affect what.

So, the actual set of policy values in effect for an invocation arises from a reconciliation of client-side and server-side policy values. To see how this is done, we need to consider the consequences of location transparency and the concept of **binding**.

In CORBA, there are a number of reasons why an object might break and reestablish its connection to a client. For example, the server may shut down the servant and start up a new one, which might be a new implementation or run on a different machine for better load balance. If it moves, it will leave a **LOCATION_FORWARD** GIOP instruction in effect at the original ORB. (**LOCATION_FORWARD** is one of the basic messages that client and server ORB exchange when connected and speaking OMG's General Inter-ORB Protocol or [GIOP]. We don't cover GIOP in this book. For details on GIOP, see the references in Appendix A.)

When a GIOP connection breaks and is re-established, it may be to a new servant running on a different POA, with different server-side QoS policies that change the way an invocation is processed. A CORBA 2 ORB, which is QoS-unaware, will transparently follow the **LOCATION_FORWARD** instruction and invoke the object at its new location without notifying the client. To keep a QoS-concerned CORBA 3 client in control of the situation when an object changes its QoS settings, the Messaging specification introduces the concept of **binding** and allows QoS-concerned applications to evaluate settings in effect at the new location before the invocation is processed. (Careful: this "bind" is not the same as the vendor-specific "bind" call that some ORBs have you do to establish a link between client and object.)

An object instance is considered *bound* once the client's ORB has followed any **LOCATION_FORWARD** instructions and has a TCP/IP connection to the server ORB of the running servant. Although binding occurs as the first step of an invocation, QoS-concerned applications will want to bind and determine true runtime server-side policies in effect *before* making any invocations. CORBA provides two operations—**validate_connection**, and **non_existent**—for this purpose. We'll tell you where to use them later in this section.

A disconnection and reconnection of a bound object that results in new QoS policies is termed a *rebind*. **LOCATION_FORWARD** instructions contain an object reference for the instance in its new location; because the object reference contains policy information, the client ORB can tell if the effective policy will change as a result. On the other hand, a simple reestablishment of a broken connection to the same servant at the same location is termed a *reconnect*.

If QoS is important to you, and the specification assumes that it may be critical, you will want to know if a rebind occurs, and be able to cope with any QoS differences that result. Here's what the spec gives you for this:

First, your client may set its RebindPolicy to one of the three values **TRANSPARENT, NO_REBIND**, or **NO_RECONNECT**. A setting of **TRANSPARENT** means "Either I don't care about QoS, or I'm positive that all locations will give satisfactory QoS, so if the instance moves, just keep processing as if nothing happened." A setting of **NO_REBIND** means "I'm concerned about QoS; if the instance moves, and the new instance has QoS settings incompatible with my client settings, raise a **NO_REBIND** exception and I'll follow up." Finally, a setting of **NO_RECONNECT** means "Not only should you let me know if policies are incompatible; I'm so concerned with QoS that I want to know if a new connection ever needs to be opened, so I can check things out myself."

Here are the tools that the spec gives you to check things out: First, a call to **get_client_policy** will tell you the policy values in effect for your client settings, by evaluating the ORB level, thread level, and finally the overriding client-side object instance level settings. (Most likely, the check will be made in the reverse order so processing for each policy type can stop when a policy setting is found.) Next, you'll want to find the policy that would actually be in effect if you made an invocation. This is where you'll want to invoke either **validate_connection** or **non_existent** on the object as a first step. This forces your client ORB to bind to the server ORB, following any **LOCATION_FORWARD** instructions to the location of the actual running servant, which updates the server-side policy values stored at the client end. Once bound, a call to **get_policy** will determine and return the policy values that will actually be in effect for your invocation by comparing the client-side policy with corresponding updated server-side values for each policy type. Conflicts raise the **INV_POLICY** exception. The system won't object if you **get_policy** before you bind with a call to **validate_connection** or **non_existent**, but this may return indeterminate, implementation-dependent results—don't make this mistake if QoS is important to you!

Most QoS policies do *not* have CORBA-standardized defaults. If you do not set policy values at either the thread or object level, your system's ORB-level policies will determine the applied policy at runtime. ORB vendors will probably establish defaults of their own, in the absence of an OMG standard, but these will surely vary from one vendor to the next. *As a result, you (the programmer or administrator) will have to establish QoS policy values at either the thread or object level in order for your application to run identically on different vendors' ORBs. You cannot rely on the default values for this, because there are none.* Why not? There are so many policies, and they apply so differently to different situations and applications, that no set of default values made sense. In addition, the various CORBA 2 ORBs on the market exhibit different QoS behaviors since there was no QoS definition in the days before Messaging. By avoiding overall defaults, the specification allows each vendor's ORB to carry its CORBA 2 behavior into CORBA 3 as its ORB-specific default so that its established user base does not have to modify its code base to retain the behavior they're used to. The price you pay is, code that relies on defaults may not run identically on different vendors' ORBs. With capability comes responsibility, so straighten up and code this right!

Now that we know the structure of the QoS policy framework, let's see what we can do with it.

II.2.1.1   QoS Policy Types

You can control a lot with CORBA 3 QoS policies. Some policy types are general enough to affect every invocation, while others either control or affect only messaging or asynchronous modes. We'll cover the general policy types first, and messaging-only afterwards.

If you're running a CORBA 3 ORB with the capabilities prescribed by the Messaging Service, but you have not installed routers on your network, you can only control **Timing** and **time-out policies.** There's a **TIMEOUT** system exception, which your ORB will return to your client if there's no reply when your invocation's time-to-live expires. It's a standard system exception, since any invocation may have a restricted time-to-live.

You can specify lifetimes of requests and replies in three ways:

- First, you may specify *Start and End times for both Requests and Replies*. All may be specified as client-overrides only, and are valid for both synchronous and asynchronous invocations. Requests and replies will be held until the specified Start time before delivery. Requests that miss their end-time deadline will not be delivered to their target; late replies will not be delivered back to the client, which will receive a **TIMEOUT** exception.

- Second, there is also a *RelativeRequestTimeout Policy* that specifies the length of time that a request may be delivered. This also applies only as a client-side override. For synchronous invocations, after the specified length of time, the request is canceled, and the **TIMEOUT** exception is raised. For asynchronous invocations, the duration refers to the length of time during which the request may be processed—if processing completes in this interval, the reply will be delivered no matter how long the return transmission takes.

- Finally, there is a *RelativeRoundtripTimeout policy* that covers the length of time when a request or its reply may be delivered. After this period, the request is canceled, or its reply is discarded. (For this particular policy, behavior of request and reply is prescribed in the specification.) This applies to both synchronous and asynchronous invocations. This would keep obsolete data from cluttering the network in, for example, financial or process-control invocations where results are useless after a predictable (and short!) time period.

That's it for QoS independent of invocation mode. The remaining QoS settings require routed delivery, and so only function on non-synchronous invocations.

II.2.2 QoS for Routing of Non-Synchronous Invocations

We covered the effects of routers on communications in Section II.1.1.2.3; here we'll discuss the effects of routers on QoS. Recall that the possible values for **RoutingPolicy**, from minimum to maximum QoS, are **ROUTE_NONE**, **ROUTE_FORWARD**, and **ROUTE_STORE_AND_FORWARD**. **RoutingPolicy** can take on a range of values; if your minimum is **ROUTE_NONE**, and your maximum is **ROUTE_STORE_AND__FORWARD**, your invocation will run anywhere and take advantage of the highest QoS of router it can. If your minimum **Routing-Policy** calls for a higher QoS than the physical network configuration can deliver, your invocation will fail with a **CORBA::INV_POLICY** exception as we pointed out already.

> **Queue ordering.** If you have routers and you've set your **RoutingPolicy** to use them, then you can use Queue Ordering to prioritize the order in which the target router forwards requests to the server. If you don't have routers installed, this setting has no effect: it does *not* directly affect the order in which servers process the requests; **RoutingPolicy** affects only routers. (To take best advantage of priority queueing, in the future some ORBs will be configured with routers either co-located on the same machine or even as part of the ORB itself.) **QueueOrderPolicy** is the policy type that controls prioritization of requests. Its possible values are
>
> - **ORDER_ANY:** the client doesn't care about the order.
> - **ORDER_TEMPORAL:** requests will be forwarded in the order they were issued, according to their timestamps. This is the default.
> - **ORDER_PRIORITY:** requests will be ordered for delivery according to their client-assigned priority values.
> - **ORDER_DEADLINE:** requests whose time-to-live is about to expire, as given by their End Times or Relative Timeouts, will move to the head of the queue.

Both server and client may select one or more of these alternatives; the policy value is calculated by ORing your selections together. Then, server- and client-side values are intersected to determine the policy in effect. (The intersection is performed on the client, using the server **QueueOrderPolicy** value extracted from the object's IOR.) A null intersection raises the **INV_POLICY** exception, of course.

Invocation priority values. These values are used by routers when the **QueueOrderPolicy** is set to **ORDER_PRIORITY**. A struct named **PriorityRange** controls priority range; you set both a maximum and minimum value at client end; there may be settings for both at the server end too. The effective value for an invocation is the intersection of these ranges. The struct **PriorityRange** is a **readonly attribute** of the interfaces **RequestPriorityPolicy** and **ReplyPriorityPolicy**.

To illustrate the benefits of routers and these policy settings, let's suppose we're using a server that is both important and overloaded, and that it processes both online customer transactions and bookkeeping requests. To keep customers happy (and coming back!), we decide to prioritize sale transactions higher than bookkeeping requests, and prioritize data analysis queries even lower than bookkeeping except at night when these have priority so that their results can be analyzed the next day.

We implement this by setting the QoS **QueueOrderPolicy** to **ORDER_PRIORITY** at both the server and all of its clients, and having each client assign a priority value to each invocation. On the clients' side, we'll set both the minimum and maximum priority values for all invocations made by customers to 300; those made by accounting to 100; and those made by marketing to 150. On the server side, we'll set the minimum priority value to 0, and the maximum to 300. This server-side range allows all of the values that we've allotted to clients, and does not allow any invocations to be prioritized higher than the customers'. The minimum value for **RoutingPolicy** may *not* be **ROUTE_NONE**, because the QoS settings require invocations to be dispatched through at least one router—that is, the server's target router, which will order the requests. The invocations and replies will, almost surely, go via intermediate routers as well.

So, all of our asynchronous invocations end up at the server's router where they get sorted by priority before delivery. The diversion to the server's router for prioritization is dictated by the routing specification in the AMI. (We do have to point out one thing here: The AMI specification dictates that QoS settings apply equally to synchronous and asynchronous invocations, at least where it makes technical sense, but AMI itself is an optional conformance point, and not all ORBs will choose to implement the full specification. If you plan to take advantage of priority queuing to order the synchronous hits on your enterprise transaction server, check with the vendor of your client ORB and confirm that it complies with this feature.)

By co-locating a router on the server machine, we avoid adding network hop overhead to prioritized invocations even where queue ordering is performed. The client ORB addresses its invocation to the server's router where it arrives without the use of intervening CORBA routers, and the reply may head directly to its destination (even if different from the client machine) directly from the server's router as well.

We expect that, as the specification itself suggests, some vendors will place routing functionality *inside* the server's ORB, avoiding even the interprocess communication step that occurs with co-located routers. Although this isn't required, it moves queuing behavior into applications and allows them to respond directly to invocations according to users' preferences. We think this is a more natural way of providing this service to clients, even if it does require some rework of the server-network interface.

II.2.2.1   oneway Invocations

Under CORBA 2, the only way to make a stub-based invocation and get control back right away was to declare it **oneway** *in your IDL*; that is, the operation had no output or inout parameters, and a **void** return value. Delivery was, according to the definition of **oneway**, "ORB best effort," and the meaning of that phrase was defined by your ORB provider.

Why would you want to use **oneway** invocations now that you have all of the asynchronous features that we've been discussing for the last few pages? There's a common pattern that involves notifying an object somewhere that something happened, and not needing to get anything back, not even a confirmation. The event service is an example and its possible use of **oneway** is a good example even if you probably won't implement this service yourself. (As we write this, OMG members are also working on an "unreliable multicast" invocation semantic, intended for the event service but also useful in other ways.) Lots of applications need to notify specific objects about something, or send a couple of values when something happens, and they'd like to be able to send the information out and not worry about doing anything afterward.

However, the loose QoS (at least up 'til now) did not give programmers confidence that they could regard **oneway** as a mode for delivering notifications in code that might be run on different vendors' ORBs, since each vendor was free to interpret the phrase "best effort" however he wished.

To fix this shortcoming, the Messaging Specification introduced the QoS policy type **SyncScope**. There are four possible values; here they are along with what they do:

SYNC_NONE. The client's ORB returns control to the client immediately after receiving the invocation from it, so there is not even a brief blocking of the client thread. On a separate thread, the ORB passes the **oneway** invocation to the network and does not expect a reply. Since no reply returns from the server, no errors will be reported and location-forwarding cannot be done.

SYNC_WITH_TRANSPORT. The client's ORB returns control to the client only after the network transport has accepted the request. For the usual transports (for example, TCP/IP), this is not much stronger than **SYNC_NONE** (although it does guarantee that your invocation will make it past a full TCP stack when your network is overloaded), but for reliable store-and-forward messaging protocols (that is, if you've installed persistent routers) it will provide a high Degree of assurance without consuming client resources. No location-forwarding can be done in this mode either, because no reply returns from the server.

SYNC_WITH_SERVER. The server-side ORB sends a reply after it has received the invocation, but before it invokes the target object; the client's ORB returns control only after it has received this acknowledgment. This form of guarantee is useful where the reliability of the network is substantially lower than that of the server. The client blocks until all location-forwarding has been completed.

SYNC_WITH_OBJECT. This is the same as a synchronous, non-**oneway** operation in CORBA 2.2. The server-side ORB doesn't send the reply message until the target has completed the invoked operation. Location-forwarding is no problem in this case, of course.

Before AMI, a major use of **oneway** invocations was to trigger operations that returned results, when their execution was finished, via a reverse **oneway** invocation of an object in the originating client's application—that is, a callback-style asynchronous invocation constructed (painfully, perhaps) in application-level code. We think that most of these instances will be replaced by true asynchronous invocations now that CORBA provides them, even though **oneway** has been improved so much. Use of **oneway** for notification, however, will continue and probably increase (until the multicast specification becomes official) now that this invocation form has determinate QoS.

II.2.3 Summary

In this chapter, we've covered CORBA's new infrastructure for QoS control: its framework, settings for timings and timeout, routing, prioritization, and the special case of **oneway** invocations. If you're working across enterprise boundaries on the Internet or a private network, you can use the specifications in this chapter to define exactly the environment you need to carry out reliable B2B e-commerce, especially if you combine them with CORBA messaging.

And, continuing our theme of re-use, you'll see that the timing and timeout policies defined here are used in the Real-Time CORBA specification presented in the next chapter.

CHAPTER 3

Real-Time CORBA

CHAPTER PREVIEW

Here we start a series of three chapters describing specialized CORBA environments. The first of these, Real-Time CORBA, relies on precise control of resources to deliver guaranteed end-to-end performance. Although we don't present a beginner's view of Real-Time computing here, we will spend a page or so describing basic concepts in the CORBA context. Then we proceed to cover the basic architecture, priorities and threading, and Real-Time communications.

Real-Time (RT) systems are, in the temporal sense, predictable. They are not necessarily fast, although many are; nor do they necessarily deal with high throughput, although many do. The defining characteristic of these systems is that they will, reliably, complete operations on time. Of course some of these systems run glamorous, high-risk, high-speed applications such as fly-by-wire airplane and missile controls, military data collection and display, and manufacturing process control; but they also run e-commerce transaction systems, materials-handling facilities, and other more mundane applications. For example, RT systems ensure that:

- When the high-fluid-level sensor in a tank is triggered, the pump will, *always*, receive a shut-down message within 10 seconds.

- When engine RPM exceeds 6,000 RPM, fuel flow will *always* be lowered within 20 milliseconds.

- 95% of credit-card sales approval requests will receive a response within one minute.

These examples also demonstrate some of the differences among RT systems: They may (as the first example illustrates) work in time intervals that are long compared to a machine cycle. Or, as the second example shows, they may be fast. (Some RT systems work in microseconds.) Or, as the last example illustrates, their reliability may be measured statistically, instead of absolutely.

Predictability is achieved through control of resources and load. RT systems are built on controllable, predictable hardware running controllable, predictable operating systems. Designers spend a lot of time identifying and removing unpredictable loads from the system. These may have nothing to do with CORBA or the application itself. For example, communications interrupts from Ethernet, ATM, or IEEE FireWire were responsible for most of the "jitter" (that is, variations in time behavior) in a tested system. Because they generate high-priority system-level interrupts, these randomly timed interrupts steal processing time from even the highest-priority threads in a RT application. But, with its Ethernet cable unplugged, this system provided reliable, predictable performance and was well-suited for RT systems. (In another system, disk access had a similar effect.) We won't talk about solutions to this problem in this book; the point here is that you have to look everywhere for the source of unpredictable behavior, even in operating systems that claim to be "Real-Time."

You won't find a lot of IDL in this chapter or the two that follow, and for good reason. You can't just read a programming manual for the first time and program a Real-Time, embedded, or fault-tolerant system. These specialized systems require a lot of study and practice in order to be programmed at all, never mind programmed well. So, we're going to restrict ourselves to descriptions of the features of these specifications, without listing IDL interfaces. If this is your first encounter with these types of systems, when you're done reading you'll have a high-level knowledge of their general capabilities, and the way they work in a CORBA environment. If you already have experience with RT, embedded, or fault-tolerant systems, reading the information about the CORBA-specific aspects here will put you in a good position to follow up with a look at the specifications themselves, or the documentation of a product that implements them.

II.3.1   Real-Time CORBA Architecture

RT CORBA does not define a magical environment that makes a non-RT CORBA application run with RT predictability with just a re-compilation and link, even if you invoke *all* of the RT facility's interfaces. You can only get predictable behavior in a controlled environment: If you know and control the load on the server CPU, and you control all of the clients—how many there are, where each one runs, and the load on each of their CPUs—and you also control the network including load and routing, then you can use RT CORBA from your application to control the way resources are allocated and used, ensuring that low-priority tasks give way to high-priority ones and that all of your important functions complete on or before their scheduled times.

You use RT CORBA for the distributed part of your application, but that's not the whole story. You'll need your local computing to run predictably as well, and for that you rely on your Real-Time Operating System (RT OS). So, even before you start worrying about RT CORBA and distribution, you're already busy trying to control your application's priorities using your RT OS's capabilities. RT CORBA doesn't help you with the operating system and basic communications. The specification only standardizes your Real-Time ORB; it's up to you to write your application to run predictably in your execution environment.

Real-Time is a set of optional extensions to the standard CORBA ORB. The RT CORBA specification was written and submitted to OMG jointly by twelve companies, a large number for such a specialized category, and eight more companies put their names on it as supporters. Only specialized CORBA products will support these extensions and you will have to shop for them explicitly, just as you shop for RT OSs now.

The goal of RT CORBA is to support end-to-end predictability for your distributed application. It tries to do this by:

- Respecting thread priorities between client and server during CORBA invocations
- Bounding the duration of thread priority inversions
- Bounding the latencies of operation invocations

II.3.1.1   Activities and the Scheduling Service

One more thing before we look at the capabilities and interfaces that RT CORBA gives us to control our system: Although our goal is Real-Time behavior from our *entire system*, RT CORBA interfaces address threads, priorities, and connections—all are at least relevant to timing and behavior, but why couldn't we just set a magical REAL_TIME policy attribute to TRUE and get RT behavior? Because, as you probably figured out, the relationship between the individual attributes that we can control and the overall system's behavior is complex.

The RT CORBA specification gives you two ways to control your system:

- You can control your system closely, by invoking the interfaces that we'll cover in this chapter. This gives you the finest degree of control, but also requires the largest amount of coding and tuning.

- Alternatively, you can invoke RT CORBA's *scheduling service*. A number of scheduling policies have been studied and implemented in software. These policies have descriptive names like "global rate-monotonic scheduling with priority ceiling"; we'll spare you the details (but provide a few references to articles about scheduling in Appendix A to get you started on your own investigation). A scheduling service raises the level of abstraction: instead of setting priorities on threads or connections, you set priorities on *activities*—sections of code that perform an application function. If you choose to let the client control the priority policy, then the priority will follow an activity even across the network on a remote invocation. The RT CORBA specification defines interfaces to a scheduling service that a vendor might implement. Different vendors may provide services with different policies and varying behavior, since the specification does *not* dictate that a particular scheduling policy must be implemented, nor what its characteristics might be, leaving this as an aspect that a vendor might use to differentiate his products from another's.

We won't discuss the scheduling service anymore in this chapter—at the level we're covering this service, it's enough to point out that the RT CORBA specification supports the service with a standard set of interfaces. In the rest of the chapter, we'll cover the thread and communications policies and attributes that you can set if you want to do it yourself, or that your scheduling service will set for you if you decide to use one.

Now it's time to take a look at how RT CORBA works.

II.3.1.2   Basic Real-Time Architecture

As Figure II.3.1 shows, RT CORBA extends the client's current interface, the POA interface, and adds interfaces for Priority settings, Threadpool

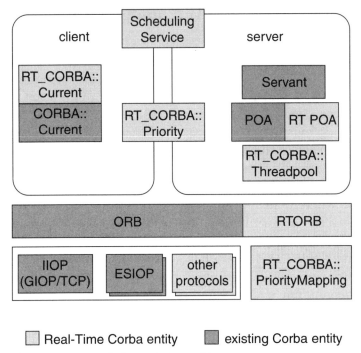

☐ Real-Time Corba entity   ■ existing Corba entity

Figure II.3.1 Real-Time CORBA architecture.

management, Priority Mapping, Communications features, and a Scheduling Service.

Real-Time reuses a lot from existing CORBA specifications: Its policy is the same as the POA policy, which it inherits, and it uses the messaging service policies and interfaces for TimeOut of invocation. However, the Real-Time priority (which has its own interface definition and allows values from 0 to 32767) is not the same as the messaging-service priority (which allows -32768 to 32767), even though both store their value in a **short**.

An RT CORBA product includes a RT ORB. To access it, you call `ORB::resolve_initial_references("RTORB")`. You can, if you want, set the priority range to less than the allowed range of integers from 0 to 32767.

Once you've initialized your RT ORB, when you call `ORB::resolve_initial_references("RootPOA")`, you get a RT POA. The RT POA has all of the features of a normal POA (which it inherits), adding operations to set object-level priorities and understand the RT priorities that we'll describe in the rest of this chapter.

In fact, the RT CORBA priority has some special features, which we'll cover next.

II.3.1.3 Real-Time Priorities and Threading

When you write a RT application, you never have enough computing resource to get everything done right away so you have to prioritize. You divide your application's activities into groups by priority and, when they run, you assign each activity a priority based on how urgent or important it is, or how often it has to be run. High-priority tasks get first crack at resource—CPU, network, even database rows. You prioritize CPU access by allocating threads with assigned priority values, a function supported by your RT OS. Then you assign priorities to these threads based on a scheduling approach, such as assigning high priority to the highest frequency tasks. Low-priority tasks run when no high-priority tasks are left in the queue, or when it is necessary to run a low-priority task in order to release some resource that a high-priority task is waiting for.

RT CORBA runs on many RT OSs. In each OS, priorities are represented by integers, running from a minimum to a maximum value. Trouble is, each RT OS defines its own minimum and maximum values and, in a distributed system, you will probably have a combination of RT OSs linked by the network. To enable interoperable and portable applications, RT CORBA defines a mapping from its own priority scheme termed *Real-Time CORBA Priority* to the scheme of the underlying RT OS.

What happens to the priority of a task that migrates over the wire from one CPU to another? There are two priority propagation models in RT CORBA: the *Client Propagated Priority Model*, in which the client's priority is propagated to the server where its invocation executes at the priority you really intended thanks to RT CORBA's priority mapping functions; and the *Server-Set Priority Model*, where the server imposes its own priority on every request based on the server's locally set prioritization rules. Servers set their priority model as a policy on a RT POA, either as a default or by including it in the policies passed to **create_POA**. Clients can bind to an object on the POA using **validate_connection** to find out a POA's priority model. (Yes, this is the same **validate_connection** that we defined in Part II, Chapter 2.)

In the Client-Propagated model, the priority value is passed from client to server and back again in a CORBA Priority service context. An object using the Server Declared model will publish its priority (along with its policy) in its object reference; the client may use but not change this information. But, on the server side, you can override the default server-declared priority value on a per-object-reference basis when you create new object instances.

Priority Transforms allow priority models in addition to client-propagated and server-declared. RT CORBA allows user-defined transforms at two locations in a server: First, where the invocation enters the server, before any processing occurs, and second, where the invocation leaves the server to make a call on an outboard object. This pair of locations allows, for example, processing to be done at a modified priority within the object while onward invocations are made at the client-set priority.

Access to RT resources including threads and connections is controlled by mutexes. The RT CORBA mutex accessed by the client or object is the same one used by the ORB, since the use of multiple, independent mutexes would lead to unpredictable behavior. The specification requires that the implementation include some form of priority inheritance protocol to limit the effects of priority inversion, and that this also be the same for the application and the ORB. There are a number of ways to implement priority inheritance, and the specification does not require any particular one.

Priority inversion (PI) is the bane of the RT programmer. Here's an example of a priority inversion: Suppose a low-priority task, as part of its function, locks a database row in preparation for a read-and-change and then stops executing because a high-priority task takes over the CPU. Suppose, further, that the high-priority task needs the same database row. The high-priority task cannot proceed because it can't get the mutex lock on the row, but the low-priority task can't get the CPU cycles it needs to finish and unlock because other medium- and high-priority tasks keep getting the CPU time. RT CORBA defines a number of mechanisms that reduce both the occurrence and duration of PIs. *Priority inheritance* sets the priority of a thread, in part, based on the priorities of other threads (and especially threads doing work which might interfere). Multi-banded communications also work to prevent PI, as we'll see in the next section.

There are two basic ways to manipulate threads in RT CORBA. One set of interfaces, derived from **CORBA::Current**, affects threads for its object (that's what **Current** refers to, of course); the other set affects Threadpools. Threads in pools can be pre-allocated and partitioned among your active POAs—the threadpool abstraction in RT CORBA is very advanced.

II.3.1.4   Real-Time Communications

Because RT systems depend on control to deliver end-to-end predictable performance, they are not subject to the same kind of multi-vendor participation that other systems must tolerate. For example, they are much more likely to run on a closed network inside an airplane or chemical plant than on the Internet. Nevertheless, the communications refinements defined in RT CORBA will support a high degree of interoperability. And, because they are based on IIOP, they also support interworking between RT and non-RT CORBA systems.

Because communications QoS is crucial to end-to-end predictability, RT CORBA gives you lots of ways to control it. First, you can set timeout values for your remote invocations, using the timeout definitions in the Messaging service specification that we described in Section II.2.1.1. These let you define timeouts for the invocation, the response, and the round trip.

RT CORBA also introduces the concept of *priority-banded connections*. Your client can open up a number of connections with a server, each handling a restricted range of priorities. Once you've set this up, your client just makes invocations normally; the ORB makes sure that each invocation goes over the connection assigned to its priority value. If you've tuned the ranges properly for the load in each range, this will keep lower-priority invocations from interfering with higher-priority work.

In addition, you can ask for a *non-multiplexed connection* from a client to a server. The low-priority connections serving the riff-raff may be totally blocked, but your connection will be clear all the way through.

Finally, client and server may *select and configure the protocols* that they use to communicate. You can't do this from your app in standard CORBA (although your sysadmin can; controlling and tuning the network is his job), but in real-time work, communication details must be exposed to the application, so here they are.

II.3.2 Summary

In this chapter, we've covered all of the basics of RT CORBA. We know that our description wasn't enough to turn you into a Real-Time programmer, but we hope that it will help you choose RT CORBA if you need a distributed Real-Time environment for a future programming project. If you were bitten by the Real-Time bug as you read our description here, you can check the appendix for references that truly will get you started programming Real-Time systems. In the meantime, we'll go on to Fault Tolerant CORBA in the next chapter.

Fault Tolerant CORBA

CHAPTER PREVIEW

Our second specialized CORBA environment is Fault Tolerant CORBA. Following an introduction to Fault Tolerant computing, the chapter describes object groups and replication, with its choice of passive and active styles. These set up a discussion of fault detection and failover semantics, recovery, fault logging, and notification via the fault analyzer. A brief discussion of system limitations teaches some important lessons as the chapter comes to a close.

In the Part II introduction, we listed a wide range of application areas that need the kind of reliable computing that Fault Tolerant (FT) CORBA provides. So, with the introductory material out of the way, we can start out here with a description of the specification itself.

The difference between running an application under normal conditions and under fault tolerant conditions is simple: Under normal conditions the application will fail occasionally. Under fault tolerant conditions, the application should *never* fail. *Every* invocation by a client should produce a response with the correct result. (We admit, there are some faults that FT CORBA does not protect against. We'll see these in Section II.4.2.)

If you're familiar with Transaction Processing (TP) systems, you know that they make each transaction robust but typically don't protect against system faults. One way to keep a system like this operating in the face of faults is to run two separate instances in parallel, on separate machines, and ideally on separate networks and power sources. Geographical separation will protect against downtime due to environmental conditions such as storms, long power outages, and even earthquakes. CORBA provides a much finer level of functionality: the object. An FT system built on object redundancy is much more efficient than one that duplicates your entire server—in fact, it's efficient enough that you can easily afford to create three, four, or in some cases even more redundant copies of important objects where that's necessary to provide the assurance that your business requires.

Programming a robust and reliable FT infrastructure is difficult, and we'll see what some of the difficulties are as we make our way through this chapter. For now, we'll ask you to take our word that an FT application supported by an FT infrastructure built by FT experts will be a lot easier to implement, less expensive, and more robust than one that a crew of business-domain experts builds themselves. That's why OMG members produced the FT CORBA specification, which standardizes a range of FT functionality and the interfaces that the service and the application use to communicate with each other. Vendors follow the specification to build products that work with standard ORBs to let you run your CORBA applications in an FT environment. (You will have to add a little something to your objects to let the FT product create multiple copies of your object instances and manage them; we'll cover this later in the chapter.) In fact, there were several FT CORBA products under development or on the market before this specification was written, and the experience gained in the writing and use of these products can be seen in the result. With the adoption of this specification, you can anticipate that these products will converge on basic functionality accessible through standard interfaces as competition moves to extensions, algorithms, and management.

The specification enables products that support a wide range of fault tolerance, from simple one-copy redundancy of key objects to highly reliable, geographically dispersed, multiply connected servers. It supports both passive and active replication. (Don't worry, we'll define these terms shortly.) Important functions including generation of instance copies and synchronization of the copies' state may be controlled either by the infrastructure, or by the application. The specification also supports Strong Replica Consistency.

FT CORBA aims to be transparent to the user, the operation of the client, and to some extent to the application programmer. The user clicks away as usual, and the client makes its usual single invocation. It's perhaps a little more surprising that the transparency extends to some extent to the application programmer who codes his usual CORBA program with the same set of objects that he would have coded for a non-fault-tolerant system, adding to each application object a few interfaces that let the FT infrastructure synchronize the state of each set of object replicas. Running this same code on reliable, redundant hardware under the control of a fault-tolerant infrastructure makes it fault-tolerant. For those of you who prefer a little tighter control, this specification also supports replication and consistency modes controlled by the application. We'll contrast this to infrastructure control in Section II.4.1.5.

Although FT CORBA does not restrict application design, allowing analysts and programmers to build the *same* object set of objects that they would have for a non-FT system, it does require that each object bear and implement participant interfaces that let the FT infrastructure create and manage copies of object instances at run time. (*Participant interfaces* are defined by a specfication but borne and implemented by objects in the application. FT CORBA uses participant interfaces to manage instances of objects that were coded by the application programmer.) If you choose application-controlled consistency, you will have a little more programming to do, building pieces of FT functionality into your objects yourself.

The transparency also does not extend to the system administrator, who must install and configure the fault tolerance product, provide redundant hardware and software, and configure the application to run redundant copies of its objects. As we'll see in this chapter, fault tolerance results from the way the application uses the redundant hardware to run redundant copies of its software.

In this chapter, we'll start with an introduction to basic FT objectives and concepts. This will include a look at the basic architectural constructs that products implement to provide fault tolerance. To close, we'll look at some known limitations of FT CORBA systems and the conformance points.

Although there is a lot of material in the specification that goes beyond what we've listed here, it's mostly for implementors, and not users, of FT systems and we're not going to cover it in detail. We will present a few items that address the heart of fault tolerance, because we know that programmers want to know something about how things work.

II.4.1 FT Basics

FT CORBA supports applications that require a high level of reliability. Under FT CORBA, applications must have no single point of failure.

FT systems provide this degree of assurance through:

- Redundancy (replication)
- Fault detection and notification
- Logging and recovery

The unit of redundancy is the *object*, not the server or TP system. The FT CORBA infrastructure allows individual object instances to be replicated on multiple processors at different locations on the network—even in different cities or on different continents—in a very flexible way. Even when calls are cascaded, with replicated objects calling other replicated objects, propagation is controlled so that each copy receives and executes the resulting call *exactly once*.

Faults are detected by a number of mechanisms, including both push (heartbeat) and pull monitoring. To avoid scalability problems, a Fault Detector on each host monitors the individual objects on it, and a global (replicated, of course) Fault Detector monitors the individual host Fault Detectors.

II.4.1.1   Replication and Object Groups

The replicas of an object are created and managed as an *object group*. To render this structure opaque to the client, the copies are created and managed by a *replication manager*, and addressed by a single Interoperable Object Group Reference (IOGR). We're not going to present details of the IOGR here—they're hidden from the application, and serve only to allow the ORB and FT infrastructure to work together to deliver FT support.

Fault Tolerance Domains make it practical to create and manage large FT systems. A FT domain may contain a number of hosts, and many object groups, although a single host may support multiple domains. There is a single (replicated) Replication Manager for each domain.

In Figure II.4.1, lightly shaded ovals denote the extent of FT domains, while darker shaded ovals denote hosts, and circles denote object instance replicas. The capital letters within an object's circle denote its object group; the set of circles with the same letter is therefore the set of replicas of an individual instance. Hosts may participate in one (Host 2) or more (Hosts 3 and 4, e.g.) domains, but all objects in a group must be in the same domain because they are all created and managed by that domain's Replication Manager. Don't get the impression that any domain in a real installation would support replicas of only one object instance, even though the Los Angeles and Wide-area domains in the figure do this. The New York domain supports two instances (D and E). Consider these to be stand-ins for the dozens or hundreds of instances, each with its one or several copies, that a real domain would support. (However, if you've wrapped a legacy applica-

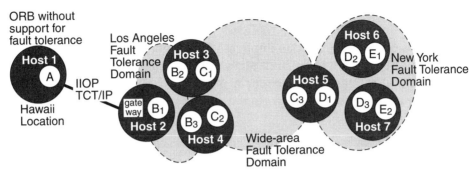

Figure II.4.1 Structure of fault tolerance domains.

tion up as a single CORBA instance and replicated it, then you really could have a domain with copies of only one or a few instances.)

The wide geographic dispersal of object groups shown in Figure II.4.1 is a demonstration of FT CORBA's capabilities but not a requirement for your implementation! By keeping your implementation simple, you make is easier to install and maintain, and one way to keep things simple is to keep your installation compact. This allows a single sysadmin to control everything, and avoids long network links with their accompanying delays and increased probability of failure. On the other hand, an installation in a single building or city can be knocked off-line totally by a fire, storm, long-term power outage (beyond the limit of your batteries or generators), or earthquake, proving that there are some good reasons to spread your FT system widely. Thus (no surprise here) your actual configuration will be a compromise between simplicity and economy on the one hand, and greater and more widespread redundancy with accompanying complexity and cost on the other. If your enterprise already extends across one continent or several, a set of domains with the wide dispersal shown in Figure II.4.1 may not be financially out of reach anyhow.

Every object group has a set of FT properties, including ReplicationStyle, MembershipStyle, ConsistencyStyle, FaultMonitoringStyle, and six others. These may be set either domain-wide, per-type, or per-group, and (unlike POA properties, for example) some of these may be modified after the group is created.

II.4.1.1.1 Active vs. Passive Replication Styles

There are two major styles of replication: *Active* and *Passive*. Passive then subdivides into two styles of its own, but let's look at the difference between Active and Passive first:

- *Every active replica executes every invocation independently*, in the same order as every other replica. (We'll discuss later how the communcations system inhibits duplicate invocations when one set of replicated objects invokes another set of replicated objects.) Active replication is faster and cheaper when the cost of computation is less than the cost of saving/restoring state, and necessary when recovery *has* to be instantaneous.

- *Only one passive replica of a set, the primary member, executes invoked methods*, saving its state periodically. When a fault occurs, a backup member is promoted to primary, and its state is restored from the log and replaying of request messages that may have followed the log entry. This restoration process takes time, and precludes use of passive replication in cases where delays are unacceptable.

The difference between Warm and Cold passive replication isn't difficult: Warm passive replication lessens the recovery delay somewhat by loading state into backup objects periodically during execution; cold passive replication does no loading until the primary member fails.

There's another mode, *Stateless*, that applies to objects that have no dynamic state.

The specification dictates the values that `ReplicationStyle` may take: `ACTIVE`, `COLD_PASSIVE`, `WARM_PASSIVE` (no, you haven't accidentally warped into Psychology 101!), `STATELESS`, or `ACTIVE_WITH_VOTING`.

`ACTIVE_WITH_VOTING`, the only one we haven't covered yet, is interesting for two reasons: First, it is not fully supported by the current specification and represents a likely future extension. Second, this mode (and the fact that it's not supported) points out a limitation of the specification: The current specification protects only against crash faults: that is, when an object issues *no* response. When multiple responses come back, as almost always happens with active replication (unless you have, for example, two objects in a group and one fails), the system does *not* compare them—it assumes that *all* responses are correct and that any one is as good as any other. So, the specification does not protect against what it terms *commission* faults, where an object generates incorrect results, nor against what it terms *byzantine* faults, where an object or host generates incorrect results intentionally. The `ACTIVE_WITH_VOTING` replication style, used with sophisticated algorithms, can protect against commission and byzantine faults, but this costs too much in terms of compute time and network transport to be practical except in some extreme cases. (The voting itself isn't costly, as the specification takes pains to point out: It's the underlying network transport.)

Strong Replica Consistency is the principle of FT CORBA that guarantees that objects have *identical* state. Supported by the specification, it guarantees that for Passive replication, all members of an object group have the same state following each state transfer, and that for Active replication, all members have the same state at the end of each operation. For this to work, applications must be *deterministic*, or must be *sanitized* so that they give the appearance of being deterministic: for a given starting state, a given invocation with a given set of parameters must produce the same output and the same internal state. (*Sanitize* means to "clean up" a set of replicas so that all give the *identical* answer to an invocation—removing *all* sources of non-deterministic behavior. Although this may be simple for a routine that queries a database row or performs a calculation, it's not so easy to sanitize a set of replicas against a query that depends on time of day or some other value that differs from one machine to another or varies with even slight differences in invocation delivery timing.)

The specification requires that the FT infrastructure deliver the *same* set of invocations in the *same* order to *every member* of an object group. The deterministic behavior of the object instances, combined with the consistent behavior of the FT infrastructure, guarantees strong replica consistency. If you're the application programmer, remember that the deterministic behavior of the application object implementations is *your* responsibility!

II.4.1.2 The Replication Manager

Figure II.4.2 shows a sample configuration for an FT system. We'll use this configuration to discuss the way each element works.

The replication manager, itself replicated as Figure II.4.2 shows by the nested boxes, inherits three interfaces defined separately in the specification: **PropertyManager, ObjectGroupManager,** and **GenericFactory.**

The **PropertyManager** interface lets you define fault tolerance properties for your object groups, possibly using a GUI. Of the properties we've already listed, two are especially relevant here: `MembershipStyle`, and `ConsistencyStyle`. `MembershipStyle` defines whether the infrastructure or application controls membership in an object group, and `ConsistencyStyle` defines whether the infrastructure or the application controls consistency of state for members of an object group.

If you set `MembershipStyle` to `MEMB_INF_CTRL`—that is, infrastructure-controlled—then the Replication Manager creates replicas in the locations you've set administratively whenever you call the generic `create` for an object type. But, if you've set `MembershipStyle` to `MEMB_APP_CTRL`, then

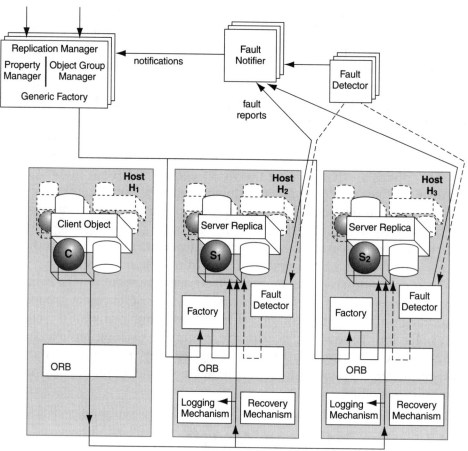

Figure II.4.2 A possible architectural configuration of an FT system.

the application can create the replicas itself, and call **add_member** to add each to its group. ConsistencyStyle works analogously.

The **ObjectGroupManager** interface lets the application add or remove members of a group. (**add_member** is one of the **ObjectGroupManager**-derived interfaces.) And, the **GenericFactory** interface lets the application invoke the Replication Manager to create new replicated objects in a transparent manner.

II.4.1.3 ORB Invocation Failover Semantics

Your client and server ORBs exchange GIOP messages as they work your invocation and reply. They do this using a handshaking style and may exchange a number of message types. The inner workings of GIOP are covered in basic CORBA books, so we're not going to repeat the explanation here. If you aren't familiar with basic GIOP, you might want to look it up when the information in this section becomes a little opaque.

II.4.1.3.1 Changes to CORBA Supporting Failover Semantics

When a client ORB makes an invocation and something goes wrong, the ORB receives a failure notification and, usually, a coded reason for the failure. The notification will include a completion status of either COMPLETED_NO or COMPLETED_MAYBE, and any one of a number of reason codes.

An Interoperable Object Reference (IOR) may contain a number of network endpoints (IP addresses, for TCP/IP-based protocols). When an invocation fails with one of four specific system exceptions and a status of COMPLETED_NO, an ORB *may*, under CORBA 2.3 and prior versions, choose to repeat the invocation using an alternative endpoint. Or, the ORB may decide to return a failure exception to the client *without* trying the alternatives; CORBA 2.3 and prior versions leave this decision to the ORB.

Starting with CORBA 2.4, however, this client ORB behavior is prescribed precisely: Under these conditions, the client ORB *must not* abandon the invocation and raise an exception to the client until it has tried to invoke the server using *all* of the alternative IIOP addresses in the IOR, unless it receives a correct response or one of the alternative error returns that do not allow retry, before exhausting the list. This behavior is required of *all* CORBA 2.4 and higher version clients. It is a change to basic CORBA, and not restricted to FT-compliant products.

Because this behavior is required of all clients, FT systems know that all alternative endpoints will be invoked when one fails. FT systems take advantage of this by listing alternative locations for the client to try. It allows any CORBA client to invoke an object in an FT system and receive some of the benefits of FT services. This is a help, but doesn't change the fact that only FT-aware clients derive full benefit from the system.

II.4.1.3.2 Failover Extensions under FT CORBA

With active replication, there are enough running copies of each object that FT CORBA does not need to provide special handling for invocations that fail. But, for Warm Passive and Cold Passive FT systems, when a primary member fails, the invocation fails and must be redirected to the backup server. And, it must be executed *at most once*, in accordance with CORBA's required semantics.

To support this, FT CORBA defines an environment that allows *transparent reinvocation* under certain conditions. The mechanisms we're going to describe in this section are executed by client and server ORBs—none of them requires client or server participation, and your application is never aware that they are being used. We're explaining them here because of the way they demonstrate the robustness of the FT CORBA specification and infrastructure.

FT ORBs insert a newly defined *REQUEST service context* into each request. (Service contexts convey parameters from client ORB to server ORB, invisible to client and server application code. They are a standard CORBA mechanism available to the CORBAservices but, because they must be implemented within the ORB, not accessible to application code. The Transaction and Security CORBAservices use service contexts.) The REQUEST service context contains a client ID, a retention ID that identifies the request uniquely, and an expiration time.

The server ORB stores IDs *and the results* of prior invocations in a table until their expiration times. (Once an invocation expires, it may be garbage collected.) Whenever an invocation arrives with a valid expiration time, the server ORB compares its ID numbers to the ones in its table. If the ID is not in the table, the ORB knows that it is a new request and passes it on to the object for execution.

FT client ORBs take advantage of this when a request that they issued comes back with a status of COMPLETED_MAYBE and raises a system exception on the list of allowed values. In this case, the client ORB *reissues* the request with the *same* ID values. When the request reaches a server ORB, even one different from the (possibly failed) server ORB that serviced the original invocation, that ORB checks its tables for those ID values. Tables are synchronized by the FT infrastructure, so the execution pathway here is the same regardless of which server ORB copy and object replica is invoked. If the ORB finds the values in its table, it knows that the request was, in fact, completed and that the failure occurred somewhere on the network between ORB and client on the return trip. To avoid duplicate execution of the request, the server ORB simply retrieves the original results from the table where they were stored along with the IDs and re-sends them back to the client *without* ever passing the duplicate invocation to the object. Of course if the ORB does not find the ID values in its table, it passes the invocation to the object for execution in the usual way.

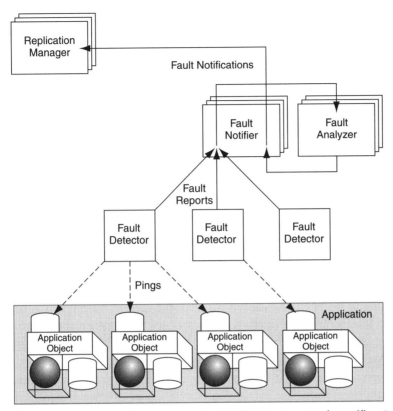

Figure II.4.3 Interactions among the Fault Detectors, Fault Notifier, Fault Analyzer, and Replication Manager.

II.4.1.4   The Fault Detector and Fault Notifier

Here's the sequence of events that ensues when a fault is detected, and the characters in this particular drama. Figure II.4.3, copied from the specification, shows this diagramatically. (We'll discuss the Fault Analyzer in Section II.4.1.6.)

As we mentioned before, there is at least one Fault Detector on each host that periodically pings each object replica on that host to see if it is functioning. Applications can configure additional fault detectors as necessary; the specification shows an example with several fault detectors arranged hierarchically within a host machine and external to it. The specification standardizes pull-style fault detection, where the Fault Detectors periodically ping each replica using the **PullMonitorable** interface that participating objects must inherit and implement. Not standardized, but allowed, is a push-style detection style where objects notify the Fault Detector over an application-specific interface.

When a Fault Detector detects a fault, it pushes a report to the Fault Notifier using the **FaultNotifier** interface. This is a subset of the Notification Service interface (The Notification Service is not described in this book, but is summarized in *CORBA 3 Fundamentals and Programming*), and the Fault Notifier is a drastically slimmed-down version of the Notification Service.

This is a standard event notification, and the Replication Manager, a Fault Analyzer, or any application object can register as consumers. Fault events can be either **CosNotification::StructuredEvent** types or **CosNotification::Event-Batch** (a sequence of **StructuredEvent**) types.

II.4.1.5 Logging and Recovery

Everything we've covered so far was introduction for this part. Here's where the service fixes up your application when an object crashes.

If you're running in one of the Passive replication styles (either Warm or Cold), only the primary member of each of your object groups actually executes an invocation and sends back replies. When the Fault Detector suspects that the primary member has failed, it signals the Replication Manager to either restart the primary member or promote a backup member to primary.

At this point, the primary member needs to have its state restored. If you've chosen application-controlled consistency style, the application must fetch and restore the state of the new primary member. This is easy to describe: it's application-dependent, and you have to code it yourself.

If you've chosen infrastructure-controlled consistency style, things are more automatic. Under this style, all invocations and replies are copied to the logging and recovery mechanisms where they are recorded in a log, which the recovery mechanism uses during recovery. In addition, the logging mechanism peridocally invokes **get_state( )** on the **Checkpointable** interface, which application objects are required to inherit and implement in order to participate in the service. Then, during recovery, the recovery mechanism invokes **set_state( )** on the new primary to set the state as it was recorded in the log. The **Checkpointable** interface with its operations **set_state( )** and **get_state( )** is another participant interface defined by the FT CORBA specification.

If you've chosen Active replication, then none of this applies at failure/recovery time—the system just has one fewer duplicate response than usual and goes on with its processing without missing a beat. That, presumably, was why you chose Active mode in the first place. However, the logging and recovery mechanisms still have a role to play: When a new member is added to an object group at run time, whether it's an additional member or a replacement for a failed member, the state of the new member must be synchronized with the state of the executing members. So, even under Active conditions, the application objects need to inherit and implement the **get_state( )** and **set_state( )** interfaces on your application objects, and the logging and recovery mechanisms must be running.

II.4.1.6 The Fault Analyzer

The Fault Analyzer registers with the Fault Notifier to receive fault reports. It then correlates fault reports and generates condensed fault reports using an application-specific algorithm.

Even though reporting is orthogonal to recovery and your system is (hopefully) chugging along without missing a beat even when redundant copies or hosts fail, you'll still want to know everything that's gone wrong during execution. The Fault Analyzer is the system component that takes care of this.

Even though the Fault Analyzer is an essential component of a complete FT system, it's not the kind of thing that can be standardized. The basics of a fault report are fixed by common sense, and the rest of the report—additional facts, and the format—are the kind of thing that vendors can implement as a differentiating feature of their product. So, with reasonable justification, the specification does not standardize an interface for the Fault Analyzer—it only standardizes a good place for your FT CORBA product vendor to put it.

The specification suggests, since a host failure will generate at least one fault report for every object that resides on it, that that the analyzer correlate reports before making its report. It's a lot easier to cope with a notice that a host failed than to read a thousand object failure notices and figure out yourself that they all result from the same host failure. You can also cope with this using the filtering mechanism within the Fault Notifier.

II.4.2 Limitations

There are some limitations to FT CORBA. Here's an abbreviated list. By analyzing the limitations listed here, you'll gain some more insight into the workings of an FT system.

- **Legacy Client ORBs:** An unreplicated client hosted by a CORBA 2.3 or earlier ORB can invoke methods on a replicated server, but will not participate fully in FT. We discussed the new requirement to retry all of the alternative endpoints included in an IOR or IOGR, and the new REQUEST service context that legacy ORBs will not insert into their requests. These are not the only limitations of legacy ORBs, although they are the most evident.

- **Common Infrastructure:** For this first release of the specification, all hosts within a domain must use the same FT product *and* ORBs from the same vendor, to ensure FT behavior. Between domains, full FT behavior is only guaranteed when all domains share the same FT product and the same ORB, although some improvement can be expected even when using different products.

- **Deterministic Behavior:** Application objects and ORBs must behave deterministically in order to guarantee Strong Replica Consistency. Sources of non-determinism must be identified and sanitized. This requires careful coding of objects by the application programmer, and may require restricting multi-threading in the ORB.

- **Network Partitioning Faults:** A *Network Partitioning Fault* separates the system into two parts, each able to operate and communicate within itself but unable to communicate with the other. When a network partitioning fault splits an FT system, each half thinks the other half failed, as both continue to chug away and their states grow more and more out of synch. The inherent nature of the problem does not allow assured detection and recovery from network partitioning faults, which are therefore not covered by FT CORBA.

- **Commission and Byzantine Faults:** We mentioned these before: Commission faults occur when an object or host generates incorrect results, and Byzantine faults occur when this happens intentionally or maliciously. These fault types are neither detected nor corrected by FT CORBA, although the ACTIVE_WITH_VOTING replication style provides a mechanism that could be used to build a solution. The solution, however, will be expensive in terms of resource.

- **Correlated Faults:** Correlated faults cause the same error to occur simultaneously in *every* replica or host, and typically result from failures in design or coding. They can happen anywhere: application, operating system, storage, network, hardware, or any other replicated part of the system. FT CORBA provides no protection against correlated faults.

II.4.3 Conformance

FT CORBA defines two conformance points. An implementation must support at least one of these, and may support both:

- **Passive Replication FT CORBA** products support only the COLD_PASSIVE, WARM_PASSIVE, and STATELESS replication styles.

- **Active Replication FT CORBA** products support only the ACTIVE and STATELESS replication styles.

II.4.4 Summary

In this chapter, we've shown how FT CORBA couples entity redundancy with fault detection and recovery to give CORBA applications the robustness they need to serve enterprise and Internet applications. We hope you'll think of FT CORBA for your company's reliable server infrastructure.

In the next chapter, closing our series on specialized environments, we'll examine a specification that takes something away from CORBA instead of adding to it: minimumCORBA, for embedded, card-based, and other small-footprint systems.

minimumCORBA

CHAPTER PREVIEW

minimumCORBA is the last of our three specialized CORBA environments. Intended for embedded and card-based systems, minimumCORBA shrinks CORBA by removing dynamic features. Because of the stability of these systems, they will never need dynamic features such as the Dynamic Invocation Interface, Interface Repository, and dynamic any. In this chapter, we'll start with a look at uses for, and architecture of, embedded systems. Then we'll list exactly what minimumCORBA eliminates from the standard ORB. To conclude, we'll examine the Smart Transducer RFP, which will standardize CORBA interfaces for networked single-chip sensors or actuators.

Computers come in many shapes and sizes. In this chapter, we'll concentrate on the small end of the size range, where CORBA will have greatest impact in terms of sheer numbers of ORBs: While large enterprise server installations may number in the high hundreds or thousands, and medium-sized servers may number in the tens or hundreds of thousands, and the total number of clients may be one to ten million if you add them all up, it's common for the production run of a single embeddable chip design to be one to ten million units. Because production of a new chip happens fairly frequently, if each chip contains an ORB then the total number of embedded ORBs could easily number in the billions of units. That's a lot of ORBs!

The amount of memory available in embedded systems when we wrote this in early 2001 was pretty small: Cell phone chips typically had as little as 200K of RAM available for an application, and perhaps 64K of ROM to store it—both ORB and application combined! And, automobile engine controllers and similar chips typically churned out in quantity are smaller yet—as small as 2K of RAM and .5K ROM. When production runs reach into the multiple millions, pennies per unit adds up! But, the future generations of chips are predicted to be much larger, with multiple megabytes eventually available on the cell phone chips and 15K on the automotive pieces.

A fully functional, fully compliant CORBA ORB is much too big to fit onto chips in this size range, even if you cut down the footprint by linking with client libraries only. And, client-only is not an option here anyhow since these embedded applications have to respond to queries and this requires them to host objects. This means that some POA functionality has to be squeezed on there somewhere. So, to enable CORBA to be a player in the world of distributed embedded systems, OMG adopted the minimumCORBA specification in late 1998.

minimumCORBA defines a compliance point for a small-footprint ORB. Even though a (strategically chosen) set of CORBA capabilities is omitted, this ORB nevertheless interoperates using IIOP with not only other minimumCORBA but also standard ORBs, plays the role of both client and server, and handles the full complement of IDL types. (We'll give details about what's left out in the main part of this chapter.) This specification lets CORBA play in some embedded-systems application areas and brings it closer in other areas. Let's take a closer look.

A typical footpprint for a minimumCORBA ORB is 150K; some compliant product configurations weigh in at 30K or so less. Link-time options offered on virtually every minimumCORBA ORB let you remove features not used by the application (even though they're required by minimumCORBA). These can reduce the footprint down even further, to as little as 80K or so.

At this size, minimumCORBA ORBs fit easily onto cards used in telecommunications switches for both established analog connections and emerging digital networks. There's enough business here to support a thriving marketplace: OMG runs two workshops each year for embedded and Real-Time CORBA, one on the east coast, and one on the west. Both attract one hundred or more attendees to a four-day program of tutorials, technical presentations, and roundtables. Vendors and developers contribute many papers to each of these workshops every year, documenting their companies' advancement of the state of the art. OMG maintains a web page with workshop information; we've listed it along with the other references in Appendix A.

Still, these ORBs are not small enough to fit onto current generation cell phones (there wouldn't be any room left for an application, once you crammed the ORB into available memory!) and are way too big to fit onto the typical automotive chip. The next generation of cell phone chip, with an expected 16 to 64 MB(!) of memory, could conceivably fit a fully functional ORB but will probably use minimumCORBA because of the inherent space limitations of a hand-held system. The next generation automotive chip, with an expected 16K or so, will still be too small to handle a fully functional ORB. We expect that, as ORBs continue to shrink and on-chip memory continues to expand, the two will meet in the middle in a generation or two.

Small ORBs are also poised to have an impact in the area of miniature smart transducers. Combining a sensor or actuator, a microcontroller, and networking functions on a single chip inexpensive enough to be used once and thrown away, these tiny devices are going to be connected by (typically simple and slow) networks and put to work measuring and controlling under conditions where this combination of functionality and low cost is the only way to carry out the work. As we write this in early 2001, OMG has just issued an RFP for a Smart Transducer interface. We'll discuss the interface requirements and other aspects of the future specification in Section II.5.4.

In the rest of this chapter, we'll start with a high-level overview of minimumCORBA, and continue with a look at the items removed or otherwise affected by the specification. Then we'll conclude with a look at OMG's Smart Transducer RFP.

II.5.1   What's Left Out of minimumCORBA

minimumCORBA defines a single profile of CORBA, originally cut down from CORBA 2.2 but updated with each CORBA release to refer to the current version. The specification also suggests that compliant ORBs can shrink footprint further by eliminating additional features at link time, but points out that link behavior is not subject to specification so this type of flexibility cannot be required. In any case, the combination of a single profile with additional space-saving tailored to the application's needs seems to fit the market extremely well.

II.5.2   minimumCORBA Overview

The single minimumCORBA profile was designed with a number of goals in mind:

- The profile was chosen to be broadly applicable within the domain of limited-resource systems.

- minimumCORBA supports all OMG IDL types. Even the **any** type is retained.

- Interoperability features were also kept; minimumCORBA and standard CORBA applications are fully interoperable.

- minimumCORBA saves space mainly by eliminating features that support the dynamic aspects of CORBA.

As a result, minimumCORBA defines an environment that is almost as easy to code in as standard CORBA; it is fully interoperable, but nevertheless produces executables with a footprint that fits easily into many of today's card-format devices and, with some effort, onto large-end individual chips.

II.5.2.1   Removal of Dynamic CORBA Features

minimumCORBA removes mainly the dynamic features of CORBA: As we'll see, these include the IFR, the DII, and individual features and interfaces that support them. Fully featured ORBs maintain many resources on the chance that an application will decide, at run time, to use a dynamic feature, either to retrieve an object's interface, or to create an invocation on-the-fly using the DII. But, if you've built an application that never makes a dynamic invocation, and burned that application into silicon, there's no chance that it's ever going to call the DII and that means there's no reason to include the DII in your executable. The removal of dynamic features such as the DII lets minimumCORBA fit an ORB onto a reasonably sized footprint.

Because dynamic features have been removed, minimumCORBA applications *must* make all of their resource allocation decisions at *design time.* Under minimumCORBA, it is not possible to invoke operations dynamically on new object types that you discover at run time out on the network. But, this has an additional benefit: because dynamic functions are slower as well as resource-intensive, applications coded under minimumCORBA run *quickly.* The small, fast applications supported by minimumCORBA typically fit perfectly into the niches where they're needed most.

II.5.3 The minimumCORBA Specification

Here is a rundown of the ORB elements affected by minimumCORBA:

- **ORB Interface.** Operations in this interface that support the DII were omitted: **create_list, create_operation_list, work_pending, perform_ work, shutdown,** and a few others.

- **Object.** In addition to the DII-related operations **get_interface** and **create_request**, the operations **is_a** and **non-existent** were eliminated because type-checking issues are expected to be resolved at design time.

- **ConstructionPolicy.** minimumCORBA applications do not organize their objects into policy domains, for either security or any other reason, so this interface is omitted.

- **Dynamic Features.** The Dynamic Invocation Interface, the Dynamic Skeleton Interface, and Dynamic **any** are omitted.

II.5.3.1 Interface Repository

Most of the IFR is omitted. However, **RepositoryIds** and part of the **TypeCode** interface are kept.

   TypeCode information supports the semantics of the **any** type. minimumCORBA applications are restricted to sending and receiving only **anys** of IDL types that were known at build time, allowing part of the **TypeCode** interface to be omitted including all of the **create_** operations.

II.5.3.2 Portable Object Adapter

Dynamic POA modes are not supported, shrinking the size of the POA while still allowing applications to port among minimumCORBA implementations and from a minimumCORBA ORB to a standard ORB.

   Omitted operations are **create_thread_policy, create_implicit_activation_policy, create_servant_retention_policy,** and **create_request_processing_policy.**

   ServantManagers and the **USE_DEFAULT_SERVANT** option are also not supported, allowing another four operations to be omitted: **get_servant_manager, set_servant_manager, get_servant,** and **set_servant.**

   The elimination of many modes of POA operation reduces a number of POA policies to a single value. Where the retained value is the default anyhow, these policy objects and their **enums** have been eliminated: **ThreadPolicy,**

ImplicitActivationPolicy, ServantRetentionPolicy, and **RequestProcessingPolicy.** For three others, only one value is allowed but it's not the default, so the policy object is retained: **ThreadPolicy** (only **ORB_CTRL_MODEL** is allowed), **ServantRetentionPolicy** (only **RETAIN** is supported), and **ImplicitActivationPolicy** (only **NO_IMPLICIT_ACTIVATION** is allowed; minimumCORBA does not support implicit activation).

minimumCORBA supports both values of the remaining POA policies: **LifespanPolicy, ObjectIdUniquenessPolicy,** and **IdAssignmentPolicy.**

The POAManager object is retained, but all declarations except the **activate** operation and **AdapterInactive** exception are dropped. The AdapterActivator supports a dynamic mode and is also dropped, as is the ServantManager object.

II.5.3.3   Interceptors

Interceptors support is omitted.

II.5.3.4   Interoperability Protocols

The DCE ESIOP is omitted. IIOP is retained.

Many minimumCORBA products allow the addition of specialized protocols. There's an active RFP at the OMG to standardize this function, but that hasn't stopped vendors from including this capability in minimumCORBA products now. And, this product experience will help these vendors write a better standard, also.

II.5.3.5   Language Mappings

A minimumCORBA ORB must support at least one language mapping, but, like standard CORBA, no particular language is mandated. Language mappings do not have to support omitted CORBA features or objects. C++ and Java have one additional quirk each:

- **C++.** The _this() member function does not cause implicit activation of a servant in minimumCORBA.
- **Java.** The Java ORB Portability Interfaces, which depend on the DII and DSI, are omitted.

This concludes our look at minimumCORBA. We'll turn briefly to the Smart Transducer RFP, underway as this book went to press, before making the bigger switch to CORBA's component-based architecture.

II.5.4 The Smart Transducer RFP

For those of us who don't work with systems-on-a-chip every day, this RFP starts out by telling us that a smart transducer is

> a device that comprises, in a compact small unit, a sensor or actuator element (possibly both), a micro-controller, a communication controller, and the associated software for signal conditioning, calibration, diagnostics, and communication.

Just issued in December 2000, as this book went into production, the RFP expands OMG's efforts into a realm far smaller than even the one we've been discussing in this chapter so far.

The key enabler is the combination of the sensor or actuator, the microcontroller, and the communications capability onto a single, low-cost chip. This allows a number of these chips—and the RFP clearly envisions configurations from just a few to many hundreds or possibly thousands—of these devices to be linked together in a cluster, using a simple low-speed network, feeding their data to a collection point using a device-specific protocol. The collection point then feeds the data to a higher-level service application using a GIOP-based (but not necessarily IIOP-based) protocol.

The RFP suggests that three levels of interface are required: a *real-time service interface* which periodically delivers that data that you're interested in; a *diagnostic and maintenance interface* for querying of log data without interfering with the real-time service interface; and a *configuration interface* for initial configuration and updates.

These devices are too small, and the interconnecting networks too slow, to support CORBA and IIOP. Still, the RFP expects as much of existing OMG specifications to be used as is practical, and for interfaces to the higher level end user application to be recognizable as CORBA-derived. With its references to the wire bus standards ISO 9141 and RS 485, though, this RFP clearly breaks new ground for OMG.

For references to this and all other active OMG RFPs, see Appendix A.

II.5.5 Summary

This concludes the Quality of Service part of the book. We've covered a wide variety of qualities of a wide variety of services, all under the CORBA umbrella, and seen how existing extensions and specializations of OMG specs allows CORBA applications to fit well into Real-Time, reliable, small-footprint, and other specialized niches. In the Part III, we'll stick to one environment—scalable servers—and see how much work the OMG has done to equip the ORB to work well in this key enterprise function.

PART

III

CCM and Supporting
Specifications

The first two chapters in this part lay the foundation for discussion of the CORBA Component Model (CCM), which we then present (at some length!) in the last chapter. The two supporting specifications are:

- The Portable Object Adapter (POA)
- The Persistent State Service (PSS)

The POA, which forms the basis for the CCM *container*, was a part of CORBA 2.2. And the PSS, which is actually a CORBAservice and not part of CORBA itself, was scheduled to complete finalization in late 2000 coincident with the CCM itself.

From a high-level architectural viewpoint, these specifications—working together with the transaction, security, event, and notification services—made CORBA a nearly-ideal foundation for scalable enterprise and Internet servers. Why "nearly"? Because these services were defined individually, and not packaged into a unified environment.

That's what the CORBA Component Model does: It packages up all of these services and specifications into a single, standard development and run-time environment. Because it pre-selects service configurations for that server environment, the CCM is able to present your programmer with service APIs at a much higher level than those of the services themselves—in fact, a CCM application can be made transactional or secure by adding a single line to a configuration file, without changing a single line of language code. This lets an enterprise migrate its server-programming work from system programmers to business programmers, who can tailor the server to sophisticated business algorithms more precisely and respond to new business opportunities at "Internet speed."

But, before we speak any more of the CCM, we have to lay the foundation by discussing the POA and the PSS.

As a part of the CORBA 2.2 release, the POA is the oldest of the specifications described in this section. We know it was designed to support scalable servers (which it does, extremely well); what we don't know is how much of the POA specification was written with a future extension to CCM in mind. In the introductory section of Part III, Chapter 1, we tell how the POA was specified during the time period when forward-looking people were first becoming aware of the possibilities of the Internet. With this as its background, its no wonder that it's so well suited for this highly stressed environment.

The POA works its greatest transformation on the architecture of the server, where it cleanly separates the client-side notion of "CORBA object" from the server-side concept of "the code that happens to be activated to service a request for this object, this time" (which, as you may have already guessed, might be different from the code that happened to be activated to service a request for that same object the *last* time, or the *next* time). This concept, an essential characteristic of a server that handles Internet or enterprise loads, only affects the implementation *beneath the encapsulation boundary* and so preserves the client view of a CORBA object as a simple, self-contained module with a single, well-defined IDL interface and no other operations. The POA term for "code that services a request, this time" is *servant*; we'll devote several pages to clarifying the difference between an object and a servant so don't fret if this short paragraph hasn't been enough for you.

OMG's new Persistent State Service, like the **valuetype**, deals with an object's internal state but in a very different way. Consider these contrasts between the **valuetype** and the PSS:

- A **valuetype**, which is a programming language object, exists only while the object is running; when its reference count goes to zero, it—and its state—vanish. In contrast, the PSS *preserves* an object's state from one activation to the next.

- A **valuetype** is designed to *externalize* its state, in a form usable by the same or another vendor's ORB. In contrast, the PSS is required to *internalize* an object's state so that only the *same* service (albeit at a later time) can restore it.

There are other differences (set out in a document written by a number of OMG members and cited in Appendix A), but you get the idea: The **valuetype** and the PSS are fundamentally different services that deal with state in entirely different ways in spite of the superficial similarity that they both deal with state.

Targeted to the needs of the CCM as well as CORBA in general, the PSS provides both transparent and programmer-controlled persistence of variables declared as an object's state. It's well-designed, in contrast to the original Persistent Object Service (POS) specification which it replaces.

So, that sums up the architecture of the three specifications in this chapter. Now, on to the technical details.

The Portable Object
Adapter (POA)

CHAPTER PREVIEW

The Portable Object Adapter standardizes the interfaces and operations that the
server ORB uses to interact with the object implementation for resource control.
To optimize resource usage, the server does not establish a permanent association between the code that services a request (termed a POA servant), and the
CORBA object reference that represents the object to the client. In the first half
of this chapter, we'll establish this concept and the mechanisms that make it
work. In the rest of the chapter, we'll examine some of the different patterns
that the POA can use to connect object reference to servant and see which ones
work best in a number of common programming situations. This chapter lays
the groundwork for our presentation of CCM: The CCM Container is a specialized POA that implements four of the most common resource usage patterns
using highly optimized vendor code.

III.1.1   Introduction

The second wall of the foundation for the CCM is the Portable Object Adapter or POA (the first was the **valuetype**). As we'll see in this chapter, CORBA keeps your application architecture manageable by deliberately keeping the client side simple, but that means that all of the features for scalability and robustness live on the server side—the side that we're about to discuss. The CCM adds programmer convenience to the model by packaging a number of things—transaction and event handling, persistence, security, and server-side resource control—into a *container*. But what's a container? It's a specialized POA, and that's why we need to understand the POA first, and well.

If you're already a CORBA programmer, or if you've read the first edition of *CORBA Fundamentals and Programming*, you're already familiar with the Basic Object Adapter or (BOA). This construct, OMG's first server-side architecture, was a good start, but neither robust enough nor precisely enough described to serve in today's complex applications. In mid-1995, OMG members issued the Portable Server RFP, and two years later adopted the POA specification. The original impetus for the RFP was programmers' complaints (quite justified) that the BOA interfaces were not written precisely enough to allow server code to port from one vendor's ORB to another's; thus the name Portable Object Adapter (POA) for the overall standard. However, while the submitters were drawing up their specification, Internet computing outgrew its training wheels and entered the mainstream, and interactive networking replaced batch jobs in serious enterprise computing. With this in mind, the submitters added many scalability features to their specification, finally coming up with the POA that we present here. Mind you, we're not criticizing the authors of the BOA specification: At the time it was written, it was the only structure of its kind and represented a major advance over any other standard architecture. In the early 1990s when it was first described and implemented, networks did not support the traffic volumes or speeds that we have today, and few people had even conceived of applications needing to respond to the hit rates that today's servers handle with aplomb.

The POA specification deprecates the BOA; that is, it replaces that part of the specification, and requires future products to provide POA support in order to claim compliance. (Products can continue to offer BOA support alongside, so you won't have to recode your applications all at once. Even so, we'd recommend that you upgrade and recode as soon as you can since the POA architecture is so much better than the BOA.) Compliant implementations of the POA started coming to market in late 1999; by the time this book reached stores in early 2001 POA ORBs from almost every vendor were well-established.

III.1.2   The CORBA Server-Side Computing Model

Even though Figure III.1.1 shows the POA as a simple blob with no internal structure, you can tell from the figure that the server side of the ORB is more complicated than the client side. In this section, we'll introduce the server-side CORBA computing model; the rest of the chapter will fill in the details.

To get started, let's consider two very different CORBA object types: One is an iterator object, created by another object during an invocation to provide access—presumably for only a short while—to a list of results that was too big to return in a single argument. The other is a customer object in our e-commerce database.

Although each of these is a CORBA object with its own unique object reference, their lifespans are very different: The iterator will spew out its list of results in a few calls and then be destroyed; neither the object nor its reference will work again after this. Because of its brief lifetime, the iterator

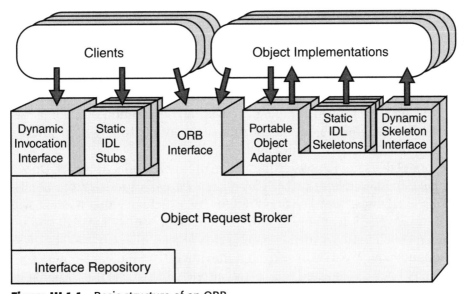

Figure III.1.1   Basic structure of an ORB.

object can keep its state in memory for the brief duration between calls; it does not need to use a persistent store. But we hope our customers will keep coming back to buy more at our electronic emporium, and so the customer objects that represent them in our system are expected to live forever. To support this, the persistent data that comprise their state are enshrined in our best database. As long as we remain in business, all of our customer objects remain active and their references remain valid, each object instance representing the same customer whose data are stored in the same row in our database. (In EJB, this object would be programmed as an Entity Bean.)

These are quite different object-use patterns, and there are others besides. A shopping cart, for example, has a lifetime intermediate between our ephemeral iterator and robust customer objects, as we'll see in Section III.3.2. To enable scalable applications, the POA supports a range of object lifetimes and activation patterns, as we'll see shortly. Before we do, however, let's consider a problem specific to object types with medium to long lifetimes.

CORBA intentionally keeps the client-side programming model simple. As we mentioned in the previous chapter, *no* object activation or deactivation operations are visible to it; from the client's point of view, *a CORBA object starts running as soon as it (and its object reference) are created, and the object runs constantly, always ready and waiting for invocations and maintaining its state, until it is irrevocably destroyed.*

This model is great for the client: Its only interface to CORBA is the IDL for the object it invokes. When it wants to make an invocation, it just goes ahead and does it. When it doesn't, it doesn't. If it wants, a client can hold on to an object reference (or the name of an object in the Naming Service) for years without invoking it. Then, whenever it wants, it can just send an invocation and expect that the answer will come back. (That is, unless the object has been destroyed. Unlike deactivation, destruction of an object is irrevocable—once an object has been destroyed, it's totally gone and its object reference will never work again.)

The model does not look as attractive on the server side, however. Do we really have to keep all of our CORBA objects active, or at least the persistent long-lived ones, so we're prepared for the off-chance that a client will send us an invocation at some random time? Suppose we have 10 million customers, each with his own shopping cart object, but only 2000 of them are shopping now. We'd be overjoyed if the other 9+ million customers suddenly came back and started to shop all at once, but this is pretty unlikely, and we don't have enough computing power to run all 10 million carts at once anyhow. What can we do?

CORBA, and specifically the POA, deals with this situation by distinguishing the concept of CORBA *object*—the client's concept of an object that runs continuously from creation to destruction—from the concept of POA *servant*: a piece of running code that services an invocation. In the POA model, object references are mapped to running code dynamically when needed—sometimes only when an invocation comes in, although there are other patterns as well (and we'll describe the common ones later in this chapter). When the invocation is complete, the resources are freed and become available for whatever the ORB needs to do next. What's true is that the object is always *available*; what's not true is that it's always *running*.

This differentiation is necessary for scalability: the ability of an ORB to service millions of clients, using a reasonable number of computers. However, we've found that this concept is confusing or disconcerting to many when they hear about it for the first time. In the next section, we'll tell a short story to illustrate, by analogy, the difference between object and servant, and demonstrate that it's perfectly possible for the client to cling to its concept of "CORBA object running all the time, waiting for me to invoke" while the server allocates a servant for it only when an invocation needs to be serviced. If you're comfortable with this concept already, you can skip ahead to the following section. If you're still a little hazy, read on here.

III.1.2.1 Santa Claus Is a CORBA Object

Until just a few years ago, my younger son (who is now 13) believed in Santa Claus. Santa Claus is a fat and jolly old man who wears a red coat and pants trimmed with white fur, and travels in a sleigh pulled by eight or nine reindeer (depending on the weather), delivering toys to children around the world by jumping down their chimneys and putting the toys into stockings hanging from the mantel. For a few days after Christmas, Santa recovers from this effort by soaking his feet in a hot bathtub and drinking hot chocolate; he spends the rest of the year making lists and collecting toys for the next Christmas. (This is the North American view of Santa Claus and the one we'll use in this story; if you're reading this book in another country with another view, please adopt our version for the sake of the analogy. We know that in Finland, for example, Father Christmas walks through the front door and hands presents directly to the children. If Father Christmas is also a CORBA object, his encapsulation boundary is very different from the one we're about to describe for the North American Santa Claus!)

The Santa Claus CORBA object that my son believes in supports a single interface with a single, well-defined operation **GetPresents**. Here is the invocation:

- Wait until December 24, in the evening. Otherwise, the invocation fails and returns the **WrongNight** exception.
- Find a stocking, preferably a very large one with your name on it, and hang it from the mantel above the fireplace.
- Fill a glass with milk, and set it on the hearth beneath the stocking.
- Cover a small plate with cookies and set it next to the glass of milk.
- Optionally, put a note requesting specific toys next to the milk and cookies. (The milk, cookies, and note are the input parameters.)
- Go upstairs to bed, and go to sleep.

Going to sleep is very important, since it defines the *encapsulation boundary*. Clients are not allowed to peek beyond this boundary: The interface is defined on it, and once the invocation has been delivered to it, the invocation is in the realm of the implementation. In object orientation, one reason for encapsulation is to enable substitutable implementations. Fortunately, encapsulation also enables scalability, as we'll see shortly. For the Santa Claus object, encapsulation is the only thing that enables the invocation to work at all.

But this invocation is not going to work if we rely on the client's concept of CORBA Santa to fulfill it. However, if we use the POA concept of servant—that is, some resource that gets activated and configured when needed, services a single invocation, and then is released—things can work out well. Parents around the world will appreciate this next concept: In this story, my wife and I are servants (okay, at least in the POA sense!). Here's how the **GetPresents** invocation is serviced at our house:

- After son completes invocation, including going upstairs to bed, Mom and Dad stay up and wrap various presents until we are sure that encapsulation requirements have been met.
- Mom fetches bag with various small gifts, and commences stashing them in stocking. New England tradition requires an orange in the toe, and family tradition requires a stuffed animal reaching out from the top, even though Dad thinks son is much too old for this.
- Dad takes the glass of milk, pours it back into the bottle, fills the glass up with eggnog and rum, grates fresh nutmeg on the top, and drinks it down.
- While drinking the eggnog, Dad may eat a cookie or two. Most of the cookies get put back into the box. Part of one is crumbled on the plate, which remains on the hearth.

- Dad rinses the glass with milk to cover up the smell of the eggnog and rum, and places it back on the hearth next to the plate of cookie crumbs.

- Dad helps Mom put the last of the toys into the stocking and hangs it back up on the mantle.

- Dad and Mom clean up their mess and go to sleep.

In the morning, son awakens and runs downstairs. Seeing the stocking full of toys and the empty glass and plate, he exclaims, "Wow, look at all the toys. Santa Claus must be real—he left all these toys, and drank the milk and ate the cookies!" And, from his point of view, this is true: The CORBA object accepted the input parameters (milk, cookies, optional note), and delivered the expected return value (toys).

Let's go over the CORBA lessons from this story:

- Client and server can have totally different viewpoints of the object implementation, but as long as invocations get serviced according to the agreed-upon definition of the operation, this inconsistency does not matter.

- In the story, Son thinks that Santa is real and always exists, as we described at the start. In reality, the Santa Claus servant comes into being only for a few minutes a year on Christmas Eve when it's needed.

- In CORBA, the client holds an object reference and acts as if the object always exists, making an invocation any time it wants and assuming that the object will maintain its state from one invocation to the next regardless of the time that elapses between invocations. In reality, in POA-based systems, computing resources may not be allocated for an object until an invocation comes in, and may be freed as soon as the invocation has completed. State is maintained on persistent storage between invocations, loaded on activation, and stored again with any changes on completion.

- There is a lesson here on scalability as well: The story about the jolly fat guy in the red suit may be charming, but as an implementation architecture, it just doesn't scale. Too many kids need presents on the same night for any one person to distribute them all, especially a fat old man who obviously doesn't keep in shape during his off-season, and the year between Christmases is too long for such a scarce resource to sit around unused even if he is out of shape. The POA implementation, however, does not have either of these problems:

Every household (well, almost) has a resource that can play the role of Santa Servant on one night a year, so there's no problem scaling to any number of households. And, the resource is flexible enough to play other servant roles during the rest of the year, whenever the household POA requires it.

The object-oriented principle that enables this is *encapsulation*: The implementation is encapsulated beneath a boundary that the client is not allowed to penetrate. Until now, we have only suggested that implementation details such as algorithm and coding reside on the far side of this boundary and may change unbeknownst to the client. Now we are adding that resource allocation efforts—some of them massive, supporting a huge enterprise application or a worldwide e-commerce shopping site—may also exist beneath this boundary.

Here's one more example of a difference between client and servant points of view: When a new object—for example, a new shopping cart or bank-account object for a first-time customer—is created, the client receives a new object reference and has the impression that the object "exists." However, on the implementation side, *no servant was activated for the object, and no resource was allocated for execution*, when the object reference was created (at least for the allocation patterns used in large, scalable applications). No servant will be allocated until the client uses the object reference in an invocation. You can "create" a new shopping cart object for every customer who browses your Web site, allowing each client to invoke "add to shopping cart" without any setup, without consuming any resource in your server, including storage, since your POA and implementation can be configured to postpone setup until the first invocation on each reference. You can even allocate account numbers at creation. We'll see later how they can be stored without consuming resources in your system. (Actually, they will be stored inside the object reference, but invisible to the client. We'll give details shortly, in Section III.1.3.1.)

III.1.3   What Is a POA and How Is It Used?

A short definition of an object adapter is:

> An object adapter is the mechanism that connects a request using an object reference with the proper code to service that request.

The POA is a particular type of object adapter specified by OMG to achieve the maximum amount of portability among ORBs that have widely differing design points.

III.1.3.1   Three-Part POA Definition

Let's analyze the three important pieces of the definition and apply them to the POA. They are:

- The object reference
- A mechanism that connects a request
- Code to service the request

It's worth anticipating the "mechanism" part of the discussion a bit. You should be aware that there isn't necessarily just one POA in a server. We'll talk about "the POA," but we really mean "the concept of the POA specified by the OMG of which there may be several instances with different characteristics." Yes, by golly, the POA itself is an object, albeit a strictly local object used only in a single server. A server programmer may create several POAs in a server, each of which helps the programmer implement objects. We'll see more details later, but for now you can think of a POA as being part of the implementation of your object, and that not all objects use the same POA.

With that introduction, let's look at the pieces of the definition.

III.1.3.1.1   *Object Reference*

An object reference is the center of all CORBA usage. It is the only means by which a client can do something with an object. We'll discuss it (again) in some detail because it is the basic concept around which all of CORBA (including the POA) is organized, and its meaning is very specific when considered by the POA.

While "object reference" is the generic term, we'll often talk about an "Interoperable Object Reference," or IOR, meaning an object reference that is understood by ORBs that can interoperate using the OMG defined protocols GIOP and IIOP (You'll have to check another reference, such as *CORBA 3 Fundamentals and Programming*, for a discussion of CORBA interoperability). Most importantly, ORBs that are written by different people can understand an IOR, which is one of the strengths of CORBA. We'll use the term "IOR" when we want to emphasize interoperability, and "object reference" otherwise. Most vendors provide object references that are indeed IORs.

Where does an object reference come from? In a POA-based ORB, an object reference can be created only in server code that is using a POA (except for the basic object references that clients are now allowed to create using `corbaloc` and `corbaname`, as we showed in Part I, Chapter 3). It is important to remember that object reference creation is server related rather than client related. Once created by a server, an object reference can be passed outside the server and can travel to any number of clients, any of which can then issue a request on it, but that's all clients can do with it.

An object reference can come only from server code because *the act of creating and giving out the reference promises the recipient of the reference that some server, somewhere, is willing to service invocations on the object represented by the reference.* The server code that creates the object reference puts information in the reference that reminds the server of what it promised.

So, what is an object reference? One thing it is not is something a client can manipulate directly or see into. It is opaque to clients. Only ORBs can manipulate it. The information in an object reference is meaningless to the client and is vital to the encapsulation, location transparency, and implementation independence of CORBA.

When a client makes a request using the object reference, the client's ORB extracts pieces from the reference and returns them to the server. Since the reference is the means by which a request is sent to the server (returned to the server from whence it came), the server (and the POA) must have created the object reference with enough information to tell the client-side ORB how to get back to the server code. So, logically (meaning we're skipping a lot of details), an object reference contains at least three pieces of information: an address for the benefit of the ORBs and two pieces that are important for a server programmer. The three pieces are:

- Something like an address
- The name of the POA that created the object reference
- An Object ID

Since a client can't see any of these pieces, they are meaningful only to the client ORB, the server ORB, and the programmer-written server code.

- *Something like an address* is necessary so that the client ORB can find the right computer to which to send the request. The "something like" weasel words cover up a lot of trickery that sophisticated ORBs provide in order to achieve proper routing, failover, load balancing, and other features that are administrative in nature and that neither client nor server code need be aware of. Programmers can feel confident that requests will eventually make their way to an appropriate machine.

- *The name of the POA* that created the object reference is the first concrete piece of information about the POA that we've run into. Server-side programmer code must create a POA (with particular characteristics) and specify a name for it before that programmer code can request the POA to create an object reference. The POA name uniquely identifies the POA (and its characteristics) to a particular computer when requests are returned to it. That computer may have several servers (processors). A server that contains a POA with the given name is the server that will service the request. A request for service will always be routed back to a POA with the same name as the POA that created the object reference. The important point is that every object implementation belongs to a POA, and the POA name is part of the identification of the code that services requests. The server programmer typically creates a named POA with the same characteristics each time it is created. This means that the POA that created an object reference has the same characteristics as the POA that will service invocations on the object.

So far, two of the three pieces of information in an object reference have gotten us to a particular computer node, to a particular server, and to a unique POA within that server. Up to this point, all the processing of a request has taken place through the "routing" function of the ORB. For example, if we have an object reference called "objref" and we invoke its "doit" operation, we might see the routing path shown in Figure III.1.2 to arrive at the POA called "POA-X."

None of the routing involves programmer-written code. It is performed entirely by the infrastructure of a CORBA vendor's system (part of it even across vendors). Routing is the "Broker" part of an Object Request Broker: Its purpose is to find the right code to execute. The quality of the routing function is one of the primary determiners of the efficiency and scalability of a CORBA system, and one of the differentiators among CORBA vendors.

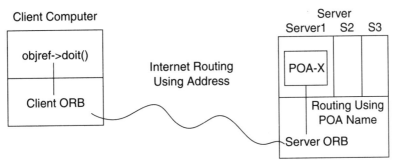

Figure III.1.2   Routing as client invokes the "doit" operation on a servant on POA-X.

- The *Object Id* was assigned when the object reference was created. After a request is routed to the POA, the Object Id may be used for two purposes: even more routing, and object identification. The further routing occurs when the POA connects the request to the right piece of code that implements the object; that is, to a servant. (Remember the Santa Claus analogy from Section III.1.2.1? We'll discuss servant in more detail later.) "Making the connection" is the third of the three pieces of the POA definition and we'll discuss it in detail later, too.

Once the servant has control, it typically (but not always) uses the Object Id for its second purpose: identification of the instance of the object. For example, the creating server may have set the Object Id to the key for a database containing the permanent state of the object. In this case, the servant receiving the request now uses that Object Id to access the permanent state.

To complete the routing picture shown in Figure III.1.2 with the last piece of object reference information, we might show the logical contents of POA-X as seen in Figure III.1.3.

Actually, this figure shows only one possible configuration for a POA and servants, but it illustrates the point. A POA is responsible for passing control for the request to the method of a servant that is prepared to handle the interface to an Object with a particular Object Id.

III.1.3.1.2 *Code to Service the Request*

In the discussion about the object reference, we've already had to start talking about servants. A servant is code written by a programmer, specifically by the server programmer, that contains the business logic of an object. All of the ORB, POA, and routing are merely administrative constructs to get a request from a client to the correct servant.

More precisely, a servant contains the methods for a CORBA object—where a method is defined in CORBA as the programming language code that implements an operation defined in an IDL interface. In OO languages

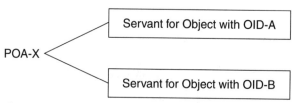

Figure III.1.3 Logical contents of POA-X.

such as C++ and Java, a servant is an instance of a class, which is a declarational entity in those languages. Creating a servant in these languages requires knowing the declaration for the class and then using the language function `new` on the class name. Since a servant implements the operations of an IDL interface, it contains computational language entities in its class corresponding to operations on the IDL interface. The computational entity for Java is called a *class method*, and for C++ it's called a *member function*. (Unfortunately, there isn't a single terminology for all of OO. As another example of terminology confusion, OMG's concept of object is not the same as C++ and Java. Objects in those languages are instances of the language class, strictly local and temporary in nature, while OMG's object is location-transparent and potentially persistent.)

For other languages, a servant might be a set of structures, pointers, and subroutines that are organized to achieve essentially the same effect. In all cases, control is transferred to code using some initialized data. For the rest of this discussion, we'll use the C++ and Java terminologies rather than that of procedural languages, but the techniques are essentially the same.

To understand servants a little better, let's review all of what an IDL interface corresponds to in, for example, the C++ language mapping. An IDL compiler first generates a definition file that is used by the client for invocations and by both client and server for access to the data types defined in the interface. Directly corresponding to that definition file, the IDL compiler also generates a stub, C++ code that intercepts object invocations on that interface and delivers them to the ORB. Programmers don't deal with stubs except to compile and include them in the client binary.

Getting closer to the servant, the IDL compiler next generates a skeleton, also called the servant base class—a class declaration and code that contains interface-specific details for runtime use on the server. A server programmer uses the servant base class in two ways: First, the servant base class code is compiled and linked into the server executable binary; like stubs, the programmer doesn't look at or modify this code. Then, after the IDL compiler has provided the servant base class declaration, the programmer codes the servant class, inheriting all the methods required for the object from the servant base class declaration and providing the code for them.

Figure III.1.4 diagrams the relationship among IDL interfaces, CORBA Object, servants, and the servant base class. This diagram is not UML—it shows what files and classes are generated by the IDL compiler and the inheritance relationships of those classes.

A new class and a couple of new methods appear in Figure III.1.4. `ServantBase` is a class definition and code provided by an ORB vendor; it

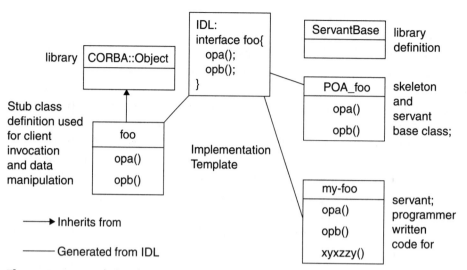

Figure III.1.4 Relationships among IDL interfaces, the CORBA Object, servants, and the servant base class.

serves as the base class for all servants. Since the ORB vendor provides this code, it can have secrets in helping the ORB vendor deal with servants in general. (Note: We're skipping over some programmer-visible details in the definition of ServantBase that might be useful for advanced users.)

POA_foo is the name of the compiler-generated servant base class (aka skeleton); it contains specific, secret information about the **foo** interface, as well as the declaration of the operations of the foo interface for use by the servant inheriting from it. POA_foo inherits from ServantBase, and the real servant inherits from POA_foo.

Finally, my_foo is the programmer-selected name of the class for the real servant. The programmer must provide the code for all the **interface foo** operations (whose definitions are inherited from POA_foo) and may contain other useful, internal code as defined by the programmer, indicated here by xyxzzy.

In summary, a servant is an instance of a programming language class that contains at least the methods for an IDL interface. The IDL compiler cannot provide the business logic for the servant but does provide the superstructure: a servant base class declaration (the skeleton). Many products also provide an example servant class declaration and an outline to be filled in with business logic, but that's only a convenience, saving a little typing.

At run time, the class definition of a servant is made into an instance of a servant (something that can be executed) by the programming language new function.

After an instance of a servant is created, the programmer must communicate its existence to a POA so that the POA can route requests to it. That takes us to the last part of our POA definition.

III.1.3.1.3   A Mechanism That Connects

Finally, we arrive at the interesting part of the POA: How does it connect a request to a servant?

The first fact about POAs worth noting is that a POA is an object. It is created, has an object reference, is invoked and is destroyed like other objects, with the only difference being that a POA is locality-constrained. That means that the POA object reference makes sense only to the ORB on the server on which the POA was created. You can't pass a POA reference to any other computer because its entire job in life is to deal with servants and requests on a particular computer; it deals with addresses, entities meaningful only within a single process.

The first thing we can deduce from what we've already discussed is that a POA doesn't just connect the request to a servant and then get out of the way. A POA is part of the implementation of an object. That is, the implementation of an object is the combination of a POA and a servant.

This statement makes more sense when we consider again that there isn't just a single object called a POA like there is a single object called the ORB. We've already seen that a request is routed to one of many possible POAs, one with a particular identity (a name). The reason for a POA having a name is that when a server creates a POA, it assigns not only a name, but also some characteristics; that is, a POA is a stateful object. The routing function of the ORB goes to a lot of trouble to deliver a request to the correct POA because that POA has the characteristics necessary for the correct implementation of an interface, such as the ability to handle transactions. In addition, in servicing a request, a servant might need to create an object reference. A servant can't do this by itself; it must ask its POA to do it because an object reference is complex and has information meaningful only to ORBs and POAs. The way in which the POA creates the right kind of object reference depends on characteristics of the POA.

For this and many other reasons, the characteristics assigned to the POA at its creation time are vital to the implementation of an object. These creation-time characteristics are called the policies of the POA. Once a POA is created, its policies are immutable. The policies govern how the POA operates. For example, POA policies control:

- What kind of object references it creates (among other things, what kind of routing is done, and how long the object and object reference might exist)

- How an Object Id is assigned and used
- Whether the object is allowed to take part in transactions
- How the POA deals with servants. (Must they be created and registered with the POA before the POA starts processing requests, or can they be created and destroyed dynamically, in one or more ways?)

In addition to policies that are assigned at POA creation, a POA has dynamically specifiable, optional behaviors that are largely administrative in nature. Finally, there are some POA features that are totally independent of a POA's role in implementations and are available primarily for convenience.

Some POA policies and optional behaviors are defined for situations that only a very small number of servers in the world will ever want to deal with. We won't discuss every possibility; a few of them could take a page of discussion to set the context for the two alternatives it offers. When you get to the point that you can imagine an option, check your manual; it might already be there.

III.1.3.2   POA Usage Patterns

We will cover most of the important aspects of the POA by considering the most common patterns of usage. After you've seen one example of code for each of these, you can probably just keep re-using it as a template. You will probably keep a set of about four or five such templates and paste them into new applications. The default POA (available without worrying about options) is quite useful too.

The most important of the POA characteristics are the policies controlling how POAs interact with servants. While there are slight variations on the theme, there are about five patterns concerning POAs and servants. These relate to the way the POA associates a servant with an Object Id so that the POA can dispatch control to the servant to service the request. These patterns are:

- Explicit object activation
- Single servant for all objects (with two variations)
- On-demand activation for the duration of a single method
- On-demand activation, indefinite duration

The last four patterns (including the two variations on single servant) are mutually exclusive. The first (explicit object activation) can be used by itself or combined with most of the others. We'll discuss each individually.

III.1.3.2.1 *Explicit Object Activation*

Explicitly activating an object means that programmer code creates a servant and tells the POA to use that servant whenever it sees a particular Object Id. The phrase *activating an object* comes from the name of the POA operations to do so: `activate_object` and `activate_object_with_id`. Programmer code can tell the POA to stop the association of a servant and an Object Id at any time by using the `deactivate_object` operation.

The two options for `activate_object` exist for alternate methods of assigning an Object Id. Most often, a programmer wants to specify the Object Id, but other times doesn't care about it. For example, the programmer might use a database key as the Object Id, to represent an object with a long lifetime. Whenever the request comes into a servant, the programmer looks at the Object Id and accesses that database record. The Object Id has meaning in this case. On the other hand, sometimes an object exists only a short time (say, for the duration of a session) and has no long-term meaning. In that case, the programmer doesn't care what the Object Id is, and lets the system assign it. This works because the object is unique and is identified by the system-assigned unique number (which has no other meaning than to cause a request to return to a particular servant). This choice is expressed by the POA policy called IdAssignmentPolicy. It has values USER_ID and SYSTEM_ID. No matter which of the patterns are used, the programmer has the choice of assigning Object Id in this fashion.

The advantage of activating an object explicitly is that the servant is always ready to service a request on the object. An object that is already activated gives the fastest response time to a request because the POA can quickly find the servant and dispatch to it (by looking up the Object Id in an internal table called the *Active Object Map*). The disadvantage of having continuously active objects is resource usage: An active object is a *stateful* object. (The terms *stateless* and *stateful* refer to *in-memory* state—that is, whether or not a servant has to maintain state in active memory from call to call. These terms do not refer to maintenance of state on a persistent storage device or in a database.) Since the servant always exists and has the state of the object in memory, it uses more memory than the other techniques that dynamically create a servant and activate an object only when needed. When there are more active objects, more memory is used, causing memory contention and reducing overall throughput.

A server main program might activate several objects when the process is started and then turn control over to the ORB. Explicit activation is typically used when the server has a predetermined set of objects (although the server may later deactivate such objects before server shutdown). Such a technique might be very useful for access to very frequently accessed objects in a stable environment, where speed of access is the primary consideration.

Rather than a main program pre-activating many objects, a servant servicing a request on one object can explicitly activate another object so that the POA will be prepared to service the other object after this method completes. A method on the active object (or any other) might later deactivate the object. Explicitly activating and deactivating objects like this allows very strong programmer control over resource utilization decisions.

The technique of explicitly activating objects under control of another object is particularly well suited for temporary objects; that is, objects that are created and destroyed in a short period of time, such as an iterator. During its lifetime, the object is stateful, but it is destroyed very quickly and has no permanent state or existence. This idea of a temporary object is further supported by the POA LifeSpanPolicy, which tells the POA to create an object reference taking into account the expected lifetime of the object and the object reference. A LifeSpanPolicy value of TRANSIENT tells the POA that any objects created have meaning only in the process in which they were created. When the process goes away, the object goes away, and the object reference is no longer valid, even if a client still holds it. An advantage of TRANSIENT is that the routing information in the object reference can be very limited. Only one process on one machine can service requests on the object reference. The routing function need make no decisions nor try to load balance or deal with failure. If the process still lives, the request can be served; if the process terminates, the request fails with no further attempts at finding an alternate server. A LifeSpanPolicy of PERSISTENT, on the other hand, means that the object is expected to be long-lived, certainly beyond the lifetime of the process creating it. The object reference must then contain more generalized routing information so the routing function has more latitude in finding an appropriate server. The LifeSpanPolicy of TRANSIENT is used almost exclusively with Explicit Activation. (I can't think of any other reasonable usage. That's a dare.)

If a POA was created with a RequestProcessingPolicy of USE_ACTIVE_OBJECT_MAP_ONLY, the only way that POA can deal with servants is through this explicit object activation technique. It is more likely that a server will use a mixture of explicit object activation and of the POA-controlled, dynamic servant finding defined later. In the case of such a mixture, the POA checks its active objects first to see if there is a servant already dealing with the Object ID; if not, the POA performs its other servant finding techniques.

Example of Explicit Object Activation

How hard is it to use a POA pattern? Well, "explicit object activation" is the easiest, but it's still instructive to see how regular the pattern is.

The default (root) POA uses only the explicit activation pattern with a LifeSpanPolicy value of TRANSIENT and an IdAssignmentPolicy with value SYSTEM_ID. If these options are suitable for your application, you don't have to create a POA. You obtain the `rootPOA` from the ORB and start using it immediately, activating objects, creating references, and preparing your process to service requests. For example, in C++, you can get an ORB reference and a reference to the root POA with these three declarations and three lines of code:

```
CORBA::ORB_ptr            orb_ptr;
CORBA::Object_ptr         obj;
PortableServer::POA_ptr   rootPOA;

orb_ptr = CORBA::ORB_init(argc, argv, "");
obj = orb_ptr->resolve_initial_references("RootPOA");
rootPOA = PortableServer::POA::_narrow(obj);
```

The first three statements declare data types. The first active statement retrieves a pointer to the ORB. The second asks the ORB for a reference to the root POA, and the third narrows the returned reference to be type—specifically a POA. Now you've got a POA.

Let's say you want to provide a server for an object with **interface Foo**. You must activate the object; that is, tell the POA to get ready to service requests made on that object reference. To do that, you first need code to service requests—a servant. Let's say you have created such a class, `FooServantClass`, for this purpose. The next code might then be:

```
FooServantClass* foo_servant = new FooServantClass();
Foo_var foo_ref = foo_servant->_this();
```

The first statement creates a servant (an instance of `FooServantClass`), and the second tells the POA to activate it, using an Object Id assigned by the POA, and then to create an object reference for it and return it. You can now hand out that object reference (`foo_ref`) to clients, perhaps through a naming service.

The POA and ORB are now almost ready to start servicing requests for that object. We start the server proper by performing two administrative functions first:

```
rootPOA->the_manager()->activate();
orb_ptr->run();
```

The first line tells the POA that it's been properly initialized and it's okay to service requests. The second tells the ORB that it now has control of the process so it can process the requests.

That wasn't so bad, was it? Only seven lines of code in all. You'll get used to just pasting this into your programs. Only the name of the interface and servant class will change in each usage. The other patterns described next require a few more lines of code, but they're just as regular.

III.1.3.2.2   *Single Servant for All Objects*

(We ignore for now the possibility that a server has explicitly activated an object. That possibility affects only one part of the POA as we've already described it.) If the POA was created with a RequestProcessing policy of USE_DEFAULT_SERVANT, the POA will dispatch control to a single servant that has been registered with it. To perform this registration, the programmer first creates a servant (using the `new` language function) and then calls the `set_servant` operation on the POA, passing the servant. This means that there is a single servant always ready to receive requests directed to the POA. Such a servant may or may not be stateful, but there is only one such servant for the entire POA, and its state is likely to be small.

The servant so registered can handle a multitude of objects, in one of two ways: servicing a single interface type in a stateless object fashion, or servicing many different interfaces in an extremely general fashion defined only by the server programmer. Which of these two cases applies depends on what kind of object references the programmer creates with the POA, and what kind of servant is registered with the POA. The latter requires more work.

Single Servant for All Objects of the Same Type

For the first case, if each `create_reference` operation invoked on this POA is for the same interface, it makes perfect sense for all invocations on this POA to be directed to the methods of a single servant. (It makes sense since every request is directed toward a servant designed to handle that interface.) That single servant can be written to service requests for any number of objects using that interface. Since each object reference created can have a different Object Id, this POA/servant combination can service an arbitrarily large number of objects, one object and one method at a time. While the servant itself exists between method invocations, it probably takes few resources. For each request that arrives, each of the servant's methods will find the request's Object Id, use it to read the object's state from permanent storage, perform the business logic on the state, and save the object's state at the end of the method invocation. This technique for POA/servant is very powerful and is explicitly designed for rapid access to stateless objects—that is, the servant is created only once; invoking it is quite cheap, and the state for the object uses memory only for the duration of a single method.

Single Servant for All Objects of Different Types

The second way of using the single servant for all objects technique is for the single servant to handle any of a variety of interfaces. For this to work, the servant must be a special kind of servant, a `DynamicImplementation` servant. (In particular, the servant must inherit from the class of that name, rather than directly from `ServantBase`.) This is the CORBA notion of DSI (Dynamic Skeleton Interface, the server-side analog of the DII that we discussed, however briefly, in *CORBA 3 Fundamentals and Programming*). When the POA dispatches control to this single servant, it obviously can't call the object's interface method directly since the only servant provided is going to handle multiple interfaces, each with potentially many methods. Instead, the POA invokes the DSI servant using a generic method and passes it an object that describes the request (the `ServantRequest` pseudo-object). It is then the job of the DSI servant to take apart the `ServantRequest`, figure out what interface and method the request is intended for, do some internal processing to create a "second level" servant (for the target interface), and then invoke a method on that servant. If this sounds complicated, it is. This is a technique for use only by advanced programmers who seek the last ounce of resource usage. Actually, it remains to be seen if the DSI servant (originally defined in CORBA 2.0 as a resource optimization technique for use with the BOA) can yield better performance than the dynamically created servants defined in CORBA 2.2 for use with the POA.

III.1.3.2.3 *On-Demand Activation for Duration of a Single Method*

Stateless objects have no in-memory existence (state) except when a method is actively servicing the object. Since a servant is the keeper of in-memory object state, even the servant does not exist at the beginning of server processing. When a request arrives, the POA must cause object activation to occur. This is completely different from the Explicit Activation technique, because the POA (not the programmer) is in control at the time when the object must be activated. The POA itself cannot create a servant out of thin air because it doesn't know what servant to activate. Thus, the POA needs the help of programmer code to create a servant and initialize the state for an object before the POA can invoke the method for the request.

Activating an object on demand requires that the server programmer configure the POA with a "callback" object reference that the POA can invoke in order to create a servant. The callback is the entry to programmer written code, since only the programmer knows how to create the servant for a particular interface (and, perhaps, for a particular Object Id).

Configuring the POA for on-demand activation requires the server programmer to do the following:

- At run time (probably in the main program for the server), the server creates a POA with two particular policy values. The first is a Request-ProcessingPolicy value of USE_SERVANT_MANAGER, meaning that the POA should invoke a ServantManager object to ask the programmer-written code to create, initialize, and return a servant. The second is a ServerRetentionPolicy value of NON_RETAIN, meaning that any servant created on demand is to be discarded after the method invocation completes (remember, the goal is statelessness). Since the ServerRetentionPolicy is NON_RETAIN, the particular kind of `Servant-Manager` that the POA will invoke will be called a `ServantLocator`.

- The server programmer codes the `ServantLocator`. A `ServantLocator` has two operations, `preinvoke` and `postinvoke`. The server programmer codes `preinvoke` to create a servant by deciding what kind of servant is needed (possibly querying the Object ID), using the new command to bring an instance of that servant into existence, and initializing the state needed for the object. The `postinvoke` operation of the `ServantLocator` cleans up any state, perhaps writing it to permanent storage, and then most likely destroys the servant.

- At run time (probably in the main program), the server programmer creates an instance of this `ServantLocator` and an object reference to it.

- A weird twist in creating the `ServantManager` callback object is that it is a real object so it has to be registered with a POA. This sounds a little strange at first, but it's really a mechanical procedure that, seen once, can just be copied into your own program. The root POA is designed with policies that are ideal for implementing `ServantManager` callback objects.

- The server programmer invokes `POA::set_servant_manager`, passing the `ServantLocator` object reference. This tells the POA how to get at the callback.

After the server programmer provides this setup and turns control over to the ORB, the ORB waits for requests. When it receives a request for a particular POA, the ORB passes control to that POA. If the POA doesn't already have an appropriate servant, the POA uses the `ServantLocator` callback to invoke the `ServantLocator::preinvoke` operation (that is, the programmer code), asking it to create a servant, initialize the object in memory, and return the servant. Upon return, the POA invokes the appropriate method on that servant. After return from the method, the POA invokes the callback's `ServantLocator::postinvoke` operation to let the programmer code clean up any state and destroy the servant.

III.1.3.2.4 On-Demand Activation, Indefinite Duration

This pattern is very similar in structure to "on-demand activation for duration of a single method," although it is intended for objects that are stateful over some period. The similarities are that the POA starts out without a servant for objects, and when a request comes in, the POA uses a callback to create a servant (as for the "… single method").

The difference is that, after calling the method on the object, the POA keeps the object activated instead of deactivating it immediately. The object thus remains activated until (most likely) programmer code deactivates it (using `POA::deactivate_object`), or the POA itself is shut down. If the POA is shutting down, all its constituents are also shut down in a graceful manner, resulting in the POA deactivating the objects that were activated on demand by invoking the callback object to do so (this is similar to the automatic deactivation for stateless, differing only in timing).

When a request for an active object arrives, the POA can find the servant for it and invoke the method on the servant directly, without having to create a new servant. Being active continuously has resource and responsiveness implications (it uses more resources, but responds faster). This statefulness is useful when the decreased response time is needed, or when the object takes part in a transaction that requires statefulness across multiple method invocations.

"On-demand activation, indefinite duration" differs from "explicit object activation" by not activating the object until it is needed. Even after this on-demand activation, the object can be deactivated and then activated on demand again later. Thus, the overall resource use may be lower because the object is active only while needed, while in Explicit Activation, the object is usually active all the time (subject to the discussion in that section).

As stated earlier, the basic programming structure of "on-demand activation, indefinite duration" is similar to stateless, with only two differences in the details:

- The POA is created with a different ServerRetentionPolicy value, RETAIN.

- The type of `ServantManager` used is a `ServantActivator`, and its two operations are `incarnate` (to create the servant and initialize state) and `etherealize` (to deactivate the object).

III.1.3.3   Code Wrappers and the POA

Given these patterns, how would you use the POA to write wrappers for existing applications, for code that was written before CORBA? (These are sometimes called *legacy applications*, but they're much more than "old-fashioned," which is what legacy often implies. They're usually applications that are vital to an enterprise and are not likely to be rewritten just to take advantage of a different technology. They're not broken and they don't need to be fixed. They just need to be used differently.) Maddeningly, as with most things, the answer is, "it depends." Each of the patterns is suitable for particular kinds of applications.

For example, if the existing application runs on a high-rate, transaction-processing backend, it probably uses a stateless programming model within itself. That is, it doesn't keep information in memory between calls to the application. It might read records from one or more databases, modify them, write them back, and return, leaving nothing in memory. In this case, your CORBA object's methods are probably stateless: They repackage their parameters suitably for the existing application and call that application using the existing API. Depending on how difficult it is to repackage the parameters and how often the object gets invoked, you might use one of two patterns to achieve this stateless operation. If the servant is simple and the repackaging is easy, you could mirror the existing application by using the pattern on-demand activation for duration of a single method. Don't bother creating a servant until it's needed, and then get rid of it right away. Alternately, if the servant is complicated, takes a long time to set up, and is called quite frequently, you might use single servant for all objects. In this case, you would initialize the servant once and have the same servant field all requests. Such a servant wouldn't have to keep state—it uses only the parameters during a single method. It stays around because you want to avoid servant setup time to get better response, and you can afford to have the servant exist between calls.

The other POA patterns are likewise usable for fronting an existing application, depending on the characteristics of the application. Wrapping existing applications in CORBA and the POA isn't something that needs special treatment. The applications just need to be called correctly, and every one of them is different. That's true of new applications, so you can usually use the same analysis techniques for both kinds of applications.

III.1.4 Summary

Although the POA became part of the official CORBA specification with release 2.2 in February 1998, we've presented it in some detail here because it's one of the foundations for the CCM, which we will present in Part III, Chapter 3. That's not all, of course: it's an important part of the architecture even if you're not using CCM and worth the discussion here.

We need to put one more wall of the foundation into place before we start on CCM itself, and that's the Persistent State Service (PSS). We'll do that in the next chapter.

The Persistent State Service (PSS)

CHAPTER PREVIEW

The Persistent State Service automates storage and retrieval of a servant's persistent state. Most useful when a servant cycles through de-activation and re-activation, this capability also comes in handy when a server is brought down (whether intentionally or not!) and up again. The chapter illustrates PSS programming using both available PSS modes: you may use Persistent State Definition Language (PSDL), or declare your objects' state directly in your programming language, termed transparent persistence. Following a description of PSS architecture and programming, we tell how to connect the persistent state described in your code with a datastore in your runtime environment. PSS products may be based on databases (relational, object-oriented, or hybrid), flat files, or any other storage method that a vendor chooses to support. Datastores may be either transactional or non-transactional. The PSS is the last of the building blocks that we need to put into place in order to present the CCM: The CCM Container connects to an implementation of the PSS to provide persistence.

III.2.1   Introduction

For almost 10 years, OMG specifications deliberately avoided anything to do with the internal state of an object (if you excuse the now deprecated Persistent Object Service or POS). With the suite of specifications described in this book, that situation has changed: The **valuetype**, already described in Part I, Chapter 1, started things off although it's not truly a CORBA object. The Persistent State Service (PSS), successor to the POS, defines storage for the persistent state of a CORBA object, and the CCM goes even further, defining a programming environment built around services that store and persist objects' state.

Storage and retrieval of objects' internal state is an important part of programming virtually every application, and CORBA programmers want to use off-the-shelf products implementing standardized interfaces to persist their objects. In mid-1997, OMG members initiated the process of replacing the POS with a totally new version, a 2.0 release. This process concluded in late 1999, defining the newly named Persistent State Service (PSS), which we present in this chapter. The new service specifies a very elegant architecture, and is expected to receive wide usage. This is also the persistence that is required by the CCM, as we'll show in the next chapter. In EJBs, the bottom (data) tier of a three-tier application is implemented as entity beans; in the CCM the corresponding role is played by entity components. Either way, the effect is to give the database row (or wherever the data are stored) a "handle" in the component system: either an EJB reference, or a CORBA component reference.

III.2.2   The Persistent State Service

Architects and programmers spend a lot of time designing ways to make objects' states persistent. Vendors provide databases, both relational- and object-oriented, and transaction processing systems. Some of these may be expensive, especially the most robust, but the need for scalability and reliability in enterprise and Internet applications makes investment in these systems a wise move.

CORBA programmers have been maintaining objects' state persistent, even across activations, for years, so why standardize a PSS now? The benefits of the PSS stem from the way it packages up the persistence layer of your application. Once you've chosen a data storage format (database or file type) and PSS product that supports it, all your programmers have to do is declare their objects' state using one of the two ways the PSS allows them to do this. At build time, the PSS generates code to store and retrieve these objects when they're needed; at runtime, this code executes and values persist. This means that your programmers don't need to be persistence experts to use whatever datastore your company prefers: relational tables, object-oriented or object-relational databases, or flat files, all supported by the PSS specification. (Individual products will support some subset of these alternatives.) Some of these methods require training and experience in order to be used well, but this expertise is built into the PSS specification and product. Programmers can concentrate on business rules and logic, not database programming. A large part of CORBA 3 is about making services more accessible to programmers, so PSS fits right in.

Another reason to standardize PSS now: Persistence is one of the four key services provided by the CCM container. Components submitters wanted to use a standard set of persistence service interfaces in their specification so the PSS is, in part, a response to their needs and wants which we discuss in the next chapter. Even so, the PSS designers did not sacrifice generality in order to support components.

Transactional semantics are an important part of persistent storage. The PSS supports transactions, and we'll look at this aspect before we're done with this chapter.

Storage object structure will mirror your object structure, with storage objects for instances of a type (your shopping carts, for example) stored together in a storage home. Even this structure is generated and managed automatically.

The two ways of declaring state to the PSS are:

- Using the new *Persistent State Definition Language* (PSDL) defined by the specification

or

- Declaring state directly in your programming language, termed *transparent persistence*

We'll go over both of these methods.

Of all the CORBAservices, this is the first time that one intrudes on what the OMG refers to as "implementation detail"—the internals of your implementation. This is a departure for OMG specifications but, as applications become more complex, it's also a big help for programmers. Of course, the CCM not only "intrudes" on the implementation also; it also codes large parts of the implementation—so at least these extensions are being made on a wide front.

The PSS concerns itself only with the interfaces between a servant and the datastore that makes its state persistent. There is no interaction between the PSS and the client of the object.

III.2.2.1 PSS Basics

The PSS stores CORBA objects' state in datastores, which may be relational tables, object-oriented or object-relational databases, or flat files. A particular PSS implementation may support only a subset of these datastore types.

The PSS implements and manages the interaction between the state members of a storage object incarnation, shown in Figure III.2.1 on the left-hand side, and the corresponding members of storage objects in a datastore, shown on the right. Therefore, changes to the state of a storage object incarnation during execution automatically result in corresponding changes to the datastore.

Suppose you're running an e-commerce Web site and your shopping carts are CORBA objects. Each individual shopping cart needs its own storage. In the datastore, the storage for an individual shopping cart is termed a storage object. Storage for a group of shopping carts (possibly all of them, although you can split this up) resides inside a storage home. In Figure III.2.1, the dots on the domino on the far right might represent storage

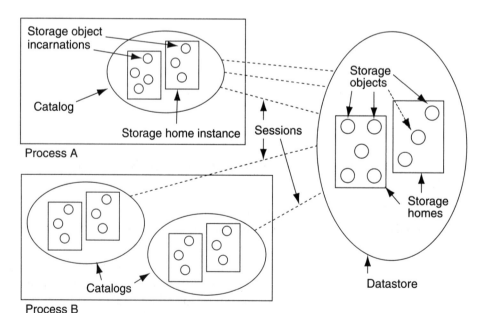

Figure III.2.1 Relationships among storage objects, storage homes, storage object incarnations, storage home instances, and catalogs.

objects for our shopping carts, while the rectangular domino boundary delineates their storage home. There will be additional storage homes for other storage object types; the other domino represents one. The surrounding oval represents the datastore that contains them. If this particular datastore is a relational database, then each storage home could be a table, and each storage object could be a row. The schema for each table has to correspond to the state of the type it represents; we will describe various ways of connecting things up shortly. Keep in mind that the representation in the datastore is generally static; we still need a representation in execution space to make things work.

Each storage object has an identifier unique within its storage home—its **short-pid**—and a global identifier, scoped to every catalog it may be implemented by (on the left in the figure)—its **pid**. You may set the **pid** and **short-pid** to identical types and values where scope allows. You identify and retrieve storage objects by their **pid**s.

In addition to a **pid** and **short-pid**, a storage object can have one or more **key**s. Each **key** consists of one or more state variables whose values, taken together, uniquely identify it in a storage home.

In order to update the storage objects in the datastore, they must be represented in code. The PSS represents them in a form analogous to the class/interface structure we've already seen in OMG IDL, and defines a new language for this: *Persistent State Definition Language* (PSDL). You declare the state variables for the smallest units of your program in **abstract storagetype**s. Then, you declare a **storagetype** (concrete; that is, not **abstract**) that implements one or more **abstract storagetype**s. This distinction was designed quite deliberately: Abstract interfaces contain information important to the PSS user—the servant programmer—while concrete interfaces collect information used by the PSS itself as it implements the storage functions in generated code.

Similarly, you declare an **abstract storagehome** that will be responsible for creating new instances of your **abstract storagetype**s. The corresponding concrete **storagehome** implements the operations that you declared in your abstract type. This structure means that your PSS work divides cleanly into two stages:

- First, you specify your storage objects' schemas—the objects' and servants' view of persistence, primarily the list of state variables—in **abstract** declarations.

- Second, you write specifications that the PSS uses to generate persistence implementation code.

This architecture lets you specify the schema of an object *once*, and use it with various datastores and implementations as your application evolves—

for example, from a small Web site to a large e-commerce emporium. It parallels the use of IDL in CORBA, where a single IDL interface can have multiple implementations.

If basic persistence functions are all you require, the PSS can generate all of the storagehome code for you. However, you are allowed to declare custom operations on storagetypes and storagehomes. If you do, you'll have to fill in the code for these yourself.

III.2.2.1.1 Declaring Abstract Types

Here's our shopping cart example, declared first in PSDL. PSDL is a superset of OMG IDL, adding five new constructs: **abstract storagetype, abstract storagehome, storagetype, storagehome,** and **catalog.** For brevity, we've included only our customer's account number, name, and address, and left out the state variables that hold the stuff that he bought. You can add these yourself as an exercise if you want. In this section, we declare the abstract interfaces as needed by our servant programmer:

```
// In file Cart.psdl:

abstract storagetype Cart {
   readonly state long cust_account_number;
   state string cust_full_name;
   state string cust_address;
};

abstract storagehome CartHome of Cart {

   Cart create (in long cust_acct_num,
                in string cust_f_nam,
                in string cust_addr)

};

catalog Emporium {
   provides CartHome cart_home;
};
```

To make our shopping cart a bit more realistic (but longer), we could have defined a few more related abstract storagetypes and included all of them in the concrete storagetype we're going to declare next. **abstract storagehome CartHome** bears the interface we'll use to create a shopping cart for each customer. **catalog Emporium** will connect our executing image with our datastore at run time; details follow a few sections along.

abstract storagetype Cart defines the schema for our cart. In this example, we've chosen to declare all of our variables as state, but there's another way to do it.

An abstract storagetype can have state members and operations. In this PSDL taken from the example in the PSS specification, **abstract storagetype NamingContextState** defines persistent types for **CosNaming::NameComponent** and **Object** from our use of them in these operation declarations. We talk briefly about how to work with them in the next section.

```
// file NamingContextState.psdl
#include <CosNaming.idl>
abstract storagetype NamingContextState {
   Object resolve(in CosNaming::NameComponent n)
      raises(...);
   void bind(in CosNaming::NameComponent n, in Object obj)
      raises(...);
   etc...
```

An abstract storagehome can define operations as well, but we won't cover that in this book.

Don't look for a declaration of the **pid** here. It's not considered part of the storage object's schema, and doesn't appear in the PSDL declaration. **pid** values are actually set by the constructor in your programming language, and this operation only appears through the language mapping. There is a PSDL operation to locate and retrieve storage objects by **pid**, but we won't describe it in this chapter except to tell you here that you can do it.

Alternatively to PSDL, a PSS implementation that supports *transparent persistence* lets you specify storage objects directly in your programming language. Here is our cart declaration in Java:

```java
// Java
public interface JCart {
    public long cust_account_number();
    public String cust_full_name();
    public void cust_full_name(String newName);
    public String cust_address();
    public void cust_address(String newAddress);
}
```

In transparent persistence, we don't have to declare storagehomes or cat-alogs—just one more step and we'll be done. There's a price to pay for this simplicity, however: We have a lot less control over the implementation, and in the way the values in our code are ultimately represented and stored in our datastore.

III.2.2.1.2 Declaring Concrete Types

There are a number of ways to define the concrete storagetypes and storagehome types that implement the abstract storagetypes and abstract storagehomes we've just declared in PSDL.

Perhaps the glitziest way is to buy a vendor's fancy PSS product with integrated interactive visual tools that let you map abstract storagehomes to tables in a relational database, and state variables in your abstract storagetypes to columns, with a couple of mouse clicks.

The "conventional" way (if there can be a convention for a specification this young) to define your concrete storagetypes and storagehomes is to use more PSDL. All PSS products must let you declare your storagetypes and storagehome types using PSDL; fancier products may also write the PSDL for you using tools or other means, or read your PSDL and help you map it to your database. PSS products use these PSDL declarations to generate an implementation that persists your state variables. Here's what the PSDL looks like for our minimal shopping cart example:

```
// In file CartImpl.psdl

#include <Cart.psdl>

storagetype CartImpl implements Cart{};

storagehome CartHomeImpl of CartImpl implements CartHome{};
```

Your PSS product will generate implementation code in your programming language based on these declarations. In Java, for example, it would generate concrete Java classes for both **CartImpl** and **CartHomeImpl**. The `class CartImpl` would implement an interface representing **abstract storagetype Cart** (and, if we had declared any other abstract storagetypes that needed to go into it, each one of them would occur as an additional interface as well), while the `class CartHomeImpl` would implement the interface **create** to **create** a **Cart**. If we were going to define keys for our **Cart** (and the account number would be a great choice, except that we would probably define it to be the **pid** instead), we would do it here.

So, our Java version of **CartImpl** would have, for every settable state variable, two accessor methods (one read-only and one read-write), and one modifier method. If the state variable is read-only, only that accessor is generated.

For the **NamingContext** example in the previous section, the **NamingContextImpl** bears the signatures we declared in the PSDL file. Although we have to fill in the code that executes these operations, storage is simple: All of the state variables are connected to the datastore; we simply refer to them in our code and storage is automatic.

Regardless of the way we declared our state (as variables or in operations), the storage object implementation is a programming language object if we're working in an object-oriented language, or a function if we're working in non-object-oriented languages. It's not a CORBA object, does not have a CORBA object reference, and can not be invoked remotely (at least not using CORBA).

The third alternative, transparent persistence, lets you define storage object implementations directly in your programming language, just as we defined our abstract storage objects in the previous section. Here is the Java for our cart implementation:

```
    // Java
public class JcartImpl implements Jcart  {
    public long _cust_acct;
    public String _cust_name;
    public String _cust_addr;
    public long cust_account_number () {return _cust_acct };
    // etc
    }
```

With transparent persistence, this is all you get. Specifically, only default storagehomes are available to you; you cannot define your own storagehome with keys and operations.

III.2.2.1.3 Connecting Things Up

To connect our programming language artifacts with their datastore counterparts, we need a session (as shown in Figure III.2.1), or, if we don't want to explicitly manage connections ourselves, a session pool. We won't show any of the code here, but will tell you that the ORB provides the references you need through a call to `resolve_initial_references("PSS")`.

You control sessions, while the PSS controls session pools. If you are not using transactions, you may want to use sessions so that you can tune the system for performance. If you are using transactions, and especially if you're using a high-performance transaction monitor system, you will almost certainly use session pools because your system will already be tuned to perform best when left to its own devices.

The PSS specification uses the terms *storage object incarnation* and *storage object instance*. What's the difference? Both terms refer to a set of data in our execution space that is connected to the datastore via a session, but storage object incarnation refers to an independently accessible set of data with a **pid**, while storage object instance may refer to a dependent set of data that were extracted from a storage object incarnation and do not have their own **pid**. The storage object instance may have a **pid**; both of these entities are instances, but only the one with a **pid** is an incarnation.

For example, consider an **Employee**, which has an **EmployeeID** (that, for simplicity, we will use for both the **pid** and **short pid**), **Name**, and **Address**, where **Address** is another storage type with Street, City, and Zip, but no identifier. In this case, **Employee** would typically have an **EmployeeHome**, and an instance of **Employee** retrieved from an **EmployeeHome** would be an incarnation. Asking the **Employee** for its **Address** would give out an embedded storage object instance, but not an incarnation because **Address** has no home and no life outside the **Employee** incarnation.

III.2.2.2 Persistent CORBA Objects

The simplest way to associate a CORBA object with a storage object is to bind the **ObjectID** of the CORBA object with the identity of the storage object. We've already seen how each storage object provides two external representations of its identity as octet sequences: a **pid** and a **short_pid**.

So, to associate the storage objects stored in storage home **CartHomeImpl** with CORBA objects representing each shopping cart, we would create for each one a CORBA object whose **ObjectID** was that cart's account number, and a storage object whose **short_pid** was also the cart's account number. Then, in our code's servant activation section, we would receive the account number from the POA as the ObjectID and invoke **find_by_pid** to associate the proper storage object with our storage object incarnation.

III.2.2.3 Transactional PSS

The PSS was designed to work with either transactional or non-transactional datastores. You have to create a session or session pool to connect your storage objects to their datastore, and this is where you tell your system if you want to operate transactionally. If you invoke **create_basic_session**, operation is not transactional, but if you invoke **create_transactional_session**, it is. Session pools may be either transactional or not; when you call **create_session_pool**, you have to input the pool's transactionality policy.

When you operate in transactional mode, reads and writes occur with transactional assurance. CORBA's Object Transaction Service (OTS), described in Chapter 13 of *CORBA 3 Fundamentals and Programming*, describes how a distributed transaction can have many participants that all have the chance to vote either to commit or rollback at completion time, and the transaction can only commit if all voted in favor. In transactional PSS stores, there is always only one participant: the storage object implementation. This means there is no need to coordinate multiple participants, so that transaction systems much simpler than those defined by the OMG OTS may support PSS implementations perfectly well.

To allow these simpler implementations to qualify as conforming to the OTS specification, the PSS specification will add a qualifying appendix to the OTS defining a PSS-capable *lite transaction service* that does not need to support the registration of more than one resource per transaction, nor support distribution of a transaction over multiple ORBs. It also defines a lite distributed transaction service that supports distribution, but still only handles a single resource.

III.2.3 Summary

This covers the basic structure of the PSS and then some. We'll present more PSDL in our CCM example, coming up in the next chapter. This will be plenty to give you an idea of what the service can do for you and how you can use it.

CORBA Component Model

CHAPTER PREVIEW

The CORBA Component Model (CCM) packages up persistence, transactions, security, and event handling, along with the POA's server-side resource handling capability, behind a set of higher-level interfaces that makes sophisticated server programming accessible to business programmers.

This chapter presents the CCM from two points of view: a programming example, presented first, followed by a set of interface and architecture descriptions.

The programming example illustrates an e-commerce application with three component types: a customer component type, a shopping cart component type, and a checkout component type. Because each customer is represented by his own customer component instance, and has his own shopping cart while shopping and checkout component while checking out, the scalability of this application is determined only by the CCM infrastructure it runs on. Text and comments surround the code, telling how a few lines of programmer code can trigger execution of optimized patterns pre-programmed in the CCM runtime. In this way, a small amount of programmer code can generate a substantial and scalable server infrastructure.

Following the example, the chapter describes the structure of a CORBA component and of the CCM container, and the CCM development and runtime environments. Programming involves not only creating and describing the component types themselves, but also specifying how they install into the container and connect up at runtime. The CCM architecture allows a component to bear multiple interfaces, and a Component Home type provides class-like operations. Four pre-coded selectable resource allocation patterns, selected from the nearly two hundred provided by the POA, simplify server-side programming while preserving flexibility.

Finally, the CCM unites the worlds of CORBA and EJBs. There are two levels of CCMs: basic, and extended. Basic CORBA components correspond to the definition of Release 1.1 EJBs, while extended CORBA components add additional capabilities, including distributed events, and multiple interfaces and navigation.

The chapter concludes with a listing of general IDL enhancements made by the CCM specification, including the raising of exceptions by IDL attributes on set and get.

III.3.1   What the CORBA Component Model Does for You

The CORBA Component Model (CCM) takes the key services you use regularly—persistence, transactions, security, notification—combines them with the POA's servant handling capability for supremely scalable servers, and wraps all of these tools with higher-level interfaces that correspond to the patterns that experienced programmers use to code enterprise and Internet server applications.

Here's what this means to you and your programmers:

■ *CCM applications are very compact.* That is, you write very little code, and the code that is required all devotes to business programming.

■ *CCM applications are easier to code.* Only the best resource-usage patterns are included in the CCM solution space. Code for these patterns and for other recurring functions is generated automatically from declarations in specially designed new languages built upon the familiar OMG IDL.

■ *CCM applications are modular.* They can be assembled from commercial CCM components, in-house programmed CCM components, or any combination. CCM components and Enterprise JavaBeans can be combined in a single application.

■ *CCM applications scale to enterprise and Internet usage levels.* Years of vendor experience with current products are embodied in the resource-handling patterns built into CCM; your applications automatically reap the benefits—high throughput, great performance, robustness—even though your programmers didn't write a single line of infrastructure code. These infrastructure functions—storing data, activating and de-activating servants—are not only performed automatically, but *coded* automatically.

We're going to start our presentation of the CCM with an example of a realistic e-commerce application, and show how compactly it can be coded up. (The entire application, including code generated by the CCM and the CCM runtime itself, may be large, but the code that *you* write will be compact, thanks to all the help you get from the CCM.) Next (and partly as we go along coding), we'll point out the automated code generation and functionality that the CCM provides. Finally, we'll review the CCM infrastructure; that is, all (well, perhaps most) of the functions that it provides, and how they fit together. There are a bunch of these, so this section will be kind of long and perhaps imposing. That's why we'll put it off until after the example: If you're familiar with some of the CCM functions before you start it, the rest will fall into place better.

Don't be put off just because you've heard that the CCM specification is 700 pages long and complicated: Most of that stuff is for the people who write CCM ORBs, and includes details on how they have to package up the infrastructure, so that your CCM applications not only work on one CCM ORB, but also port to any other that you might decide to use in the future. Once they put all of these details into a CCM development and run-time product, it's simple to program and delivers enterprise-level scalability automatically. We'll spare you these system implementor details—consider this chapter a CMM *application programmers' guide*, not a CCM product developer's manual!

III.3.2 CCM Shopping Cart Example

We're going to illustrate CCM programming with an e-commerce Web site shopping cart application. We'll present the example as code, but we admit that it hasn't been tested: We wrote this just after the final draft of the CCM submission was being completed, and there were no compilers that we could use to check out our CIDL (Component Implementation Definition Language). When you get your CCM ORB and development environment (lucky you!), if you type this example in, you'll probably have to make some adjustments to get it to compile and run, but the basic structure will be right and the application really will have the scalability characteristics that we will describe later in this chapter.

What's a CORBA component? Strictly speaking, it's any piece of functionality that runs in the CCM environment, and takes advantage of the services that the environment provides. Before we go into details, let's consider two aspects of components. First, do we really deploy *components*? The answer is, usually not—instead, we typically deploy component *factories*. For example, we don't deploy a thousand, or a hundred thousand, shopping cart components in our e-commerce shopping application. Instead, we deploy a single shopping cart *factory*. Clients invoke the factory to create a shopping cart instance that is *theirs alone*; at any instant, our application contains exactly the number of shopping carts that it needs. When a cart's work is done, the client application will destroy it, allowing its resources to be reclaimed by the server.

Second, are components large or small? A component can be any size you write, but *the most efficient applications will be built of relatively small components.* That's because the component (or, to use a word before we've defined it, the *segment*) is the smallest unit that our CCM runtime can swap in and out to optimize throughput; by keeping your components small, you give your runtime a leg up as it struggles to run your Internet or enterprise application, keeping up with your thousands of employees or millions of customers. By "small" we don't mean "tiny"; take a look at the size of the customer, shopping cart, and checkout components in our example to see what we think of as a good size.

That's not the whole story, though, because components are also the unit of re-use, and you can lose some of the benefits of re-use if your components are too fine-grained. Fortunately, the CCM gives you a number of ways to get around this: You can either keep your components small and group them into *assemblies*, which can be re-used just as components can, or you can make your components larger but divide them into *segments* (as we hinted in the previous paragraph), allowing your CCM runtime to activate and passivate segments instead of entire components for efficiency. We'll cover assemblies and segments as part of our CCM discussion.

You write components in different categories, depending on how long they and their object references are expected to last, whether or not they have persistent state, and how this state is exposed to the client. These have names like *service, session, entity,* and *process.* (Yes, some of these category names are the same as those used with EJBs, quite intentionally.) We'll use three in this example and describe each one as we introduce it; later in the section, we'll present a table with all of them and their characteristics.

In our example, we'll have a *Customer* component, a *Shopping Cart* component, and a *Checkout* component. Actually we'll have many of each of these, since each customer will have his own persistent customer component to maintain account information, and his own shopping cart whenever he's shopping. (A shopping session starts when a customer puts the first item into his shopping cart, and ends when he checks out.) The Checkout component generates a bill and a shipping order from the contents of the shopping cart, so its existence is fleeting. As with many component-based applications, our deployed application consists of component *factories*, and not the component instances themselves. At runtime, the factories create component instances on-the-fly as we need them. The ability to create, activate, passivate, and destroy components as needed is the key to the CCM's scalability.

Each component type (not instance) has its own ComponentHome type—kind of a class object for the type. ComponentHomes bear lifecycle interfaces for their type: create, find (for entity components only), and remove. We'll have to declare the ComponentHome types in our IDL file also, but we get a lot for our efforts: IDL *and code* for ComponentHome operations will be generated automatically from our simple declaration.

We'll start by defining our three CORBA components and their homes in an IDL file. We'll define the Customer component first. This component makes available the customer information that resides permanently in our database; when a customer comes to our site and logs in, the application will find his record and account number for use during the session, and return a component reference for a new shopping cart so he can start shopping.

We'll design the Shopping Cart component to last for one shopping session, regardless of how long the session lasts (even if the customer logs out, and logs back in again days or weeks later). The Cart component will only come into memory for execution when the customer adds something to it or checks out, and be swapped out in between times. When it's swapped out, its contents (the component's state) are stored persistently in our database. This allows us to service many more customers with a given amount of hardware than any other pattern would—a typical customer spends most of his time browsing, and relatively little time actually putting items into the cart. After the customer checks out—that is, buys the stuff in the cart—his particular Cart component is destroyed and its resources reclaimed by the system. The next time he shops, he gets a new Shopping Cart component, just as he would at a physical store.

When our customer finishes shopping, he clicks the "purchase" button, which activates the Checkout component, charging his credit card and notifying the shipping department to send his stuff out. We'll design the Checkout component to be *stateless*—it does all of its work on a single invocation, using only the information we pass in at the start. This gives our CCM a lot of freedom in allocating resources, since it doesn't have to find a special servant for the task—any Checkout servant that's not busy can be pressed into service.

To illustrate how components can work together, we've tied the Shopping Cart component and Checkout component together with **uses** and **provides** statements, declaring that the Checkout component *provides* the **CheckoutIntf** interface, and the Shopping Cart component *uses* the **CheckoutIntf** interface. To illustrate that there are other ways to tie components together, we've used the client part of the application to tie the customer's account object to the shopping cart. To do this, we've used a number of new component capabilities, but we won't give details until later.

We've tied our three-component application into an *assembly*, comprising our executables, configuration information including how the shopping cart uses the checkout component, and installation information. Why does the CCM define the assembly? Because it will be rare for a component-based application to be complete with only a single component type. Most, like ours, will be composed of many component types working together. The commercial CCM applications you buy will surely be assemblies. You can combine purchased and in-house programmed components in an assembly, for deployment as an application.

A component is not a CORBA object with super powers; instead, it's a new CORBA meta-type that *supports* or provides interfaces that you define separately in your IDL. This means we need to pre-declare all of our interfaces before we declare their components, as you'll see in this file. Once we've declared their interfaces, we can declare our components using the new IDL keyword **component**. For each, we'll have to declare the interfaces they support or provide, and we'll need to declare a Component Home.

This IDL file looks a lot longer than it really is: When you use components, the CCM development environment generates a lot of IDL and code from your input. In this file, we present a lot of the generated IDL in comments, so you'll be prepared when we use it later. This makes the file about three times longer than it needs to be.

Here's the IDL for the three components and their homes:

```
// IDL

// First, some general typedefs:

    typedef    long      CustAcctNum;
    typedef    string    CustName;
    typedef    string    CustAddress;
```

```
typedef    string    CustCity;
typedef    long      CustZip;
typedef    string    CustCredCdNum;

typedef    long      ItemNum;
typedef    long      ItemQty;
typedef    float     ItemPrice;

typedef              struct    CartItem {
ItemNum              thisItem;
ItemQty              thisQty;
ItemPrice            thisPrice;
};

typedef sequence<CartItem> CartItemList;
```

```
// We need to define our customer interface
// before we can declare its component:

interface  CustomerIntf {
    CustAcctNum      AcctNum();
    CustName         Name ();
    CustAddress      Address ();
    CustCity         City ();
    CustZip          Zip ();
    CustCredCdNum  CredCard ();
}

// Now we can define the customer Component:

component Customer  supports CustomerIntf { };

// The "equivalent IDL" for this declaration is:
//    Interface Customer : CustomerIntf, CCMObject {
// };

// Next we declare a CustomerHome. This declaration will generate IDL
// for operations to manage the lifecycle of our Customer components:
// that is, to create, find, and destroy instances. We won't show the
// equivalent IDL here.

home CustomerHome manages Customer primaryKey CustomerKey { };
// definition of the primary key for our Customer component.
    valuetype CustomerKey : Components::PrimaryKeyBase {
      public CustAcctNum custKey;
    };

// We need to define the operations for our ShoppingCart interface
// before we can declare its component:
interface ShoppingCartIntf {
    void setCust  (CustAcctNum cust);
    void addItem (ItemNum n, ItemQty q, ItemPrice p);
    void buyContents ( );
```

```
        // operations to remove items from cart, and list items,
        // have been left as an exercise for the reader!
};


// Forward declaration – we'll define this fully afterwards:
interface CheckoutIntf;


// Now we can declare our Shopping Cart Component.
// It provides the ShoppingCartIntf interface on a separate facet,
// and uses the CheckoutIntf interface of the Checkout component,
// which we will define next:
component ShoppingCart {
        provides ShoppingCartIntf Cart1;
        uses CheckoutIntf CheckOut1;


// The ShoppingCart interface generates operations that permit
// the client to access the ShoppingCartIntf facet of the ShoppingCart
// component, and to connect to the Checkout component.
// In this case the generated operations look like:
// interface ShoppingCart : CCMObject {
//     ShoppingCartIntf provide_Cart1 ();
//     void connect_CheckOut1 ( in CheckoutIntf MyCheckout );
//     CheckoutIntf disconnect_CheckOut1 ();
//     CheckoutIntf get_connection_CheckOut1 ():
//   };
// }


// Next we declare a ShoppingCartHome. This declaration will generate IDL
// for operations to manage the lifecycle of our Shopping Cart components:
// that is, to create, and destroy instances. The Shopping Cart is a process
// component with no primary key, so no find operation is generated (unlike
// the CustomerHome, above). Again, we won't show the equivalent IDL here.

home ShoppingCartHome manages ShoppingCart { };


// Need to define the operation for our Checkout component:

Interface CheckoutIntf {
   boolean buy (in Customer cust, in CartItemList cartStuff);
};


// Now we can define our Checkout Component:
component Checkout {
   provides CheckoutIntf Check1 ;
// This is equivalent to the following IDL:
//   interface Checkout  : CCMObject {
// The Checkout interface supports an operation to access the
// CheckoutIntf facet. In this case the generated interface looks like:
//     CheckoutIntf provide_Check1();
//   };
};


home CheckoutHome manages Checkout { };
```

III.3.2.1 Making Our Components' State Persist

Our Customer components' state persists from session to session, hopefully for a long time (as long as we keep our customers happy!). Shopping carts' state may also persist. In CCM, persistence can be managed by the new Persistent State Service (PSS) and declared using Persistent State Definition Language (PSDL), which were defined and presented in Part III, Chapter 2.

In our system, we represent the customer using a component with state that persists from every session to the next, and exposes its key (the account number) to the client. In the terminology of the CCM, this is an *entity* component. Architecturally, this is a departure for CORBA, which up to now has never used the infrastructure to maintain instance identity that was visible to the client: CCM clients may invoke **find_by_primary_key** on the ComponentHome (a part of the CCM that we'll define shortly), passing in a key that might be an account number or social security number, and receive the reference for that component instance in return. In the past, identity of this sort has been maintained by CORBAservices (Naming, Trader) that are distinct from the ORB infrastructure; in the CCM, these aspects are allowed to merge.

Before we go into detail on persistent state, let's review objects and identity: We now have *four* ways to identify different aspects of an object or component's instance, and it's important to keep track. Here they are:

- *The CORBA object reference.* Every instance of a CORBA object, and every interface on a CORBA component, has its own unique object reference.

- *The POA ObjectId.* When we **create_reference_with_ID**, *the POA lets us assign an ObjectId of our choosing to the instance. At activation time, the POA hands the key value to our servant, which uses it to find and restore the proper state for that instance. This applies regardless of the persistence method we're using.*

- *The PSS Object Key.* If we're using the PSS for persistence, we get yet another key: the PSS key, which may be distinct from the ObjectId. This key identifies the instance to our PSS schema. If we're using both the POA and the PSS, it makes sense to assign the PSS key and the POA ObjectId to be identical. (They're both strings.)

- *The CCM Key.* For entity components only, the CCM supports component identity, letting us assign a key valuetype to each instance. The ComponentHome maintains a table of keys and component references, and supports an operation that accepts a key as input and returns the component's reference.

Of the three component types in our application, two have persistent state: the Customer and the Shopping Cart. However, only the Customer is an entity component with a CCM key (and the other three identifiers also, of course); the Shopping Cart has a PSS key that identifies its persistent store, but no CCM key so you can't ask the Shopping Cart ComponentHome to pick your shopping cart out of the flock in the electronic parking lot by giving it a key! In the PSDL that follows, watch for the assignment of PSS keys to both Customer and Shopping Cart. Later in the CIDL, look for Customer to get a CCM key, while Shopping Cart does not.

We almost don't have to write the implementation of the customer entity component at all. In our abbreviated presentation of this example, we're not including the interactive I/O that asks a new customer for his name, address, and other data, but if we did, all we would have to do is assign these data to their variables in our component. Then, by declaring these variables to be the component's state using PSDL, we cause the CCM to generate code to store and retrieve the values whenever they're used; that is, to generate nearly our entire implementation. That's why we called CCM applications—that is, the part you have to write yourself—"compact."

Here are the PSDL declarations for the Customer component:

```
// PSDL:
// This defines the state variables of our customer account, in a way that
//   lets the PSS generate code to store and retrieve them automatically:

abstract storagetype CustomerState {
        state long   AcctNum;
        state string Name;
        state string Address;
        state string City;
        state string Zip;
        state string CreditCard;
};

// The PSS needs a storagetype object; this implements the abstract storage

storagetype PortableCustomerState implements CustomerState { };

typedef sequence <Customer> CustomerList;

// The primary key in this code is the PSS key:
abstract storagehome CustomerStorageHome of Customer {
        primary key AcctNum(AcctNum);
        factory create(AcctNum, Name, Address, City, Zip, CreditCardNum);
// You can define operations on the storage home. For example:
        CustomerList find_customers_by_zip(in string Zip);
// This is handy, but we won't explain it any further in this example.
// See the PSS Chapter for more.
};
```

```
storagehome PortableCustomerStorageHome implements CustomerStateHome { };
```

Since the Customer component accepts, stores, and furnishes the customer's personal information and does nothing else, our CCM development environment can produce the *entire* implementation from these declarations.

The client side of our application will either log in an existing customer or initialize a new one. (We show some of this code in Section III.3.2.6.) If this is a new customer, the client will find the CustomerHome and invoke its create operation, getting back a new component reference. At create time, the factory will assign a new account number, which it encapsulates in the component reference and simultaneously stores in the database as the key to that customer's record. Doing triple duty, the account number is also the primary key for the Customer component. The client then collects name, address, and credit card data from the customer and assigns each piece to a declared state variable by invoking the component using interfaces that we didn't show here. The CCM stores these state values automatically using code generated by the PSS. For an existing customer, the client application asks the customer to input his account number and then invokes **find_by_primary_key** on the CustomerHome component.

Now for the shopping cart. Since this is a *process* component, it does not have a CCM primary key, but since it's persistent, it will have a persistence key and a POA ObjectId. Fortunately for us, the PSS and CCM work together to generate these and use them to tie each shopping cart's state to its servant, so we don't have to do anything here—not even declare them. Here's the PSDL for the shopping cart:

```
//PSDL
// Embedded storagetype (no home definition)
// More on embedded storagetypes in PSS Chapter.
abstract storagetype CartItem {
      state long item_number;
      state long quantity;
      state float price;
};

storagetype PortableCartItem implements CartItem { };

typedef sequence<CartItem> CartItemList;

abstract storagetype CartState {
      CustomerState get_Customer();
      CartItemList get_items();
      float calculate_total();
};

storagetype PortableCartState implements CartState {
      readonly state long AcctNum;
```

```
         state CartItemList  ItemList;
};

// Since we won't declare a primary PSS key on the
// ShoppingCartStateHome, the PSS and POA will
// automatically generate and use a common key that couples
// the state of our shopping cart instance with its component
// reference.
abstract storagehome ShoppingCartStateHome { };

catalog ShoppingCatalog {
     provides CustomerStateHome;
     provides ShoppingCartStateHome;
};
```

There is no PSS declaration for the **Checkout** component, which has no persistent state.

III.3.2.2   Implementing the Customer Component

Since we're not including the registration of a new customer as part of our abbreviated example, there isn't much to show here. Our client code (which we'll show last) invokes the **Customer** component to ensure that there really is a valid account associated with each shopping trip. We've shown the IDL and PSDL that maintains this state persistent. Here's the CIDL that declares our implementation to be an entity component:

```
// CIDL:

  composition  entity  CustomerImpl {

     implements Customer;
     home  executor  CustomerHomeImpl  delegatesTo
         abstractstoragehome CustomerStateStorageHome;
};
```

Finally, there's an XML-based component configuration file that tells the CCM about our component. This is where we declare its servant activation policy to be per-method, as well as other runtime info: Interface Repository ID, threading and transaction policies, and more. These files will be generated by interactive visual tools, and use a lot of defaults, so you'll never have to code one up yourself. But, they're in XML so you can read them if you're truly curious. Since we're writing this to satisfy curiosity, here's at least part of the file for the Customer component. Remember, you won't have to write this yourself!

```
<corbacomponent>
    <corbaversion> 3.0 </corbaversion>
    <componentrepid repid="IDL:Customer:1.0" />
    <homerepid repid="IDL:CustomerHome:1.0" />
    <componentkind>
        <entity>
            <servant lifetime="method" />
        </entity>
    </componentkind>
    <threading policy="multithread" />
    <configurationcomplete set="true" />

    <segment name="Customerseg" segmenttag="1">
        <segmentmember facettag="1" />
        <containermanagedpersistence>
            <storagehome id="PSDL:CustomerStorageHome:1.0" />
            <pssimplementation id="ACME-PSS" />
            <catalog type="PSDL:CustomerCatalog:1.0" />
            <accessmode mode="READ_ONLY" />
            <psstransaction policy="TRANSACTIONAL" >
                <psstransactionisolationlevel
                        level="SERIALIZABLE" />
            </psstransaction>
        </containermanagedpersistence>
    </segment>

    <homefeatures
     name="CustomerHome"  repid="IDL:CustomerHome:1.0">
        <operationpolicies>
            <operation name="*">
                <transaction use="supported" />
            </operation>
        </operationpolicies>
    </homefeatures>

    <componentfeatures name="Customer" repid="IDL:Customer:1.0">
        <supportsinterface repid="IDL:CustomerIntf:1.0">
            <operationpolicies>
                <operation name="*">
                    <transaction use="supported" />
                </operation>
            </operationpolicies>
        </supportsinterface>
    </componentfeatures>
```

III.3.2.3 Implementing the Shopping Cart Component

To conserve resources, we'll make ShoppingCart a *process component* and give it a method activation policy. While customers browse, their shopping carts are swapped out, so even millions of browsing customers won't consume any resources (for carts, at least) on our server. When a customer clicks the "Add to Shopping Cart" button on a product's Web page, the CCM runtime and PSS do everything we'd like them to do, automatically: The CCM activates our Shopping Cart component, assigning a servant, retrieving its state from persistent storage, and starting its execution. We're executing the `addItem` operation with parameters `ItemNum`, `ItemQty`, and `ItemPrice`. These are declared state variables in our PSDL, and come in as parameters in the invocation. All we need to do is increment the number of items in the cart, and assign the `ItemNum`, `ItemQty`, and `ItemPrice` to their corresponding state variables. Because the PSS couples state in execution space with its image in storage, this automatically updates our database. When this is done and we return, the cart is automatically deactivated by the CCM runtime, which then reclaims its resources.

To do this, the ShoppingCart component must also implement the **Components::Basic::EntityComponent** interface. (Process and entity components, which both have persistent references and state, share the **EntityComponent** interface, which is defined by the CCM specification. Entity components have an additional interface that gives them their Primary Key, which we'll see later on.) When we declare `ShoppingCart` to be a process component, the CCM assigns it the **Components::Basic::EntityComponent** interface. Here's the CIDL for this:

```
//CIDL
    composition process ShoppingCartMgr {
        uses catalog {ShoppingCatalog Scart};
    };
    home executor ShoppingCartHomeImpl {
        implements ShoppingCartHome;
        bindsTo Scart1.ShoppingCartStateHome;
        manages ShoppingCartImpl;
    };
};


class ShoppingCartImpl  implements  ShoppingCart;


// PSEUDOCODE:
// You will have to fill the code for the business operations of
// your components into the skeletons that come from your IDL compilation,
// in your chosen programming language.  Here, in pseudocode, are the
// operations that you'll have to fill in:

// setCust imports the customer's account information into the
// ShoppingCart, based on the account number that came in
// as an input parameter:
setCust operation:
    sc.acct = cust.acctnum;
```

```
        sc.name = cust.name;
        sc.address = cust.address;
        sc.city = cust.city;
        sc.zip = cust.zip;
        sc.cc = cust.cc;

// addItem adds selected items to the cart:
addItem operation:
    for I=1 to number_of_items do;
        sc.item[I] = item[I];
        sc.qty[I] = qty[I];
        sc.price[I] = price[I];
    end;

// buyContents creates a Checkout component and buys the contents
//  of the ShoppingCart:

// This is the "Factory Pattern" and there are two ways to code it:
// Do everything explicitly ourselves, or let the CCM runtime take
// care of the details by declaring a connection. In either case, the
// Checkout ComponentHome is invoked to create a Checkout
// component instance whose reference is returned to the
// Shopping Cart component.
// In a real application, we'd only do this one way and most likely
// the easy way using a connection. Here, we'll show you both.

// Here's the easy way, using a Connection:

// buyContents creates a Checkout component and buys the contents
//  of the ShoppingCart:
buyContents operation;

// PSEUDOCODE, USING CCM CONNECTION:
    // This is the "Factory Pattern" using the connection declared
    // in the configuration file. At run time, the CCM will
    // locate the checkout Home, create an instance, and connect it
    // to the Checkout1 receptacle of our Shopping Cart:
    // We don't save the reference, which is not valid after
    // this single invocation since Checkout is a Service
    // component type.

    CheckoutIntf co = sc.get_connection_CheckOut1 ();

    // Buy the contents of the ShoppingCart;
    status = buy.co (in customer cust, in cartItemList list);

    // If we were building a robust application, we'd check the boolean
    //  status return value here.
    return;

// END OF CONNECTION FACTORY PATTERN.

// PSEUDOCODE, CREATING CHECKOUT COMPONENT OURSELVES:
```

```
// This is the "Factory Pattern" coded explicitly: Our ShoppingCart
// finds the Checkout ComponentHome which is a checkout component
// factory, and invokes it to create a checkout component which it
// invokes to check out.
// It doesn't save the reference, which is not valid after this single
// invocation since Checkout is a Service component type.

// Locate a CheckoutHome;

HomeFinder hf = orb.resolve_initial_references("ComponentHomeFinder");

CheckoutHome coh = hf.find_home_by_comp_type
   (CheckoutHome co_repid);

// Create a Checkout component. This is implemented
// as a Service component –

Checkout co = create.coh();

// Buy the contents of the ShoppingCart;
status = buy.co (in customer cust, in cartItemList list);

// If we were building a robust application, we'd check the boolean
// status return value here.
return;


// END OF EXPLICIT FACTORY PATTERN.

class ShoppingCartStateMgr  implements  Components::Basic::EntityComponent;

// COMPONENT CALLBACK INTERFACES: The operations that follow are all
// callbacks: your component implements these interfaces, and they're called by the
// CCM when it is activated, or about to be passivated, or when it needs to load
// or store persistent state. Skeletons for these operations are generated by the
// CCM for process and entity components. Code for the persistence-related
// operations will be generated automatically by the PSS from your PSDL
// declarations. In our example here, the other operations don't need anything
// except for set_session_context, which needs its value saved. This is still
// pseudocode.

set_session_context (in SessionContext ctx);
   sc = ctx; // save in local instance variable
return;


ccm_activate operation
// If we had anything to do on activation, in addition to the persistence operations,
// which are generated automatically, we'd put it here.
return;


ccm_load operation
// This code will be generated automatically from the PSDL
// declaration. It consists of a series of accessor operations
// for the defined fields.
```

```
return;

ccm_store operation
// This code will be generated automatically from the PSDL
// declaration. It consists of a series of accessor operations
// for the defined fields.
return;

ccm_passivate operation
// If we had operations to do before passivation, we'd put them here.
return;

ccm_remove operation
// Last chance to do anything (besides persistence, which is automatic) before
// our instance is destroyed!
return;
```

Because our shopping cart is persistent, we've made it a Process component. A Process component can have transactional persistent state, but does not expose it to its clients. It is intended to model business processes that have a beginning and an end, like the act of shopping at an e-commerce site. If we declare the activation policy to be *component*, the servant will stay in memory from the first invocation until the object is destroyed, but we think this will leave too many idle carts in memory. So, we'll declare the activation policy to be method. This allows our CCM runtime product to swap out carts, except when shoppers are in the act of adding something to them or checking out, and, since we made it a process component, the code that is necessary to save the state on passivation, and restore it on activation, is generated automatically. We think it would be effective to create a permanent database table with a pool of rows for this temporary storage, and allocate from it as carts need. We haven't shown this level of detail in the example code, but your PSS documentation will tell you how to code up something like this.

There has to be an XML-based configuration file for the **ShoppingCart**, just as there was for our Customer component. In it, we declare the servant activation policy to be per-method, allowing inactive carts to move out of the way while others swap in to have stuff dropped into them.

We've taken good advantage of the Transaction Policy here, by requiring that everything the **ShoppingCart** does occurs in the context of an active transaction. Look for the line in the next code listing that reads `<opera-tion name="*"=>`, and the few lines that follow, to see how this is done. With this declaration in the configuration file, the CCM will examine every invocation of every **ShoppingCart** component to see if it carries a transaction context. If it does—that is, if the operation is already transactional—the CCM does nothing. If it's not, the CCM creates a transaction that covers everything the ShoppingCart component does during the invocation, and commits just before it returns. *Every* call to the Transaction Service is generated and executed automatically by the CCM.

The ShoppingCart component has only two operations (thus far, anyhow): **addItem** and **buyContents**. This simple declaration makes the adding of items, and the *entire* purchase procedure (including everything that happens in other components that get called, including the CheckOut component), transactional. If you follow our suggestion and add an operation to delete items from the **ShoppingCart**, that operation will automatically become transactional, too.

Let us point out one more time: You won't have to write this file yourself; it's generated automatically. Here it is:

```
<corbacomponent>
    <corbaversion> 3.0 </corbaversion>
    <componentrepid repid="IDL:ShoppingCart:1.0" />
    <homerepid repid="IDL:ShoppingCartHome:1.0" />
    <componentkind>
        <process>
            <servant lifetime="method" />
        </process>
    </componentkind>
    <threading policy="multithread" />
    <configurationcomplete set="true" />

    <segment name="ShoppingCartseg" segmenttag="1">
        <segmentmember facettag="1" />
        <containermanagedpersistence>
            <storagehome id="PSDL:ShoppingCartStateHome:1.0" />
            <pssimplementation id="ACME-PSS" />
            <catalog type="PSDL:ShoppingCatalog:1.0" />
            <accessmode mode="READ_WRITE" />
            <psstransaction policy="TRANSACTIONAL" >
                <psstransactionisolationlevel
                        level="SERIALIZABLE" />
            </psstransaction>
        </containermanagedpersistence>
    </segment>

    <componentfeatures name="ShoppingCart"
                repid="IDL:ShoppingCart:1.0">
        <ports>
          <provides providesname="Cart1"
                    repid="IDL:ShoppingCartIntf:1.0"
                    facettag="1">
            <operationpolicies>
              <operation name="*"=>
```

```
                     <transaction use="required" />
                   </operation>
                 </operationpolicies>
               </provides>

               <uses usesname="Check1"
                   repid="IDL:CheckOutIntf:1.0" />
             </ports>
       </componentfeatures>

       <homefeatures
        name="ShoppingCartHome"
        repid="IDL:ShoppingCartHome:1.0">
           <operationpolicies>
               <operation name="*">
                   <transaction use="supports" />
               </operation>
           </operationpolicies>
       </homefeatures>
```

III.3.2.4 Implementing the Checkout Interface

We've implemented **Checkout** as a service component—a very low-resource component with no state. The POA can keep a pool of initialized **Checkout** servants around and assign an incoming request to any one of them since they're all the same, functionally. Based solely on information in the input parameters, the **Checkout** component will charge the amount of the sale to the credit card and produce a bill of lading, which the shipping department will use to assemble and ship the order. This is all encapsulated behind the **buyContents** operation that the client invokes on the **Shopping Cart**, which invokes the **Checkout** component.

```
// CIDL
    composition service CheckoutMgr {
        home executor CheckoutHomeMgr {
        implements CheckoutHome;
        manages CheckoutImpl;
        }:
    };

class CheckoutImpl implements CheckoutIntf;


//PSEUDOCODE:
// Here, in pseudocode, are suggestions on how you would code up the Checkout
// component functionality in your programming language, inserted into the
// skeletons generated by the CCM from your IDL and CIDL.
// The implementation of the buy operation is shown here as invocation of two
// additional components which we won't show: A CreditInvoice component
// which bills the customer's credit card, and a Lading component which
```

```
// generates a bill of lading for the shipping department. Both of these are
// created and invoked using the Factory pattern, since they're session
// components. We've assumed that they were declared as used interfaces
// in our IDL, allowing us to find the component home and create our instance
// in a single call for each one.
// However, we haven't shown any of the declarations for the CreditInvoice
// or Lading components in this oversimplified example.

buy operation:
    // Locate a CreditInvoiceHome and create a CreditInvoice component:
    CreditInvoice ci = co.get_connection_CreditInvoice1;
    // Copy billing information from ShoppingCart to CreditInvoice and submit.
    // All of this is in the scope of the client's transaction;
    submit.ci ();
    //
    // Create a Bill of Lading for the order;
    Lading li = co.get_connection_Lading1();
    // Copy order information from ShoppingCart to Bill of Lading and submit
    // All of this is in the scope of the client's transaction:
    submit.li ();
    return;


class CheckoutStateMgr implements Components::Basic::SessionComponent;
    set_session_context (in SessionContext ctx);
    sc = ctx; // save in local instance variable
    return;


ccm_activate operation
    return; // nothing to do;


ccm_passivate operation
    return; // nothing to do;


ccm_remove operation
    return; // nothing to do;
```

III.3.2.5   Component Assembly

The last thing we need to do to the server side of our CCM application is assemble it into a single unit that we can deploy, install, and run. Like the component configuration file we examined earlier, this is a file that will be generated by an interactive tool using a lot of defaults, but it's in XML so we can read it if we want. If detail doesn't scare you, read through it and look for the location of the executable files, the partitioning information, and especially the details of how the "buy" invocation made by the **Shopping Cart** (through its receptacle) is connected to the interface and implementation provided by a **Checkout** component.

```
<componentassembly id="7823828d878a7878c">
    <description>Assembly descriptor for web store example
```

```
        </description>
    <componentfiles>
        <componentfile id="ShoppingCartFile">
            <fileinarchive name="shoppingcart.car"/>
        </componentfile>
        <componentfile id="CheckOutFile">
            <fileinarchive name="checkout.car"/>
        </componentfile>
        <componentfile id="CustomerFile">
            <fileinarchive name="customer.car"/>
        </componentfile>
    </componentfiles>

    <partitioning>
        <homeplacement id="ShoppingCartHome">
            <componentfileref idref="ShoppingCartFile"/>
        </homeplacement>

        <homeplacement id="CustomerHome">
            <componentfileref idref="CustomerFile"/>
        </homeplacement>

        <homeplacement id="CheckOutHome">
            <componentfileref idref="CheckOutFile"/>
            <componentinstantiation id="CheckOutSingleton"/>
            <registercomponent>
                <registerwithnaming name="CheckOut"/>
            </registercomponent>
        </homeplacement>
    </partitioning>

    <connections>
        <connectinterface>
            <!- connect the "uses" ports of all ShoppingCarts
                created out of ShoppingCartHome to the "provides"
                port of CheckOutSingleton ->
            <usesport>
                <usesidentifier>Check1</usesidentifier>
                <homeplacementref idref="ShoppingCartHome"/>
            </usesport>
            <providesport>
                <providesidentifier>Check1</providesidentifier>
                <componentinstantiationref
                    idref="CheckOutSingleton"/>
            </providesport>
        </connectinterface>
    </connections>

</componentassembly>
```

III.3.2.6   Coding the Client

Now that our application is complete, we can write a client to invoke it. (If we had completed an Analysis and Design before we started coding, we could have coded our client in a parallel effort, of course.)

In real life, the client will be a GUI application, but we won't show any of that here, nor will we show the small amount of coding that saves the **ShoppingCart** reference in a cookie, enabling a shopping trip to be spread over two or more logins. The server-side application is ready for this, but our client won't be. You can code this yourself, if you want, as an exercise.

Here's the client, in C++ with liberal comments:

```
// We need to start by using the finder pattern
// to get the CustomerHome for our customer
// account component.
//
// There are two ways for this client to find
// the CustomerHome: Through the Home Finder,
// or via the Naming Service. Of course for the
// Naming Service method to work, we had to save
// the reference of the Customer Home in the
// service beforehand.
//
// We've already shown how to find the CustomerHome
// using the initial service ComponentHomeFinder,
// so this time we'll use the Naming Service:

// Initialize the ORB
    CORBA::ORB_var orb = CORBA::ORB_init(argc, argv);

// Get initial naming context
    CORBA::Object_var obj;
    obj = orb->resolve_initial_references("NameService");
    CosNaming::NamingContext_var nameContext;
    nameContext = CosNaming::NamingContext::_narrow(obj);

// Look up CustomerHome using our agreed-upon name:
    CosNaming::Name homeName;
    homeName.length(2);
    homeName[0].id = CORBA::string_dup("MyHomes");
    homeName[1].id = CORBA::string_dup("MyCustomerHome");
    obj = nameContext->resolve(homeName);
    CustomerHome custHome_var = CustomerHome::_narrow(obj);

// We need to get the Customer Account Number
// from the user to find his account component.
// This isn't very friendly, but it keeps the
// example short. You'll have to be friendlier
// than this in a real e-commerce application:
```

```
//
// Code to get customer acct from user goes here
// but we won't show it.
// Use acct number to find the customer's record:
// CustomerAcctKey holds valuetype which contains
// primary key.
   Customer_var cust =
     custHome->find_by_primary_key (CustomerAcctKey);


// Get a reference to the ComponentHomeFinder:
     obj = orb->resolve_initial_references("ComponentHomeFinder");
     Components::HomeFinder_var homeFinder;
     homeFinder = Components::Homefinder::_narrow(obj);


// Now use the Factory Pattern to get a shopping cart:
// Look up a ShoppingCartHome:
     Components::CCMHome_var ccmHome;
     ccmHome = homeFinder->find_home_by_component_type
       ( "IDL:ShoppingCartHome:1.0");
     ShoppingCartHome_var shopCartHome =
       ShoppingCartHome::_narrow(ccmHome);


// Create a ShoppingCartIntf:
     ShoppingCartIntf_var shoppingCart =
       shopCartHome->create();


// Tell it who the customer is:
     shoppingCart->setCust (CustAcctNum);


// Do some shopping. This is a loop, where our
// customer browses our website and occasionally
// drops something (or a number of somethings)
// into his cart. When that happens, the operation
// looks like this:
     for (i = 1; i < total_number_of_items; i++)
         shoppingCart->addItem
           (ItemNum n[i],
            ItemQty q[i],
            ItemPrice p[i]);


// This is the end of the shopping loop. If
// you were to allow shopping trips to be interrupted
// and re-started without losing the contents of the
// cart, code for this would go here too.


// When the customer finishes shopping and presses
// the "Purchase" button on our web page, buy the
// contents of the shopping cart:

       shoppingCart->buyContents();
```

```
// Now we're done with this shopping trip. In a clever
// application, we'd ask the customer if he wanted to
// do some more shopping, and loop back to create another
// shopping cart.
```

One important thing to remember: The client—that is, the desktop or other remote application that initiates our CCM invocation—will not be a component! We pointed out, near the beginning of this chapter, that the CCM environment was too heavy to be practical for running clients. Since the client is not a component, it does not have receptacles, and cannot connect to our components automatically. It can, however, make full use of the factory and finder patterns, at least if it's running on a CORBA 3.0 or later ORB, as we'll now see:

There are some things a client *cannot* do if it is running on a CORBA 2.X ORB, including navigation operations. Such a client is referred to as *component-unaware*; it lacks the ability to do certain operations whose IDL is generated automatically from the component declaration. We'll discuss this more in Section III.3.3.16.2. Clients must execute on CORBA 3 ORBs to access the full capabilities of the CCM.

In this client, we've used the Naming Service to find the **CustomerHome**, and the finder pattern to find the Customer component we want using the customer's account number as the primary key. We admit, it's not user friendly to require your customer to memorize his account number in order to log in, and we suggest that you save it in a cookie or something to rescue your customers from memorizing yet another string of seemingly random numbers.

The operation `find_by_primary_key` is a departure for CORBA: For the first time, the CORBA runtime is managing object identity *for, and visible to, the client*. It's as if the CCM is running its own mini Naming Service, at least for primary keys and only for components within the control of this particular CCM runtime. We'll discuss this further in a couple of places in the rest of this chapter.

Once we have the reference to our Customer component, we can use the factory pattern to create a shopping cart instance. We invoke `find_home_by_component_type` to find the `ShoppingCart` Home, which we invoke to create the cart. As soon as we have the cart, we invoke `setCust` so it knows that it's our cart. The cart will use this information when we check out. If we had coded this robustly, the cart would not accept items unless it had been set up with a valid customer account number. If we were resuming an interrupted shopping trip and already had a cart, we would retrieve its component reference here (probably from a cookie).

Now we browse away, dropping items into our shopping cart whenever we see something we like. The server-side code allows us to interrupt our shopping trip and come back to it later without losing the contents of our cart, but we're not going to show the client-side code for this here. We don't have to do anything special to save the contents of the cart, since it's saved automatically every time we drop anything into it. All we have to do is save the Cart component reference in a cookie, for retrieval when we resume shopping.

When we're done shopping, we trigger the `buyContents` operation, presumably by clicking the "purchase" button on our Web page, although we haven't shown the GUI code for this. The `buyContents` operation was defined on the ShoppingCart back in our IDL, and in our implementation it triggers the creation of an instance of a Checkout component that charges our credit card and creates a bill of lading for the shipping department.

Even though our entire shopping trip executes with transactional assurance, there is no invocation of the Transaction Service in the client. In fact, the only place we needed to specify transactionality was in the XML-based configuration files for our components. With these declarations in place, the CCM took care of all of the details.

III.3.2.7 Running Our Component Example

That's our component example—quite a compact bit of code for a scalable, Internet application. Here's what we did.

We started out by coding the interfaces to our components in OMG IDL, using the new keyword **component** instead of **interface**, and declaring a home to manage each of our various components. Using these declarations, our CCM product can start to set up a structure in which it can instantiate and manage each of our component types.

Next, we declared state for each of our components that have state, in PSDL. Our CCM product, perhaps working with a separate persistence product, will use these declarations to generate code to store and retrieve state variables during execution.

Then, we declared some implementation in CIDL. Our CCM implementation will use this to construct more of our implementation.

We weren't quite done; we also had to declare some configuration information in our XML-based component descriptor files. This file is where we declared runtime characteristics, including servant lifetime policy, security, transactions, and more.

Although the functionality of this shopping-cart application may be barebones, it's fully scalable just the way it's written: Our customer list will scale to the size of the database that holds it; if we buy a multiprocessor distributed database to implement our PSS, we can handle millions. Similarly, the scalability of our shopping site will depend on the CCM implementation we buy to run it, and these will come in versions that run load-balanced on a roomful of interconnected machines.

Scalable patterns are built into CCM implementations by the specification, and we've demonstrated how to use several of them in this brief example. Customer is an entity object with persistent state and a key (the account number) that is exposed to the client. Its operation is very simple: Once it has been properly filled in, all it does is pop into memory for an instant to trigger and sanction the creation of a shopping cart with its account number. This ensures that all shopping carts are associated with active accounts.

Shopping Cart is only slightly more complex, and we did this partly to demonstrate this server activation pattern. Carts are process components that save their state in a database when they are not active; this lets them activate only for the brief instant when a customer is adding something or checking out. (We've left the programming of "Remove item from shopping cart" and "List contents of shopping cart" for you to add as an exercise, if you want.) This pattern uses our server resource extremely economically; even with hundreds of thousands of customers actively shopping, there will be only a small fraction of that number of carts executing at any instant.

Alternatively, we could have implemented our shopping cart as a session component and kept intermediate values in memory. Session components maintain their values in memory across invocations in the same session (thus their name), from the time they are created until they are destroyed, so our values would be preserved if we gave our session carts the activation policy of component as well. This has the disadvantage that every shopping cart occupies memory—or at least virtual memory—from the time a customer starts shopping until he either checks out, logs out, or times out. If we're successful enough to have a million people shopping our site, this means a million active shopping carts compared to perhaps a couple of thousand using the activation-per-method pattern. For lower-traffic sites, however, per-session is a perfectly reasonable activation pattern to use.

For checkout, we used a service component. Service components are stateless—they have neither identity nor state; nothing persists from one call to the next. This makes them very cheap (in resources, at least) to activate (or create, actually), and just about free to deactivate, increasing your server's efficiency. Of course you can only use them with the factory pattern; there's nothing to find! We thought about using a process component for this step; this would have used more resource in exchange for a slight increase in robustness that we thought wasn't really necessary.

Once we've declared these component types to have these activation patterns, our role as programmer is done and our CCM implementation takes over. CCM products may range from small, single-machine implementations with simple datastores, to large multimachine, multiprocessor implementations that couple to distributed databases and transaction engines. Your CCM application will run with all of the power of your CCM engine, since the high-level code you write does not over-specify how it's supposed to run, and the engine has already been tuned for your environment.

As CCM applications go, this one is pretty simple: The CCM has features that we didn't use, quite intentionally, since this example was meant to be only an introduction. In the rest of this chapter, we'll introduce the entire CCM. It won't be a complete treatment—the specification itself runs over 700 pages, and we don't have space. We're sure that books devoted entirely to CCM will be out soon; in fact, we're planning one ourselves.

III.3.3   Description of the CCM

CCM is designed for large, distributed enterprise and Internet applications that need to run with transactional assurance, security, and high throughput, and are best coded by programmers whose skill and knowledge is of business rules and processes, rather than the esoterics of server-side scalability patterns and the nuances of two-phase commit and rollback. Although CORBA gives architects and developers everything they need to develop these applications (as we know from the large number of successful CORBA installations running now), it may give you too much because POA policies, transactions, security, and other resources combine in thousands of different ways, and it requires considerable skill to select the best combination out of all the alternatives. Of these combinations, a relatively few patterns have proven successful—so successful that it's usually not necessary to consider the others; all you have to do is pick one of these and get on with your development.

The CCM packages up this subset of successful use patterns into a new OMG specification that defines a comprehensive server-side development and runtime architecture. Because all component-based applications fit the CCM's pattern space, they will be expressed very compactly in the new languages that the specification defines, plus a minimal amount of code in a language with a CORBA language mapping. (Vendors will support C++ or

Java initially, adding more CORBA-mapped languages as CCM products mature.)

The CCM consists of a number of interlocking conceptual pieces that, taken together, comprise the complete server computing architecture. These pieces are:

- *The Components* themselves, including
  - An Abstract Component Model, expressed as extensions to IDL and the object model
  - A Component Implementation Framework, centered on the new Component Implementation Definition Language (CIDL)
- *The Component Container Programming Model* expressed alternatively in the specification as
  - The component implementer and client view
  - The container provider view
- *Integration with persistence, transactions, and events*
- *Component Packaging and Deployment*
- *Interworking with EJB 1.1*
- *Component MetaData Model*—Interface Repository and MOF extensions

In the rest of this chapter, we'll summarize most of these pieces. We'll skip the container provider's view; if you're a vendor building a CCM product, you'll need to read and understand the specification itself and not a summary like this one (or maybe you *wrote* the specification). We'll also skip the metadata model, since this book is written more for programmers than for modelers. But, we'll point out that there's an entire part of this book—Part IV—that discusses OMG's modeling specifications.

III.3.3.1   Stages in a CCM Development Project

Here are the steps in a CCM development project. For each one, we've listed the things you write, the CCM tools you use, and the artifacts that the step produces.

III.3.3.1.1   Analysis/Design Phase

CCM projects, in general, will be large so you'll want to do an analysis and design before you start to code. Chances are you'll use OMG's standard analysis and design (A&D) language, UML, for this. (For a description of

UML, turn to Part IV, Chapter 1.) Right now, the connection from UML to CORBA and CCM hasn't been fully standardized: Although you can construct a UML model and use it for your CORBA or CCM application, you have to subset UML (which is a very general language) yourself, and map some of the UML constructs to coding constructs yourself.

OMG is working on this problem, and expects to have a connection within a year or two. The work goes under the name "Business Object Initiative"; currently there are three RFPs underway and one that will be issued when these complete since its piece builds on them. They were issued by OMG's Analysis and Design Task Force; you can watch their progress on the OMG Web site. See Appendix A for the URLs. OMG's anticipated move to the UML-based Model Driven Architecture (MDA) will formalize the connection between design and coding even more than the BOI; look ahead to Part IV, Chapter 3 for details.

This step includes all the modeling and analysis work that happens before a developer is even ready to start designing CORBA components. It produces a UML model of the application in several parts including an architecture, possibly a set of Use Cases, and other artifacts. Check out Part IV, Chapter 1 for an introduction to UML that includes a model of one of the objects implemented in our previous book, *CORBA 3 Fundamentals and Programming*.

III.3.3.1.2 *Component Declaration*

As we've seen in our mini-example, you declare your CORBA component's methods and home (a type manager, basically) in OMG IDL using the component extensions. Then you compile it using the CORBA 3 IDL compiler that came with your CCM product. (You'll declare its state and some additional aspects in PSDL and CIDL, but we'll cover those in their own steps.)

Because we're in the CCM environment and not just CORBA, our interfaces include more than the operations we declare. For example, every component interface includes operations to navigate around its various interfaces, and stubs for these were generated automatically when we compiled our IDL. When we code our clients, we're free to invoke any of these automatically generated methods, in addition to all of the ones we declare and write explicitly ourselves.

Server-side products of this step include skeletons, IR entries (in the new component keywords that we present later in this chapter), some automatically generated code, and an XML component description that we'll use later for packaging and deployment.

III.3.3.1.3 *Component Implementation*

The first part of the implementation step is to declare each component's persistent state in PSDL (an extension of OMG IDL, presented in Part III, Chapter 2), and some behavior in CIDL (an extension of PSDL). This integrates your components with the CCM's transaction, persistence, event handling, and other features.

You map components' declared state to your persistent store using an interactive tool, or by writing some simple code.

Compilation of the CIDL generates component skeletons that you fill in with business logic in your chosen programming language. Some CCM products may assist this step with interactive tools; others will let you use your favorite text editor. You may also have to write a few lines of code to tie together some of the CIDL declarations.

From this step, once we compile the code we and the CCM wrote, we get still more compiled libraries.

III.3.3.1.4 *Component Packaging*

Next, you generate a component *descriptor*: a file, in XML, that tells the CCM runtime how to connect up and manage the implementation that we've just created. Again, you may write this using a text editor, but many CCM products will provide an interactive tool that does most of the work and ensures that the file produced is error-free.

Then you package up the implementation and the component descriptor into a *Component Archive File* (CAR; the file extension is `.car`), using a packaging tool (again, probably interactive) provided with your CCM product.

The CAR is deployable, as is, but we can optionally use the CAR in an *assembly*.

III.3.3.1.5 *Component Assembly*

This optional step allow us to assemble a number of components into a *component assembly*—that is, an application or part composed of a number of components with predefined interaction pathways—that will be packaged in an assembly archive file (`.aar`) to be distributed and deployed together.

The specification says this step is optional, but it won't be left out of very many development projects. As we've already mentioned, efficient CCM applications will be made up of many different, small components, and they'll be put together in assemblies for distribution and deployment.

In this step, you custom-configure each component in the assembly, describe how it connects to the other included components, and tell how the different component types will be partitioned among a set of computers if the installation is designed for a multimachine execution environment for load balancing. You will probably do this using one or a set of interactive tools, but a text editor will work too, in a pinch.

The output is a component assembly archive file that contains a set of component archives and an XML-based descriptor that describes the assembly.

You can't nest assemblies, but you can extend an existing assembly by pulling it into your assembly tool, adding stuff to it, and saving the result as a new assembly.

III.3.3.1.6 *Component Deployment and Installation*

Now we leave the development space and enter the runtime environment. CCM product vendors must provide a runtime that supports transactions, security, and event handling. (In fact, many CCM runtime products will be built upon vendors' current TP, TM, or OTM products, packaging up the years of experience embodied in these products in the best possible wrapper.) These systems may support persistence as well, although the CCM specification allows a runtime to rely on a separate compliant PSS implementation.

Before you can install your components, you (or your system administrator) have to install and configure your component runtime, get its transaction processing system and security system working properly, and connect it up to your persistence service whether it's built in or separate.

CCM development and runtime products will be quite distinct, even though most CCM product vendors will provide both. Some component applications will be constructed in-house, built, deployed, and supported by the same crew. For these, it's likely that a site will deploy the runtime of the same vendor that provided their CCM development environment. But, many other component applications—perhaps most, if the specification is as successful as we hope—will be built by application vendors, packaged (perhaps even shrink-wrapped), and sold either at retail or through industrial channels, to be deployed and run at many different sites.

The component runtime includes an installer program that reads the CAR and installs the components or assemblies, connects up provided and required interfaces, and supplied and consumed events. When the installer tool is done, the component application is ready to run.

III.3.3.1.7 Runtime: Component Instance Activation

For most component-based applications, you won't deploy the components themselves. Remember, most components will be ephemeral beings: shopping carts (as in our example) or other objects that come and go along with the customers or other users that need them. What you really deploy are the component *factories* and managers that create and manage the components during their lifecycle, as we pointed out 'way back in Section III.3.2. At runtime, components are activated by the container POA using the subset of modes available, and are invoked by clients via their IDL interfaces.

Once deployed and installed, the component factories are available to be activated and used via the standard CORBA ORB mechanisms.

III.3.3.2 The CORBA Component Model and CCM Extensions to OMG IDL

Component is a new basic meta-type in CORBA; when you define a component in IDL, you declare a **component** and not an **interface**. The CCM specification extends IDL and the IR with the new keywords and concepts required by its model. At runtime, a component is represented by a component reference, which is derived from the CORBA object reference.

There are two levels of components, *basic* and *extended*, that differ in the range of capabilities they support:

- **Basic components**, whose characteristics correspond nearly exactly to those of Release 1.1 Enterprise JavaBeans, enable an extremely close relationship between CCM and EJB. They also provide a simple mechanism for converting existing CORBA objects into components.

- **Extended components** add a number of new features, as we'll see later on. As in the specification, we'll tell you when we're describing basic components; if we don't say, we're referring to extended.

There's more about the difference between basic and extended components later in the chapter; we'll postpone our explanation because the details involve CCM features we haven't covered yet.

Figure III.3.1 summarizes the structure of a component and how it interacts with the outside world. We'll add to this as we work through the rest of this chapter, but the features on this diagram will get us started.

The various stubs and skeletons a component bears are referred to as *ports*. Four types have special names:

Facets are the potentially multiple interfaces that a component provides to its clients.

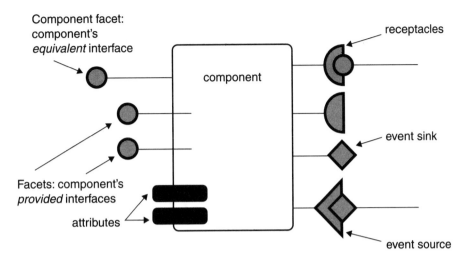

Figure III.3.1 Structure of a component, showing the various ways that it can interact with the outside world.

Receptacles are the client stubs that a component uses to invoke other components, as described in its configuration file.

Event sources are the named connection points that emit events of specified type to one or more interested consumers, or to an event channel.

Event sinks are the named connection points into which events of a specified type may be pushed by a supplier or an event channel.

A component may also incorporate client stubs used to invoke other (non-component) CORBA objects—for example, the naming or trader service. These interfaces do not have a special name.

Other new features of the model include:

Primary keys, values that components (that have persistent state; not all component types do) expose to their clients to help identify themselves—a customer account number or social security number might be a primary key

Attributes and **configuration**, named values exposed through accessors and mutators, primarily used for component configuration

Home interfaces that provide standard factory and finder operations

At runtime, a CCM *container* supports components' lifecycles from instantiation, through execution (which may entail a number of activations and deactivations), to destruction. You can think of a container as a specialized POA with some added features, but you'll see as we work our way through the specification that it's sometimes hard to tell when one container stops and another one starts. (CCM allows applications to span machines, for load-balancing.) A CCM application will, almost always, include a number of component types with different activation and persistence characteristics, requiring a number of different POAs and, therefore, containers. Component types have names including "session" and "entity" that you remember from EJB. There are a total of seven types, as we'll detail in Section III.3.3.7.

III.3.3.3 Multiple Facets (interfaces) and Navigation

Here's the structure of the multiple interfaces—that is, facets—that an extended component may support, as shown in Figure III.3.2.

The interface named in our component declaration—**component Shopping-Cart** in our mini-example—is the component's *equivalent* interface and, for each instance as soon as it is created at runtime, bears its *distinguished reference*. We could have also declared that the component *supports* additional interfaces defined elsewhere in our IDL file; each of these interfaces is inherited by the equivalent interface and augments it by adding operations to the distinguished reference.

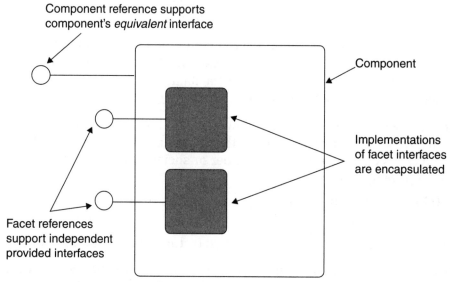

Figure III.3.2 A component supporting multiple facets; that is, interfaces.

We can also declare that the component *provides* additional interfaces. Each is independent of the equivalent interface and has its own reference, and is referred to as a *facet*.

The entire implementation is encapsulated within the bold line that delineates the component, but you shouldn't assume that the implementation of each facet is distinct from all of the others, and from the distinguished interface, since this is up to the developer. In fact, we'll see later that there are two ways to program multifaceted components—segmented and non-segmented—depending on whether or not you intermingle implementation of the various facets.

Component-aware clients can navigate from any component interface—distinguished or facet—to any other, using functionality provided by the CCM through standard interfaces.

Basic components only bear the equivalent interface; no additional facets are allowed.

III.3.3.4 Component Homes: CORBA Finally Gets Some Class

For years, OMG members who write enterprise applications have been asking for standard operations on the extent of a type. (*Extent* is the set of instances of a type.) In an object-oriented language, these are typically class operations. With all instances residing in the same process, class operations are no problem: All instances are created within the process, and there's no way for one to escape. In CORBA, however, applications are distributed: Instances of a CORBA type can be created anywhere, coming and going at the whim of their clients. This makes the concept of extent so hazy that CORBA never bothered to define anything resembling a class operation. (Nothing prevented individual applications from providing this functionality for themselves, at least within a restricted domain; it was just not defined as a standard part of CORBA.)

With CCM, things are different: We know in advance that all of the instances are going to run in the scope of our CCM runtime. This may be spread across several machines to provide load-balancing and redundancy for fault tolerance, but at least our scope is well defined and managed. The architecture virtually demands that we define a factory to create these instances, making it easy to keep a list of their component references as they get created. If we can just cross them off the list as they're destroyed, we'll always know the extent, and it's easy to write an operation that lets an instance take itself off the list as it destroys itself. We do, indeed, have everything we need to define class-type operations, at least for the extent within the scope of our CCM runtime.

So, the CCM defines another new meta-type, the **ComponentHome,** that takes on these responsibilities—basically, a type manager for its instances. You declare the home type the same way (except using the keyword **home**), and at the same time, as you declare the component type. There must be at least one home type for each component type; you may define additional home types for the same component type if you want (for instance, homes defining different state variables as the primary key), but each component instance must consider only one of them to be its home at runtime.

The home bears lifecycle operations to manage instances of the type it was designed to manage: factory operations that create instances and associate a primary key value with each one (if it's an *entity* component, as we'll show soon); finder operations based on this key value; and destructor operations. These basic operations are defined and implemented by the CCM, via generated code. You can define and implement any other factory and finder operations you want.

You can also define operations—for example, queries—on the extent, in a component home; on invocation, the home could contact every instance, query whatever you wanted to know, collate the answers, and report the result.

III.3.3.5   Receptacles

In one sense, we already know what a receptacle is: It's the client side of an interface, born by an object.

What's new in the CCM is the *management of the connection.* In your component IDL, you can declare that a component type uses one or more interfaces. CCM automatically generates a standard **connect** and **disconnect** operation for each interface, and generates code to manage the setting (**connect**) and unsetting (**disconnect**) of the object references at runtime. You can declare that instance connections be set up, for example at creation time, and the CCM will generate code to set the values at run time too, although you'll have to do this yourself if program logic for this gets a little opaque. Then in your business application code, when your component is ready to invoke the interface, the object reference is already set.

III.3.3.6   Events

The CCM event model is based on publish/subscribe. It supports a subset of the semantics of the CORBA Notification Service, using simplified inter-

Table III.3.1   CCM Componet Categories

COMPONENT CATEGORY	CORBA USAGE MODEL	CONTAINER API TYPE	PRIMARY KEY	EJB BEAN TYPE
Service	Stateless	Session	No	—
Session	Conversational	Session	No	Session
Process	Durable	Entity	No	—
Entity	Durable	Entity	Yes	Entity

faces. Only push semantics are supported. We'll discuss events later, in Section III.3.3.12.3.

III.3.3.7   Component Usage Patterns

Everything that you do with the CCM is part of one or another pattern that it supports, but there is one place where this comes to the fore, and that is in the selection of *component category*. There are seven categories: four supported by the CCM, two by EJB, and an "empty" category that you can declare and support yourself, if you're up for the work.

Table III.3.1 lists the four CCM categories. We'll define all of the new terms and explain everything in this section.

Every component type that you define (using IDL, PSDL, and CIDL) must have a category; you'll declare its category in its **composition** CIDL. You'll also declare its Container API Type; you declared its Container Category indirectly when you declared its category.

The component category is built up from a *CORBA usage model* and a *Container API type*, so we'll review those first.

- **Container API types.** There are two, and they differ depending on the durability of the component's object reference. *Session* container API types support *transient* references; these expire and are not valid across session boundaries. *Entity* container API types support *persistent* references, valid across session boundaries. Your container derives its API type from your component category declaration, following the third column of Table III.3.1. Session and Entity container APIs are defined in the CCM; they provide the services that the CCM defines for the type. Your CCM documentation will list the container APIs that you're allowed to use for each type.

- **CORBA usage models.** These refer to the interaction patterns between the component and its container on the one hand, and the rest of CORBA—especially persistence and transactionality—on the other. There are three: *Stateless* uses transient references, and the POA assigns an incoming request to any servant of the proper type. *Conversational* uses transient references, but the POA dedicates a specific servant to each component reference. This lets your client invoke an instance of a conversational component more than once, although not across a session boundary. *Durable* uses persistent references and also dedicates a specific servant to each one.

Now for those component categories. There are four:

- *Service* components have no state and no identity; every execution starts with a clean slate and has to finish everything it starts because nothing persists from one invocation of a service component to the next. In our mini-example, we used this category for the Checkout component and it fit well; in another application, a service component could execute a transaction, or a command. The *stateless* designation of its CORBA usage model indicates this. Its *Session* Container API type indicates that its component reference is transient: that is, clients cannot store it and use it again in a subsequent session. And, of course, service components cannot have a primary key since they don't have persistent storage.

- *Session* components have transient state, and non-persistent identity. We could have used this category to implement a ShoppingCart component for an application where shopping trips are always limited to a single session; the client could hold onto its object reference and count on the component to maintain its state for that duration, but not much longer. This is indicated by the conversational designation of its CORBA usage model: The object reference is transient, but it is assigned to a specific POA servant. The Session container API type confirms that its object reference will not survive from one session to the next and, having no persistent state, it cannot have a primary key.

- *Process* components have persistent identity and state that may span sessions, but no key is visible to the client. A client can save the reference for a process component and invoke it repeatedly to complete a task, but the instance and reference expire once the task is complete, so it doesn't make sense to register the reference in a Naming or Trader Service. Also, process components do not support the **find_by_ primary_key** operation. They are useful to represent a process with a beginning and an end; we could have used a process component in our mini-example to collect name and address data from a new customer to create an account if we had included this stage of the customer interaction in the example. The account-creation piece would be a process component, while the resulting account would be represented by an entity component (presented next). The entity container API type supports persistent object references, and the durable CORBA usage model signifies in addition that the reference is assigned to a dedicated POA servant for execution. Process component may be transactional.

- *Entity* components have persistent state and identity, visible to their client through a primary key. We used an entity component for our customer object, keyed by the customer's account number. Like the process component type, entity components use an entity container API type and durable CORBA usage model. It's good programming practice, and an efficient use of resources all around, to use an entity component to represent the data in a row of your database to the other component types in your application, as we did with the customer component in our example.

The CCM supports four *Servant Lifetime Policies:* Method, Transaction, Component, and Container:

- Servants with a **method** lifetime policy are activated on every operation request, and passivated as soon as the operation has completed. For components that spend only a small fraction of their existence computing (such as our Shopping Cart, that spends most of its time waiting for a customer to order something), this benefit of the memory savings outweighs the cost of the activation/passivation.

- Servants with a **transaction** lifetime policy are activated at the beginning of a transaction, and passivated upon completion. Memory remains allocated for the duration of the transaction which is virtually always kept short in order to minimize consequences of resource-locking.

- Servants with a **component** lifetime policy are activated on an operation request, and remain active until the component implementation asks to be passivated. This is useful when the executing servant has the information it needs to determine when passivation is in order.

- Servants with a **container** lifetime policy are activated on an operation request, and passivated when the container decides that it's time. This is useful when information that the container has, which might include the active servant count, affects the decision. For example, you could leave container-policy servants in memory if only a few are active even if invocations come slowly, but passivate servants faster during busy times when memory is scarce.

Servants for service category components can only be assigned the method lifetime policy; all other categories of components can have any of these four lifetime policies. This makes sense; service components only live for a single invocation anyhow.

III.3.3.8 Component Attributes and Configuration

Components are *configurable:* You can design and write your components in a flexible way, and use features of the CCM to configure them to fit a particular application at install time (and, to a lesser extent, at runtime).

You can indicate which interfaces of a component are intended for configuration, and which are primarily for runtime use, although the distinction becomes blurry at times. At the end of installation, you call **configuration_complete**. Before the call, operations on configuration interfaces are allowed, and on operational interfaces are disallowed. After the call, the reverse is true.

IDL **attributes** hold configuration information, and the CCM recognizes their special role. Because of their critical role, the CCM adds **exceptions** to **attributes'** set and **get** operations. Any CORBA 3 application, and not just those using the CCM, can declare and use these **exceptions**.

The CCM collects all of the configuration information in a **configurator** object, which it saves. There's an operation to apply a configurator, with its collection of settings, to a component in a single operation.

III.3.3.9 Component Implementation

The CCM uses the term *Component Implementation Framework* (CIF) for the programming model that your programmers use to construct component implementations.

The core of the CIF is the CIDL, which we've already used in our miniexample. CIDL is an extension of PSDL, which adds persistent state declaration to OMG IDL.

The PSDL subset of CIDL allows the CCM to take care of your component's persistent state, through the mechanisms defined in the new Persistent State Service (PSS) described in Part III, Chapter 2. One thing PSDL lets you do is declare the implementation variables that make up your instances' persistent state; the PSS uses generated code and service functions to store and retrieve their values, as we've already shown in its own chapter.

At runtime, the CCM environment takes care of a lot of things for your components: navigation, identity (via the primary key), activation/deactivation, persistent state management, creation/destruction, and other functions. You declare these in CIDL; the CCM then generates code called *skeletons* (an extension of the IDL skeletons defined by basic CORBA) that implements the automated CCM functions. You have to fill in the skeletons with code for the business part of your application—the only part that the CCM can't do for you!

III.3.3.10   Composition

For every component type that you define, you need to declare a *composition* that binds its various elements together. This is where you declare your component's name and category—service, session, process, or entity. This is also where you bind to its executor and home executor—the code for its behavior. There are optional parts to the composition: binding to PSS artifacts, and division into segments. Here are a few example composition declarations.

III.3.3.10.1   Minimal Composition

Here's an example of minimal composition. (We took this example from the specification.) It declares a name for the composition, the component's category (service, session, process, or entity), the home type (which implicitly identifies the component type), the name of the generated home executor, and the name of the generated component executor.

A minimal composition definition (with no state management) looks like:

```
// CIDL
composition <category> MyComposition {
    home executor MyHomeExecutor {
        implements MyHomeType;
        manages MyExecutor;
    };
};
```

Figure III.3.3 illustrates this composition. After declaring the category of the composition and its name, the definition identifies the Home Executor that defines the composition. The Home Executor is CCM-generated code in your programming language, that implements the operations of your Component Home—**create**, **remove**, and **find_by_primary_key** are provided and implemented by the CCM. You can add your own operations, as we show in the following sections.

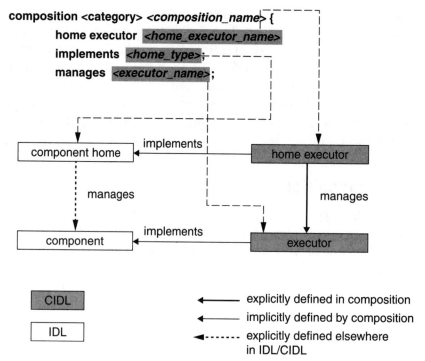

Figure III.3.3 A minimal composition.

III.3.3.10.2 State Management

Now we'll add persistent state management, still keeping things simple. Here's an example with a *catalog* (which, as we saw in Part III, Chapter 2, manages a connection from our execution space to our storage space, which is probably in a database), and various types and homes that, together, manage our storage.

We won't explain all of these terms here; we're including this example to show that you can add persistent storage management with only a few lines of code. We presented an explanation of Abstract Storage Homes and the like in Part III, Chapter 2.

```
// CIDL
composition <category> MyComposition {
  uses catalog {
    MyCatalogType MyCatalog;
  }
  home executor MyHomeExecutor {
```

```
      implements MyHomeType;
      bindsTo MyCatalog.MyAbstractStorageHome;
      manages MyExecutor;
   };
};
```

III.3.3.10.3   *Home Operations*

We've already mentioned that the **Component Home** acts as a type manager, providing factory, finder, and other operations on its extent. Here's an example of how you declare your own factory, finder, and other operations and delegate them to homes. Since the CIF cannot guess what you intend these operations to do, it (wisely!) does not attempt to generate implementation code. Instead, you use the **delegatesTo** construct to redirect these operations to, for example, an abstract storagehome (defined in Part III, Chapter 2) or an executor where they are either implemented or delegated one step further down. Here's a sample of the CIDL for this:

```
// CIDL:
composition <category> MyComposition {
   home executor MyHomeExecutor {
      ... // storage management specification goes here...
      delegatesTo abstract storagehome{
        MyHomeOp1 : MyStorageHomeOp1,
        ...
      };
      delegatesTo executor {
        MyHomeOp2 : MyExecutorOp2,
        ...
        abstract(MyHomeOp3, MyHomeOp4, ... );
      }
   };
};
```

III.3.3.10.4   *Defining the Component Executor*

Now that we've defined our home executor, it's time to define the component executor that it manages. There are two kinds of executors: A *monolithic* executor is a single programming artifact. Its persistent state is a single unit, and it is activated and deactivated all at once. In contrast, a *segmented* executor is made up of parts, each with its own defined persistent state and execution unit. A segment corresponds to one or more of a component's facets. This is one way to increase the efficiency of a heavily used server: The unit of activation/deactivation during execution is the segment. You can only segment entity and process components; there's no reason to use this trick on components without persistent state anyhow.

In the section of CIDL that declares your executor, you have to specify its name and one or more segments. Additional lines control code generation of receptacles (CCM-controlled client-side interfaces), and declare delegation relationships between component features and the PSS.

Here's a sample CIDL declaration of a component executor with a single segment, bearing two facets:

```
composition <category> MyComposition {
   ...
   home executor MyHomeExecutor {
     ... // storage management specification
     manages MyExecutor {
     segment MySegment0 {
       storedOn MyCatalog.MyAbstractStorageHome;
       provides ( MyFacet1, MyFacet2 );
     };
   ...
   };
};
```

III.3.3.11   Container Programming Model

Now that we've defined the composition of our component, let's examine the programming environment that CCM gives us—that is, the container programming model. The container is the server's runtime environment for a CORBA component implementation, offering CCM services to the components it services.

Figure III.3.4 shows the container programming architecture. We'll go through its features one at a time.

External API Types (labeled "external" in Figure III.3.4). These are the APIs that clients use to invoke operations on the component or its home. You defined the operational interfaces in your IDL; the standard factory and finder interfaces on the home were defined by the CCM, but (as we've already pointed out) you were able to define additional ones if you wanted.

Container API Types (labeled "Container" in Figure III.3.4). These are local interfaces that allow either component-to-container or container-to-component invocations. Component-to-container invocations request the container-provided services shown in the diagram: Transactions, Security, Persistence, and Notification. Container-to-component invocations primarily concern activation/deactivation and informing the servant of its Primary Key so that it can restore the required state. The form of the container API types will vary depending on the type of your component: *session* or *entity*.

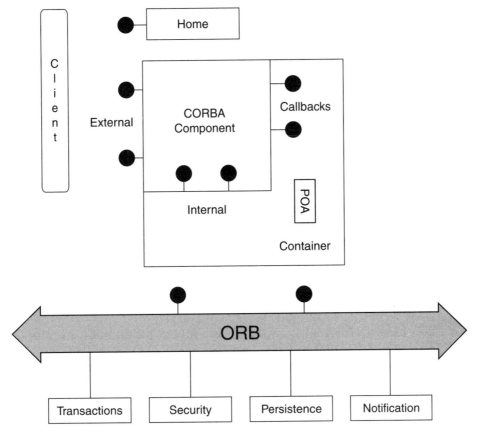

Figure III.3.4   The container programming architecture.

III.3.3.12   The Container-Provided Services

The four services provided to components by the container are Transactions, Security, Event Handling, and Persistence. Here's a little more information about each one.

III.3.3.12.1   *Transactions*

You can manage the transactions your component takes part in yourself, or allow the container to do it. If you select self-managed transactions, you must declare the transactions' start and end boundaries yourself by invoking either the container's **UserTransaction** interface or the CORBA Transaction Service. If you select container-managed transactions, you declare transaction policies in the component's descriptor as we did in our example. The container follows these policies, executing the component's operations in the context of a transaction.

III.3.3.12.2 Security

The CCM container relies on CORBA security to retrieve security policy declarations from the deployment descriptor and to check the active credentials for invoking operations. You define your security policies at the operation level; in fact, it's done in the configuration file in the `ComponentFeatures` section, right next to the transaction declaration.

You define the access permissions for a component in its deployment descriptor. You've also defined a set of rights recognized by the CORBA security when you installed your CCM runtime. You have to align the component's permissions with the CCM security installation's rights; otherwise, the security system won't be able to process access requests.

III.3.3.12.3 Events

Your Component IDL (not your CIDL) generates operations for emitting and consuming events; the container maps these to the CORBA notification service. Components and component-aware clients can use either the CCM event APIs or the Notification Service APIs to publish and receive events. Component-unaware clients (described soon) must use the notification service APIs, and must stay within the subset supported by CCM. The CCM runtime includes an implementation of the notification service, or at least the subset required by the CCM.

The CCM defines two types of event channels: one shared, the target of the **publishes** designation; the other dedicated, and the target of the **emits** designation. The dedicated channel is intended primarily for use during configuration, while the shared channel is designed for runtime.

A component event is represented as a **valuetype** embedded in an **any**. This way, emitters and publishers can be matched to consumers by event type, but untyped channels can still be used. Containers set up the channels, accept a component event and push it to a channel as a structured event, and receive structured events and convert them to component events.

III.3.3.12.4 Persistence

There are two basic ways you can handle persistence:

- **Container-managed persistence**, selected in CIDL by connecting a state definition defined using PSDL (as specified in the CORBA Persistent State Service) to a component segment in CIDL. The container, using code generated from these declarations, automatically saves and restores state as required.

■ **Self-managed persistence**, selected by suitable CIDL declarations (which we don't have space for in this chapter). The container still invokes defined interfaces when it needs to save or restore state, but in this case you are responsible for implementing the code that does the work.

If you're replacing an existing application with components and your database schema already exists, you'll have to use self-managed persistence and map the variables in your components to the database yourself. But, if you're starting from scratch, you can let the container manage the persistence and end up with an object-oriented schema that matches your object model.

Persistence is implemented via the Persistence Service, which we already covered in Part III, Chapter 2. In fact, persistence is the only one of the container-provided services that you may have to purchase separately and integrate with your CCM runtime—when you select yours, make sure you understand whether you have to buy a separate PSS, and which ones the vendor knows work well with it: Transactions, Security, and Event Handling are all provided by built-in container functions, so there's nothing extra for you to buy here.

The container vs. self-managed persistence works about the same in CCM as in EJB but the CCM makes less of a fuss about it, possibly because the distinction actually happens in the PSS.

III.3.3.13 Component Levels and Integration with Enterprise JavaBeans

Near the beginning of this section, we said that there were two levels of components: basic, corresponding to the EJB programming model, and extended. We didn't say much about it at the time, because the details involved concepts that we hadn't presented yet—primarily segments and services. Now we have, so it's time to add some detail.

A basic component has only a single interface and may use transactions, security, and simple persistence for a single segment. It relies upon the container to manage the construction of CORBA object references and uses only a single thread (the *serialize* threading model).

An extended component has all the functionality of a basic component, plus multiple facets and advanced persistence assigned

individually to multiple segments. It may use the event model, participate in the construction of CORBA object references, and use multiple threads (the *multithreaded* threading model).

OMG members, including Sun (which is a supporter of the CCM specification), wanted to integrate Enterprise JavaBeans (EJBs) with CORBA Components as closely as possible. That, as things turned out, was extremely closely indeed, as we'll describe now: You will be able to mix EJBs and basic (*not* extended) CORBA Components in the same application.

The basic level of the CCM specification corresponds, nearly feature for feature, to the 1.1 release of the EJB specification. In fact, the required programming API for Java CORBA Components is EJB 1.1. The EJB 2.0 specification, released after the CCM, requires that EJBs interoperate over the network using OMG's protocol IIOP, using equivalent IDL generated from Java objects via the reverse Java-to-IDL mapping (described in Section I.1.4).

Building on this foundation, the CCM specification includes a comprehensive forward and reverse mapping of EJB operations to CCM operations. The correspondence, as you might expect, is extremely close; a thin bridge can span the gap. It encompasses not only method invocations, but also container, factory, finder, and other infrastructure operations.

With suitable bridges in place, an EJB running in a CORBA EJB container can look like a CCM component, and a CCM component running in a CCM container can look like an EJB. Figure III.3.5 shows, conceptually at least, what such a system might look like.

This allows you to build up applications from both CCM components and EJBs, which is something you might want to do for many reasons. For example, staff skill levels may dictate use of one or the other environment, or you may find commercial components or EJBs that you can incorporate into your application.

You don't declare a component to be basic or extended; instead, the compiler identifies which one you mean by the format of your component declaration. The authors of the specification felt that, in the future, either CCM or EJB or both might develop in a way that renders this distinction moot, and IDL with the declarations of basic or extended obsolete.

III.3.3.14   Component Assembly and Packaging

Component applications with more than one component type—and that's every one that we can think of—have to be *assembled* into a unit that works together. You can do this in layers if you want, assembling assemblies into

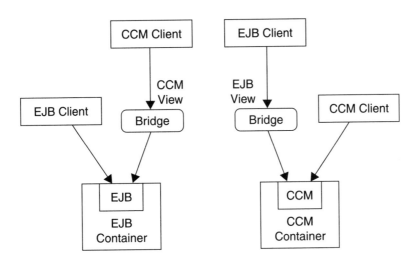

Figure III.3.5 Interoperating between CORBA Components and EJBs.

still larger assemblies, or do it all at once. (This comes in handy when you get an assembly from a vendor or other software supplier, and need to add more functionality to get what you need.)

When you're done, you need to *package* up everything for deployment. The CCM defines, finally, a multiplatform software distribution format for CORBA. It's in layers, and can support the heterogeneous environments that the rest of CORBA handles so well. It's all built around a *component archive file (*.car*)*, which is a zip file with a prescribed contents.

The bottom layer is the *component package*. This centers around a descriptor file, written in XML, that points to the various files in the package and describes them in a standard way. The most important files in the package are the executables: You (or your vendor) can compile a component for different platforms and operating systems and put all of the executables into the package, telling in the descriptor file which platform each one supports. At deployment time, an installer in your CCM runtime will read the descriptor file and pull off the executable it needs. The descriptor for a component will also list and describe its ports, and how it wants to connect to other components, although the package descriptors (coming next) build on this.

You can install a component package into a CCM runtime, if the single component in it does something useful, or you can assemble it with other component packages into the much more useful *component assembly package*. This package is a set of component packages with a package descriptor that describes them and the way they interconnect—provides/uses for receptacles and interfaces, and emits/publishes/consumes for events.

III.3.3.15 Component Deployment

The CCM specification places the onus onto CCM runtime vendors to build an installer that reads the component assembly archive file, including its descriptors at various levels, extracts and installs the proper executables, instantiates homes on the server, and registers them with the home finder that comes back from **resolve_initial_references**. Some ports can be connected at installation time, but ports on service, session, process, and dynamically created entity components will have to be connected at runtime based on information in these configuration files. Since the CCM explicitly allows assemblies to be deployed onto multiple-machine configurations for load balancing, you can expect installers to be fairly sophisticated pieces of software in their own right. The CCM expects that installer software will gather some information interactively from the sysadmin at install time, using interactive tools.

III.3.3.16 Client Programming Model

The CCM specification devotes some space and effort to differentiating and describing *component-aware* and *component-unaware* clients. Component-unaware clients are not somehow stupid or forgetful; they're the best you can write if you can only find a CORBA 2.X ORB on your client platform. Even though there are ways to compensate for the shortcomings you encounter, you'll still miss the client-side functions that the CORBA 3 ORB provides. We'll describe the more elegant component-aware client first, and follow up with the unaware and some ways to overcome its deficiencies.

III.3.3.16.1 *Component-Aware Clients*

CCM provides clients with many new ways to access remote functionality, but the basic component interface is still just a regular CORBA interface accessible via a regular CORBA object reference. The differences are in the additional things you can do, and not in changes to the stuff you've been doing already.

Service, session, and process components have to be created afresh for every use. Even entity components have to be created, although they stick around and can be used in later sessions. For this, CCM provides the *factory design pattern*: Our client starts by invoking **resolve_initial_references** for a **HomeFinder**. The **HomeFinder**, implemented by the CCM runtime, maintains a table of references and types of every **ComponentHome** in the system, and so is able to provide our client with the reference of the **ComponentHome** for the type that we need. Our client then invokes the **create** operation on the **ComponentHome**, creating a new instance of the type we want and returning its reference to us. There may be several create operations on the **ComponentHome**, differing in signature. The **ComponentHome** acts as manager for its type in many ways, and not just as factory, so our client may use the reference for more than just **create**.

To locate existing instances of entity components, CCM provides the *finder design pattern*. To use it, our client still needs the reference for the **ComponentHome** which it finds the same way, but instead of invoking **create**, we invoke **find_by_primary_key**. Because entity components stick around, we can store their references in our Naming or Trader Service (described in *CORBA 3 Fundamentals and Programming*) and retrieve them by name or characteristics.

You don't have to find your **ComponentHome** using the **HomeFinder**; homes have CORBA object references and can be registered with the Naming Service and found by clients that look them up using the name you establish in your application. EJBs use this pattern too, substituting JNDI for the CORBA Naming Service.

Component-aware clients may use CCM-specific interfaces to delineate transaction boundaries, and manage security. They may also use the notification APIs defined by the CCM to post or consume events. But clients, no matter how component-aware, do *not* participate in persistence operations; only the component itself interacts with the PSS!

Finally, there are a number of operations provided by the CCM runtime: Navigation among multiple interfaces (for extended components); an operation to determine if a reference is a component or a CORBA object; and another to determine if two references refer to the same component.

The component's equivalent interface bears operations for functionality declared using the **supports** clause, plus operations to discover and navigate to all of its facets. Each facet bears operations declared using the **provides** clause, plus operations to navigate to its equivalent interface or any other facet.

III.3.3.16.2 *Component-Unaware Clients*

Because component interfaces are, under the covers, regular CORBA interfaces with CORBA object references, they can be invoked by a component-unaware client. One reason why you might end up writing component-unaware clients for your CCM application is CORBA version mismatch between client and server platforms; there are other reasons as well. Here's how this could happen.

It's likely that your CCM server-side application will run on a different platform than your clients, especially if it's aimed at a large enterprise or the Internet. If your CCM provider doesn't market a development environment on your client platform, you'll have to use a different ORB. Interoperability is no problem because client and server both generate the IIOP protocol, but if your client-platform ORB vendor hasn't upgraded his line to CORBA 3, you may have to write component-unaware clients for your first deployment. Remember, the keywords that generate the navigation and service stubs, and the stubs themselves, are defined in CORBA 3 and your CORBA 2.X client-side ORB doesn't know that they exist, or what they're for!

There are a few strategic things that a CORBA 2.X client cannot do in a CCM environment (navigation, HomeFinder operations, and a few other things) either because these operations are performed by the ORB at least in part, or because their stubs are generated automatically from the component IDL. These clients can use the factory pattern to create component instances, but only if the operations they need are on a supported interface. (There's no way for them to find and navigate to a provided interface.) They can find entity components using the Naming or Trader Services, but not by invoking **find_by_primary_key** on the **ComponentHome** because they won't have a stub for it.

In spite of the shortcomings of the CORBA 2.X clients that you'll have to field, we suggest that you design and build your CCM server for component-aware clients. If you designed your CCM server architecture for CORBA 2.X clients, avoiding client navigation operations and segmented servants, you would keep your CCM runtime from delivering the efficiency it's designed for.

To let your component-unaware client cope, you can split it in half: Put the CCM-specific calls in a wrapper component on the server. Register the wrapper factory with a Naming or Trader Service, so that the desktop part of your split client can find it easily and create a new wrapper component for each session. The interfaces between the true client and the wrapper client component may not be elegant, but at least they'll let you tread water until you get a CORBA 3 ORB on your client platform and can compile and deploy the client you wanted. And, even from the beginning, platforms with CORBA 3 ORBs can run the true client, bypassing the wrapper component and going straight to work.

III.3.3.17   Other IDL Extensions

That's all we're going to say about the CCM. We've covered both design and programming aspects, in considerable detail for a specification that was just coming to market as we finished writing the chapter. Before we turn completely away from programming and look at modeling and design in the last volume of the book, there are a few general improvements that the CCM specification makes to CORBA, and we want to present them here:

Local Interfaces. Sometimes it's necessary to declare an object as "local"; that is, constrained to the same process as its ORB. Because references for these objects cannot be passed outside of their creating process, these objects can never be invoked remotely. These object types are typically used more to implement ORBs than to implement applications, so you may never need to use the new IDL declaration local interface that declares this characteristic.

Import. A new **import** statement imports only the declarations from another IDL scope or compilation into your IDL. Without import, you had to use **#include**, which brought in the IDL as well as the declarations.

Repository Id Declarations. The CCM adds **typeid** and **typePrefix** declarations to IDL, allowing you to declare repository ID values without using **#pragma**.

Exceptions for Attribute set and get operations. We already mentioned it, but this one fits here and is worth mentioning again. Attribute set and get operations raise exceptions: **getRaises**, and **setRaises**. No longer do you have to use the Property service (again, described in *CORBA 3 Fundamentals and Programming*) to declare attributes that raise exceptions on **set**s and **get**s.

III.3.4 Summary

This chapter on the CCM brings our presentation of CORBA 3, but not this book, to a close. Starting with an example and moving on to descriptions of the CCM interfaces and architecture, we've shown how CORBA supports the kind of component-based programming that lets business programmers build scalable enterprise servers.

But enterprise-sized servers—the kind that take best advantage of CCM's features—need to be designed before they are programmed. We've all heard the stories of large projects delivered after deadline, or over budget, or not delivered at all. To give your project the best chance of success, you need to analyze the problem and design the solution before anyone starts to code; and the world standards in OO analysis and design come from OMG: They are the Unified Modeling Language (UML), the Meta Object Facility

(MOF), Extensible Markup Language Metadata Interchange (XMI), and the Common Warehouse Metadata (CWM). In the final part of this book, we'll take a look at the modeling standards that you can use to get the best advantage out of the CORBA features that we've just covered.

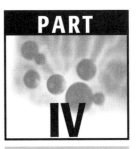

PART

IV

Specifications Supporting Modeling and Design

Mention the Object Management Group to a programmer and he or she thinks, right away, about CORBA: Object request brokers, Interface Definition Language, Object Adapters. But, since late 1995, OMG has had another group of members who think first of something else: Analysis, modeling, and design specifications, including what is probably OMG's most popular standard, the Unified Modeling Language (UML). And, now that we've covered all of the new CORBA standards, we're going to devote the rest of this book to the analysis, modeling, and design side of OMG, for a number of reasons:

- **OMG's A&D standards are more widely used than CORBA.** Why is that? Because, for one thing, the application and data models generated by UML-, MOF-, and CWM-compliant tools can be implemented on *any* platform: CORBA, Java/EJB, XML/SOAP, COM/DCOM, and others. The MOF can standardize a repository and metamodel for *any* modeling environment. And, in the area of data modeling, the Common Warehouse Metamodel (CWM) standardizes metamodels for *any* form of data repository including relational, object-oriented, hybrid, and other modes.

- **Analysis, Modeling, and Design pays off big.** As your application grows in size and scope and your server scales to increasingly large numbers of objects and higher hit rates, the payback from using CORBA grows with it. And, as applications grow, the payback from modeling and design grows as well. In fact, without a design for a guide, a large programming project risks outright failure.

- **Not everyone reading this book is a programmer.** Architects as well read books like this one because they need to know what's out there that programs and programmers can take advantage of, to buy instead of build. That's why we write each chapter in "drill down" style, putting architectural and structural aspects first, interfaces and programming details last. The best tools in the world for architects are those that come from OMG's Analysis and Design Task Force so, in the rest of this book, we're going to address the architects directly and describe OMG's standards addressing analysis, modeling, and design.

- **Modeling holds the key to integrating the enterprise.** We've saved the most important reason for last: When OMG members first conceived of CORBA in 1989, there was no such thing as middleware, and OO was a research technology given only a small chance of penetrating the mainstream. (My, how things change!) OMG's goal was to integrate the enterprise, once and forever, by building a foundation based on platform- and language-independent object technology.

Now, in spite of the success of CORBA in the enterprise (and, on the server side, there is no arguing with CORBA's status in enterprise computing), it's clear that CORBA did not become the universal platform that OMG anticipated. Every year or two, a new "silver bullet" emerges seemingly from nowhere, promising painless interoperability, and captures the industry's fancy. You know what these technologies are; XML (described in Part I, Chapter 2) was the latest when this book went to press but has probably been superseded by the time you read it. Typically introduced with the goal of displacing all of the technologies that preceded it, each Silver Bullet displaces nothing but settles down eventually into a niche where it may, in fact, provide a good solution as just another one of the set of technologies that systems architects can choose from and (whether they chose it or not) that they must cope with forever after.

So, as middleware platforms come and stay (they never seem to go!), we start to recognize commonalities among them. There has to be a large area of overlap, since each provides the same functionality as its predecessor (only better! better! better!), and as its successor (promised to be better still, of course).

Since commonality is the key to integration, OMG members have just started a major integration effort based on the common features of the assortment of middleware technologies. Termed the Model Driven Architecture (MDA) and based on UML, the MOF, and associated OMG modeling standards, this new effort will allow enterprises to integrate what they've built, with what they're building, with what they're going to build. Part IV, Chapter 3 is devoted to the MDA. This book went into production just as OMG members endorsed a general statement starting the group's official migration toward the MDA, but before they had a chance to adopt the architectural specifications that will officially define it. Thus our chapter is a strong indication of the members' direction but could not be a reflection of official OMG policy, which still remained to be set. For the latest word, check out the MDA's own home page, www.omg.org/mda.

Impact of OMG's A&D Standards

Widely recognized as the only standard representation for analysis and design (A&D) results, UML is supported by an incredible array of tools from a large assortment of vendors. For example, there's a list of 30 UML-based and UML-related tools at http://dmoz.org/Computers/Software/

Object-Oriented/Methodologies/UML/Tools/ and a much longer list of about 80 tools and versions at http://www.objectsbydesign.com/tools/ umltools_byCompany.html. We present UML in the next chapter, Part IV, Chapter 1.

Two things you might wonder about an application model are first, what do you build it from and second, where do you put it once it's finished? Addressing both of these topics in a single specification, OMG members adopted the Meta-Object Facility (MOF) as the first follow-up to UML. Because the foundation for any modeling work is its meta-model, the MOF rapidly became the centerpiece of OMG's A&D toolbox. The XML Metadata Interchange (XMI) and Common Warehouse Metamodel are both based on MOF meta-models, as is UML now.

Support for XMI is growing rapidly. Ten of the tools listed on the Objects By Design page support XMI; we suspect that many others do as well. And, tools don't need to support UML in order to still use XMI—for example, tools for data modeling that support OMG's Common Warehouse Meta-model (CWM). We present the MOF and XMI in Part IV, Chapter 3.

With the adoption of the Common Warehouse Metamodel, OMG expanded its standardization efforts to include data modeling. With support for

- Relational data resources
- Record data resources
- Multidimensional data resources
- XML data resources
- Data transformations
- OLAP (On-Line Analytical Processing)
- Data mining
- Information Visualization
- Business nomenclature
- Warehouse process
- Warehouse operation

the CWM is *the* standard this important field, thanks in part to the merger of the Meta-Data Coalition into OMG during the standardization process, which reduced the number of standards in this area from two to one.

Unfortunately, the recent adoption of CWM did not give us time to prepare a chapter describing it. But, OMG maintains a Web page on this important standard at www.omg.org/cwm. If you're interested in standards-based data modeling and the advantages that it brings, check this page out.

In spite of its recent arrival on the scene, we have included a chapter on OMG's new Model-Driven Architecture. The MDA is so important that, starting now, no book on OMG's standards is complete without a mention of MDA and, we believe, soon the MDA will be the centerpiece of both OMG's efforts and of any work describing them. (We're looking forward to writing a book centered on MDA-based standards in just a few years.) Our description of the emerging MDA appears in Part IV, Chapter 3. We've already said why we believe MDA will be important; for details, turn ahead to that last chapter.

One more thing: Before we move on to the chapters that present each of OMG's A&D standards separately, let's take one last look at all of them *together*: OMG derives a major advantage from the fact that all of these standards come from one group in one organization. By deriving all from a common meta-metamodel (there we go with the "meta"s again; sorry!), using a common procedure, OMG goes as far as it can to enable models built using any of them to work together. Because an enterprise's application and data modelers typically work independently, not to mention the possible lack of communication between groups working on different applications within an enterprise, this common foundation provides a basis (necessary although, we admit, not sufficient) for interworking and interoperability down the road. Each chapter will point out where its standard either derives from, or works with, the others. Pay attention; the benefits from this multiply your payback from A&D.

While it's true that analysis, modeling, and design are one layer higher in abstraction than programming and implementation, this does *not* make their impact somehow less "real." The analogy that compares the design of a software application to blueprints for a skyscraper rings true: The design, expressed in standard UML, is the only thing that ensures that the pieces of your large distributed software application, worked independently by different programming groups, will fit together properly. Analysis, modeling, and design work pays off; programming "blind" without benefit of an underlying model and design is a frequent cause of project failure. Here, in this final volume, are the OMG's standards for A&D.

Modeling Distributed Applications with UML

This chapter was written by Cris Kobryn, a co-author
of the UML specification.

In a relatively short period of time, the OMG's Unified Modeling Language (UML) has emerged as the software industry's dominant modeling language. The UML is a general-purpose visual modeling language that is being used to specify applications in a wide range of domains ranging from healthcare and finance, to telecommunications and e-commerce. This chapter explores how the UML can be used to specify distributed applications, in particular those implemented with CORBA.

IV.1.1 UML and IDL

In order to understand how UML can help you build more correct and robust distributed applications, it may be useful to first compare it with CORBA's specification language, OMG IDL. The CORBA architecture provides a standard framework that you can flexibly extend to build robust distributed applications. This prefabricated architecture insulates you from the details of interprocess communication and distributed operating system services. However, it does not buffer you from the minutiae associated with real business applications, which can sometimes rival distributed operating systems in size and complexity.

Of course, you can use OMG IDL to specify your business objects and components. IDL is a pure specification language; it allows you to define the interfaces to objects without constraining their implementations. Consequently, you can use IDL to define the structure of your application and to separate the definitions of your business objects from their implementation details. By separating object specifications from their implementations, you obtain the benefits of information hiding, implementation neutrality, and platform independence.

For these reasons, IDL is an important tool for the application architect and programmer as well as for the system architect. However, IDL has some significant shortcomings. First, it does not allow you to specify object behavior or class relationships other than generalization. Consequently, you can specify the operations associated with an interface but you cannot define methods, use cases, collaborations, state machines, workflows, or the various relationships typically associated with real business objects. Second, IDL is a textual language with no graphic representation. While this may be satisfactory for specifying simple structures, it is an undesirable limitation for defining complex structural relationships and behavior.

In this chapter, we'll explore how the UML addresses these shortcomings. We'll begin with an overview of the UML specification, and then investigate both the modeling language and the model interchange facility. The chapter will conclude with a discussion of the future evolution of UML.

IV.1.2   What Is the UML?

The UML is a language for visualizing, specifying, constructing, and documenting the artifacts of software systems. It is a general-purpose modeling language intended to be used with all major object methods and applied to all application domains. The multiple facets of the UML are explained here:

Visualizing. The UML's syntax is graphic, based on a rich set of graphic icons, symbols, and connectors. When properly applied, the graphic notation has a high semantic "signal-to-noise" ratio so that a single UML diagram can concisely express what may otherwise require many pages of text.

Specifying. The UML's graphic syntax is matched by powerful semantics that allow you to specify static structure, dynamic behavior, and model organization. As previously explained, the UML's specification capabilities significantly exceed those of IDL.

Constructing. UML models can be directly mapped to various programming languages, protocols, and platforms. These mappings can support forward engineering—that is, the automated generation of executable code from object models. (UML also supports reverse and "round-trip" engineering, but these topics are beyond the scope of this chapter.)

Documenting. UML models can be used to produce documentation for all phases of the software lifecycle. UML diagrams can function as artifacts for requirements gathering, analysis, design, testing, and project planning.

The UML represents the convergence of the best practices in object modeling. It is the historical successor to the object modeling languages of three leading object-oriented methods: Booch, Object Modeling Technique, and Objectory. UML was designed to meet the following goals:

- Define an easy-to-learn but semantically rich visual modeling language.
- Unify the Booch, OMT, and OOSE modeling languages.
- Include the best ideas from other modeling languages.
- Support industry best practices for modeling.
- Address contemporary software development issues, such as scale, distribution, concurrency, and executability.
- Provide flexibility for applying different software processes.
- Enable model interchange and define repository interfaces.

The next section describes the benefits of modeling in general, and UML modeling in particular.

IV.1.3   The UML Modeling Advantage

If you were commissioning a high-rise office building, you would expect your architect to provide you with detailed blueprints that describe the proposed structure from various views (e.g., elevations, site plans, floor plans, sections). These detailed plans allow you and the other stakeholders to evaluate how the proposed building will meet your needs, and will help the contractors to calculate their time and material costs. Similarly, if you were going to commission an aircraft, a ship, or a supercomputer, you would expect an architect to produce detailed plans before you started work.

Those outside of the software profession may be surprised to learn that people commissioning large software systems do not always require detailed blueprints before they start a project. Software projects are frequently initiated with only high-level sketches (conceptual architectures), which consist of some simple box-and-line diagrams along with some informal prose. Of course, we recognize that software systems are substantially different from hardware and building systems in that they are far more malleable and dynamic. However, they are not so different that their builders wouldn't benefit from more thoughtful and detailed planning. The lack of detailed blueprints may be one of the major reasons why software systems tend to be less reliable and more difficult to estimate than their hardware and building counterparts.

The UML is a powerful language for specifying software blueprints. Consider the following simple analogy between building blueprints and UML software blueprints: The UML counterpart to a building is a physical system, the subject of a software model. An example of a physical system is an online car buying service, which includes software, hardware, and wetware (people). The UML analog for a building blueprint is called a *model*, which is an abstraction of a physical system with a certain purpose (e.g., allowing users to compare and buy cars on the Web). UML models show different viewpoints and can be decomposed into diagrams (e.g., class diagrams, use case diagrams, statechart diagrams) and model elements (e.g., classes, interfaces, components), just as building blueprints show different perspectives and can be broken down into plans and architectural elements.

If you are considering a major software project at your enterprise, you should consider using UML to specify your software blueprints. There are several advantages to this approach:

- It provides an excellent notation for software problem solving.
- It furnishes a rich set of abstractions for managing system complexity.
- It supports concurrent exploration of multiple solutions.
- In a manner similar to software prototyping, it facilitates project risk management.

From a business perspective, the ramifications of these advantages include reduced time-to-market, decreased development costs, and diminished risk.

In order to obtain the most benefit from UML, you should apply it using a rigorous software development process or method. Choose a method that is iterative, incremental, and also architecture-centric. By selecting a method that is iterative and incremental, you can better synchronize the concurrent activities of your modelers and your programmers, thereby increasing their efficiency. By choosing a process that is architecture-centric, you will increase the likelihood that your model is consistent with the physical system it represents, thereby improving the system's architectural integrity.

The UML is a general-purpose language that supports many methods over the full software lifecycle. Look for methods that show you how to apply UML modeling to business requirements analysis and testing, not just to software analysis and design. UML also supports many levels of sophistication in modeling techniques. Make sure that you select a method that matches the sophistication and culture of your development team.

The next section provides an overview of the UML specification, which includes language extensions for software development processes.

IV.1.4   OMG UML Specification

Although the core of the UML specification is the definition of the language's syntax and semantics, the specification also includes related definitions for model interchange and constraints. The major sections of the specification are shown in Figure IV.1.1 and described below.

UML Semantics. Specifies the semantics of the language using a meta-model. The language is organized by packages, and the metaclasses are described in a semiformal style that combines graphic notation, constraint language, and natural language. Both the semantics and graphic syntax (notation) are elaborated upon further in Section IV.1.5.

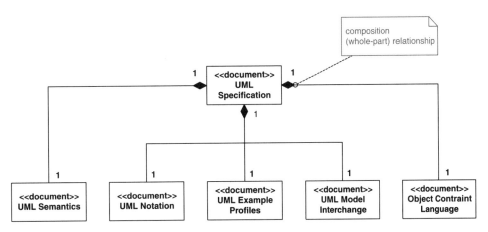

Figure IV.1.1   The UML specification structure.

UML Notation Guide. Defines the graphic syntax for expressing the semantics described in the UML semantics specification.

UML Example Profiles. Shows how UML can be customized for specific domains, such as software development processes and business modeling.

UML Model Interchange. Specifies how UML models can be exchanged via the XML Metadata Interchange (XMI) and CORBA IDL. The Model Interchange facility is discussed further in Section IV.1.8.

Object Constraint Language (OCL). Defines the syntax and semantics of the OCL, a declarative language for specifying object constraints.

The following sections describe the modeling language, the relation of UML to other modeling standards, and model interchange. If you are interested in learning more about OCL or profiles, you should explore the references provided in Appendix A.

IV.1.5   The Modeling Language: Syntax and Semantics

In keeping with the principles of good language design, the UML's graphic syntax and semantics are defined separately. The semantics constructs are the foundation for the syntactic constructs, since there is a well-defined unidirectional mapping from the graphic syntax to the semantics. Consequently, we discuss the UML semantics first.

The UML semantics are defined with a metamodel that is decomposed into several logical packages: Foundation, Behavioral Elements, and Model Management. Figure IV.1.2 shows these packages as folder icons, with the dependencies between them illustrated as dashed arrows. The package at the tail of the arrow (the client) depends upon the package at the head of the arrow (the supplier). The top-level packages are decomposed into subpackages, indicated by nesting the folders. For example, the Foundation package consists of the Core, Extension Mechanisms, and Data Types subpackage.

The scopes of the top-level packages are:

Foundation. Defines the semantics for static structural models. The Foundation package supports various structural diagrams including class diagrams, object diagrams, component diagrams, and deployment diagrams. It consists of the Core, Extension Mechanisms, and Data Types subpackages.

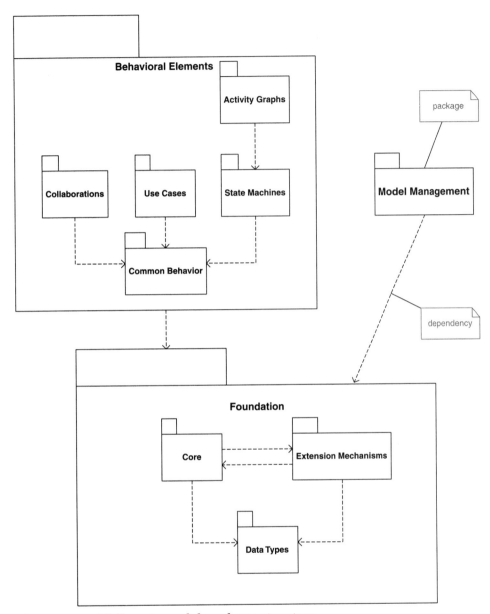

Figure IV.1.2 UML metamodel package structure.

Behavioral Elements. Defines the semantics for behavioral models. This package supports various behavioral diagrams including use case diagrams, sequence diagrams, collaboration diagrams, statechart diagrams, and activity diagrams. It consists of the Common Behavior, Collaborations, Use Cases, State Machines, and Activity Graphs subpackages.

Model Management. Defines the semantics for managing UML models. This package supports various grouping constructs including packages, models, and subsystems. It has no subpackages, but in the future it may be grouped with other packages that are also general mechanisms.

The metamodel is described in a semiformal manner using a combination of graphic notation (UML), constraint language (OCL), and precise natural language (English). The description is presented in three complementary views:

Abstract Syntax. Defines the semantic constructs, where complex constructs are built from simple constructs. The abstract syntax is presented in UML class diagrams that show the metaclasses that define constructs along with their metarelationships. The diagrams also present a limited number of well-formedness rules (mostly multiplicity and ordering constraints) and short informal descriptions in natural language.

Well-Formedness Rules. Specify the constraints on each semantic construct (except for multiplicity and ordering constraints) as a set of invariants on an instance of the metaclass. These rules are expressed in both OCL and English.

Detailed Semantics. Defines the detailed meanings of the constructs using natural language. The constructs are organized into logical groups that are discussed together.

UML's graphic syntax or notation is the concrete syntax that is mapped onto the semantics. The notation is defined in terms of four basic graphic constructs: icons, two-dimensional symbols, paths (connectors), and strings. At its most basic level, a UML diagram is a graph containing "boxes" (icons and two-dimensional symbols) connected by "lines" (paths) and labeled with strings.

UML supports the following diagrams:

Structural diagrams. Show the static structure of the model. Structural diagrams present the entities that exist (e.g., classes, interfaces, components, nodes), their internal structure, and their relationships to other entities. The kinds of structural diagrams include:

Class

Object

Component

Deployment

Behavioral diagrams. Show the dynamic behavior of the model. The kinds of behavioral diagrams include:

Use case

Sequence

Collaboration

Statechart

Activity

Model Management diagrams. Show how models are organized into packages, models, and subsystems. These grouping constructs are typically applied to the various structural diagrams. When a structural diagram is dominated by package constructs, it is sometimes referred to as a "package diagram."

IV.1.6   Structural Modeling Example: The POS System

Although a UML tutorial is beyond the scope of this chapter, we include a simple example that shows how you can use UML to define OMG IDL interfaces and modules. Figure IV.1.3 is a class diagram that shows a subset of the interfaces and classes for the Point of Sale (POS) tutorial example as presented in the book *CORBA 3 Fundamentals and Programming*.

In this diagram, the POS IDL module is shown as the package labeled Point_Of_Sale. IDL interfaces are shown as rectangles labeled with the keyword **IDLinterface**. We have chosen to model the IDL interfaces as a «CORBAInterface» stereotype of the Class base model element, rather than use the standard **interface** construct. (Note that guillemets, or Romance language quotation marks, are used here to indicate that «CORBAInterface» is a stereotype.) Stereotypes are a lightweight extension mechanism for customizing the semantics and syntax of UML model elements. We say they are lightweight because they are restricted in their use when compared with a heavyweight extension mechanism, such as a metaclass.

We have defined a stereotype for CORBA interfaces because UML interfaces are more restricted than CORBA interfaces. A UML interface is defined as a named set of operations that characterize the behavior of a model element. Since IDL interfaces include attributes as well as operations, we found it convenient to define a stereotype that does the same. In this example, we follow the convention that all interface names are prefixed with the letter I, such as **IPOSterminal**, **IInputMedia**, and **IOutputMedia**. The

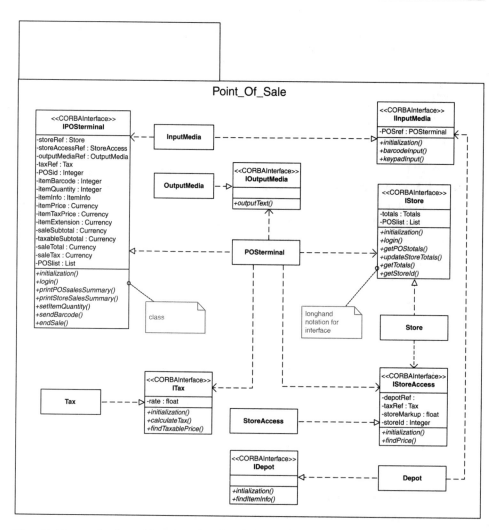

Figure IV.1.3   A class diagram for the POS example.

attributes of the IDL interfaces are shown in the middle compartment of the rectangle, and the operations are shown in the lower compartment. For example, the attributes of the **IStore** IDL interface are **totals** and **POSlist**, and its operations are **initialization**, **login**, **getPOStotals**, **updateStoreTotals**, **getTotals**, and **getStoreId**.

The CORBA interfaces are realized by (i.e., are implemented by) classes, which are shown as rectangles without special keywords. For example, the POSterminal class realizes the **IPOSterminal** CORBA interface. The realization relationship is shown by a dashed line with a closed triangular arrowhead connected to the specification element, and the tail connecting to the realization element.

The CORBA interfaces are also used by the various classes. For example, the `Store` class uses the **IStoreAccess** CORBA interface. The usage relationship is shown by a dependency arrow—a dashed line with an open arrowhead.

Figure IV.1.4 shows how the class diagram might evolve into a deployment diagram during a later lifecycle phase, such as the implementation phase. In this diagram a node is represented as a rectangular solid, and a component is represented as a rectangle with two smaller rectangles protruding from its side. Component interfaces are shown using the shorthand "lollipop" notation, and the use of interfaces is shown by dependency arrows. The example shows how the classes in the class diagram might be implemented as components and deployed on nodes during an implementa-

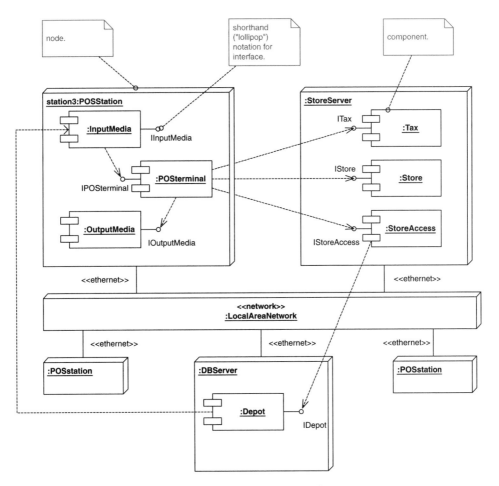

Figure IV.1.4   A deployment diagram for the POS example.

tion phase. For example, instances of the **Tax**, **Store** and **StoreAccess** components are deployed on an instance of the **StoreServer** node.

The preceding translation of IDL to UML structural diagrams shows you only a small part of the specification capabilities of UML. In order to appreciate UML's expressive power, you should consider the elaboration of the POS example with relationships between the various classes and the specification of behavior with use cases, collaborations, statecharts, and activity graphs. Since this exercise is beyond the scope of this overview, we suggest that you explore modeling and methods books that feature UML if you need more complete examples.

IV.1.7   Relationship of UML to other Modeling Standards

The UML is not the only OMG modeling standard. In addition to UML, the OMG has adopted the Meta Object Facility (MOF) for specifying metadata and the XML Metadata Interchange (XMI) facility for exchanging models. In addition, many OMG task forces are in the process of customizing UML for various domains via *profiles*. A profile is a package that contains model elements that have been customized for a particular domain or purpose using UML extension mechanisms: stereotypes, tagged definitions (compare property lists), and constraints.

The relationship of UML to these other modeling standards is shown in Figure IV.1.5. There are three layers in this diagram: the metadata layer, the specification layer, and the customization layer. The specification layer in the middle consists of UML and its model interchange definitions: UML XMI DTD and UML CORBA IDL. Since the UML is general-purpose, this specification layer is expected to be sufficient to model most common software problems and to support the exchange of modeling solutions among any tools that support the UML XMI DTD and UML CORBA IDL specifications.

The metadata layer at the top of the diagram provides metadata infrastructure support for the UML specification layer. As you will see shortly, the MOF meta-metamodel is used to define the UML metamodel, as well as various other metamodels and metadata facilities, such as the XMI facility for exchanging models. The customization layer at the bottom allows users to customize UML profiles for particular domains and purposes. Platform Technology profiles tend to be infrastructural or general purpose (e.g., UML Profile for CORBA) while Domain Technology profiles are typically domain-specific (e.g., the UML Profile for Telecom).

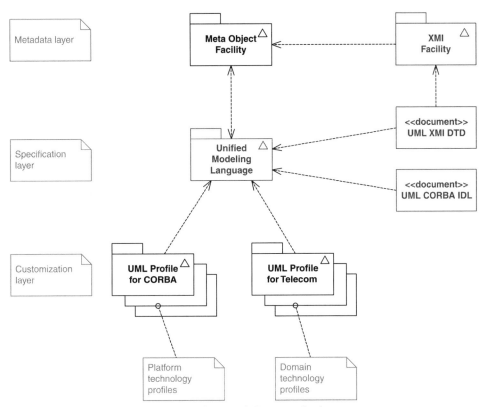

Figure IV.1.5 Relation of UML to other modeling standards.

In addition to functioning as a specification layer, UML may also be considered one of the layers of a four-layer metamodel architectural pattern. The other layers in this pattern are the meta-metamodel layer, the model layer, and the users objects layer. The metamodel layer is derived from the meta-metamodel layer, which for UML is defined by the Meta Object Facility's meta-metamodel. In particular, metaclasses in the UML metamodel are instances of the MOF meta-metaclasses. An instance of this architectural pattern is shown in the class diagram in Figure IV.1.6. In this diagram, the various model layers are shown as package symbols with a triangle symbol in the upper-right corner. (Models can alternatively be shown by inserting the keyword **model** above the model name). The models that are also metamodels (i.e., MOF Meta-Metamodel and UML Metamodel) are stereotypes on the Model base element and are indicated with the keyword **metamodel**. The metaclasses in the MOF Meta-Metamodel and UML Metamodel layers are shown as metaclass stereotypes on the Class base model element.

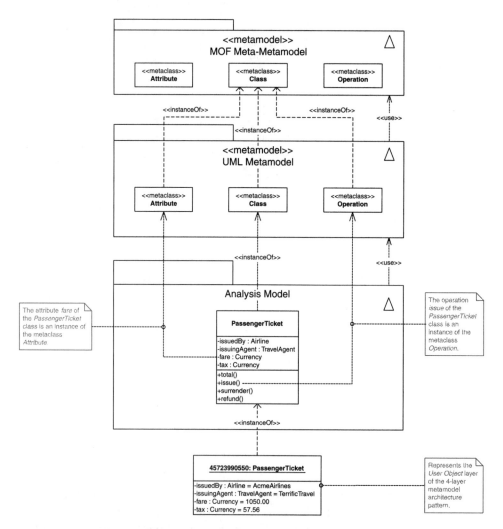

Figure IV.1.6 The four-layer metamodel architectural pattern.

Instance-of metarelationships between elements in the various metamodel layers are shown by the **instanceOf** keyword on the dependency arrows. The instance in the lowest layer (the user objects layer) represents an executable instance, which is shown by underlining its name and including the class name after the colon: **45723990550: Passenger Ticket**.

The **instanceOf** metarelationships between the various metamodel elements imply usage dependencies between the metamodel layers. These are shown explicitly with the **use** keyword on the dependency arrows between the models.

The metamodel architectural pattern is a proven infrastructure for defining the precise semantics required by complex models that need to be reliably stored, shared, manipulated, and exchanged across tools. There are several advantages associated with this approach:

- It recursively refines the semantic constructs at each metamodel layer, resulting in more concise and regular semantics.

- It provides an infrastructure for defining future metamodel extensions.

- It architecturally aligns the UML metamodel with other standards based on a four-layer metamodeling architecture, such as the XMI facility for model interchange.

IV.1.8   UML Model Interchange

The UML specification provides two mechanisms for exchanging UML models between tools: XMI and CORBA IDL. The XMI mechanism, based on the XMI specification, exchanges models as streams or files with a standard XML format. The CORBA IDL mechanism, based on the OMG IDL specification, provides CORBA interfaces that can be used to dynamically create, access, and modify UML models. Of these two mechanisms, the XMI facility is more widely implemented, so we will focus on it.

Perhaps the best way to understand how the XMI mechanism works is to examine how it translates models into a standard XML format. Consider the model fragment from the POS example class diagram shown in Figure IV.1.7. This model fragment consists of a **Tax** class that realizes an **ITax** CORBA interface.

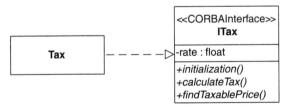

Figure IV.1.7   Model fragment from POS example class diagram.

The following is an edited version of the XML that an XMI-compliant export utility generated from the model fragment. Some of the details have been elided to improve readability.

```
<?xml version = '1.0' encoding = 'ISO-8859-1' ?>
<!DOCTYPE XMI SYSTEM 'UMLX13.dtd' >
<XMI xmi.version = '1.1' xmlns:UML='//org.omg/UML/1.3' ...>
 <XMI.header>
  <XMI.metamodel xmi.name = 'UML' xmi.version = '1.3'/>
 </XMI.header>
<XMI.content>
<!-- POS_Example_R2    [Model]  -->
<UML:Model xmi.id = 'G.0'
  name = 'POS_Example_R2' visibility = 'public' isSpecification = 'false'
  isRoot = 'false' isLeaf = 'false' isAbstract = 'false' >
 <UML:Namespace.ownedElement>
   <!-- POS_Example_R2::Tax    [Class]  -->
   <UML:Class xmi.id = 'S.1'
     name = 'Tax' visibility = 'public' isSpecification = 'false'
     isRoot = 'true' isLeaf = 'true' isAbstract = 'false'
     isActive = 'false'
     namespace = 'G.0' clientDependency = 'G.1' />
   <!-- POS_Example_R2::ITax    [Class]  -->
   <UML:Class xmi.id = 'S.2'
     name = 'ITax' visibility = 'public' isSpecification = 'false'
     isRoot = 'true' isLeaf = 'true' isAbstract = 'false'
     isActive = 'false'
     namespace = 'G.0' supplierDependency = 'G.1' >
     <UML:Classifier.feature>
       <!-- POS_Example_R2::ITax.rate    [Attribute]  -->
       <UML:Attribute xmi.id = 'S.3'
         name = 'rate' visibility = 'private' isSpecification = 'false'
         ownerScope = 'instance'
         changeability = 'changeable' targetScope = 'instance'
         type = 'G.2' >
         ...
        </UML:Attribute>
       <!-- POS_Example_R2::ITax::initialization    [Operation]  -->
       <UML:Operation xmi.id = 'S.4'
        name = 'initialization' visibility = 'public' isSpecification = 'false'
         ownerScope = 'instance'
         isQuery = 'false'
         concurrency = 'sequential' isRoot = 'false' isLeaf = 'false'
         isAbstract = 'false' specification = '' />
       ...
     </UML:Classifier.feature>
   </UML:Class>
   ...
   <!-- POS_Example_R2.CORBAInterface    [Stereotype]  -->
   <UML:Stereotype xmi.id = 'XX.1'
     name = 'CORBAInterface' visibility = 'public' isSpecification = 'false'
     isRoot = 'false' isLeaf = 'false' isAbstract = 'false'
     icon = '' baseClass = 'Class'
     extendedElement = 'S.2' />
```

```
    </UML:Namespace.ownedElement>
  </UML:Model>
  </XMI.content>
</XMI>
```

The mapping of the elements in the model fragment to their XML counterparts is straightforward. For example, the Tax class maps to the XML element `<UML:Class xmi.id = 'S.1' name = 'Tax' visibility = 'public' ... />`. Likewise, the CORBAInterface stereotype maps to the XML element `<UML:Stereotype xmi.id = 'XX.1' name = 'CORBAInterface' visibility = 'public' ... />`. The mappings of the other model elements to their XML counterparts is left as an exercise.

IV.1.9   UML Futures

The speed at which the UML is being adopted and applied is encouraging. Developers are using UML for a wide range of business and scientific applications in a variety of domains. It is being applied to enterprise information systems as well as commercial products and embedded real-time systems.

As software continues to evolve, so will the UML. It is a "living language" in the same sense that human languages such as English, Japanese, and Swahili continuously evolve to meet the changing needs of their speakers. We can expect future revisions of the UML to provide better support for the model-driven development of large and complex systems. Improvements in executable models, implementation language translations, and model change management will make round-trip engineering practical. Advances in architectural modeling and formal specification techniques will increase the rigor and scalability of UML blueprints.

The trends toward distributed enterprise architectures and component-based development will drive many other improvements in UML. The demands of distributed enterprise architectures will help us improve how we model systems-of-systems, distribution, and concurrency. Similarly, advances in component-based development will help us refine how we model interfaces, classes, components, and containers. We can look forward to UML not only tracking, but also enabling, these and other advances in software development.

Implementing Metamodels and Repositories Using the Meta Object Facility

This chapter was written by Sridhar Iyengar,
a co-author of the MOF specification.

Within the OMG's Object Management Architecture (OMA), the use of IDL and the CORBA services to specify distributed interoperable applications is now the norm. These technologies help in implementing object interoperability using standardized Object Interfaces specified in OMG IDL. However, there has historically been a lack of standard modeling techniques, application development, and management infrastructure within the OMA. The increased complexity involved in the process of designing and implementing distributed object applications has been an additional motivation for standardization of application infrastructure. The use of metadata repositories for data administration (1980s), data warehouse management and year inventory management (mid-1990s), and more recently for managing distributed object components, frameworks, and business objects (late 1990s) is indicative of the growing role of metadata in the enterprise.

The OMG Object Analysis and Design Task Force (ADTF) was chartered in 1995 to address the problems of lack of standardization in these areas. Soon after, OMG members responded with the Unified Modeling Language (UML) and the Meta Object Facility (MOF) in November 1997. You've just read our overview of UML and how it can be used to model CORBA applications in the previous chapter. In fact, UML is the most widely known and implemented metamodel and has been formally defined using the MOF. In addition, OMG members have standardized a set of CORBA Interfaces used to manipulate UML repositories known as the *UML CORBAfacility.* These CORBA Interfaces are derived from the MOF-to-IDL mapping, which is part of the MOF specification.

The OMG standard for metamodeling and metadata repositories is the MOF, which is fully integrated with UML and, in fact, uses the UML notation for describing repository metamodels. In March 1999, the OMG standardized XMI—XML Metadata Interchange—a specification used to interchange metadata among tools, repositories, and applications in a vendor- and middleware-neutral way. XMI allows the interchange of metadata using the World Wide Web Consorium eXtensible Markup Language (XML) among MOF-compliant applications. The MOF, XMI, and UML form the core of the OMG metadata management as well as component-based development architecture.

This chapter focuses on the use of MOF-based metamodeling, a formal technique for designing and implementing modeling languages such as UML, and metadata repositories that are used for tool and application integration in distributed object environments. The MOF provides modeling constructs and a set of CORBA interfaces that can be used to define and manipulate a set of interoperable metamodels and their implementations.

IV.2.1   The OMG Metadata Architecture

Even before the adoption of the MOF, the OMA had several metadata specifications: the CORBA Interface Repository, the Trader Service, and the COS Naming Service. However, these specifications did not have a unifying metadata architecture. The MOF formally introduced the four-layered, object-oriented metamodeling architecture that is shown in Figure IV.2.1 using the UML package diagram notation. You can expect that, over the next few years, many of OMG's unaligned metadata specifications will gradually evolve to the MOF-based architecture. The MOF is the most fundamental layer (the M3 layer) of the four, defining the modeling primitives such as MOF::Class (MetaClass) and MOF::Attribute (MetaAttribute) needed for defining object-oriented metamodels. Metamodels defined using the MOF (such as UML and the Common Warehouse Metamodel—CWM) are at the metamodel (or M2) layer. The metamodel layer describes modeling concepts in a particular domain.

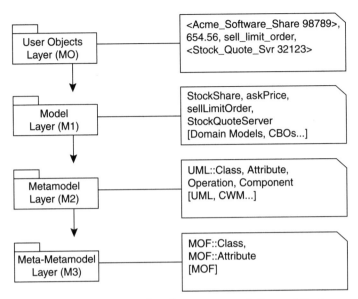

Figure IV.2.1 The OMG four-layer metamodeling architecture.

In the case of UML, modeling concepts include Package, Class, Collaboration, and Usecase. In the case of a data warehousing metamodel such as the CWM, concepts include Table, Column, Cube (for multidimensional databases), and Transformation.

The dependency arrow between the M3 and M2 layers implies an "instance-of" relationship, indicating that metamodels can be stored and managed in a MOF repository in an implementation sense. The dependency can also be used to imply "The Metamodel is-defined-by the MOF." Figure IV.1.6 shows a more complete example of the metamodel architectural pattern using the UML notation. The next layer is the Model or M1 layer, which typically corresponds to application models. In this example, we've described a stock trading application using UML. This model has concepts such as Stockshare and Askprice, and can be managed in a UML repository or an XML document allowing multiple developers to share, use, and exchange consistent definitions of these key quantities. Finally, the user objects layer is referred to as the M0 level and typically corresponds to the information captured in an operational database for a specific stock trade.

While the layers appear complicated, they are primarily an artifact useful in the analysis and design phase of designing and implementing complex model-driven systems. At runtime, all of these models are CORBA, Java, or COM objects. The traversals across the levels happens by navigating these relationships or by invoking operations on MOF objects.

Metamodeling has been used over the years in metadata repositories for a number of reasons:

- Metamodeling provides the basis for recursive definition of semantic constructs.

- Metamodeling provides the basis for introspection and reflection of not just attributes and operations, but also relationships, constraints, and additional semantics. The MOF Reflective module specifies metadata reflection within the OMG architecture.

- Metamodeling provides an architectural basis for extending existing metamodels and introducing new ones in a coherent manner.

- Metamodeling can be used to architecturally align metamodels in different but related domains to maximize reuse. This technique was used in the alignment of the modeling concepts in UML and the MOF as well as in the design of new MOF-based metamodels.

- Metamodeling can be used to ease tool and application integration by formally describing the tool and application models as metamodels. You can then relate the concepts and subtype them in these related metamodels, and still get a cohesive view across the metamodels.

Figure IV.2.2 shows the runtime architecture of the MOF and how it fits within the OMA. Once again, we've used the UML notation to architecturally depict the dependencies between the various components and/or subsystems.

In Figure IV.2.2 Metadata (XMI) and Metamodels (UML, MOF) are shown as horizontal technology frameworks (CORBAfacilities) that provide modeling and metamodeling services in the OMA. These services and modeling frameworks can be used to implement various metadata repositories, component repositories, application development frameworks, and similar modules. These frameworks have been modeled as UML subsystems using the <<subsystem>> UML notation. The arrows imply either CORBA interface calls between the various systems or, in some cases, interchange of metadata using XMI that may not have to use CORBA.

Within this architecture, the roles of the MOF, XMI, and UML are as follows:

- The MOF defines one or more metamodels and their CORBA interfaces for manipulating metadata in a distributed environment.

- XMI provides an XML-based metadata interchange format. The XMI specification defines a MOF to XML mapping for specifying XML Document Type Definitions (DTDs) and XML streams.

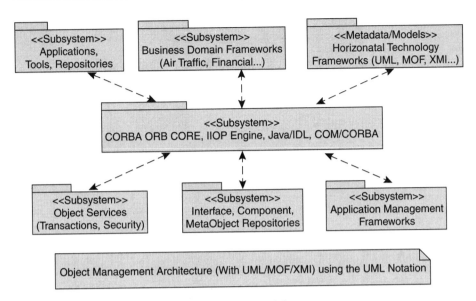

Figure IV.2.2 The MOF, UML, and XMI as part of the OMA.

■ UML is used to design and analyze the metamodels or models that are implemented using CORBA.

The OMG metadata architecture is concretely expressed in Figure IV.2.3, which shows how application development tools, repositories, and CORBA work together. Tools and applications can be implemented in any programming language supported by CORBA, and can directly manipulate the metadata. In addition, tools and repositories that use XMI can also exchange metadata as XML documents without necessarily using CORBA. A typical scenario would be for a designer to create a UML model that represents the problem domain and to manage it in a MOF-compliant UML repository. A Java Integrated Development Environment (IDE) could read the classes and interfaces in the model using a Java program and automatically generate the Java Class and Interface definitions (or even implementations, if the model is precise enough). These could be passed to a deployment tool that reads XML documents that describe the deployment metadata. This metadata would be used to configure the application components. Such as scenario is quite common in component-based runtime architectures such as the CORBA Component Model, JavaSoft EJB, or Microsoft COM+ environments.

The UML-based modeling tools shown in Figure IV.2.3 can store and manage models in a UML repository (which could be a flat file, or relational or object-based repository) using CORBA interfaces. Once the model has been

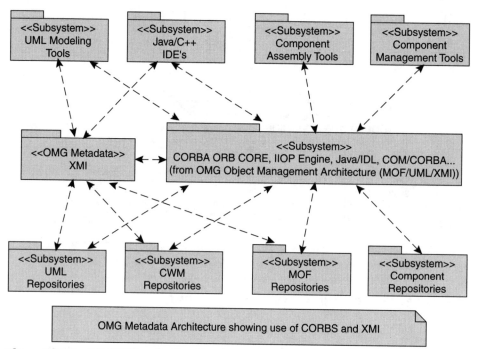

Figure IV.2.3   A CORBA application development environment architecture.

saved, a second tool could use XMI to read this information and refine the model with additional detail (for example, providing actual Java code that corresponds to an implementation), and a third tool could use CORBA to manipulate the same metadata. This could happen over a network, thus enabling collaboration in a virtual development environment.

We will now dive a little deeper into the architecture of the MOF itself, to give you a better understanding of how to design and implement metamodels.

IV.2.1.1   What Is the MOF?

The MOF specification provides a set of modeling constructs and IDL interfaces that can be used to define and manipulate a set of interoperable metamodels. The MOF enhances metadata management and interoperability in distributed object environments in general, and in distributed development environments in particular.

The MOF also defines an abstract model called a *meta-metamodel* (because the MOF is used to define metamodels!) with sufficient semantics to describe metamodels in various domains starting with the domain of object analysis and design for which the UML metamodel has been defined. Since its adoption, the MOF has been used to specify metamodels in a range of domains including data warehousing (work leading up to OMG's new CWM specification), business objects, the CCM, and proprietary metamodels. Integration of metamodels across domains is required for integrating tools and applications across the lifecycle using common semantics. The abstract model is, in essence, a metalanguage with rich semantics (classes, relationships, constraints, and operations) but with precise mappings to OMG IDL (in the MOF specification) and XML (in the XMI specification).

The MOF is an evolution of object-oriented repository and metamodeling research in Unisys, IBM, Oracle, DSTC, and other companies that designed the MOF specification.

The architecture of the MOF is shown in Figure IV.2.4. The MOF is composed of two major standardized parts: the MOF Model, which includes the MOF-to-IDL mapping; and the MOF Reflective Interfaces. (A MOF Facility, included in early versions of the specification, was deprecated in version 1.3 but is still shown in Figure IV.2.4.)

IV.2.1.2 The MOF Model

The MOF Model is the built-in meta-metamodel and is the abstract language for defining metamodels. You use the UML notation to design and describe MOF-based metamodels. The key modeling concepts in the MOF are:

Classes, which can have attributes, references, and operations to model state, relationships, and behavior. The MOF supports multiple inheritance as well as constraints. References allow direct navigation from one class to another.

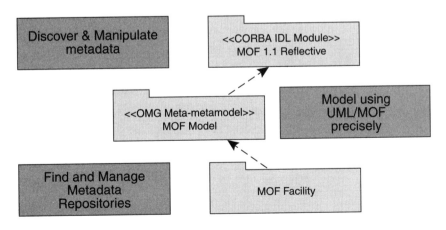

Figure IV.2.4 The MOF architecture.

Binary Associations (Relationships), which are links between Class instances and can model relationships between two classes in a model, or between classes in separate models. The latter is typically used to integrate tools and applications supplied by multiple vendors. Associations have two AssociationEnds which can have constraints on multiplicity (cardinality), aggregation (shared or composite), and semantics.

Packages, which are collections of related Classes, Associations, and Packages (nested packages are supported by the MOF) and typically correspond to metamodels. Packages can be composed by importing or inheriting from other packages.

Data Types for describing state or parameters. The MOF supports all the CORBA data types.

Constraints, which are used to define well-formedness rules in OCL or other languages.

Figure IV.2.5 shows the MOF model using UML notation.

By design, the MOF model is well aligned with the UML metamodel, making it possible to use UML-compliant modeling tools to design MOF-based metamodels.

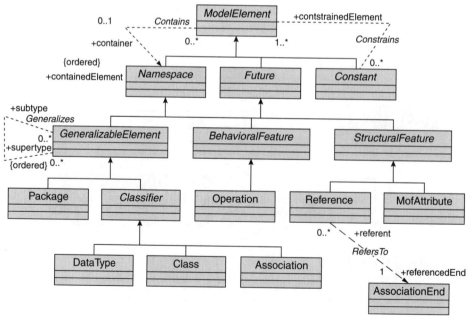

Figure IV.2.5 The MOF model.

IV.2.2   The MOF and CORBA: MOF-to-IDL Mapping

The MOF-to-IDL mapping provides a standard set of templates that can be used to map a MOF metamodel to a corresponding set of OMG IDL Interfaces. For a given metamodel (that corresponds to certain types of metadata), the resulting IDL interfaces are for CORBA objects that correspond to the metadata. The IDL interfaces are typically used to store and manage metadata in a repository.

The main mapping algorithms are as follows:

A **Package** in a metamodel maps onto an IDL interface for a package proxy that is used to manipulate the package contents (packages, classes, and associations).

A **Class** in a metamodel maps onto two IDL interfaces: one for the Class object that provides factory operations for meta objects, and the other for the interfaces that support the attributes, operations, and references in the metamodel.

An **Association** in the metamodel maps to an IDL interface for a metadata association proxy object.

The semantics of the mapping are defined precisely enough to allow interoperability between metadata repositories from multiple vendors. In fact, it is possible to generate the CORBA server implementation for a metadata repository from a well-formed MOF-based metamodel.

IV.2.2.1   The MOF CORBA Interfaces

The MOF CORBA interfaces come in two categories: they may be tailored to a specific metamodel based on the MOF IDL mapping, or Reflective. The MOF Model itself has tailored interfaces that can be used to create and manipulate models. Similarly, for a given metamodel (such as UML or Electronic Data Interchange [EDI]), the tailored IDL interfaces can be generated based on the MOF IDL mapping patterns. These interfaces reflect the metamodel structure and are roughly proportional in number to the complexity of the metamodel.

The MOF Reflective Interfaces, on the other hand, are a fixed set of four interfaces: **RefbaseObject**, **RefObject**, **RefAssociation**, and **RefPackage**, as shown in Figure IV.2.6. These four interfaces form the core of the MOF that allows manipulation of any metadata in any MOF-compliant CORBA server. The Reflective Interfaces allow introspection of any MOF-based metadata across metamodel layers.

The Reflective Interfaces are used by general-purpose metadata management tools such as browsers and report generators, and are a bit cumbersome to use compared to the tailored interfaces. They also require a deep understanding of the structure of the MOF itself. The ability of the MOF to integrate metamodels that have been independently developed takes advantage of the modeling concepts in the MOF as well as the power of the Reflective Interfaces. The Reflective Interfaces have all the machinery you need to manipulate arbitrary metadata: create, delete, update, invoke, and introspect metadata.

The interface **MOF::RefBaseObject:meta_object()** allows traversal across meta levels. The **Refpackage** interface is used to manipulate Packages, Classes, and Associations. **RefObject** is used to manipulate Objects and Classes. **RefAssociation** is used to manipulate links between Objects.

Next we'll review the latest OMG metadata standard, XMI-XML Metadata Interchange, adopted in March 1999 as a vendor- and middleware-neutral standard for exchanging metadata among tools, applications, and repositories. Once we have done that, we will use a simple EDI model to demon-

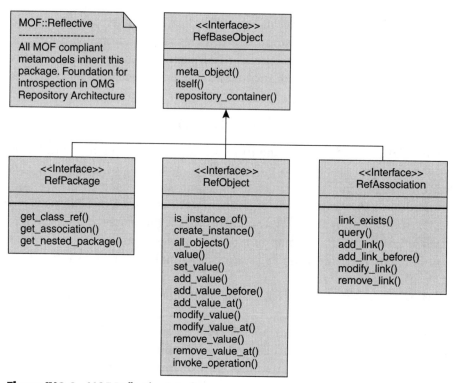

Figure IV.2.6 MOF Reflective Interfaces.

strate how to use the MOF and XMI along with UML to design and implement MOF-based repositories and tools that also support XMI as a metadata interchange mechanism.

IV.2.2.2 XMI Overview

XMI, which stands for *XML Metadata Interchange*, is the OMG standard used for interchanging metadata among tools, applications, and repositories. While XMI was initially defined to exchange UML models, the architecture of XMI is generic and can be used to interchange any metadata described using the MOF. In fact, because of the extensibility of XMI and MOF, you can even exchange metadata where the tool needs to go beyond what is in the standard. Many tools have a need for these extensions for their legacy needs or to provide value-add over competing tools.

When the UML and MOF were standardized by OMG in November 1997, an important piece of work was not completed. At that time, only CORBA-based access to metadata was supported; due to time constraints as well as lack of consensus, no file- or stream-oriented interface was specified. The OMG Stream-based Model Interchange Format (SMIF) RFP was issued to solve this problem. XMI was proposed by Unisys, IBM, and several other companies, and was adopted by the OMG. The XMI specification allows easy exchange of metadata among tools, repositories, and applications using XML.

XMI integrates three key industry standards:

- XML, a W3C standard
- MOF, which we've just covered
- UML, described in the previous chapter

The integration of these three standards into XMI marries the best of OMG and W3C metadata and modeling technologies, allowing developers of distributed applications to share object models and metadata over networks anywhere. The benefits of XMI over traditional interchange mechanisms stem from the ubiquity of XML technology, the inherent extensibility of both XML and MOF, and the fact that XML is human readable and easy to implement.

The XMI specification consists primarily of:

- A set of XML Document Type Definition (DTD) production rules for transforming MOF-based metamodels into XML DTDs.
- A set of XML document production rules for encoding and decoding MOF-based metadata.

- Design principles for generating XMI-compliant DTDs.

- Design principles for generating XMI-compliant XML documents. (XMI documents are XML documents. No extensions to XML have been proposed or used.)

- Concrete XML DTDs for the MOF (to exchange metamodels) and UML (to exchange models).

Starting with versions MOF 1.3 and UML 1.3 of these two specifications, the DTDs and streams are maintained as part of the MOF and UML specifications.

IV.2.3   Using MOF and XMI to Implement Metamodels

The process used in defining and implementing MOF- and XMI-based systems is straightforward. First you need to thoroughly understand the domain before you design a model or a metamodel. Use a UML-compliant tool (or you can do it manually or programmatically) to define your metamodel. If you are familiar with the Class Diagram part of UML, you know enough to define MOF-based metamodels.

Apply the MOF-to-IDL mapping rules to generate the OMG IDL interfaces. If your project uses advanced programming tools, they will automate not only IDL generation but also CORBA server generation. Use Reflective Interfaces to write generic tools and Tailored (generated) Interfaces to write more concrete tools.

If you need to exchange metadata using a stream- or file-based mechanism, use the MOF-to-XML mappings defined in the XMI spec to automatically generate an XML DTD that can be used to validate the metadata that is being exchanged between systems.

We will use a simple EDI model (we will pretend it is a metamodel!) to show how the concepts in the MOF apply to metadata as well as data within the constraints of what you can model in the MOF. For more complex examples, check out the MOF 1.1, MOF 1.3, XMI, and UML 1.3 specifications on the OMG server. You'll find URLs for these references in Appendix A.

IV.2.3.1   The EDI Model

Figure IV.2.7 is a simple model of an EDI system that shows Customers purchasing products over the Web. We've purposely used a model different from UML and the MOF to demonstrate the MOF's generality. By the way, this model was used in the XMI proof-of-concept demonstrations during the OMG XMI adoption process in November 1998. This model uses all the major MOF modeling constructs.

IV.2.3.2   The OMG IDL for Portions of the EDI Model

Once the model in Figure IV.2.7 has been designed and verified as being MOF-compliant (either by hand or automatically by a UML/MOF-based modeling tool), the model can be imported into a MOF repository server and the MOF-to-IDL mapping can be applied.

The following IDL fragment shows the generated IDL for the Customer Class. **CustomerClass** is the factory interface that inherits **Reflective::RefObject**. The object interface is **Customer**, which inherits **CustomerClass**. The EDI model, generated IDL, XML DTD, and the XML stream for the model can be found on the Web site for *CORBA 3 Fundamentals and Programming*, www.org/library/corfun/corfunhp.htm. This shows how relationships and the more complex mappings are handled.

```
interface CustomerClass : Reflective::RefObject
  {
    readonly attribute CustomerSet all_of_type_customer;
    readonly attribute CustomerSet all_of_class_customer;
    Customer create_customer (
```

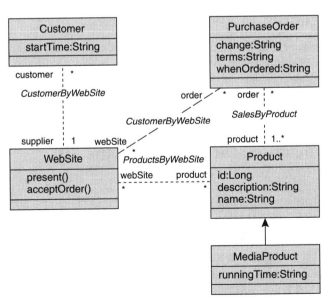

Figure IV.2.7   A MOF model of a simple EDI system.

```
      in string start_time)
      raises (Reflective::MofError);
};
interface Customer : CustomerClass
{
  string start_time ()
    raises (Reflective::MofError);
  void set_start_time (in string new_value)
    raises (Reflective::MofError);
  WebSite supplier ()
    raises (Reflective::MofError);
  void set_supplier (in WebSite new_value)
    raises (Reflective::MofError);
}; // end of interface Customer
```

IV.2.3.3   The XML DTD for Portions of the EDI Model

Once the EDI model has been loaded (or registered) in a MOF repository, if there is a need to exchange EDI metadata (or in some cases, data), an XMI-compliant XML DTD can be generated. This DTD would be used to validate the contents of the message to be validated by either an XML parser in a Web browser or part of an application.

Here is a fragment of the XML DTD generated for the Customer Class. The complete DTD is found on this book's Web site.

```
<!-- _____       -->
<!-- METAMODEL CLASS: EDI.Customer                         -->
<!-- _____       -->
<!ELEMENT EDI.Customer.startTime (#PCDATA|XMI.reference)*>
<!ELEMENT EDI.Customer.supplier (EDI.WebSite)?>
<!ENTITY % EDI.CustomerProperties '((EDI.Customer.startTime)?)' >
<!ENTITY % EDI.CustomerAssociations '(EDI.Customer.supplier?)' >
<!ELEMENT EDI.Customer ( %EDI.CustomerProperties;
        ,(XMI.extension* ,   %EDI.CustomerAssociations; ) )?>
<!ATTLIST EDI.Customer %XMI.element.att; %XMI.link.att; >
```

IV.2.3.4   The XML Document for Portions of the EDI Model

This example was generated by applying the MOF-to-XML DTD mapping rules in the XMI spec. How did we get the EDI model into a MOF repository server? Very simply: We loaded an XML document into a MOF repository server in the first place. The way we generated the XML document corresponding to the EDI model was by applying the MOF-to-XML stream mapping rules to the EDI model. A fragment of the Customer Class appearing as an XML document is shown below. This document was of course validated against the MOF 1.3 XML DTD that is part of the MOF 1.3 specification. This example will also show clearly that DTDs are how you specify the schema in XML, while the document itself appears as an XML stream. Work is under way within the World Wide Web Consortium (W3C) to unify these two syntaxes as part of the XML Schema work. When this work completes, the XMI specification will be extended to support the W3C adopted specification.

When the XMI specification was adopted by OMG, the XML Namespaces work was still in progress. One of the directions for improving the readability of XMI is to use XML Namespaces. Another feature being considered is to use default values in the XML stream so that the stream is more compact.

```xml
<!-- _____ -->
<!-- Contents of Class: Customer                       -->
<!-- _____ -->
<Model.Class xmi.id='a2'>
    <Model.ModelElement.name>Customer</Model.ModelElement.name>
    <Model.ModelElement.annotation> </Model.ModelElement.annotation>

<!-- Portions deleted for simplicity                   -->
<Model.Class.isSingleton xmi.value='false'/>
    <Model.Namespace.contents>
    <Model.Attribute xmi.id='a3'>

<Model.ModelElement.name>startTime</Model.ModelElement.name>
    <Model.ModelElement.annotation> </Model.ModelElement.annotation>
    <Model.Feature.visibility xmi.value='public_vis'/>
    <Model.Feature.scope xmi.value='instance_level '/>
      </Model.StructuralFeature.multiplicity>
    <Model.StructuralFeature.isChangeable xmi.value='true'/>
    <Model.Attribute.isDerived xmi.value='false'/>
    <Model.TypedElement.type>
    <Model.DataType xmi.idref='a17'/> <!-- EDI.String -->
      </Model.TypedElement.type>
      </Model.Attribute>
    <Model.Reference xmi.id='a28'>

<Model.ModelElement.name>supplier</Model.ModelElement.name>
    <Model.ModelElement.annotation>From Rose
    </Model.ModelElement.annotation>
    <Model.Feature.visibility xmi.value='public_vis'/>
    <Model.Feature.scope xmi.value='instance_level '/>
    <Model.StructuralFeature.multiplicity>
    <XMI.field>1</XMI.field>
    <XMI.field>1</XMI.field>
    <XMI.field>false</XMI.field>
    <XMI.field>false</XMI.field>
      </Model.StructuralFeature.multiplicity>
    <Model.StructuralFeature.isChangeable xmi.value='true'/>
```

```
<Model.TypedElement.type>
<Model.Class xmi.idref='a14'/> <!-- EDI.WebSite -->
  </Model.TypedElement.type>
<Model.Reference.referencedEnd>
<Model.AssociationEnd xmi.idref='a25'/>

<!-- EDI.CustomerByWebSite.supplier -->
  </Model.Reference.referencedEnd>
   </Model.Reference>
   </Model.Namespace.contents>
   </Model.Class>
```

IV.2.4   Futures

Development of the MOF and XMI will have to keep up with the demands that come from the widespread use that OMG's modeling specifications enjoy. Members are already considering a number of new features for both of these specifications. Here is a look at possible future developments:

IV.2.4.1   The MOF

The MOF specification has evolved over the last two years based on the experience of various MOF implementors. The main enhancements from MOF 1.1 to MOF 1.3 made it easier to manage complex metamodels and their relationships to other metamodels (or parts of them) by introducing a package clustering concept. The MOF model itself has remained stable.

Some of the features being considered for future versions of the MOF include:

- MOF Schema Evolution and Versioning
- Support for mappings between metamodels
- Support for higher order relationships
- Tighter integration with UML and XML
- Mappings from the MOF to Java and COM to enable better interoperability with Java- and COM-based metadata repositories
- Integration with Naming and Directory Services

IV.2.4.2   XMI

The XMI specification was adopted in March of 1999, but the designers are already looking at enhancements to make it more usable over a wide range of technology and business domains. XMI is already being used to specify metadata interchange standards for middleware, data warehousing, document management, and other application areas. During the next several years, you will see the use of XMI expand into business domains.

Some of the features being considered in the future for the XMI include:

- Use of XML Namespaces to improve management of multiple XML metamodels
- Improving the readability of the DTDs and documents
- Shrinking the size of documents through better choice of default values
- Better integration with W3C XML Schema efforts
- Maintaining the tight integration with UML and MOF specifications as they evolve

IV.2.5   Summary

The introduction of MOF, UML, and XMI into the OMA is a big step forward for OMG and the software industry. Now you can analyze, model, and design applications with UML; manage, discover, and integrate your application metadata using the MOF; and interchange metadata among tools and applications in both CORBA and non-CORBA environments using XML. Figure IV.2.8 summarizes these roles of XMI, UML, the MOF, and XML within the OMG environment.

Using UML and the MOF, you can implement software designs at a higher level of abstraction and precision. In addition, the MOF and XMI automate

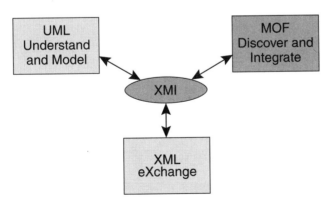

Figure IV.2.8   Roles of XMI, the UML, MOF, and XML within OMG.

the definition and implementation of standard metadata repositories with common interchange formats for specific technology and business domains. This integration of OMG and W3C metadata and modeling standards eases the modeling, discovery, management, and sharing of metadata over the Internet and networks everywhere.

Expanding OMG's Reach: The Model-Driven Architecture

CHAPTER PREVIEW

This final chapter does not describe an OMG specification. Instead, it describes what OMG members expect, as this book goes to press, will become OMG's future direction.

The specifications originally labeled CORBA 3, described in the first three parts of this book, define a powerful, standard, operating system- and language-independent middleware infrastructure. But, regardless of the power or applicability of any middleware platform, it seems that the industry will always look beyond to a platform that seems better, in some way or other. As a result we have been subject to a succession of middleware platforms, each one proclaiming itself to be perfect, universally applicable, and therefore the last in the line. And each one *is*, until the next one comes along.

It's time to recognize that *this* is the steady state: The line has no end! Every "silver bullet" technology will eventually be followed by another, and enterprises will always take advantage of new developments even as they complain about the speed and cost of doing so.

Enterprises need a point of reference—a stake that remains fixed in the ground as the computing environment around it shifts over time. *This stability exists at the model level*. Taking advantage of this, OMG's Model Driven Architecture (MDA) will establish normative standards for services and facilities as UML models, and extend them via mappings to define interfaces and structure on a number of platforms expected to include EJB, XML/SOAP, and others. While availability on multiple platforms aids acceptance, the common basis of these services and facilities in the MDA eases both interoperability and portability of services and the applications that use them.

Establishing the MDA will take a lot of work. This chapter sets out the basic architectural concepts and direction; OMG members will spend the next several years filling in the details. Partial implementations of this concept exist today at forward-looking companies. We think that the end result will be well worth the effort.

What's middleware? Middleware environments started out providing interoperability via architectures that were either standard (CORBA), proprietary (DCOM or MQseries), or somewhere in the middle (JMI or HTTP/XML/SOAP). Essential services such as transactions, directory, persistence, event handling, and messaging were added over time. Recently, more powerful middleware has emerged that builds on the basic interoperability environments to make it easier to construct transactional enterprise components (CORBA Component Model, EJB, MTS/COM+) that execute on application servers.

It's difficult—in fact, next to impossible—for a large enterprise to standardize on a single middleware platform. Some enterprises find themselves with more than one because their different departments have different requirements, others because mergers or acquisitions created a mix. Even the lucky enterprise with a single middleware choice still has to use other technologies to interoperate with their customers and suppliers, and B2B markets.

The middleware environments that are most visible today are CORBA, EJBs, message-oriented middleware, XML/SOAP, COM+, and .NET. However, over the past decade or so, the middleware landscape has continually shifted. For years we've assumed that a clear winner will emerge and stabilize this state of flux, but it's time to admit what we've all suspected: The sequence has no end! And, in spite of the advantages (sometimes real, sometimes imagined) of the latest middleware platform, migration is expensive and disruptive. (We know an industry standards group that, after migrating their standard infrastructure twice already, is now moving from their latest platform *du jour* to XML.)

So, enterprises have applications on different middleware that simply have to be integrated even though this process is time-consuming and expensive. And, the middleware they use continues to evolve as the enterprises continue to integrate.

To make matters even more complicated, enterprises have used different technologies depending on whether communication was within or beyond the firewall. A component built on the assumption that it communicates within a firewall might have to be exposed beyond the firewall for B2B e-commerce, and a component exposed via an extranet might be moved behind the firewall because of an acquisition or merger. Thus, in addition to the basic integration problem, IT organizations must find ways to preserve the development investment made in new components as enterprise boundaries shift, forcing the underlying technology to change accordingly.

IV.3.1   The Role of Modeling at OMG

Although we've spent many pages looking at OMG's specifications, we haven't devoted any time to looking at how those specifications are expressed. But now we need to, so let's have a look:

OMG IDL defines interface syntax very precisely, so OMG uses its own official language to specify syntax for every part of the OMA: CORBA, the CORBAservices, and all of the CORBAfacilities all have interfaces officially defined in OMG IDL.

Specifying behavior and constraints, however, was not so easy. Programming language implementations are an expression of behavior, of course, but an implementation in one language is not necessarily a clear or unambiguous specification for an alternative implementation in another, and constraints are not easily recognized when expressed as executable code. So, because a search for a formal semantic specification language turned up nothing suitable either, OMG started out specifying behavior and constraints in English text along with the syntax in IDL. Until UML and the MOF came along, this was it for OMG's specification vocabulary.

With the adoption of UML and the MOF in 1997, OMG members had the possibility of refining the expression of their specifications. Although use of UML and the MOF is optional in this pre-MDA era, a number of current specifications augment their textual description of behavior and constraints with UML diagrams, and the meta-model for the ORB's Interface Repository has been formalized using the MOF.

Because of the richness of UML and its accompanying Object Constraint Language (OCL) in describing structure, behavior, and constraints, specifications expressed (even in part) in UML and OCL convey their intent much more clearly than those expressed only in English text. For one thing, because the application or facility is visualized as a model, architectural aspects of the design can be refined before the interfaces are realized in IDL (which remains a necessary part of a CORBA specification, of course). In addition, some aspects of a specification remain ambiguous in all but perfect textual description but are rendered precisely in UML and OCL, including

- Invariant rules
- Pre- and post-conditions for operations
- Whether a single-valued attribute or parameter is allowed to be null
- Whether an operation has side effects
- Whether a set of subtypes of a common supertype is disjoint or overlapping; i.e. whether it is permissible to define a type that inherits from more than one of the subtypes
- Whether a type is abstract; i.e., whether it is permissible to create instances of the type that are not instances of some subtype.

Pre- and post-conditions are parts of a rigorous software design formalism referred to as contract-based design; the other conditions and rules in our list go beyond this to add to the rigor of designs produced using UML and OCL. We're still not totally free of English text descriptions of behavior and constraints, but the combination of UML and OCL, augmented by text where necessary, is much richer and more precise than text alone.

Figure IV.3.1 shows a fragment of a UML diagram specifying the invariant rule that number must be between 1000 and 9999. We've included the rule in both English and OCL for clarity. Figure IV.3.2 shows a different fragment including a number of pre- and post-conditions (in OCL only) for the operation XFerFromChecking.

IV.3.1.1   Mapping Models to Platforms

In Part IV, Chapter 1, Cris Kobryn pointed out that UML interfaces were more general than CORBA interfaces. In fact, the scope of UML is much greater than the scope of CORBA, or EJB, or any single middleware platform (or other type of computing platform). That's because UML was designed, from the outset, to model an application that might be realized on *any* platform.

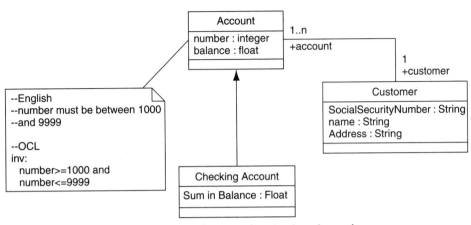

Figure IV.3.1 A fragment of a UML diagram showing invariant rules.

This might make it easy for us to model, but it also means that, once we're done with the first modeling step, we still have some decisions to make: Elements of a general UML model don't map unambiguously to elements of a CORBA implementation, so we'll have to specify where we want, for example, UML classes to map to OMG IDL interfaces, and which elements map to IDL **struct**s and which to **valuetype**s.

We could have avoided this ambiguity if we had constructed our UML model in a CORBA environment from the beginning. To make this possible, OMG has just standardized a *UML Profile for CORBA*. Using UML *stereotypes* and *tagged values*, a profile adapts the full, perhaps over-rich UML modeling space by subsetting and specializing elements to match the capabilities of a particular development and execution environment.

Why stop with just one profile, since UML can easily support profiles for other environments as well? Work on these, it turns out, is already underway: A profile for Enterprise Distributed Object Computing (EDOC) will adapt UML to the CCM (which we presented in Part III, Chapter 3), and a profile for Enterprise Application Integration (EAI) will address messaging-based distributed environments (including CORBA messaging, presented in Part II, Chapter 1). The Java Community Process is working on a UML profile for EJBs (JSR #26); several OMG members are participating.

What about profiles for COM/DCOM, XML/SOAP, .NET, and other middleware environments not so closely connected with CORBA? We don't know of any current work to define these profiles, but we suspect (as will you, once you've finished this chapter) that work on these profiles will start fairly soon.

Our newly expanded capacity to model, with all of the precision and power of OMG's suite of modeling specifications, plus the concept of profile that allows us to tailor our modeling to a particular target, are the building

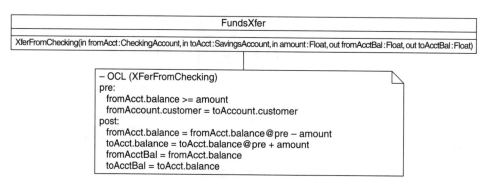

Figure IV.3.2   A fragment of a UML diagram showing pre- and post-conditions.

blocks for an extension of OMG's specifications that copes with today's real problem: the continual evolution of middleware—the ground shifting under our feet, keeping us from ever finding and adopting the "best" middleware as a stable environment for our enterprise. We've put the building blocks into place, and it's time to see what we can do with them.

IV.3.2   Addressing the Problem: The Model Driven Architecture

Even if the increased precision were the only benefit that modeling brings to the table, it would be worthwhile to use UML, OCL, and MOF metamodels in OMG specifications. But, it turns out, we get something else: Having a precise model decreases the amount of work we have to do to achieve interoperability between implementations of the same specification on different middleware platforms. That's nice, but what we really need is interoperability between *different* applications on different platforms. Would this be easier to achieve if we had precise models of the two applications? We think it would be, and this principle is the motivation for the **Model Driven Architecture** (MDA) that is the topic of this chapter.

Basing its new architecture on the core modeling standards that we described in the last two chapters, OMG will leverage the precision, richness, and power of UML, the MOF, XMI, and CWM to define a foundation *model layer* where the representation of an application remains constant even as the middleware layer evolves over time.

This proposal (which had just started its movement to become an official OMG direction as this book went to press) will *expand*, and not replace, the Object Management Architecture (OMA) that has organized OMG's work until now.

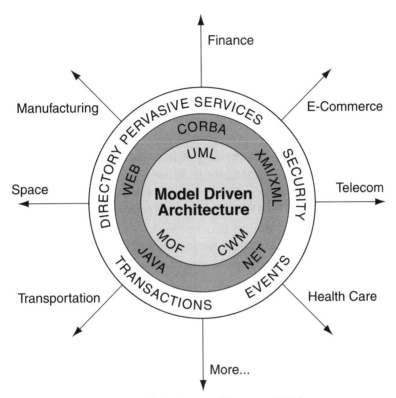

Figure IV.3.3   OMG's Model Driven Architecture (MDA).

Figure IV.3.3 lays out the Model Driven Architecture (MDA), which is language-, vendor- and *middleware*-neutral.

The core of the architecture, at the center of the figure, is based on OMG's modeling standards: UML, the MOF, XMI, and CWM. Although we spoke until now of only one core model, there will actually be multiple core models, realized as UML profiles: One will represent Enterprise Computing with its component structure and transactional interaction; another will represent Real-Time computing with its special needs for resource control; more will be added to represent other specialized environments but the total number will be small.

Each core model, of course, will be *independent* of any particular platform. The number of core models stays small because each core model represents the common features of *all* of the platforms in its category—in modeling terminology, each is a *metamodel* of its category. So, for example, the Enterprise core model is a meta-model of the component space and represents the commonalities of CCM, EJB, MTS, and all other component-based platforms.

IV.3.2.1 Platform-Independent Application Model

This is step one of the MDA development process. Whether your ultimate target is CCM, EJB, MTS, or some other component-based platform, the first step when constructing an MDA-based application will be to create a *platform-independent application model* expressed in terms of the Enterprise UML core profile. (If you're creating a Real-Time or other non-Enterprise application, then you'd pick its core profile instead, of course.)

This model, in the core profile, is the key to application stability over time. Incorporating all of your business logic, basic application structure, and interactions with existing MDA services (such as directory, distributed events, and security) and with other applications that you've built or imported into your MDA environment, this model takes advantage of the richness and power of OMG's modeling environment to represent everything there is to your application except the fraction that is purely platform-specific.

You can—and will—do a lot with this model: The first thing you'll do, of course, will be to use it as the basis for a full implementation in your enterprise's current middleware of choice. Later, when this application needs extension or modification, you'll modify the model and propagate the changes to the working code; eventually MDA functionality will include "round tripping" where updates to the code can be propagated back to the model with some degree of automation. Still later, when your enterprise designs (in the same core profile) and builds a new application that has to interoperate with this one, you'll engineer the interaction at the model level. Regardless of which middleware platform you choose to implement the new application, the ability to fine-tune the interaction between the two applications as models in the same core profile ensures that the MDA can give you lots of help getting them to interoperate smoothly. And finally, if your enterprise ever finds a middleware platform that's *so* much better than the one you originally chose for this application, you'll be able to use your up-to-date model as a basis to re-implement on the new middleware with minimum (albeit not zero) effort.

IV.3.2.2 Platform-Specific Application Model

In step two, we transform our platform-independent model into a *platform-specific* model: For our enterprise application example, we'd transform to a model in the UML profile for our enterprise's currently favored component-based platform which might be CCM, or EJB, or XML/SOAP, or COM/DCOM, or some other alternative. In Figure IV.3.3, these platforms occupy the innermost thin ring surrounding the core.

The transformation is guided by a *mapping*, standardized by the MDA. The objective is to automate the transformation as much as possible. Consider these three ways that the transformation could be done:

- A person could study the platform-independent model and derive a platform-specific model from it.

- An incomplete or skeletal platform-specific model, which needs to be completed by a person, could be produced by applying an algorithm (that is, an implementation of the mapping).

- A complete platform-specific model could be produced by applying an algorithm.

Complete automation is a goal, but partial automation is more feasible especially in the early stages of the MDA. Some types of applications are easier to automate than others (the setting and getting of attributes is simple to model and easy to automate, while behavioral features are more difficult). Models that leave out essential parts of an application can never be transformed into a complete platform-specific model. Legacy functions, which may not represent faithfully in the core model, will be difficult to deal with. And, transformation algorithms (mappings) will improve as they mature—early versions will be necessarily incomplete.

So, in this step, we start by running our platform-independent model through a process that applies an OMG-standardized mapping to our chosen middleware platform, producing the skeleton of a platform-specific model. This output will be more or less complete depending on the complexity and suitability of our application, the richness and completeness of our model, and the maturity of the mapping and implementation. To finish this step, platform specialists "flesh out" the skeleton by filling in the parts that the mapping didn't cover.

When complete, the platform-specific model is a remarkably complete representation of our application. It's still a model, rendered in UML diagrams and OCL, but the richness of OMG's modeling standards ensures that business rules and constraints, program structure, and invocation syntax are all represented precisely.

IV.3.2.3 The Application Itself

The next step is to produce the application itself. If the target environment supports components, for example, the system will have to produce many types of code and configuration files including interface files, component definition files, program code files, component configuration files, and assembly configuration files.

Once again a mapping, standardized by the MDA, defines the transformation from our model in a platform-specific UML profile (itself standardized by the MDA) to interface definitions and to a greater or lesser extent, running code.

The transformation from platform-specific model to working code may be automated to a greater or lesser extent, in parallel with the possibilities we faced in our previous step when we transformed our platform-independent model to a platform-specific model. For example, an application that mostly sets and gets attribute values and stores and compares data will produce a more complete set of code files than one requiring the implementation of new mathematical computations. And, even though the amount of code required for a typical component application is large, these applications typically spend most of their time executing, over and over, a limited number of patterns that have proven successful in the past.

So, one way to maximize code generation is to tailor the target middleware environment for it. For example, as we saw in Section III.3.3.7, the CCM limits the user to four patterns of servant activation/de-activation instead of the nearly 200 allowed by the POA. It's easy for a CCM development environment to include executable code for all four patterns, allowing a developer to simply select the pattern he wants to use instead of coding the activation/de-activation mechanism himself. In fact, this usually improves performance because the included activation/de-activation code is written by system-level experts instead of application-level business programmers.

Think of this technique as the decades-old practice of linking and invoking code from function libraries, albeit with a slightly more sophisticated selection mechanism. In principle, any standard computer science technique, or mathematical or domain algorithm, is a candidate for inclusion in a core model where it can be inserted into an application just by selecting from a menu on a modeling tool.

Anyhow, the activation/de-activation patterns are part of our platform-specific model and may even be present in the platform-independent core model if they represent a common feature. So, pattern selection at the modeling stage carries through to the generated code. And, as middleware environments grow richer over the years, application models will become simpler—as more functionality is included in the development and runtime environment and reflected in the model profile, the process of modeling involves increasingly more selection from a palette of patterns that have proven successful in the past and less detailed application-specific work.

The more precisely the platform-specific UML profile reflects the actual platform capabilities, the more completely all aspects of the application can be included in the platform-specific application model and the more complete the generated code can be. In a mature MDA environment, code generation will be substantial or, perhaps in some restricted cases, even complete. Early versions are unlikely to provide a high degree of automatic generation, but even initial implementations will simplify development projects and represent a significant gain, on balance, for early adopters, because they will be using a consistent architecture for managing the platform-independent and platform-specific aspects of their applications.

So, working in a way similar to the previous transformation, we will input our platform-specific model into an MDA tool that implements the mapping to our middleware platform, producing a skeleton application that is more or less complete. Platform specialists will then fill in the skeleton, finding that they must devote most of their effort to areas that are less well defined by the platform. Areas that are well-defined, such as the servant activation/de-activation patterns that we've already mentioned, will surely emerge from the code generator ready-to-run or nearly so.

IV.3.2.4   Multiple Middleware Technologies

As Figure IV.3.3 shows, many of today's connection technologies will be integrated by the MDA, with a space perpetually left open for tomorrow's "next best thing." CORBA provides the best middleware choice because it is vendor- and language-neutral and bridges easily to all of the other middleware environments. But, to accommodate those enterprises with multiple middleware platforms on their network, many non-CORBA platforms will be incorporated into the MDA. One of the first will be the Java-only EJB.

Because the MDA is platform-independent at its core, adding new middleware platforms to the interoperability environment is straightforward: After identifying the way a new platform represents and implements common middleware concepts and functions, OMG members will incorporate this information into the MDA as a new platform-specific profile plus a mapping from its platform-independent core profile. Various message-oriented middleware tools, XML/SOAP and .NET, will be integrated in this way; going one step further, by rationalizing the conflicting XML DTDs that are being proposed in some industries, the MDA can even help you interoperate across them.

IV.3.2.5   Interoperability in the MDA

As representations of multiple middleware platforms are added to the MDA and mature over time, generation of integration tools—bridges, gateways, and mappings from one platform to another—will become more automated as well. The draft OMG MDA document, in the version current as we wrote this, points out that MDA could help produce bridges that couple alternative implementations of an application generated from the same base model and implemented, via the standard mappings, on two different middleware platforms. We think that, eventually, MDA will also generate skeleton code for cross-platform invocations from an application in one middleware environment to a different application in a different middleware environment, as long as both derive from models in the same core profile.

Interoperability will be most transparent within a core category: Enterprise applications with other Enterprise applications; Real-Time applications with other Real-Time applications. This follows from our basis on a separate core model for each category; differences between application categories prevent us from basing all of our applications on a single core model. Further off into the future, by identifying and exploiting concepts common to two or more categories, even these boundaries can be smoothed somewhat.

IV.3.2.6   Integrating Legacy Applications

Our discussion so far has assumed that we were building our application—and its model—from scratch. Legacy applications do not fit this pattern. With many in this category built before component environments were even an idea, these applications typically will not fit smoothly into any of our core models. However, legacy applications may be brought into the MDA by wrapping them with a layer of code consistent with the MDA Enterprise component core model, or another core model if appropriate. Integration into the MDA, and interworking with other MDA-based applications, will be smoothest for applications whose underlying meta-model is most consistent with the middleware architecture that it must work with. Lacking this measure of commonality, interworking can be helped by providing a wrapper that provides a middleware-model view of the legacy application's functionality.

IV.3.3   Integrating the Next-Generation Internet

As the foundation for the next generation of OMG standards, the MDA integrates across all middleware platforms—past, present, and future. OMG, the organization that knows vendor-, operating system-, and programming language-independence better than any other, is the ideal organization to extend standardization beyond middleware to a platform-neutral, model-driven approach. MDA users gain these specific advantages:

- The choice of middleware platform for new MDA-based applications will not have the irrevocable quality that it has today. You will have the security of knowing that the essential structure, behavior, and constraints of your application have been systematically distilled and archived in the form of a platform-independent model and that any future need to migrate to different middleware (or even new versions of the same middleware) will thus be reasonably manageable. Interoperability bridges and gateways to other MDA-based applications within your enterprise as well as interconnections with customers, suppliers, and business partners can be produced methodically, using a consistent architecture and some degree of automatic generation.

- Your legacy applications—that is, the ones that keep your business in business—will interoperate with your current applications once you wrap them as we described and incorporate their functions into the MDA. You can leave them on their established platforms; the MDA will help automate the construction of bridges from one platform to another. If the legacy application's platform meta-model differs greatly from your enterprise middleware, however, automation benefits will be limited.

- Industry standards—in your industry and others—will include platform-independent models defined in terms of the MDA core profiles: Standard facilities performing standard functions, which you can buy instead of build, with interoperability and evolvability improved by their MDA roots. We'll describe these facilities and their role in the next section of this chapter.

- As new middleware platforms emerge, the OMG's rapid consensus-based standardization process will incorporate them into the MDA by defining new standardized mappings. MDA tools will thus be able to expand the list of platforms that they can target when they assist in converting a platform-independent model. The tools will also be able to expand their support for bridges to incorporate the new platforms.

- *Developers gain the ultimate in flexibility, the ability to regenerate applications from a stable, platform-independent model as the underlying infrastructure shifts over time. Return on Investment (ROI) flows from the reuse of application and domain models across the software lifespan—especially during long-term support and maintenance, the most expensive phase of an application's life.*

- Models will be built, viewed, and manipulated via UML, transmitted via XMI, and stored in MOF repositories.

- Because all applications will be realized initially in the modeling environment with its rich declarative power, formal declaration of systems' structure, behavior, and constraints will increase software quality and extend the useful lifetime of designs, and thus increase ROI.

Taking advantage of our standards and tools that exploit them, OMG members have this integration task well underway. The Enterprise Computing core model is being defined and mapped to the most-used middleware platforms. A core model is also being defined for Real Time computing.

IV.3.4   Standardizing Domain Models

Since January 1996, about half of the OMG members who attend our meetings have been participating in Domain Task Forces, communities focused on standardizing services and facilities in specific vertical markets. Until now these specifications have consisted of interfaces written in OMG IDL with accompanying description of behavior and constraints in English text. Standardizing components at a platform level, in terms of standards such as CORBA, is certainly a viable contribution to solving the integration and interoperability problem, but the MDA will enable OMG's domain task forces to go beyond this.

Most—perhaps all—of OMG's domain facilities are elegantly designed. Even though the specifications express syntax as a set of OMG IDL interfaces and behavior and constraints in English text, it is possible to read between the lines and discern their underlying models which are virtually never expressed. And, these models are of particularly high quality.

Because their models are hidden, and not every company has chosen CORBA for its enterprise middleware, OMG's domain facilities have not always received the recognition or widespread use that they deserve. Extending these implicit models beyond CORBA just makes sense. Demonstrating that this concept is realistic, several of these facilities have already been realized in non-CORBA environments, ported by hand by programmers working without benefit of an explicit model. The Healthcare Resource Access Decision Facility, already implemented in Java and EJB in addition to CORBA, is one example. There are more.

So, in order to maximize the utility and impact of OMG domain facility specifications, under the MDA they will be adopted in the form of normative, platform-independent UML models augmented by normative, platform-specific UML models and interface definitions for at least one target platform. The common basis on MDA will promote partial generation of implementation code as well, but implementation code of course will not be standardized.

Today OMG has 10 Domain Task Forces with several more "in the chute"; more are added from time to time. Rather than show them all in a static diagram, we've only included a representative sample in Figure IV.3.3 where they appear as rays emanating from the center.

The Domain Task Forces (DTFs) produce standard frameworks for standard functions in their application space. In the MDA, a future Finance DTF standard for an accounts receivable facility might include a platform-independent UML model, a CORBA-specific UML model, IDL interfaces, a Java-specific UML model, and Java interfaces. XML DTDs or schema generated via XMI-based mapping rules could be included as well. All of these artifacts would be normative. Such a standard would have broad impact, in that the platform-independent model would be useful even in middleware environments other than those targeted by the platform-specific parts of the specification. Since accounts receivable is an Enterprise Computing application, the normative, platform-specific artifacts would be derived at least partially via standard mappings of the Enterprise Computing core model to the platforms.

As another example, the Manufacturing DTF could produce normative MDA UML models, IDL interfaces, Java interfaces, XML DTDs, etc., for (Figure IV.3.4) CAD/CAM interoperability, PDM (Product Data Management), and a Supply Chain integration facility. Once the MDA models for these have been completed and adopted, their implementation can be partially automated in any middleware platform supported by the MDA.

The three facilities that we're using for this example—CAD/CAM, PDM, and Supply Chain—demonstrate a benefit that only the MDA can provide: CAD/CAM and PDM applications are tightly integrated and so will probably be implemented by an individual enterprise or software vendor in, for example, CORBA or EJB. Supply Chain Integration, on the other hand, is more of an inter-enterprise facility so we might expect an XML/SOAP-based implementation supported by an industry market-maker or trade organization to become popular. But, it will be essential to interoperate among the three: CAD/CAM designs feed into PDM production facilities which drive the supply chain; in turn, the supply chain will refer back to CAD/CAM for details on a particular part. By starting all three out as UML models in the

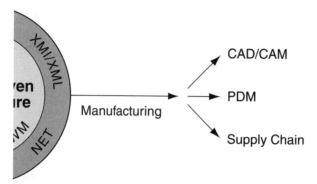

Figure IV.3.4 UML models of frameworks for vertical facilities.

MDA, we may eventually be able to generate a significant portion of the implementation of each on its preferred platform, as well as the bridges we need to integrate each of the facilities with the other two.

IV.3.5   Pervasive Services

Enterprise and Internet computing rely on a set of essential services. The list varies somewhat depending on the source but typically includes Directory services, Event handling, Persistence, Transactions, and Security.

When these services are defined and built on a particular platform, they necessarily take on characteristics that restrict them to that platform, or ensure that they work best there. To avoid this, OMG will define Pervasive Services at the platform-independent model level in UML. Only after the services' features and architecture are fixed will platform-specific definitions be generated for all of the middleware platforms supported by the MDA.

At the abstraction level of a platform-independent business component model, services are visible only at a very high level (similar to the view the component developer has in CCM or EJB). When the model is mapped to its designated platform, the MDA will map service calls to their native platforms. The pervasive services would be visible only to lower-level applications, i.e. applications that write directly to services.

In Figure IV.3.3, we've shown the Pervasive Services as a second thin ring around the core to emphasize that they're available to all applications, in all environments. True integration requires a common model for directory services, events and signals, and security. By extending them to a generalized model, implementable in the different environments and easily integrated, the Model Driven Architecture becomes the basis of our goal of universal integration: the global information appliance.

IV.3.6   Expanding the Role of the OMG

To accomplish its goal of enabling true, universal, cross-platform interoperability via the MDA, OMG plans to extend its focus from a middleware-centric to a modeling-centric organization. The foundation for the new role of the organization will be the current Analysis and Design Task Force and its work on UML, the MOF, XMI, and CWM, along with work in progress on the various profiles that we've mentioned in this chapter.

IV.3.6.1   OMG Specifications in UML and on Non-CORBA Platforms

The MDA will not only change the OMG's architecture in a fundamental way—it will change the nature of the organization's specifications as well. Let's have a look:

Currently, only CORBA artifacts (OMG IDL interfaces and English text behavior and constraint descriptions) of services and facilities can be adopted as OMG specifications. Modeling specifications are the exception: UML, the MOF, XMI, and CWM. Because these do not define executable services or facilities (for the most part), there's no conflict with OMG's requirement for CORBA artifacts. Where modeling specifications do define facilities (such as the MOF repository) the interfaces are, in fact, defined in OMG IDL.

There has always been another important requirement: The company (or companies) that propose an OMG specification (typically, although not necessarily in response to a Request for Proposals or RFP issued by the membership) must produce and market a commercial implementation within a year of its adoption. This requirement applies across the entire architecture: Services and facilities (Fault Tolerant CORBA, for example), and modeling languages and tools (UML-compliant modeling tools).

According to the documents being considered by OMG members as we write this, adoption of the MDA as OMG's direction will change the requirement for CORBA artifacts, but *not* the one for commercial availability. Before we get to the requirements statement, we need a few definitions:

- A *Platform-Independent Model* (PIM) is defined in UML, although other notations are allowed "where appropriate." Additional description—behavior and constraints, primarily—can be defined using either UML or natural language.

- There are two ways to define syntax for a *Platform-Specific Model* (PSM):

    - UML diagrams using an officially adopted platform-specific profile, or

    - Interface definitions in a concrete implementation technology (OMG, IDL, XML, Java)

- In either case, additional description—behavior and constraints, primarily—may be specified in either UML or natural language.

Under the MDA, all OMG specifications will be model-based. Therefore, every new service or facility specification will have to include a PIM, which will be normative.

Because the commercial availability requirement will continue in force under the MDA, every specification will also have to include at least one PSM (expressed as either alternative in our definition above). Although a PSM *defines* a set of implementation artifacts (e.g., IDL interfaces if the profile is for CORBA), until tools become available to generate the artifacts automatically, the interface definitions must be submitted to OMG to be adopted with the PSM. The PSM and the implementation artifacts (but not the complete implementation; only the interfaces, constraints, and behavioral description) will be normative. The submitting company or companies will have to produce and market an implementation conforming to the PSM.

It is also possible to standardize a PSM on a new platform for an existing PIM.

In case you didn't figure out what's allowed by these rules, let us point out: *Under MDA OMG can adopt, as official specifications, PSMs and implementation artifacts on non-CORBA platforms so long as they derive from an officially adopted PIM.* In fact, it is possible under the MDA for an OMG specification to consist of a PIM and only one, non-CORBA, PSM.

This change in policy makes it possible for industry groups to gather under OMG's auspices and create standards in, for example, EJB or XML/SOAP (or whatever the XML protocol turns out to be), as long as every specification includes or conforms to a PIM. To support this effort, the OMG plans to concentrate extra effort on conformance testing, certification of architects, designers, and programmers, and certification of products (branding).

IV.3.6.2 CORBA's Role in the MDA

So where does that leave CORBA? CORBA is a foundation of this new architecture. As the only vendor- and language-independent middleware, it is a vital and necessary part of the MDA superstructure; software bridges would be hard or impossible to build without it. OMG and its members will continue to extend and maintain the CORBA specification suite, including both the core and the various facilities. Extending this superstructure, the MDA is expressed completely in terms of modeling concepts, moving the reuse equation up one level.

IV.3.7 Prologue

In contrast to most books, which work themselves through a climax and an ending, in this book the climax—the description of the CCM at the end of Part III—is sustained by our look at a new beginning: OMG's MDA. This chapter may be the end of this book, but it's the prologue to the next stage of the OMG's development.

CORBA will continue to develop: It represents the only vendor- and platform-independent middleware on the market, and is the foundation for enterprise interoperability. Its expansion into the specialized Real-Time and embedded markets has only just begun, numerous implementations of the CCM are underway but have not yet emerged. OMG will continue to give CORBA its full support.

But, even as this activity goes on, OMG members will develop the MDA. Working in UML, they will establish standard profiles for every middleware with enough market presence to warrant, and map these profiles to implementation artifacts. Pervasive services—directory, transactions, security, events—will be expressed in platform-independent UML and then mapped to multiple middleware platforms. Domain standards, such as the excellently designed Person Identifier Service (PIDS) adopted by OMG's Healthcare Domain Task Force, will suddenly become available to companies that decided, for whatever reason, not to base their middleware on CORBA. Look for an XML/SOAP version of PIDS, for example, if XML/SOAP continues its pre-eminence.

OMG welcomes new members. If the MDA sounds like a good idea to you, then go to the OMG's Web site and check out the pages that list membership benefits and tell how to join. Anyone is welcome to come to an OMG meeting or two before joining, to collect the information you need to make a membership decision. Every meeting registration form tells how to attend as a guest observer. (You'll still have to pay the meeting fee, though!)

But the MDA will be defined and established by OMG's members whether you and your friends join or not. It's a sound idea, and has near-universal support among OMG's 800-odd member companies, so this is a given. We're excited by the prospects, and are even thinking, a few years down the road, that the MDA might be the theme of our next book.

Sources and References

In this appendix, we've collected all of the URLs and references that we've pointed out in the text. We've also included pointers to each of the OMG specifications that we've written about.

The first section presents this book's Web site; the second section covers the OMG Web site; and then we start the chapter-by-chapter coverage of references and sources.

A.1 This Book's Companion Web Site

We've added a tree of pages for this book to the home page for our other two books, *CORBA Fundamentals and Programming* (1995) and *CORBA 3 Fundamentals and Programming*, second edition (2000). The home page for all three books is

```
www.wiley.com/compbooks/siegel
```

On this page, you'll see a heading that takes you off to a tree of pages specific to this book. This is where to look for updates to Part I, Chapter 2 (where the specification, as you recall, needed an update on finding initial references) and other chapters as the need arises. This is also where we'll post errata as we notice those little *mistrakes* that tend to pop up occasionally despite our best efforts to be perfect, at least in print.

You may e-mail the author directly at `siegel@omg.org`.

A.2 OMG's Web Site and Contact Information

OMG maintains a Web site where you can access lots of things, including

- Downloads of all OMG specifications, for free
- Up-to-date information and documents for specifications in progress
- A CORBA tutorial, written by Jon Siegel
- Meeting and Workshop schedules
- White papers and other material on OMG and OMG specifications
- Information on OMG membership—how and why to join OMG

There are two places you have to look to find an OMG specification, depending on how far it has moved along the standardization process. For details, look at a page that we wrote:

`www.omg.org/gettingstarted/specsandprods.htm`

To find out about work in progress, go to:

`www.omg.org/techprocess/meetings/schedule/`

OMG makes even the preliminary documents for a specification available to everyone via this page.

My CORBA tutorial starts with these two pages:

`www.omg.org/gettingstarted/gettingstartedindex.htm`
`www.omg.org/gettingstarted/index.htm`

If you've never been to the OMG Web site or need to learn about OMG starting with the basics, go to the first of these pages. If you're through that part and want to find out about specifications and where they come from, go right to the second.

Meeting and workshop schedule and location information is given on:

`www.omg.org/news/schedule/upcoming.htm`

And for other information, browse through the many pages listed on the pull-down menu, which you can access by mousing over the bar just below the OMG logo at the top of every page.

Some pages are password-protected, restricted to OMG members only. Membership is by company, so you may access these pages if the company you work for is a member. OMG has about 800 member companies, and most of the people who work for them don't know about their membership. To find out if your company is a member, pull down the leftmost menu (mouse over **About Us**) and click on **Membership List**. On the page that comes up (eventually—there's an intermediate page that does some automatic pointing), leave the selector set to **All Members** and click on **Search**. If your company's name appears on the list that appears when the search completes, you're a member. To find out the membership "owner" at your company (referred to as the Primary Contact by OMG), send an email to `info@omg.org`. We'll send back the contact info you need right away, and your primary contact will send you the password and probably some other information about what your company is doing with OMG.

You can contact OMG by snail mail or phone if you insist:

Object Management Group
First Needham Place
250 First Avenue, Suite 250
Needham, MA 02494
U.S.A.
Telephone: (781) 444-0404
Fax: (781) 444-0320

A.3   CORBA and UML Sources

We maintain a CORBA resource page as part of the tutorial (check out the tutorial Web pages, already cited, to find it), but there are others with more references. CETUS is an organization of several people that maintains a site with references to as many OO sources as they can find. Their main CORBA page is at:

`www.cetus-links.org/oo_corba.html`

This page points to their ORB page, which is

`www.cetus-links.org/oo_object_request_brokers.html`

Even though this page listed 60 ORBs when we last checked, it's almost certainly not complete; companies and groups are continually springing up, implementing CORBA on some platform or other, and making their product available either on the Web or some other way. Because there's no "central clearinghouse" that these groups have to notify when they implement, it's impossible for any person or group to keep a comprehensive list of ORBs. The CETUS folks come closer than any other group that we know about, but even they cannot keep up-to-the-minute.

CETUS maintains a UML page too, at:

```
www.cetus-links.org/oo_uml.html
```

OMG maintains a page for some of its OOA&D specifications. Check these out for pointers to specifications, tutorials, and information:

```
www.omg.org/uml/
www.omg.org/cwm/
www.omg.org/mda
```

Look for pages devoted to MOF and XMI, coming soon.

A.4 Sources and References, by Chapter

Prologue

You can read the original press release that tied the various CORBA 3 specifications together at:

```
http://cgi.omg.org/news/pr98/9_9.html
```

For additional related material, look under the heading "Future of CORBA" on this page:

```
www.omg.org/news/releases/pr1998.htm
```

The valuetype, and Java-to-IDL Mapping

The **valuetype** is part of CORBA core. You can download the latest CORBA core specification from this special page, which is updated by OMG to always point to the most recent release:

```
www.omg.org/technology/documents/formal/corbaiiop.htm
```

If you choose to download by chapter, look in Chapters 5 and 6 for the **valuetype**. This does not include the language mappings; for those you need to surf to:

```
www.omg.org/technology/documents/formal/corba_language_mapping_
specifica.htm
```

This is also the page that contains the pointer to the Java-to-IDL mapping specification.

Mapping XML to CORBA

As we went to press, the XML/Value specification was newly adopted and available only as a submission. The easiest way to get access was using this URL:

```
http://doc.omg.org/orbos/00-08-10
```

The IDL in this document is not completely correct; for the IDL as adopted, check out:

```
http://doc.omg.org/orbos/00-11-01
```

This version will be updated within a year, as we mentioned in the text. We'll maintain a pointer to the latest version on this book's Web page.

XML Specification and Resources

XML is a W3C specification. The W3C home page for XML is, logically enough, at:

```
www.w3.org/XML/
```

From this page, it's only one click to the specifications for XML and all of its associated features, and to software implementations, books, tutorials, and papers. There's so much that we're not going to give any more XML references here.

DOM Specification and Resources

The DOM is also a W3C specification. The W3C home page for the DOM is, also logically enough, at:

```
www.w3.org/DOM/
```

The ancillary DOM specifications that we mentioned in the text—events, traversals, range, and views—all have pointers on this page under the header "Public Release of Specifications."

OASIS maintains a page of DOM information at

```
www.oasis-open.org/cover/dom.html
```

Both W3C and OASIS have exchanged memberships with OMG, indicating a significant level of cooperation among these groups.

Interoperable Naming Service

The features adopted collectively under the name *Interoperable Naming Service* have been incorporated into the core CORBA specification starting with release 2.4. For example, the `corbaloc` and `corbaname` URL formats are defined in Section 13.6.10, and the new ways to input initial services are in Section 4.5.3.

Messaging and Quality of Service

CORBA Messaging has been incorporated into the core specification starting with CORBA 2.4. It's all in Chapter 22: asynchronous and time-independent invocations, routers, and all of the QoS features that we discussed in Part II, Chapter 1 and Part II, Chapter 2.

The Object Transaction Service is written up in Chapter 13 of *CORBA 3 Fundamentals and Programming*. The OTS specification is available from the OMG Web site, where it's the last chapter listed on the page:

```
www.omg.org/technology/documents/formal/corba_services_available_
electro.htm
```

For an introduction to transaction processing, read Jim Gray and Andreas Reuter, *Transaction Processing: Concepts and Techniques* (Morgan Kaufman, 1992).

GIOP and IIOP are explained in Chapter 6, Section 8 of *CORBA 3 Fundamentals and Programming*. The GIOP and IIOP specifications appear in CORBA core, Chapters 11 (on the IOR) through 15.

Real-Time CORBA

Real-Time CORBA is part of Release 2.4, where it appears as Chapter 24.

The seminal reference for scheduling algorithms is this 1973 paper: C. Liu and J. Layland. "Scheduling Algorithms for Multiprogramming in a Hard Real-Time Environment." *Journal of the ACM.* 20(1):46–61. Jan. 1973.

There's also a book with coverage of the subject: Klein, M.H., T. Ralya, B. Pollak, R. Obenza, and M.G. Harbour. *A Practitioner's Handbook for Real-Time Analysis.* Kluwer: 1993. ISBN 0-7923-9361-9.

And if you're looking for even more references, surf to the Real-Time resources page at

    www.real-time.org/no_frames/rt-resources.htm

Fault Tolerant CORBA

The FT CORBA specification was not part of CORBA 2.4, the release current with the printing of this book, but you can download the specification from OMG's Web site where it appears as:

    http://doc.omg.org/ptc/00-03-04

and

    http://doc.omg.org/ptc/00-03-05

minimum CORBA

A list of upcoming OMG workshops (and upcoming OMG meetings!) appears at:

    www.omg.org/news/schedule/upcoming.htm

The minimumCORBA specification is part of the CORBA 2.4 release, where it appears as Chapter 23.

The Work in Progress page, referred to in the last few paragraphs of the chapter is:

    www.omg.org/techprocess/meetings/schedule/

The Smart Transducers RFP is listed in the first section on that page. The URL given there for this particular RFP is:

    www.omg.org/techprocess/meetings/schedule/Smart_Transducers_RFP.html

CCM Section Introduction

The paper about Valuetypes and Persistent State is:

```
http://doc.omg.org/orbos/98-12-21
```

The POA

The POA was introduced with the 2.2 release of CORBA core. It appears in the CORBA specification as Chapter 11.

The PSS

The PSS is a CORBAservice. On OMG's Web site, it appears under "Recently Adopted Specifications":

```
www.omg.org/technology/documents/recent
```

The PSS is listed as:

```
http://doc.omg.org/orbos/99-07-07
```

The CCM

The CCM was still a "Recently Adopted Specification" when this book went to press. In that category, it's listed with the other CORBA/IIOP specifications on this page:

```
www.omg.org/technology/documents/recent/corba_iiop.htm
```

It's listed in the top row of the table. It's an extensive specification, contained in ten(!) different documents.

The BOI RFPs are listed on the Work in Progress page under the Analysis and Design Platform Task Force:

```
www.omg.org/techprocess/meetings/schedule/
```

They are the UML Profile for EDOC RFP at URL:

```
www.omg.org/techprocess/meetings/schedule/UML_Profile_for_EDOC_RFP.html
```

and the UML Textual Notation RFP at URL:

```
www.omg.org/techprocess/meetings/schedule/UML_Textual_Notation_RFP.html
```

The first of these RFPs was the UML Profile for CORBA, which is a "Recently Adopted Specification" and available from the page:

```
www.omg.org/technology/documents/recent/omg_modeling.htm
```

The last will be a mapping of the UML profile for EDOC to CORBA. This RFP had not been issued when we went to press; look for it to appear on the Work in Progress page in early 2001.

The UML

UML Release 1.3 was current when this book went to press and is available at:

```
www.omg.org/technology/documents/formal/unified_modeling_language.htm
```

A 1.4 revision was being prepared for publication in early 2001, and RFPs had been issued for the 2.0 major revision. Look for the 1.4 revision to appear on the "Recently Adopted Specifications" page in mid-2001, and follow progress on UML 2.0 on the Work in Progress page.

Here are the references cited in the chapter:

- *OMG Unified Modeling Language Specification v. 1.4* draft, scheduled to be adopted by the OMG in 2001.

- J. Warmer, et al. *The Object Constraint Language: Precise Modeling with UML*, Addison-Wesley, 1999.

- www.omg.org/uml: OMG UML Resource Page.

- www.celigent.com/omg/umlrtf: OMG UML Revision Task Force home page.

The MOF and XMI

These modeling specifications are available from the Modeling Specifications page:

```
www.omg.org/technology/documents/formal/omg_modeling_specifications_
avai.htm
```

The MDA

The seminal MDA paper, which had not been adopted as official by OMG members when we went to press, is:

```
http://doc.omg.org/omg/00-11-05
```

In spite of its non-technical nature, this paper gives a good introduction to MDA intentions and plans.

A more technical MDA paper appears at:

```
http://doc.omg.org/ab/01-02-04
```

Just before we went to press, OMG members unanimously adopted a resolution endorsing the directions expressed in this last paper, and supporting development of documents necessary to make this an official OMG architecture.

Index